FISHING IN NORTHERN CALIFORNIA

Ninth Edition

The Complete Guide

Ken Albert

ISBN 0-934061-43-2

Cover Design: Electric Art Studios
Mountain View, CA

RKOE / MARKETSCOPE

P.O. BOX 3118
HUNTINGTON BEACH, CA. 92605-3118
(714) 375-9888

*" The leading publisher of
fishing books for California Anglers"*

ISBN 0-934061-43-2

51495

9 780934 061438

Great Books (for more details see p.236)

Fishing in Northern California

RKOE / MARKETSCOPE publishes the bestselling **Fishing in Northern California** (8 1/2 x 11 inches, 240 pages). It includes "How To Catch" sections on all freshwater fish as well as salmon, steelhead, sturgeon, shad, kokanee, lingcod, clams, sharks, rock crab, crawdads, stripers, etc. Plus, there are sections on all major NorCal fishing waters (over 50 lakes, the Delta, Coastal Rivers, Valley Rivers, Mountain Trout and the Pacific Ocean). All these waters are mapped in detail!

Fishing in Southern California

RKOE / MARKETSCOPE also publishes the bestselling **Fishing in Southern California** (8 1/2 x 11 inches, 256 pages). It includes "How To Catch" sections on all freshwater fish as well as barracuda, bonito, calico bass, grunion, halibut, marlin sea bass and yellowtail. Plus, there are sections on major SoCal fishing waters (45 lakes, the Salton Sea, Colorado River, Mountain Trout and the Pacific Ocean). All these waters are mapped in detail!

Bass Fishing in California

At last, a bass fishing book just for Californians—both beginners and veterans. This book explains in detail how to catch more and larger bass in California's unique waters. But, most valuable, it includes a comprehensive guide, with maps, to 40 of California's best bass lakes, up and down the state. 8 1/2 x 11, 240 pages.

Trout Fishing in California

Trout fishing is special in California and now there is a special book for the California trout anglers. It covers, in detail, how to catch trout in lakes or streams, with line, bait or flies, by trolling, casting or still fishing, from boat or shore. And even better for California anglers, this is a guide to the best trout waters all over the state. Detailed info and precise maps are featured. 8 1/2 x 11, 224 pages.

Saltwater Fishing in California

California is blessed with over 800 miles of Pacific Ocean coastline. This is a marvelous resource for all Golden State anglers. And now there is a book that covers it all. Surf fishing. Kelp fishing. Harbor and Bay fishing. Poke poling. And more. Don't go saltwater fishing without it. Both veteran anglers and beginners are finding this book a necessity. It explains, in detail, how to catch albacore, barracuda, bass, bonito, halibut, rockfish, sharks, salmon, stripers, yellowtail and striped marlin. And there is a large "How-To and Where-To" Guide for hot spots all along the coast. And don't be without the Saltwater Sportfish I.D. Section. This book has become a standard because it explains in simple, straightforward language how to catch fish in the Pacific, off California. 8 1/2 x 11, 256 pages.

Order your Copies Today!

	Price	Sales Tax	Total Price	Qty	Total Amount
____ **Fishing in Northern California**	$14.95	$1.20	$16.15	____	_____
____ **Fishing in Southern California**	$14.95	$1.20	$16.15	____	_____
____ **Bass Fishing in California**	$14.95	$1.20	$16.15	____	_____
____ **Trout Fishing in California**	$14.95	$1.20	$16.15	____	_____
____ **Saltwater Fishing in California**	$14.95	$1.20	$16.15	____	_____
				____	_____

Postage & Handling (1st book $3.00; no charge on 2 or more books) . . . .   _____ *

Check Enclosed . . . .   _____

*Special Offer** (order 2 books, any combination, and we'll pay **all** postage & handling)

Name _____   Address _____

Send Your Order To: **RKOE / MARKETSCOPE, P.O. Box 3118, HUNTINGTON BEACH, CA 92605-3118**

fnc   (Permission is granted to xerox this page.)

Contents

continued . . .

Contents (continued)

Specials	

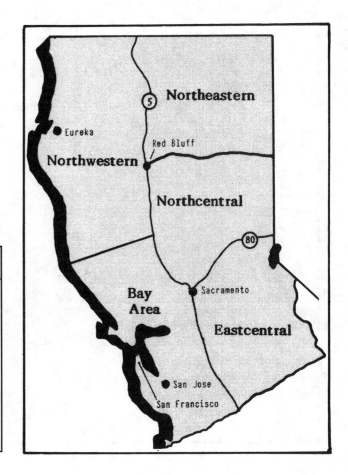

RIVER and STREAM FISHING

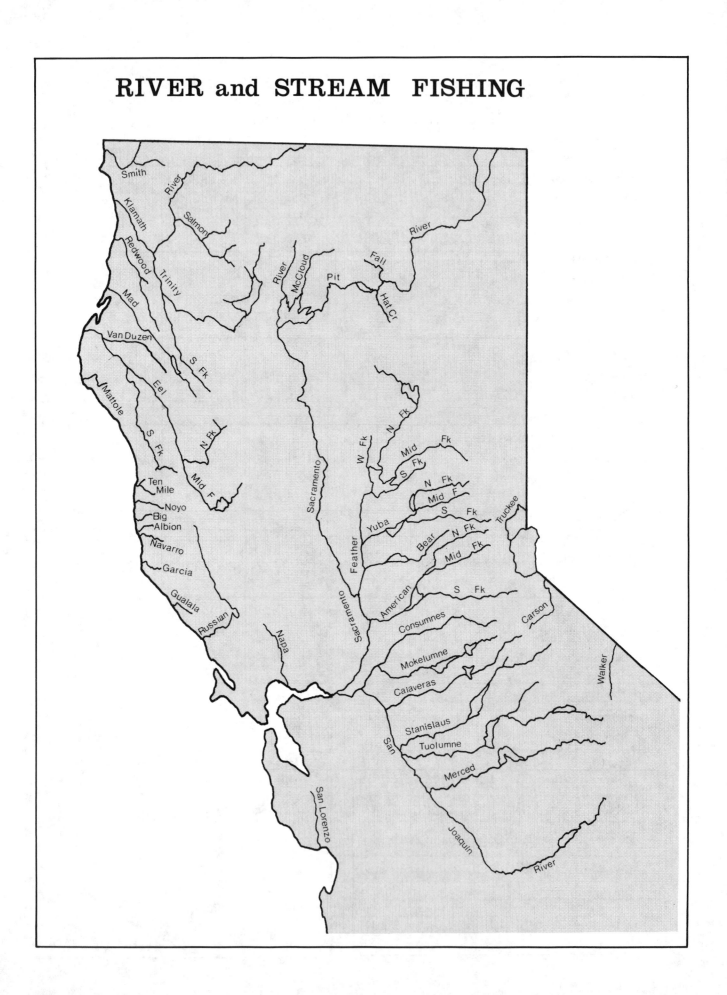

PACIFIC, BAY and LAKE FISHING

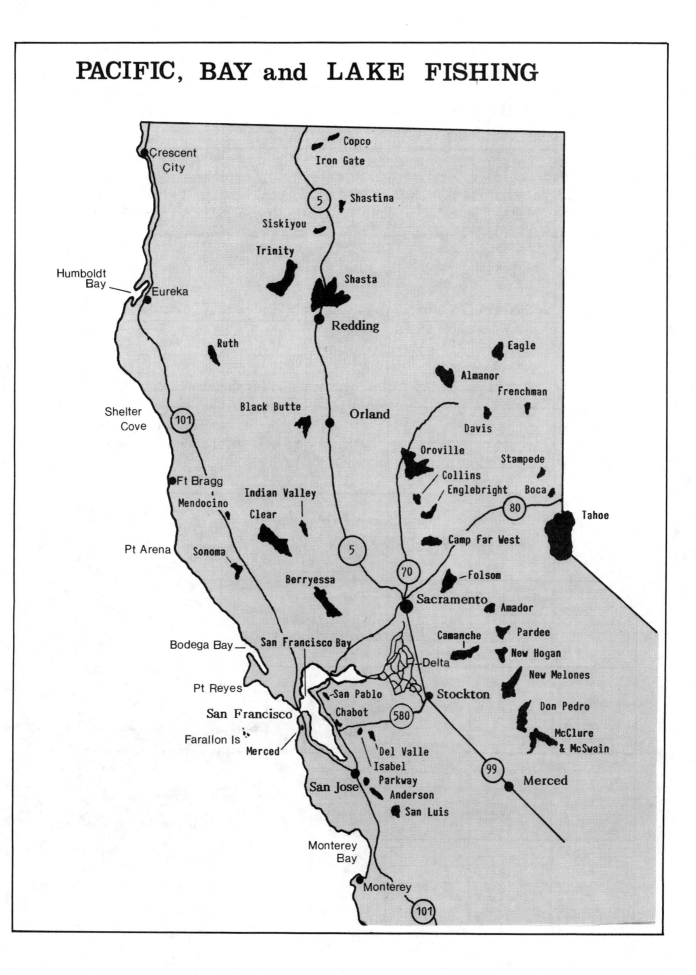

Ramblings...

Sometimes when a book is layed out, a wonderful thing happens. It's the luxury of having a page that the author can call his own, to use for a dedication, acknowledgements, personal reflections, etc. Well, that's what happened this time. So here goes...

- This book is dedicated to my mother, who died recently. You'll always be in my thoughts and in my actions.

- Marketscope has become the largest publisher of fishing books for California anglers. A special thanks to all our friends in the fishing tackle marketing business and in the bookstore trade. We'll keep the cookies coming. Also, we send our thanks and gratitude to the tens of thousands of anglers who have decided that our books are worth buying.

- The ultimate fishing experience may not be to "take a limit," but rather to catch and release as many fish as possible.

- Eat all day long . . . not possible.
  Drink all day long . . . not good.
  Sex all day long . . . not any more.
  Fish all day long . . . why not!

- And finally to Carol, my wife and best friend—
  In the two previous books, in the dedication, I promised we'd do something really important for a change . . . I promised we'd fish more often. This time let's really, really do it!

. . . Happy, our Beagle (1980–1993)

Take a Kid Fishing—One Story

My thirteen-year-old son Bruce had been after me for months to go fishing with him in tiny Lake Freedom, about four miles from our home. He'd heard at school that kids had caught some nice bass there. So late one Saturday afternoon we loaded our rowboat in the pick-up and drove to the lake.

I took my big, old metal tackle box. It had been my father's box and was packed with everything that was "state of the art" in the 1930's. He was killed in an industrial accident when I was a teenager. I inherited his love for fishing and his big, metal tackle box.

All the lures that my father used 40 and 50 years ago to entice the lunker bass are still in that metal box. But actually I hardly ever use any of his lures, since they're almost antiques and I don't want to lose them. Besides, I score most with spinnerbaits and plastic worms. This is what Bruce and I were using at Lake Freedom and we were getting skunked. The sun had set and I was ready to go home for dinner.

For some reason Bruce looked into his grandfather's tackle box and spotted an old red bucktail with three small fish-shaped flashers that protected the hook. "Dad, why don't you try this? It's sort of like a spinnerbait, isn't it?" he asked.

"Yea, I guess it is," I responded as I continued to work my worm."

"Come on, try it. Let's see how it swims."

"Okay, we'll give it a try."

I decided to humor him so I put it on and pulled it beside the boat to watch the action. "It looks pretty good. Like a spinnerbait," I said. Bruce agreed.

My first cast with this well-built relic landed near some overhanging branches. When I began my retrieve, the line stiffened and my rod arched. "Damn, I've snagged an underwater branch," I said under my breath. I was upset. I didn't want to lose that lure. For some reason, I didn't want to lose anything from the old, metal tackle box. But then the snag began to "run" and take line against my drag. What do you know, I had a strike on the first cast of a lure that hadn't been in the water since before World War II.

We landed the bass. It was a beauty. Bruce couldn't resist the temptation to say, "See Dad, I told you so. Those old lures are good."

"They sure are," I said, grinning.

Then we agreed that the fish should be released. Lake Freedom needed that bass, and we needed to know that it was alive and well. After all, it and that old lure performed 3 minor miracles. It was that old lure that gave Bruce and I a wonderful moment together. That old lure made me cherish my father's tackle box even more. And, it tied together a grandfather and grandson who never knew each other, except for a few moments at Lake Freedom.

Bruce switched to one of his grandfather's spinnerbait-like lures and we each made a few more casts into the twilight. Then Bruce said, "Dad, let's go home. I don't want to risk losing this lure. We can't see the overhanging branches." I nodded and we rowed to shore.

During the drive home, Bruce chattered about how to tell Mom our fishing story, and how to convince her with no fish as proof. But I was thinking about something else. I was thinking that someday Bruce would be a loving keeper of that big metal tackle box and those old lures.

See the "Teaching Kids How to Fish" section starting on page 14.

About this Expanded and Updated Edition

The man who will use his skill and constructive imagination to see how much he can give for a dollar, instead of how little he can give for a dollar, is bound to succeed.

Henry Ford

Henry Ford delivered an awful lot for each dollar in his Model A and Model T automobiles. And we're believers in Henry's philosophy. So we've worked very hard and long to "see how much we can give for a dollar" in developing this book. There is much more "How to Fish" info. There is way more "Where to Fish" coverage. More lakes, rivers, streams and saltwater. More maps and illustrations. More of everything. Quite simply, this expanded and updated edition is bigger and better. And guess what? It has the same cover price as the previous edition!

The Editor

Fishing Success

In earlier editions of this book we proclaimed that fishing is great in Northern California. Well, guess what? **Fishing is still great**.

There are 5,000 lakes and 30,000 miles of streams in California, and the vast majority of these lakes and streams are in Northern California. And then there are the hundreds of miles of coastline, San Francisco Bay and 700 miles of waterways in the Delta. Anglers here are fortunate to have an immense variety of quality fishing opportunities:

- Thousands of mountain streams and lakes for trout.
- Numerous lakes and reservoirs for bass, trout, catfish and panfish.
- Steelhead and salmon in coastal rivers.
- Valley rivers for striped bass, salmon, steelhead, shad and catfish.
- Bay waters for striped bass, sturgeon and halibut.
- Salmon, albacore, rockfish and lingcod in the Pacific.

Most of this great fishing is close-to-home, quite simple, and requires only modestly priced tackle. An added benefit, fishing is a wonderful way to share the outdoor experience with family or friends.

But the immense variety of Northern California fishing experiences does raise many questions, some major and others just puzzling:

- What size hook (or line) do I use for trout (or catfish)?
- Where are the bass hot spots at Folsom or Clear Lake?
- If I catch a halibut (or a catfish, or a . . .), how do I clean and cook it?
- When is the hot halibut season in San Francisco Bay?
- Can I fish from shore at San Pablo Reservoir?
- Where are the best spots to fish along the Sacramento River?
- What are the surest producers for largemouth bass?
- What rod and reel do I need for steelhead?
- When is the best time to go on an albacore trip?

Fishing in Northern California answers all these questions and many, many more. For all the types of fish and for each location, it tells how to fish, where to fish and when to fish. It also tells what equipment, tackle, rigs, bait and lures to use, how to clean and preserve your catch and how to cook each fish.

But there are common elements to fishing success. Elements that apply to many Northern California angling situations, from mountain trouting to saltwater pier fishing. And that's what this first chapter is all about.

Confidence

There is one element of fishing success that can't be taught or learned. Rather, it must be self-instilled. I'm talking about self-confidence. Often "how to" fishing articles end with a pep talk on the importance of fishing with confidence—that old Positive Mental Attitude. You know it's corny, but somehow it works.

I personally feel so strongly about the need to have faith in your approach and your tackle that I've reversed things and put this topic first. I love fishing even when I don't catch fish. But I love it even more when I do. Often the only difference between an angler who puts fish on the line and one who just wets his line is attitude. So fish with confidence.

Confidence will make you more attentive and more aware. It keeps your mind in gear. But, most importantly, it will encourage you to experiment, to change baits, or lures, or depths, or location until you find fish. This book tells you all you need to know to catch any kind of fish in Northern California. Just add self-confidence. The positive effects of perseverance, confidence and variety of approach can't be over emphasized.

But you say, "How can I fish with confidence if I'm not sure of what I'm doing." And I say, "Learn all you can, and then put what you've learned to work. You might not know it all, but you probably know enough to catch fish and have fun. And isn't that what it's all about?"

When to Fish?

There is no question that the time of year, the time of month and the time of day all impact on fishing success. More so for some species than others. All life moves in cycles. Fish are no different. For example, it's no coincidence that most of California's fishing records were set in the spring months. March, April, and May are probably the best months to fish. These are the spawning months for most species. Simply stated, here are the best times to fish.

Time of Year: Spring is best all around, followed by fall. Winter is surprisingly good. Summer, for many species is the worst. Yes, I know about summer vacations; the weather is beautiful and fishing seems to be a natural, warm weather sport, but often the fish don't know this. Or maybe they do! However, some fishing is good in summertime, especially if the proper approaches are followed. The table in the next column highlights the best time of year to fish for each species. It's easy to see why fishing if a four season sport in Northern California.

Time of Day: For most types of fish, during most times of the year, there is little doubt that early morning (from first light until 8 a.m.) and late evening (the 2 to 3 hours before dark) are the best times of day to catch fish. These are the times of day when fish are active and feeding. For some situations nighttime is also good. For example, bass fishing after dark on warm summer nights, using noisy, dark surface plugs (in shallow water) can be good. Also, summertime catfishing can be good after 9 p.m. and during the two hours before daybreak.

Time of Month (The Tides): Some would say that the phases of the moon have a great deal to do with fishing success, in any environment. This may or may not be true. But, there is no doubt that tides do impact fishing success in shallower tidal waters like bays. Surf, rock and pier anglers know how tide movements effect fishing. In tidal waters, it's always best to fish on days when there is a big change between high and low tide. Waters move faster, bait and bait fish get moved around, so game fish feed more actively.

The height of the tide varies according to the positions of the sun and moon in relation to the earth. These influences are illustrated below. The best fishing is during spring tide periods. Fish the hours before, through and after a high tide change for peak action.

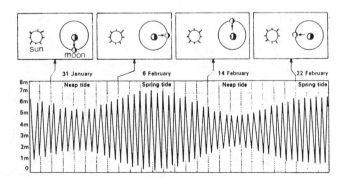

Fishing Seasons

	J	F	M	A	M	J	J	A	S	O	N	D
Abalone												
Albacore												
Bass*												
Bat Rays												
Bluegill												
Carp												
Catfish												
Clams												
Crappie												
Flounder												
Halibut												
Kokanee												
Lingcod												
Perch+												
Rock Cod												
Salmon												
Ocean												
S.F. Bay												
Rivers												
Lakes												
Sanddabs												
Shad												
Sharks												
Smelt												
Steelhead												
Striped Bass												
Ocean												
Bays												
Rivers												
Sturgeon												
Bays												
Rivers												
Trout												
Streams												
Lakes												

* Largemouth & Smallmouth
\+ Saltwater

Fair ▨   Good ▨

More on the Moon: There is a school of fishing thought that says that the position of the moon (or some say the moon and the sun), on a daily basis, has an effect on the feeding and activity level of fish. These peak activity periods coincide with the moon's strongest gravitational pull which occurs twice each day when the moon is directly above or below a particular point on earth. When the moon is above, it's a major period, and when it's below, it's a minor period according to the theory. These activity periods are published in California outdoor newspapers and in magazines. Or a guide can be purchased to calculate major and minor activity periods each day. If nothing else, it's fun to see if the activity periods coincide with one's own fishing experience.

Where to Fish

This book has tons of "where to fish" information in it. But there are three generalizations about "where to fish" that apply so universally, that they are worthy of special attention.

Fish on the Bottom!: To catch many varieties of Northern California fish you've got to fish on or near the bottom. This is true for the following fish:

Bass	Rockcrabs
Catfish	Salmon (in rivers)
Crayfish	Steelhead
Halibut	Striped Bass
Lingcod	Sturgeon
Rock Cod	Trout (most often)

Steam trout will rise up for food, but then retreat to the bottom. Trout near shore in lakes are on the bottom. I'd like to emphasize the truism, "fish on the bottom," with this analogy. Most creatures that live on land, actually live on the bottom of a vast sea of atmosphere. This atmosphere is about 100,000 feet deep, yet most creatures live right on the bottom of the atmosphere. Of course, people and all fur bearing animals live on the bottom, but so do most birds and insects. Birds and insects spend most of their time in and around the ground, plants and trees that are part of the atmosphere's bottom structure. Well, the same is true of most fish. Water is their air. And the bottom of the water provides food, shelter and security.

The primary Northern California game fish that are consistently caught in open water (not near the bottom) are salmon (in the ocean), albacore, kokanee (a land locked salmon), trout (in lakes) and some sharks.

Fish at the Right Water Temperature: In big Northern California lakes and reservoirs, the key factor in finding fish during the summer months is water temperature. Lakes stratify into three distinct layers with the coming of summer and stay that way until fall. The middle layer of water, called the thermocline, has a large concentration of dissolved oxygen, bait fish and therefore, trout, salmon and even bass. The thermocline, which provides the right temperature for trout and salmon metabolism, is down from 10 to 80 feet, depending on season and lake characteristics.

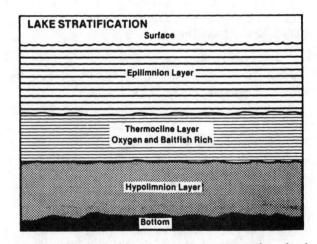

Gauges for measuring water temperature at various depths are available for as little as $5-10. Below is a chart showing the temperatures where you are likely to find fish.

Species	Optimum Temp.	Temp. Range
Salmon	55 °F	44-58 °F
Trout (lake)	50	43-53
Trout (brown and rainbow)	55-60	44-75
Bass, striped	70-72	60-78
Bass, largemouth	70-72	60-73
Bass, smallmouth	64-66	-
Panfish	-	-
Catfish	-	75-80

Fish Don't Like Direct Light: This is one reason why fishing drops off when the morning sun hits a lake. But there are things you can do. For instance, if you're catching fish in a lake early in the day, try deeper down as the light increases. Or, if you're fishing a trout stream, work the shady side. This also applies to lake shores.

Teaching Kids How to Fish

My father died when I was a teenager. But many times he shared his love of fishing with me. In the front of this book I've told a very personal fishing story. It was about how my youngest son came to know and love his grandfather's old lures and tackle box. This story was special to me, but not unique. Fishing brings families together. Teach your children how to fish. Do it for them and for yourself.

Kids and fishing just seem to be made for each other. It's hard to find a youngster that won't jump at the chance to "go fishin'." A good starting age is 3 to 7 years old. And we're not just talking about boys going fishing with their fathers, or older brothers. Over a third of U.S. fishing licenses are sold to women. So a lot of girls learned to fish along the way, and the fathers and mothers are teaching their daughters how to fish in record numbers. One caution: It is not easy, but children can be "turned off" to fishing if parents don't follow some simple guidelines.

Know the Basics: Many parents, who aren't experienced anglers, find out the basics by going fishing with friends who are veteran anglers. And don't be proud. Ask questions. And fish for the same species in the same type of waters, where you are planning on taking your youngster. A fishing guide is another alternative. He or she can teach both parents and youngsters at the same time. They are listed in phone books and they advertise in outdoor publications. Be sure to ask for references, and explain what you expect to achieve on the trip.

Equipment: Youngsters fishing tackle should be easy to operate, light weight, "kid-sized" and somewhat durable. Most experts recommend a spincast reel. These are closed-faced reels that cast and retrieve easily and don't backlash (or tangle the line). One hint: These reels need a little tension on the line to retrieve properly. This is usually of no concern while retrieving in water where a lure or sinker provides the tension. But for "driveway" practice casts and retrieves in store isles, the line right in front of the reel opening should be lightly squeezed between the index finger and thumb of the non-cranking hand. This provides the needed tension so that the line pick-up mechanism in the reel can function. Damage can result if this simple practice is not followed.

Older children, say 9-11 years old, may want to start with an open-faced spinning reel. These are the kind used by most adults. Ask the dealer to explain how to operate them.

Match the spincast reel with a short pistol grip rod. Often this combination can be purchased as a package for as little as $10-20. A good rod length is 3 1/2 to 4 feet. Most reels have line already on them. 8-10 pound test line is the best.

A good, well-fitting life jacket is highly recommended for shore, pier or boat fishing. Some kids might put up a fuss, but it's an easy battle to win, and you might just be preventing an unnecessary tragedy.

Practice: And I don't mean practice at the lake or stream. Practice at home, before going fishing. Concentrate on casting and retrieving. Practice plugs are available at tackle stores, or use a small lead sinker. Kneeling behind and slightly above the youngster might be useful on the first attempts. Pick out a target and make a game out of trying to land near it. If you're going to be bait fishing it might also be a good idea to "rig-up" at home. Then when you get to the water, anxious kids can start fishing right away. For kids, I like to use a small snap swivel as the first item at the end of the line. This allows quick change of lures, and easy replacement of lost bait rigs that have been pre-tied and stored in small sandwich bags.

Where to Go: Go close to home. Long drives are just too much for the nervous systems of little anglers. Choose a place where fish are abundant and easy to catch. The size of the fish is secondary. Good possibilities in the Bay Area are the fish-for-pay lakes like Merced, Del Valle, Chabot, San Pablo, and Parkway. These are well stocked and employees at the lake will provide up-to-date tips and hot spots. Bay piers are also a good possibility. Call first to assess the bite. In other parts of the North State, check for public information on recent trout plants. Recent plants' locales are usually hot spots. Finally, shore anglers need an open shoreline. The only way to keep kids from casting into trees is to have no trees within 100 yards.

Attitude: Simply stated, don't get upset when things go wrong. And they will go wrong. Just try to solve each problem as it comes along, and provide tons of encouragement. And, by all means, when a little guy or gal gets a fish on, don't grab the rod and land it yourself. This advice seems stupid, but in the excitement of the moment many well-meaning parents do this very thing. Let the child try bringing in the fish alone. Give calm advice, based on instructions you communicated earlier (maybe on the ride to the fishing grounds). After a few lost fish, fate will intervene and a fish will be landed. The laughing and cheers will be worth your commitment to patience. And your little one will be very proud.

Final Thoughts: Instill positive values in your children. For example, release undersized fish (a camera will capture the thrill of even a teeny first fish), and follow other fishing regulations. Don't litter. Don't trespass. Buy a fishing license for yourself. Kids under 16 don't need one. One last piece of advice—bring lots of favorite foods and beverages. Little anglers get very hungry.

Casting

Casting is an integral part of most fishing activities. This is true whether you bait fish with a sliding sinker rig for trout in a lake, or live bait fish for striper on a party boat. And it's also true that better, more accurate casts catch more fish.

Casting with spinning or spincast equipment is quite straightforward, but accurate casting takes some practice. Freshwater or saltwater conventional reel rigs are more difficult to master because of backlash, but good equipment and practice will pay off here too. Novice anglers should read up on the subject at the library and observe more experienced casters whenever possible. Excellent fishing videos are also available for rent or sale, especially at larger tackle dealers.

Fly casting is different. In spinning or bait casting the weight that is cast is concentrated in the lure or bait. And it is the weight that pulls line off the reel. But in fly casting, the offering is virtually weightless, and it is the fly line that is the weight. Fly casting is probably the most difficult casting skill to develop. A good book on the subject is *Fly Fishing From the Beginning*. There are also excellent fly casting videos.

Playing and Landing

A variety of fishing techniques are needed to entice a fish to bite or strike. Once this is accomplished, whether you've got a bass or sturgeon on the other end of your line, there is a certain commonality in playing a larger fish. Here are the elements:

1. Pull the rod up and back forcefully to set the hook. Don't be tentative. Hold the reel handle firmly, so no line is given. After setting, adjust the drag, if necessary.

2. Hold the rod tip up when playing a fish. The rod butt can be held against the stomach area. Lower the rod tip and reel in simultaneously. Stop reeling and pump the rod upwards to move the fish in. Then, reel in again on the down stroke. This rod "pumping" allows you to reel in when tension on the line and terminal tackle is not at its maximum.

3. Never give a fish slack. If it charges, reel in fast. Try to guide fish away from your boat with rod tip high. But if the fish does get under your boat, put the rod tip down into the water to prevent line abrasion or twisting around the outdrive.

4. If your fish runs, let him go against the reel drag. That's what it's for. Then slowly bring him back by reeling in, or if necessary, using the pumping technique. Never reel in when the fish is running against the drag—it twists the line.

5. Keep the rod tip high while landing. This allows the rod to act as a shock absorber and prevents the chance of slack line. Net the fish from below and in front.

Catch and Release

There is a growing awareness among anglers that the fish resource is limited. And some anglers now feel that the ultimate fishing experience is not to "take a limit" but to catch and release as many fish as possible. Of course, no one should keep more fish than they can use, or keep a fish that they don't enjoy eating.

Obviously, catch and release is a personal decision. It's also a practice that can be and should be exercised on a selective basis. Sometimes a fish shouldn't be released; for example, a badly hooked, bleeding fish, or a small rockfish that has been brought up from 50 fathoms, and is dead on arrival. For some reason, I personally don't like to take fish that are about to spawn. I know this is somewhat irrational since it's absolutely true that no matter when you take a fish in its life cycle, you're forever preventing that fish from spawning. But I guess I just feel that when a fish has made it through all the hurdles and survived all the predators and all the hazards, that is has a right to spawn without me interfering. On the other hand, I don't mind taking fish that are in abundant supply or even those that are planted regularly.

When you do want to release fish, there are several things you can do to improve the chances for the fish:

1. Use barbless hooks (or flatten down barbs with pliers) and avoid fishing with bait, if possible. If you do use bait, don't use a sliding sinker rig. Hooks with sliding sinker rigs are often very deep.

2. Time is of the essence. Play and release fish as rapidly as possible. A fish played gently for too long may be too exhausted to recover.

3. Keep the fish in the water as much as possible. A fish out of water is suffocating and, in addition, is twice as heavy. He may seriously injure himself if allowed to flop on the beach or rocks. Even a few inches of water under a thrashing fish acts as a protective cushion.

4. Gentleness in handling is essential. Keep your fingers out of the gills. Do not squeeze small fish . . . they can easily be held by the lower lip. Nets may be helpful provided the mesh does not become entangled in the gills. Hooks and lines catching in nets may delay release, so keep the net in the water.

5. Unhooking. Remove the hook as rapidly as possible with long-nose pliers. If the fish is deeply hooked, cut the leader and leave the hook in. Be quick but gentle—do not roughly tear out hooks. Small fish are particularly susceptible to the shock of a torn-out hook.

6. Reviving. Some fish, especially after a long struggle, may lose consciousness and float belly up. Always hold the fish in the water, heading upstream. Propel it back and forth, pumping water through its gills. When it revives, begins to struggle and can swim normally, let it go to survive and challenge another fisherman.

Fishing Photography

It is no coincidence that this section on Fishing Photography follows the Catch and Release discussion. You see, photography provides a wonderful way to have your fish and release it too. Actually there are several ways to use photography to "keep" fish and release them at the same time. Beyond this, photos are a great way to capture all kinds of fishing memories, even for catches headed for the frying pan.

Skin mounting of trophy fish is now being replaced, by many sportsmen, with acrylic mounts. These plastic mounts are extremely attractive and require that the angler provide good color photos to the taxidermist. A good side view and another looking down along the back are necessary. Measure the fish's length, its girth at the gills, the dorsal fin and the wrist ahead of the tail. Also measure the breadth of the spread out tail. Keep the fish in the water as much as possible while snapping photos and using the tape measure.

If you're not planning on mounting the fish, different photo guidelines are in order. That's because the photo itself becomes the end of the story. Fishing magazines publish a wide array of the best fishing photography. Browse through some of these and pick out the ones that appeal to you. Now, work at developing your ability to see things the way the camera lens sees things. Soon you'll be taking snaps that far surpass the full-length shot of the angler posing with his fish.

Fishing Guides

There are many fine fishing guides in Northern California. Most are specialists and operate in a fairly narrow geographical area, for example, steelhead on the Klamath, or striper in the Delta. Guides are listed in phone books and they advertise in outdoor publications. Charges can range from $100 to $150 per angler per day. Most guides require two anglers per boat.

Earlier it was suggested that use of a skilled guide was one good approach to teaching children how to fish. Well, it's great for adults too. It allows the angler to learn firsthand about new waters, an unfamiliar technique (e.g. backtrolling) or an untried species (e.g. sturgeon).

Telephone prospective guides in the evening. They're out on the water in the daytime. Ask specific questions about charges and what's provided. Often the fee includes boat, tackle, bait and a box lunch. Communicate clearly your purpose in making the trip. Is it for a trophy fish or for knowledge about a specific technique? Ask the guide for two or three references. Be on time the day of your guided trip. Guides are under a great deal of pressure to produce. And they know it will be easier to catch fish earlier in the day.

Hook, Line, Knots and Swivels

Fishing rigs have two ends—the angler's end and the fish's end. On the angler's end you've got rods, reels, clothing, electronics, nets, etc. On the fish's end you've got hooks, line, knots and maybe swivels and lures. Much more money is invested on the angler's end, but when you get a fish on, success often depends on the "loose change" items on the fish's end and how well they've been assembled.

Hooks: An often neglected item is the fishing hook. First, it's important to keep them sharp. Inexpensive little sharpeners are made just for this purpose. Both bait hooks and lure hooks get abused, in use, and in tackle boxes, so do sharpen them regularly.

The designation system used in fishing hook sizing can be confusing for those who don't deal with it regularly. Large hooks (1/10 and up) increase in size as the number increase. (So a 4/0 is a larger hook than a 2/0). Small hooks (1 and down) decrease in size as the number increases. (So a 6 is a larger hook than a 10).

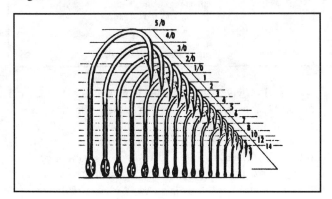

A leading hook manufacturer (Eagle Claw) makes the following hook size recommendations:

Panfish	Bluegill	8 down to 12
	Crappie	4
Bass	Smallmouth	3/0 down to 4
	Largemouth	8/0 down to 4
	Striped	3/0 up to 10/0
Catfish	up to 5#	4 down to 12
	large	4 up to 8/0
Trout	Rainbow	5 down to 14
	Brown	5 down to 14
	Steelhead	2 up to 6/0
Salmon		about 6/0

Sometimes hooks get caught in people rather than in fish. Another leading hook manufacturer (Mastad) provides two hook removal techniques (see diagram). Following removal,

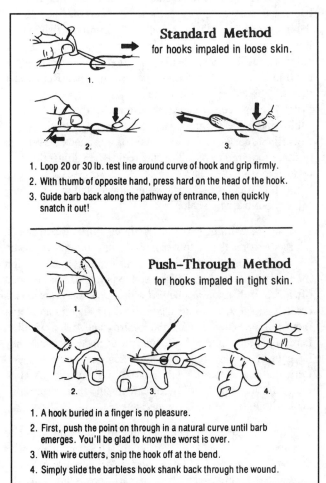

Standard Method
for hooks impaled in loose skin.

1. Loop 20 or 30 lb. test line around curve of hook and grip firmly.
2. With thumb of opposite hand, press hard on the head of the hook.
3. Guide barb back along the pathway of entrance, then quickly snatch it out!

Push-Through Method
for hooks impaled in tight skin.

1. A hook buried in a finger is no pleasure.
2. First, push the point on through in a natural curve until barb emerges. You'll be glad to know the worst is over.
3. With wire cutters, snip the hook off at the bend.
4. Simply slide the barbless hook shank back through the wound.

allow the wound to be bled freely for a couple of minutes. Then wash thoroughly, clean with alcohol and bandage. Check to see if your tetanus shots are up-to-date. The tips provided apply to routine hook removal only. For serious impalement, see physician immediately.

Finally, a note on terminology: Hooks are sold snelled or unsnelled. A snelled hook has a factory-applied leader attached to it. Unsnelled hooks are bare. Most anglers find snelled hooks to be more convenient for most uses.

Fishing Line: Good quality fishing line is a wise investment. And many anglers replace the line on all their reels at the beginning of each fishing season. Monofilament is appropriate for most fishing, and consider the fluorescent feature. It helps immensely in seeing where your bait and line are. Don't use line that is heavier than conditions require. Heavy line impedes the movement of trolled or retrieved lures and it is easier for fish to see.

Many strong fish have snapped good line and escaped because the reel drag was set too tight. After the line absorbs the impact of the strike, the drag must permit the fish to take line off the reel as it makes a run, yet be tight enough to slow it down and eventually tire it out. A good rule is to set the drag at no more than half the pound/test of the line. Remember that the breaking action increases as the spool empties. When fishing deep or in heavy currents, set the drag to about a third of the line's pound/test. To set the drag, attach the line to a reliable spring scale, apply tension and check the pounds of force required to pull it off the reel. Then adjust the drag control to give the desired value. With some experience, a "feel" for proper drag setting is developed, and then it can be set without use of a scale.

Among the things we can do without, along stream banks, lake shores or at the bottom of bays are beverage cans, plastic six-pack holders and monofilament fishing line. Nylon monofilament degrades slowly so the tangle of line stripped off a reel will remain where it's dropped for years. This creates an eyesore, a nuisance to foul the fishing area, and most telling, a lethal hazard for birds and other wildlife. Birds and other animals suffer and die each day because they have been snarled in carelessly discarded monofilament. Let's put an end to this! Discard old line properly. And go a step further—pick up the discarded line that yesterday's air-head angler dropped on the bank.

Knots: A good fishing knot is one that stays tied and one that doesn't weaken the line too much. There are many knots that fit these criteria, but most veteran anglers use only one or two basic knots. The best overall knot is probably the

improved clinch knot. It can be used to tie hooks to leaders, swivels to line, etc. There are two versions:

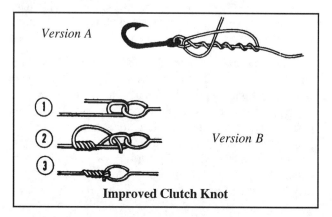

Improved Clutch Knot

The other popular knot is the Palomar knot. It is especially useful for super lines, but it is also popular for use among saltwater anglers. Here is how it is tied:

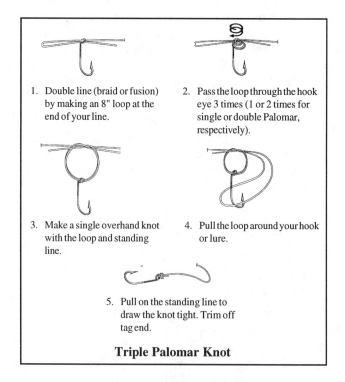

1. Double line (braid or fusion) by making an 8" loop at the end of your line.

2. Pass the loop through the hook eye 3 times (1 or 2 times for single or double Palomar, respectively).

3. Make a single overhand knot with the loop and standing line.

4. Pull the loop around your hook or lure.

5. Pull on the standing line to draw the knot tight. Trim off tag end.

Triple Palomar Knot

Swivels: Swivels are available in a number of shapes and sizes. Their primary purpose is to prevent line twist. Some models have eyes on both ends, while others, called snap swivels, feature a locking device on one end. It is very handy for quickly changing lures. However, the action of some finely tuned lures, like premium brand imitation minnow type lures, may be inhibited by using a snap swivel. Tie these lures directly to the line. One tip: Even the highest quality swivels are very inexpensive. Cheap foreign swivels often fall apart, and sometimes don't swivel. So buy good quality.

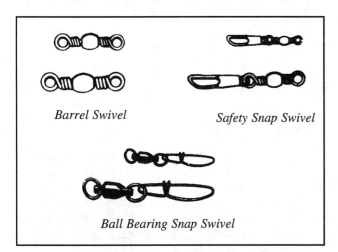

Barrel Swivel   *Safety Snap Swivel*

Ball Bearing Snap Swivel

Fish Attractants and Artificial Baits

There is little doubt that fish have a highly developed sense of smell. Salmon return to their place of origin to spawn by following the faint smell that is unique to each waterway. Attractant and bait manufacturers have done a great deal of experimenting to isolate compounds that attract fish to strike. And there is a growing number of these products on the market. They come in liquid, moldable, formed and even "slime" consistency. Anecdotal evidence among anglers suggest that some of these products, especially the newer ones, are effective in some situations. Liquids and slimes can be sprayed on lures or natural baits. Moldables are packed into or on lures or hooks. It's generally agreed that scented offerings are most effective in slower presentation modes. This gives the scent a chance to be spread in the water. It's always fun to experiment with fish attractants. Put some on one rod and not on another, and see what happens.

Downriggers

More and more anglers in Northern California are using downriggers, in both freshwater and saltwater. Salmon, trout, stripers and sharks are among the game fish being targeted. Often these fish, and others, are down deep. Traditionally, cannonball sinkers, trolling planes, leadcore line and keel sinkers have been used to troll offerings down where the fish are lurking. Often heavy line, stout rods and

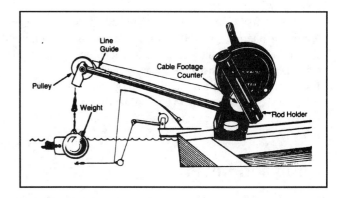

large reels are required. The advantage of the downrigger is that it enables the angler to regulate fishing depth while allowing the fish to be fought using relatively light gear.

A downrigger is essentially a winch with a heavy (usually 6 to 10 pounds) weight attached to a cable. The cable allows the weight to be raised or lowered to the desired fishing depth. The line holding the bait or lure is attached to the downrigger weight using a spring loaded release clip. When a fish hits, the line is released from the weight allowing the fish to be fought on unencumbered tackle.

Downriggers, like the rest of your tackle, should be tailored to the kind of fishing you expect to do. For offshore saltwater fishing you'll want a heavy-duty model made exclusively of non-corrosive materials. For most freshwater fishing from smaller craft, you'll want to choose something lighter and more convenient.

Fishing Electronics

There was a time, not too long ago, when fishing electronics meant just a fish finder, either with a paper graph output or a flasher output. But now fish locating electronics means a whole lot more. First, fish finders have been available with paper graph, video, LCD (liquid crystal diode) and flasher outputs. Today, LCDs dominate the market. Beyond profiling the slope of the bottom and identifying bait fish schools and individual game fish, some units offer boat speed and surface water temperature read out, split screens, dual frequency operations, integral Loran C, etc. Recently, I was in the market to replace my fish finder with some of this current technology—the options and alternatives were mind boggling! I almost drove my wife crazy by pouring over catalogs and asking questions of salespeople. It took me several months to finally make a choice!

Beyond fish finders, there are other fishing electronics worth considering. A VHF marine radio is essential on the ocean, bays and Delta and not a bad idea on large inland waters. Loran C instruments are great for returning to favorite fishing grounds, and for helping find your way home in the fog. Some largemouth bass anglers also use PH guides and Color-C-Lectors to improve their success.

Rods and Reels

In the "How To Catch . . ." chapter of this book, detailed catching instructions are provided for each Northern California game fish. There are 27 of them in all. Rod and reel recommendations are made in each section. Not only are the most desirable rod and reel combinations noted, but also alternatives that often work just as well. Happily, you don't need 27 rod and reel sets to enjoy all the fishing experiences in this book.

Often, one rod and reel are useful in several types of fishing. For example, a boat rod and conventional saltwater-sized reel can be used for salmon trolling, striper trolling, sturgeon, halibut, lingcod and rock cod. This may even be overkill in some situations since a lightweight spinning outfit can be used to troll or cast for average striper (6-10 pounds). This same light spinning outfit can be used for trout (both lake and stream), bass casting, panfishing, even steelhead in smaller coastal streams. In fact, an angler doesn't even need a fly rod and reel to fly fish, but don't tell avid fly anglers this. A casting bobber on spinning equipment will deliver a fly. See the Trout (in Streams) section of this book. And talking about stream trout fishing, one hot item now is the mini-spinning outfit—a 5 foot rod and tiny reel. It's fun to use. But spinners can also usually be delivered effectively using about a 7 foot rod and normal-sized reel filled with 4 pound test line.

Fortunately, rods and reels of good quality (not gold-plated, but good quality) are not that expensive. But, before considering a specialized rod and reel, first consider using what you've got on hand. Look at what others are using when you get to the water. I'm always surprised at the variety. Besides, the fish doesn't know what's on the other end of the line. Good line, tied well, a decent drag and know-how will land most fish.

Maps

First, let me emphasize that none of the maps included in this book (or in any fishing book, for that matter) are to be used for navigational purposes. Their only intent is to indicate where the fish can be found. Navigational maps for coastal and bay waters are available at marine and boating stores. These are published by the National Oceanic and Atmospheric Administration (U.S. Department of Commerce).

There are other good maps that are especially useful to anglers:

U.S. Forest Service Maps—especially useful in determining which land is publicly owned, and to locate access to public waters.

U.S. Geological Survey—good for detailed topographical features, and for locating out-of-the-way fishing spots.

U.S. Bureau of Land Management—for streams and lakes in this agency's jurisdiction.

Park Scenic Maps—both federal and state parks publish maps that can be quite helpful.

Hal Shell's Delta Map—comprehensive map of the entire Delta waterways including facilities.

Topographical Maps—these are very useful for underwater lake terrain and mountain topography.

Fishing . . . NorCal Style

Fishing in Northern California is much like a sumptuous smorgasbord. And what's so wonderful is that there are so many ways to participate in this feast. Some of the most popular and productive options are profiled in this chapter. It starts out with a collection of San Francisco Bay and Pacific Ocean techniques. Then there's a selection of freshwater techniques, from night fishing and fly fishing to ice fishing. Finally, there's a potpourri of unrelated, but key topics.

Party Boat Fishing

Tens of thousands of anglers enjoy ocean fishing on a party boat, or on a chart sport fishing boat, each year in Northern California. To say the least, this is a popular and relatively inexpensive way to pursue saltwater fish.

Most party boats take reservations from individuals and operate on a daily schedule. Charter boats are available for group rental. Party boat anglers range from regulars, who go out every week, to vacationers from Wyoming who have never even seen the ocean, let alone fished it. One appeal to newcomers is that no equipment or prior knowledge is needed. Rod and reels can be rented (for about $3.00-5.00 a day). Burlap sacks to hold the catch are available. Bait is included in the price of the trip, and fish filleting services are available at dockside at a modest cost. And there are plenty of helpful people around to explain the best way to catch fish. Observing those anglers who are the most successful helps the newcomer with the finer points.

Party boats are large, safe, well-equipped fishing machines. They have bathrooms, lounges and other amenities. No matter what season it is or what the weather is like on shore, it's best to bring along warm clothing. It gets cool out on the water. Dress in layers. Then you can build up or strip down depending upon conditions. One of the attractive aspects of NorCal party boat angling is the wide variety of fishing experiences that are offered. There are open ocean trips for salmon, albacore, rockfish or lingcod. Then there are what are called "potluck trips" on San Francisco Bay for striper and halibut. These trips use the live bait drift fishing techniques described later in this chapter, and also, on occasion, take rockfish, lingcod or even salmon. These same live bait boats also offer trips for striper off Pacifica when this action is hot. And there are, at times, trips in San Francisco Bay for sturgeon or even shark. The fishing techniques used on all these trips are those described in the "How To Catch . . ." chapter of this book. Ocean salmon trips are offered whenever the fish are hitting between March and October. Albacore trips are usually in August and September. Rockfish trips are offered throughout most of the ocean fishing season, while most lingcod trips are fall and early winter. Potluck trips are in summer, as are the Pacific striper trips. Sturgeon fishing is best in winter. Trip costs vary depending on travel time to the fishing grounds and the actual fishing time, but most run between $30 and $40, with albacore being higher.

Party boats operate out of several locations (or landings) along the Northern California coast. Here are the major landings: Morro Bay, Monterey, Santa Cruz, Half Moon Bay, San Francisco (Fisherman's Wharf), Emeryville, Richmond, San Rafael, Bodega Bay, Fort Bragg and Eureka. Most advertise in local yellow pages and in NorCal fishing newspapers.

Surf Fishing

Surf fishing is man and nature at their best. It's just you, the roaring breakers, the sea birds, salt spray and hopefully the fish. For those who demand more than sea birds and salt spray, there are practical reasons why so many people enjoy surf fishing: there are miles and miles of accessible beaches to fish; it can be done year-round; the necessary equipment is inexpensive; bait is often free; and the fish can be caught without a great deal of skill.

Bait Fishing Techniques: Northern California anglers catch a good variety of fish. The most common are surfperch (redtail, walleye and barred). But California halibut, flounder, striped bass and even salmon can be taken. The basic approach for catching all these fish is the same. Cast out a rig consisting of a 2-6 ounce pyramid sinker at the end of a leader that has 2 or 3 baited hooks on it. They then set the rod in a sandspike rodholder and wait for the bite. If nothing happens in a few minutes, slowly move the rig in about 3 to 5 feet and try this new location. Some novices are tempted to run back from the beach, especially when a large fish is hooked. This is not a good idea. Rather, reel the fish in steadily, and move back only if the fish is charging faster than you can take in line. When a large fish is near shore, time your retrieve with the surf so the momentum of a breaker will skid the fish up on the sand. Run and grab the fish under the gill cover and quickly move back to higher ground.

Tackle and Equipment: As mentioned earlier, tackle and equipment requirements are quite minimal. All you need are the following:

- Rod—10-12 foot surf spinning rod with two-handed grip

- Reel—Saltwater spinning reels are most popular. It should hold 200-250 yards of 15-20 pound monofilament line.

- Other—Pyramid sinker (assorted 2-6 ounce—use the smallest that tide and wave conditions will allow), surf leaders (available at most tackle counters), hooks (#2 or #6), sandspike rodholder, and a big pail (for bait and your catch).

Bait and Rigging: The basic rig is straightforward as illustrated in the diagram below.

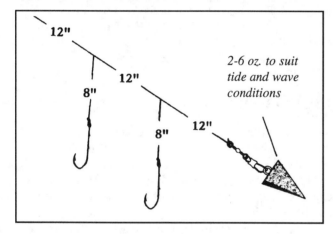

The hook size depends on the fish:

Fish	Typical Catch (lbs.)	Hook Size
California halibut	4-8	#2
Striped bass	4-10	#1/0
Barred surfperch	1	#6
Walleye surfperch	1/4	#6
Redtail	1/2	#6

Most anglers prefer frozen anchovies when fishing for halibut and utilize a slow and continuous retrieve through holes and slopes. Perch, both barred and walleye, are suckers for blood worms and sand crabs. Blood worms are natives of Maine and are available from bait shops. Soft-shelled sand crabs and another free bait, mussels, are gathered by anglers themselves. Hook the sand crab up through the tail end with the hook tip barely showing. Hook the mussel through the tough gristle-like edge. If possible, it's probably best to be prepared to toss out several of these baits and let the fish decide. Cut pieces of frozen squid is another good alternative. These strips stay on the hook very well.

Surf Casting: The most aggressive surf anglers are the cast and retrieve people. They cast plugs and spoons that weigh 2-4 ounces into the surf, and then retrieve them, alert for a striper or occasional salmon strike. Halibut can also be taken. Surf casters typically use a two-handed grip rod of about 10 feet in length. A shorter rod lacks the needed distance while a longer one is slower and more difficult to control.

Effective offerings for casters include Pencil-Poppers, Zara Spooks, Hopkins No-Eql, Krocodiles, Kastmasters, and bucktail and bug-eye jigs. Plugs are best in rocky areas and spoons are preferred on beaches. Heavy-duty saltwater spinning reels with rear drag are popular. The reel used should hold 200-250 yards of 15-30 test monofilament line. Conventional reels with a free spool and star drag (like the Penn Squidder) are for traditionalists who have mastered the art of thumbing the spool to prevent backlash. Freshwater bass tackle rigged with soft largemouth bass jigs and plastic worms is becoming popular for surfperch.

Striper anglers watch for birds like gulls, sheerwaters, pelicans or cormorants diving into the surf in pursuit of bait fish. These bait fish are driven into the beach by feeding stripers. These birds are the casters main clue as to when the stripers are feeding and in which direction they may be moving. The key is to cast the line where the bait fish are and to retrieve it so it duplicates a wounded bait fish. Early mornings and dusk are often the best times to use the birds as trackers.

Where to Fish: Some of the best surf fishing spots are listed on the next page. But exactly where on a beach to fish is important. It's best, if possible, to scout a beach at low tide. Steeply sloping beach areas are best. Look for holes and channels where the surf is not breaking. When the tide floods in, these become the feeding grounds for fish. The rising tide, up to high tide and an hour or two after, are usually the best times to fish. Actually, any accessible surf has the potential of being a good surf fishing location, but some locations are more accessible and have developed a reputation as productive fishing stretches. Starting from the Oregon border and working south, the following is a list of some of the best:

North of Humboldt: Prairie Creek Redwood St. Pk., Trinidad St. Beach, Mad River Beach Co. Pk.

Humboldt Bay: No. Spit (take Hwy. 225), So. Spit (take Table Bluff Rd.)

Mendocino County: MacKerricher St. Pk., Manchester St. Beach

Sonoma Count: Coast State beaches north of Bodega Bay

Marin County: Pt. Reyes Natl. Seashore (north and south beaches), Stinson Beach

San Francisco City and Count: Baker, Ocean and Fleishhacker Beaches

San Mateo County: Thornton St. Beach, Mussel Rock, Sharp Park St. Beach, Rockaway Beach, Linda Mar Beach, Montara St. Beach, Half Moon Bay St. Beach

Monterey Bay: Twin Lakes, New Brighton, Seacliff, Sunset and Moss Landing St. beaches, Carmel River St. Beach

San Luis Obispo County: Hearst Memorial St. Beach and Pismo St. Beach

Drift Fishing

Here's another instance of a confusing name. As used in San Francisco Bay waters, drift fishing means fishing from a drifting boat over productive areas (reefs, drop-offs). Water movement and wind move the boat, with the engine used just to position the boat to start a drift (or correct it). Drift fishing is included here rather than in the Striped Bass section because this technique is useful for more than stripers. Halibut, rockfish, lingcod, sharks and even salmon, at times, are caught this way.

Tackle and Equipment: Drift fishing tackle is quite basic. Most anglers use a 6-7 foot boat rod with a sensitive tip (to detect bites) and a conventional saltwater reel loaded with 25-30 pound test monofilament line. Reel line capacity should be in the 200-300 yard range.

Terminal tackle is also straightforward. Here's the setup:

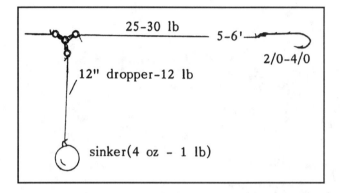

Sinker size depends on current speed. An 8 ounce cannonball sinker is most common, but in a fast current up to a pound is needed to keep the rig in contact with the bottom.

How To: San Francisco Bay drift fishing is actually a second cousin to open ocean bottom fishing. In both instances, the idea is to drift over structures while keeping the rig on the bottom, but without getting snagged too frequently. The terminal tackle is different because live anchovies are the bait of choice (most ocean bottom fishing is done with cut pieces of squid or anchovies). Most anglers bait the anchovies up through both lips—not too deep or the bait life and effectiveness will be diminished.

Lower the baited rig until you feel bottom. Then, take up slack and actually lift the weight off the bottom a reel turn or two. By raising and lowering the rod tip, or even by reeling in or letting out a little line, the key is to stay in contact with the bottom without getting hung up. Gently lower the weight to the bottom every few seconds to make sure your offering is still close. Remember, the fish are feeding near structures. You want your bait to be there too. Don't lapse into daydreaming or just drag your weight along the bottom. Rather, try to imagine the shape of the bottom as you drift over it. Try to picture its shape. "Feel" the bottom and its changing depth and adjust your depth accordingly.

Where to Fish: Some of the prime drift fishing locations in San Francisco Bay are listed on the next page. See the NOAA Nautical Chart 18652—which you should have on board for safe boating on San Francisco Bay. Also see the fishing map in the "San Francisco Bay Fishing" chapter of this book.

Alcatraz Island—south side

Arch Rock

Blossom Rock

Buoy #8

Harding Rock

Lime Point and Yellow Bluff—off Marin

Peanut Farm

Point Bonita

Raccoon Straits

Shag Rock

Sharks Point

South Tower of Golden Gate Bridge

Treasure Island and Pier 21—north and east of island

Pier Fishing*

Pier fishing is a special way to fish the Pacific Ocean and its bays. Often there is a fellowship and spirit among these anglers that you don't find in other situations. Maybe that's because a number of people share the same experience and the same piece of ocean. Or maybe it's just because there are so many regulars. One fun way to get to know more about this type of fishing is to stroll out onto a pier and observe for an hour or two. You'll see all ages and types of people enjoying pier fishing. And don't hesitate to strike up a conversation or two, especially with anglers who look like regulars. A hint—look for older people with more equipment and more skill. Many anglers are happy to talk. It's part of the whole scene. Slip in the questions that come to mind between their fish stories. Pier anglers do quite well depending on season, locale and conditions. Among the species caught are halibut, rockfish, mackerel, surfperch and salmon. Often the fish caught are quite large.

Fishing Techniques: There are a number of fishing piers along the NorCal coast. A list is included later in this section and there is additional information in the "Pacific Ocean Fishing" and "S.F. Bay Fishing" chapters of this book. One of the pleasant surprises about pier fishing is that many of them are public. At these facilities fishing is free and no fishing license is required. Piers offer good facilities including benches, bait (some have live bait), beverages and food, washrooms, fish cleaning tables, etc.

Fishing techniques vary depending on the species being sought. Many times anglers cast out a baited rig (like a surf fishing rig) and wait for a bite. Fishing straight down from the rod tip is also popular. Perch which frequent the pilings are taken this way. Halibut anglers know that they must keep their offerings moving, so they cast out a halibut rig or jig and slowly retrieve it through likely spots—like depressions. Salmon and some other species can be caught using a bobber and hooked anchovy. Specific questions aimed at seasoned pier anglers are a great way to learn.

Tackle and Equipment: Any type of rod and reel made has been used by pier anglers, but since we're talking possible good-sized fish, tackle should be hefty enough for the fish being sought. For good-sized fish (like striper or halibut) use a heavy freshwater or light-medium saltwater rod (6-8 feet) and a reel capable of holding at least 100 yards of 10-25 pound line that has a decent drag system (either spinning or conventional). For bottom fishing you can use a rockfish rig or a striper rig (see these sections for details). Bobbers are also used to drift bait. Popular baits include anchovies, squid, clams, pile worms and blood worms.

Other things you'll need are a big pail (for your catch), a long piece of clothesline and a crab net. The net is used to raise up good-sized fish from the water line to the pier level. Have a fellow angler operate the net and be sure the fish is tired out before netting and raising it.

When and Where to Fish: Timing is all important to successful pier fishing. Since we can't take the pier to the fish, we've got to go to the pier when the fish are there. And, most fish are not there most of the time. They come and go, often in as little as several days or several weeks. This is where local, timely information is essential. Keep in frequent telephone contact with local bait shops and piers. When fish are there, go after them. As with all ocean fishing, at many piers, tide movements can also affect the bite. A large swing in tides (a large difference between high and low tide) marks a good day to fish, and just before, during and after high tide is a probably the best time. A

---

* For lots more info on California pier fishing, go to www.pierfishing.com.

morning incoming tide is good, but this isn't always so. Some days the fish are just there and biting no matter what, especially if the bait fish are near the pier.

San Francisco Bay Piers: There are dozens of fishing piers on bay waters. (See the following list.) One of the best is Berkeley Pier which is a major producer. Catches include perch, jack smelt, kingfish, bottom fish, rays, sharks and striper. Best times are from dawn to 9 a.m. or so, and at night under the lights. Grass shrimp, pile worms and cut bait are good here and at other piers. The pier runs about a mile out into the bay at the foot of University Avenue at the Marina.

Bay Area Fishing Piers

Antioch: Take Hwy. 4 eastbound to Antioch Bridge. Take the Wilbur Ave. off-ramp just before the toll plaza. Follow the frontage road to the pier which is just to the right of the bridge.

Antioch: Located at the foot of "H" St. in Antioch.

Berkeley Fishing Pier: City of Berkeley. Hwy. 80 to University off-ramp, follow the signs to the Berkeley Marina. The pier is at the foot of University Ave., just past the bait shop and marina.

Point Benicia Fishing Pier: Locatd in Solano County.

Brisbane Fishing Pier: Off Hwy. 101, 2.5 miles south of San Francisco city limit.

Capitola Fishing Wharf: Take Bay Ave. exit off Hwy. 1 and follow to Capitola Village.

China Camp Pier: Located at China Camp State Park. Take north San Pedro off-ramp from Hwy. 101 near Marin County Civic Center and proceed east approximately four miles.

Dumbarton Bridge Fishing Pier: Neward at Dumbarton Bridge.

Emeryville Fishing Pier: City of Emeryville. Take the Powell St. Exit from Hwy. 80 to Emeryville. Travel west on Powell St. to its end in the Emeryville Marina. The pier is at the foot of Powell St.

Fort Baker: On the Marina side of the Golden Gate Bridge.

Fort Mason Piers: Golden Gate National Recreation Area. Located in the northern end of Fort Mason, off Marina Blvd., San Francisco.

Fort Point Pier: Golden Gate National Recreation Area. Located near Fort Point in the Presidio. From Hwy. 101 near the Golden Gate Bridge toll plaza, take the view roads to Lincoln Blvd., then to Battery E Road to the pier.

Fruitvale Bridge Park: City of Oakland. Take SR 17 to the High Street exit. From High St. turn onto Alameda Ave. and travel west to the intersection with Fruitvale Ave. The pier is on the southeast shore of the Oakland Estuary next to the Fruitvale Bridge.

Marina Green Jetty: Located in San Francisco, at the end of East Harbor. Take Marina Blvd., to Gashouse Cove and then to East Harbor.

Martinez Fishing Pier: Martinez Marina; take Hwy. 4 to Alhambra off-ramp. Travel through Martinez to the end of the road. Follow signs to the parking area and pier.

McNear Pier: Off San Pedro Rd. east of San Rafael.

Middle Harbor Park: City of Oakland. Take SR 17 to Oakland. If traveling south, take the Cypress St. exit and follow it west to the intersection with Seventh St. Turn left and continue south to the intersection of Adeline St. Turn right onto Adeline and continue west. Adeline turns into Middle Harbor Rd. Continue on Middle Harbor to the intersection with Ferro St., near the Middle Harbor Terminal. Turn left onto Ferro St. and follow it around the terminal on the Oakland Estuary. If traveling north, take the Oak St. exit, turn right onto Oak St., travel one block east, and turn left onto Seventh St. and go north to the intersection of Adeline St. Proceed on Adeline.

Monterey Municipal Wharf: Monterey, at Fisherman's Wharf.

Municipal Pier: City of San Francisco. Located at the foot of VanNess Ave.

Pacifica Pier: Located in Pacifica. Entry from Beach Blvd. and Santa Rosa. Extends into the ocean from Sharp Park State Beach.

Paradise Pier: Marin County Parks and Recreation. Vehicle entry fee collected on weekends. From Hwy. 101 near Mill Valley, take Tiburon off-ramp and proceed on Paradise Drive to the pier.

Pittsburg: Take Hwy. 4 to Railroad Ave. Head north until you reach the city marina. Turn left 1/2 block and follow the road to the parking area.

Point Pinole: East Bay Regional Park District. From Interstate 80 take the Hilltop exit in Richmond. Proceed west on Hilltop to the intersection with San Pablo Ave. Turn right onto San Pablo Ave. and proceed north to the intersection with Atlas Rd. Turn left onto Atlas. Take the park shuttle bus or walk to pier.

San Leandro Fishing Pier: Take SR 17 to Marina Blvd. exit in San Leandro. Travel west on Marina to an intersection with Neptune Dr. Turn left onto San Leandro Marina and Marina. The pier is on South Dike Rd. in the marina.

Santa Cruz Municipal Wharf: Located right by the Boardwalk in downtown Santa Cruz.

Seacliff Pier: In Seacliff Beach State Park, just south of Capitola.

Twenty-Fourth Street Pier: Located at the east end on 24th St. in San Francisco near the PG&E plant.

Werder Pier-Foster City: Located at the end of Hillsdale Blvd. next to the Hwy. 92 Bridge.

Piers at the Golden Gate Bridge, on both sides, offer a chance at an assortment of ocean-going species including salmon, stripers, rock cod, and cabezon, as well as perch and smelt. Fort Point Pier is located near Fort Point in the Presidio. East Fort Baker Pier, on the Marin side of the bridge, as an added bonus, offers a fantastic view of the city.

Yes, it is even possible to catch monster sturgeon from bay piers. 60 to 80 pounds are landed, at times. The newer McNear Pier, located off San Pedro Road east of San Rafael, is a good bet. Other San Pablo Bay sturgeon piers include Point Pinole Pier and Vallejo Pier on the Napa River (just up from the bay). As with sturgeon fishing from a boat, pier sturgeon fishing is best in winter. On up towards the Delta, the piers at Crockett, Benicia and Martinez also offer a shot at sturgeon. South Bay anglers pursue sturgeon at the San Mateo Pier and the Dumbarton Pier. Dumbarton Pier extends into the bay from both East Palo Alto and from Newark. Most anglers, for safety reasons, feel it is unwise to fish from the East Palo Alto side. Don't overlook the wide variety of other species at these "sturgeon" piers.

Ocean Piers: Northern California ocean fishing piers, as well as San Francisco Bay piers, are covered in the "Pacific Ocean Fishing" and "San Francisco Bay Fishing" chapters of this book. Each is highlighted on the maps in these sections and there is also a table that lists Bay Area ocean fishing piers. One pier in this category that is in a class by itself is Pacifica Pier. Because of its unique location, salmon and striper are caught here regularly. Contact Pacifica bait and tackle shops to find out when the bite is on. Consider getting a pier gaff and ask about the local sliding bobber rig. Note that, with some exceptions, any number of hooks and lines may be used in ocean waters.

Rock Fishing and Poke Poling

Rock anglers, even before going fishing, know that they'll catch some fish, that they'll get wet sooner or later, and that the experience at the margins of land and sea will be special. But there are some things they don't know. For instance, they don't know what kinds of fish they will catch or how many hooks, sinkers, jigs and fish they will lose because of snags and hang-ups on the rocks. Fortunately, the best bait is free, sinkers and hooks are cheap, and a dry change of clothing just takes some forethought. So the good side of rockfishing surely outweighs the bad.

But a word of caution is necessary. People die every year walking along slippery, moss-covered ocean side rocks and cliffs; therefore, exercise caution and wear shoes that provide good traction.

Fishing Techniques: Rockfishing is one of the first ways man took food from the sea. But today rock anglers

work both natural rock formations as well as jetties and breakwaters. Rockfish (several varieties), perch, eel, and flatfish are all caught. It's not unusual to catch a half dozen varieties on one outing. And the nice thing is that only one basic approach is needed.

Most say that rockfishing is at its best on an incoming morning tide. Anglers sometimes like to arrive before sunrise to gather bait and scout the rock formations before the water covers them over. Fishing is often good up to one hour past high tide. Good spots to fish include deep slots or passageways between rocks and pockets where there is some wave action and surging. Quiet water is usually not productive. Another tip: You usually don't need to cast long distances to find fish. The best spot is often right below where you are standing. The fish you're after have moved in with the tide to feed in and about the rocks. Sometimes anglers drop a jig straight down in water 5 or 10 feet deep.

Another key to successful rockfishing is to keep moving. Try a good looking spot for only a short time and then move to another. If the fish are there they'll hit right away. Speaking of hits, fish in this habitat are aggressive eaters. They hit hard and then shoot for cover, so set the hook immediately and don't give any line. Keep the fish moving in slowly and steadily. Abrupt yanks can tear out the hook. Landing a hooked fish is often a challenge. Smaller ones can be lifted out of the water. If you're lucky, there will be a good miniature bay or shallow where you can guide your catch. Another good approach is to use a surge of water to bring the fish up on the flat that will be aground when the water recedes.

Casting is the basic technique used in rockfishing. A baited hook or jig is cast out to a likely spot and then retrieved. The slowest possible retrieve is usually the best. Keep the line taut on the retrieve, always being alert for bites and snags. Maneuvering or speeding up a retrieve for a brief moment will often prevent a snag. If the pool is open, allow the offering to settle a little before retrieving. If you're fortunate enough to be fishing straight down, yo-yo your offering up and down. In some situations a bobber can be used to help catch fish. Put it about 2 feet above the hook. Now you can bait fish in spots where a sinking rig would result in snags. Kelp-covered areas are one possibility.

Tackle, Bait, Lures and Rigging: Most rock anglers use light tackle. A 6-7 foot medium spinning outfit loaded with 10-15 pound test line is popular. Bait casting equipment is also used. Heavier rods and reels are used by some. Accurate casts are a must, so use equipment that allows you to accomplish this. A backpack is good for carrying hooks, sinkers, bobbers, pliers, knife, towel, snacks and maybe a second pair of tennis or jogging shoes. A gunny sack is fine for holding your catch. Keep it wet and in the shade, when possible. Some anglers use tide pools, safely above the swells, as a good spot to put fish, once on a stringer.

The most popular rockfishing bait is probably mussels. Pry them off the rocks and open them with a knife. Now use the knife to cut out the strong portion in the middle along with the adjoining more delicate portion. Thread the hook through the tougher section and you're set to fish. Don't forget to check your bait frequently. Other baits that work include cut pieces of frozen squid or anchovy.

Rigging for rockfishing is best when kept simple. This prevents lots of snags. Most anglers use a single hook, often tied directly to the main line. Weight is provided by a sinker up about a foot above the hook. Split shot, rubber core sinkers or clinch-on sinkers are all used. An egg-shaped sliding sinker, put on the line before the hook is tied on, is also a workable rig. The cardinal rule for all of these is to use as little weight as possible. Use just enough to make the cast. Then your offering will settle slower, a slower retrieve will be possible, and less snags and hang-ups will result. Bait holder hooks in the #1 and #6 size range are best. The bigger hooks (like #6) are good for fish like opaleye. Speaking of hooks, they're the cause of most hang-ups. It often helps to use a pliers to turn in the tip of the hook (toward the shank) a little ways.

If you're willing to take the risk of losing somewhat more expensive offerings, lead-head jigs are very effective rockfishing lures. Jigs like Scampi, Clouts, Scrounger and Fat Git Zit are popular, for example. Twin tail and curly tail models are both good. Make short casts, let the jig sink, and bump it right back. In kelp beds use largemouth bass flipping techniques.

Poke Poling: Poke poling is a variation of rockfishing that goes back a long way, and is becoming more and more popular. Most poke polers use a homemade pole. Start with a fairly stiff bamboo pole about 8-12 feet long. Stiff fiberglass will also work. Tape a 1-2 foot piece of heavy coat hanger wire to the light end of the pole. Loop the end of the wire and tie on a 1-2 foot piece of 30-40 pound monofilament leader and #2 or larger hook.

Opposite from rod and reel rock anglers, poke polers work the rocks around low tide. The lower the tide the better. A minus 0.5 low tide or more is good. Work the 3 hours before low water. Poke polers roam the rock laid bare by the receding ocean, and lower their baited hook into holes and cracks in rocky reefs, sandy bottom tide pools and kelp beds. Fish and eel are lurking in these locations, ready to ambush whatever moves by. Deep probing in cracks and kelp provide instant strikes. Work deep holes even if they are small. These could widen out or even be tops of caves open to the ocean. After a thorough probing, move on to the next likely spot.

The obvious advantage of poke poling over rod and reel fishing is that there are very few hang-ups. Poke polers most often use mussels, pile worms or cut pieces of squid for bait.

Where to Fish: Many good rockfishing locations (for rod and reel and poke poling) are described in the "Pacific Ocean Fishing" chapter.

Night Fishing

Nighttime is the right time to fish in Northern California. Yes, I know there is a common perception that night fishing is illegal in California. And, it is in some waters and for salmon and trout in some districts and waters. But legal night fishing has much to offer. First, and most important, fishing is probably better in most waters and for most species than at any other time. In lakes, large fish move up to feed in shallow water losing much of their caution. In fresh and salt water, pier lighting attracts bait fish and pursuing game fish. Additionally, night fishing offers a level of tranquility and solitude not often available in the daylight.

Nighttime fishing locales should be scouted in the daylight. After dark or before dawn boat anglers should move at slow speeds and always use running lights. Shore anglers, in most spots, need lanterns and flashlights. Surface fishing techniques work well for trout, largemouth bass, and stripers, even in the heat of summer. Cast surface plugs for trophy-sized bass. Troll plugs for trout and stripers. Often the best nights are on or around full moons. Be sure to check with a current copy of *California Sport Fishing Regulations* before planning your nighttime angling outing.

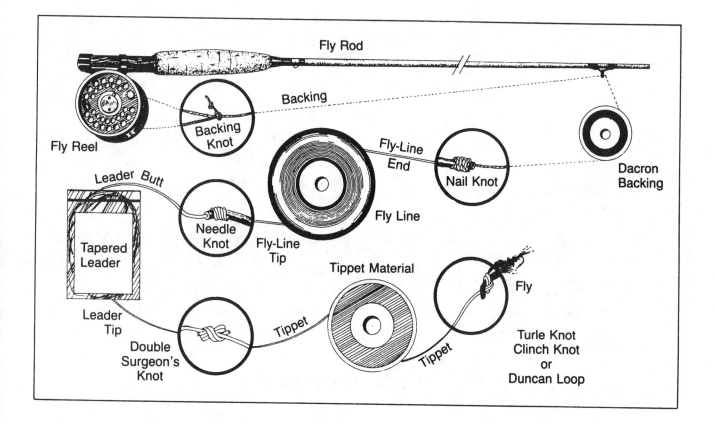

Fly Fishing

Fly fishing to most people means mountain stream trout fishing. But fly fishing in Northern California can and does mean much more. Fly anglers pursue NorCal trout, panfish, black bass, striper, steelhead, salmon and shad. But anglers considering getting into fly fishing should weigh the pluses and minuses. Fly fishing is an active sport. It involves wading, continuous casting and working the water. A good deal of walking to good spots and wading on slippery rock is required. On the plus side, the scenery is often breathtaking. But fly fishing tackle and gear is generally more expensive than spinning equipment, and fly anglers have more of it. Fly anglers tend to lose more hooked fish than bait or lure anglers because the single small hook that is used is almost always set in the lip area. But this makes the catch and release process much easier for the angler and the fish. Maybe the most important consideration is that fly fishing probably requires more practice and knowledge than most other kinds of angling—for some this is a plus, for others a minus.

Artificial lure fishing of any kind involves the deft presentation of a man-made product that simulates food items in the fish's normal diet. In fly fishing, adult insects, immature insects, crustaceans and forage fish are simulated by various "flies." Dry flies emulate adult insects; wet flies suggest drowned adult insects. Nymphs depict immature aquatic insects, while streamers are designed to simulate bait fish, water worms or leeches. Casting skills need to be developed to get the "fly" at or near the ideal fishing location, and good retrieval techniques are essential to impart the most enticing and natural action to the fly as it is moved through the strike zone.

Tackle selection is critical for good results. Unbalanced equipment can make life miserable. Here are some guidelines.

Fish	Rod (length, ft.)	Line (weight)	Reel Spool (diam., in.)
Trout	7 - 9	5, 6, 7	3 - 3 $\frac{1}{2}$
Steelhead	8 $\frac{1}{2}$ - 9 $\frac{1}{2}$	8, 9	3 $\frac{1}{2}$ - 4
Salmon	9 - 9 $\frac{1}{2}$	9, 10	4
Panfish	(same as trout)		
Bass	8 - 9	7, 8	3 $\frac{1}{2}$
Light Saltwater	9 - 9 $\frac{1}{2}$	9, 10	4
Heavy Saltwater	9	11, 12	4

Casting classes often provide balanced outfits that give a beginner a taste for proper setups. Matched outfits (including rod, line and reel) are also marketed by several companies.

There are literally thousands of flies on the market. Here are categories for each game fish.

Fish	Dry Flies	Wet Flies	Nymph Flies	Stream Flies
Rainbow Trout	X	X	X	X
Brown Trout	X	X	X	X
Brook Trout			X	X
Steelhead		X		X
Salmon				X
Panfish	X	X		
Smallmouth Bass			X	X
Largemouth Bass	X		X	X
Striped Bass				X
Shad				X

Fly fishing skills are easy to learn because of the numerous clubs, classes and seminars that are readily available. There are dozens of fly fishing clubs in California, many of which offer reasonably priced instruction at various skill levels. Fly fishing shops provide instruction on casting, fly tying and fishing techniques. Several leading tackle manufacturers and magazines also offer fly fishing schools. There are even some excellent video tapes available for rent or sale.

For more information on fly fishing see the Trout (in Streams) section of the "How to Catch" chapter.

Light and Ultralight Fishing

There is a growing movement in California towards the use of lighter fishing tackle, lighter line and smaller, more subtle baits. And it's taking place across the fishing spectrums from mountain trouting to saltwater bottom fishing. Reasons for this trend are numerous. Many anglers consider fishing with lighter tackle to be more of a challenge and more exciting. Others feel it's more sporting in this period of increased pressure on fishing resources. Some anglers are using more ultralight tackle and techniques because it produces more hook-ups. That's because small offerings match the fishes' feeding habits more closely and simply because the fish can't see the light line.

For all these reasons the march to lighter tackle is on. Here are some examples. 1) Largemouth bass anglers are finding that bucketmouths, who are used to eating 2 to 3 inch crawdads and shad, are more likely to strike artificial offerings in this same size range. Ultralight bass tackle matched with 2-6 pound monofilament line is used to deliver these plugs and soft baits. 2) Traditional freshwater largemouth bass tackle is being used in the Pacific Ocean for rockfish, kelp fishing and so on. 3) Striper trollers are using medium-weight trout outfits. 4) Trout anglers are using 2-4 pound monofilament teamed with 5 to 5 1/2 foot graphic spinning rods. 5) More salmon trollers are using light tackle matched with downriggers.

But there is a down side to lighter fishing tackle. Obviously, when you hook a lunker, it's more likely to break off. Ultralighters will respond, "Therein lies the challenge and excitement." And they have a point. For example, a New York state ultralight advocate just set the record for landlocked Atlantic salmon for 2 pound test line. The record fish weighed in at 7 pounds 1 ounce! Most anglers have never caught a bass or trout that large on any tackle. For more information on the trend towards lighter fishing tackle and line see the "How To Catch . . ." chapter of this book.

Float Tubing

Here is another trend in NorCal angling. For those not familiar, a float tube is a refined "inner tube." The angler "sits" in the center of the tube on a built-in crotch affair. Suspenders are used to hold the tube up when the wearer is walking on shore. Waders are good in colder water. Small foot-mounted swim fins are used to move around in the water. These single-person belly boats are marvelous for shallow-water pond and lake fishing. Anglers can silently maneuver along shore while spin or fly casting for trout, bass or panfish. The solitude and closeness to the water, birds and fish make float tubing a unique and very pleasant fishing experience. It's also very productive—just ask a float tuber. One caution: An offshore wind is the enemy of the float tuber. Some belly boaters even use a 100-200 yard rope tethered to shore to make sure they don't get blown too far out into a big lake. Pack-in anglers find float tubes to be a great asset on small, back-country lakes.

Pack-in Fishing

The Sierra Nevada Mountains and the other Northern California mountain ranges cover lots of territory. Most of it is accessible by car, pick-up, or 4-wheel drive. But there are some great fishing spots that can only be reached on foot or on horseback. These high mountain lakes and streams combine good-to-excellent trouting with breathtaking scenery. The Department of Fish & Game plants back-county waters with goldens, brookies, browns and rainbows. They've been doing this since the early 1900s since many waters were without natural trout and cannot support reproduction. Much planting utilizes aerial drops of fingerlings. In these cold waters where food is often minimal it takes about 2 years for plants to reach catchable size. So don't expect to catch trophy-sized fish. Pan-sized is the rule.

Pack in a good quality ultralight spinning outfit or lightweight fly rod. Spinning enthusiasts are well served with a 5 1/2-6 foot ultralight rod rigged with 2 or 4 pound test line. Cast shiny spinners and spoons like Panther Martin, Super Duper, and Kastmaster. Crystal clear water and pan-sized quarry make light line a good choice. Bait anglers also do well, as do flies cast with a casting bubble.

Fly anglers use 8 1/2-9 foot pack rods, about a WF6F line, 9 foot leader and 4x to 7x tippet. Mosquitoes, Royal Wulffs, Renegads, Muddlers and Zug Bug all work. Some pack-in tips: Backpacking is not the only way to go. There are numerous packing services available. Most use horses, but llamas are coming into vogue. A good way to find these services is through local Chambers of Commerce. Outdoor shows, mostly held in the spring, are also good. Wilderness permits are required for all overnight trips. They are free and can be obtained from Forest Service Offices. There is an entire chapter on the topic of "Wilderness Troutin' " in Marketscope's book, *Trout Fishing in California*.

Ice Fishing

Ice fishing is not the big deal in California that it is in the upper midwest part of the country. But it is a refreshing (no joke intended) change of pace, and often quite productive. Some of the more popular lakes for ice fishing include Prosser, Boca, Stampede, Davis, Frenchman, Castle and Caples.

You'll need an ice auger or pick to make a hole in the ice. A sieved ladle or ice spoon is then used to clear the water of floating ice crystals. Use a short rod (it keeps you closer to the hole for good control) and 6 to 10 pound monofilament. Also, you'll need some split shot sinkers, number 6 or 8 baitholder hooks, or number 10 to 12 salmon egg hooks. Some trout lures like Rooster Tails, Super Dupers, and Hopkins Spoons are good too.

Where to fish? Near dams or at stream inlets are often good. Yesterday's partially frozen-over hole is also worth a try—they're usually easy to re-open. Some anglers bring along portable fish finders to locate fish through the ice.

Lower lures to the bottom and then jig them in a 2 to 3 foot zone above the bottom. Raise the lure up 2 to 3 feet from the bottom and then release it so it flutters back down. Split shots are placed about 1-1 1/2 feet above the hook for bait fishing. Nightcrawlers, salmon eggs or cheese are jigged in the same manner, just off the bottom. Warm clothing is a must, especially footwear and gloves.

Drinking Water

It's probably not a good idea to drink untreated stream or lake water, even in the high country. The intestinal parasite giardia lamblia may be present in any surface water. It causes a very unpleasant disease called giardiases that is not unlike Montezuma's Revenge. Anglers should either carry water or treat local water. Boiling is one way. One minute of boiling is needed at low altitudes and 5 to 10 minutes at high altitudes. Filtering using small, portable pumps also works, if you have the right equipment. You need a filter pore size of 3 microns or smaller. Ask for advice from knowledgeable store personnel. Finally, chemical treatment may also be used. But only iodine treatments are widely recommended for wilderness water purification. Follow the instructions that come with these products.

Seasickness

And now for another unpleasant topic. Seasickness ruins many a boat fishing trip each year, on both the high seas and inland lakes. It also takes its toll on fellow anglers. For example, party boats at times return to port to put ashore one seasick customer, consuming several hours of fishing time for all the other patrons.

Cures for seasickness are possible. But probably the best course is prevention. And prevention starts on shore before the fishing trip begins. Medications are available that greatly reduce the possibility of seasickness. It is thought that they prevent motion sickness by inhibiting the flow of nerve impulses to the brain. Two categories are marketed: antihistamines and scopolamine. Both are effective but they have different side effects and dosages. Most people find the recently available scopolamine patches to be the best bet. These patches, used behind the ear, slowly release minute quantities of the drug at a steady rate over a period of three days. Apply the patch the night before your trip. Once aboard, there are a few more things to do, especially if you begin to feel a little bit queasy: Keep your eyes on the horizon or on any stationary object such as the shoreline or the horizon itself; if and when possible sit near the center of the boat where there is less motion—but don't go below or in a closed cabin.

Licensing and Regulations

Fishing regulations in California are simple and straightforward, but they are also detailed and specific. A Fish and Game Commission publication, *California Sport Fishing Regulations*, is available free at any location where fishing licenses are sold. This is a fact-filled, well-

organized brochure that has all you need to know about current regulations. Read it over and know the rules. I'm always bothered when I see a young child on a family camping trip unknowingly violating regulations that are designed to protect the young fish. A stringer full of 10-12" dead stripers caught in the Delta in July is not the youngster's fault, but his or her uninformed parents. Fishing licenses are sold at most places where fishing tackle or bait are sold. They are required for anglers age 16 and older.

California Angling Records

Athletes always say "records are made to be broken." Maybe that's still true of fishing records too. Eighty percent (or 21 out of 26) of the records listed below were set in the 1970s and 1980s. Nine were set since January 1980!

Species		Weight (lb+oz)	Where Caught	Date
Albacore (tuna)		90	Santa Cruz	Oct 97
Bass,	largemouth	22	Lake Casitas	Mar 90
	smallmouth	9-1	Trinity Lake	Mar 76
Carp		52	Lake Nacimiento	Apr 68
Catfish,	blue	59-4	Irvine Lake	Jun 87
	channel	82-2	Lower Otay	Apr 96
	flathead	60	Colorado River	Mar 92
Halibut,	California	53-8	Santa Rosa Island	May 75
Kokanee		4-13	Lake Tahoe	Aug 73
Lingcod		56	Pt. St. George	1992
Panfish,	bluegill	3-2	Lower Otay	July 91
	black crappie	4-1	New Hogan Lake	Mar 75
	white crappie	4-8	Clear Lake	Apr 71
Rock Cod,	cabezon	23-4	Los Angeles	Apr 58
Salmon,	chinook	88	Sacramento River	Nov 79
	coho	22	Paper Mill Creek	Jan 59
Shad,	American	7-5	Feather River	May 85
Shark,	blue	231	Santa Cruz Island	Aug 74
	bonito	298	Anacapa Island	Jul 70
	thresher	527	San Diego	Oct 80
Steelhead*		27-4	Smith River	Dec 76
Striped Bass		65	San Joaquin River	May 51
	landlocked	67-8	San Luis Reservoir	May 92
Sturgeon		468	San Pablo Bay	Jul 83
Trout,	brook	9-12	Silver Lake	Sep 32
	brown	26-8	Upper Twin Lake	Apr 87
	lake	37-6	Lake Tahoe	Jan 74
	golden	9-8	Virginia Lake	Aug 52
	rainbow*	27-4	Smith River	Dec 76

Rainbow and steelhead are not separated.

Recently, the California Department of Fish and Game in its publication, *Outdoor California*, described how to apply for a state fishing record, should you land a whopper. The following description is by Curt Taucher.

"Applying for a State Record: Have you ever dreamed of setting a new record for fish caught by California anglers? These tips will help you protect your record-size catch from any chance of not being included in the record books.

To ensure a legal *catch*, be sure you are the only person to handle your line, tackle or the fish during the time after you've hooked the fish and are reeling it in. Disqualification of your fish could occur if others are involved with landing your prize, with the exception of help in netting or gaffing the fish.

After you land the fish, save the first 10-20 feet of line above the hook or lure for later testing. If necessary, wrap the line around a creel or small tackle box for preservation.

The next very important step is to take the suspected record fish to a place with a certified scale (legal for trade), as soon after the fish leaves the water as possible. The fish will lose moisture and weight rapidly. Do not gut, decapitate, de-fin or scale the fish. Weigh the fish once, and measure total length, tail fork length and the circumference, with two disinterested witnesses in attendance. Be sure to get their complete names and addresses.

It would be best at this time to have color photos taken as a matter of record. Lay the fish on either side and place a yardstick, ruler or some other measuring device (if possible) just below the fish. Be sure the photo is taken close-up, with all the color and outstanding features clearly displayed.

The next vital step in preserving record status is to have the fish's species properly documented by a professional fishery biologist (or person involved with fisheries) or a taxonomist (a person who studies species of wildlife as a profession). Again, be sure to document the name, address and employer of the person identifying your catch, along with the determination of species.

During all the legwork documenting your record, it is advisable to keep the fish as cold, or frozen, as possible. Do not mutilate the fish in any way until you're sure that your record is secure and DOCUMENTED—in other words, keep it in the freezer until properly notified by the record-keeping authorities!

For stat records applications on salt or freshwater fish, contact any Department of Fish and Game office for the proper forms. Of course, at anytime the DFG is more than willing to help you document your record-size fish."

Organizations and Publications

Some of the most active fishing organizations and some of the best publications for up-to-date Northern California fishing information are

Fishing & Hunting News, Northern California Edition
511 Eastlake Ave. E, Seattle, WA 98109
(206) 624-2738

United Anglers of California
5200 Huntington Ave., Richmond, CA 94804
(510) 525-3474

The Fish Sniffer (newspaper)
P.O. Box 994, Elkgrove, CA 95624
(916) 685-2245

California Striped Bass Association
P.O. Box 9045, Stockton, CA 95208

Western Outdoor News—N. California edition
3197-E Airport Loop Rd., Costa Mesa, CA 92626
(800) 290-2929

How to Catch . . .

Many fishing books are jam packed with interesting, colorful information. But they have one glaring shortcoming. They never answer the question "how." Our purpose in the next 27 sections is to remedy this problem. So if you want to know "how to catch . . ." just look in the appropriate section. The explanations are simple, straightforward, complete and understandable. The following fish are discussed in alphabetical order for easy reference:

How to Catch. . . Abalone

An abalone is a rock-clinging, single-shelled creature that inhabits shoreline waters (especially where there are concentrations of rocks and kelp) all along the coast and islands of California. It has a large, fleshy foot and sensory projections on its underside. Most all seaside gift shop browsers have seen an eye-catching display of abalone shells. And those who have ordered it on restaurant menus know how delicious it is. But it's possible for anyone with some insight and a little luck to enjoy catching, preparing and eating abalone.

Fishing Techniques

There are three basic techniques for taking abalone:

1. **Rock Picking**—searching the rocky shore on foot.

2. **Free Diving**—diving near shore with a snorkel only (no aqualung).

3. **Scuba Diving**—diving with an aqualung.

North of Yankee Point (at Monterey) only rock picking and free diving are allowed. Scuba divers are not permitted to take abalone anywhere along the Northern California coast from Monterey Bay to Bodega Bay to Fort Bragg to Crescent City, near the Oregon border.

Rock pickers operate at low tides—preferably a minus low tide and a calm ocean. They start about an hour before the low tide and quit before the incoming tide threatens a soaking or being stranded away from shore.

The basic technique is to comb an area looking for abalone attached to rocks. Often it is best to feel under water in crevices and cracks that other rock pickers have missed.

Free divers operate in the water. The wise ones in pairs take turns diving down to rocky bottoms in 5-30 feet of water. Abalone are pried off the rocks with a metal bar. Since this can fatally injure an abalone, it is best to be sure the abalone is of legal size before prying it off. Rock pickers must also make this judgment. To pry the abalone off the rock and avoid injuring it, slip the bar under the abalone. Then lift the handle end up, pushing the tip of the bar against the rock. This prevents injury to the abalone's foot. If it is undersize, hold the abalone back on the spot where it was taken until it grabs hold itself.

Free diving lessons are available at selected locations along the coast. No one should attempt to free dive without proper instruction. Some tips: Dive only on an outgoing tide. Incoming tides create rips that can carry you out to sea. Make sure you are familiar with the weight belt release and the dive area. And dive with an experienced partner.

Tackle and Equipment

The equipment needed for rock picking and free diving are an abalone iron (of legal dimension), a fixed caliper measuring gauge, a state fishing license, a catch bag (or at least a gunnysack), neoprene boots, neoprene gloves and an inflatable buoyancy vest. In addition, for free diving, you'll need a wet suit, hood, snorkel, mask, fins, knife (for escaping from kelp) and a weight belt.

Where to Fish

Abalone can be found all along the Northern California coast from Monterey to the Oregon border. Good areas are scattered all along between Santa Cruz and Fort Bragg. North from Fort Bragg to Westport are the best bets. Check with dive shops and experienced abalone rock pickers and divers for more specific information.

Cleaning and Cooking

Cleaning abalone is different from most other seafood, but it is not actually difficult. Insert the abalone iron between the meat and the shell at the pointed end of the abalone. Now pop out the meat. Next, trim away the flanged edges and all the intestines. A pot scrubber can then be used to rub off the black skin. Scrape off the suction cups with a knife. Now it's time to tenderize the meat. Before slicing pound it with a big mallet. Then slice it 1/8 to 1/4 inch thick. Use the mallet again for a final tenderizing. The end of a bottle may also be used. Some anglers suggest leaving the cleaned abalone in the refrigerator for a day or two before slicing and pounding to allow the muscle to relax, making it more tender and easier to handle.

Most people feel that the only way to prepare abalone is quick pan frying. Tenderized steaks are usually floured, or dipped in egg and sauteed over high heat for less than one minute on a side. Fry only enough to heat clear through and slightly brown.

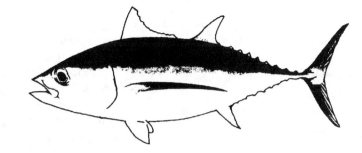

How to Catch . . . Albacore

Albacore, or long-finned tuna, often take commercial fishing boats a couple of hundred miles from shore. Commercial boats stay out until their freezers are full. Fortunately, there is a time each year when albacore come close enough to shore (usually 35-50 miles) so that sport fishermen can get in on the fun. These fish migrate up the coast of California, typically hitting the waters off Monterey and San Francisco about late August. Following their arrival, good fishing may last for as little as a week or two, or may extend for several months.

There are years when albacore fishing gets hot as close as ten miles from shore. These are the only times most sport fishermen consider albacore fishing in their own boats. At other times it's probably best to venture out on a well-equipped, fast, large party boat especially rigged for albacore. Typically the boats leave in the wee hours of the morning (about 3 a.m.) and are back in port by 7 p.m. Cost ranges from $50 to $100. There are also overnight-one day ($150) and two-day ($300) trips available.

Fishing Techniques

Trolling is the most popular technique for taking albacore. But before we get into trolling specifics, a word about where to troll. After all, it's a big ocean! First, albacore congregate and feed in warmer water. Most experts look for water in the 63-65°F range with 60°F being the minimum. The second good fish finder is bird activity. Birds actively pursuing bait fish means that albacore may be doing the same thing from down below the forage fish swarm. When birds are spotted, run the boat through the edge of the activity, not through the center. No need to chance scattering the bait fish and feeding albacore.

Albacore trolling is characterized by the following:

1. Trolling close to the boat. (The theory goes that to the albacore, the wake looks like a bait fish feeding frenzy.) Put the lure right in the white wafer wake of the boat about 50 to 70 feet behind the stern.

2. Fairly rapid boat speed (perhaps 7-10 knots) to move along the feathered or rubber-skirted jig at a good pace.

3. Party boat captains usually troll in square grids of about 20 minutes per leg until fish are located. A zigzag pattern is also a good approach.

The other method of albacore fishing is used on party boats and some private boats after a school of fish is located by trolling. The boat is stopped and scoops of bait fish (usually anchovies) are tossed into the water to raise the albacore up to the surface. This technique is called chumming. Fishermen drift live bait near the surface. Since albacore move in schools, it's always a good idea for even private boats to try drift fishing after a trolling hookup is landed. Frozen anchovies often work even without chumming. Drift, facing the wind, so that the rig is not under the boat. Casting out a Salas or similar jig can also work.

Tackle and Equipment

Albacore are big, fast, open-ocean sport fish. They are one of the most sought after game fish in California ocean waters. A good fish averages 15-30 pounds with some ranging up to 40 pounds or more. Essential equipment includes the following:

1. Large, iced, fish storage box (or cooler, or plastic trash container) and a good-sized gaff.

2. A 6-6 1/2 foot medium to heavy trolling rod with roller tip and a 4/0 to 6/0 sized reel filled with at least 300 yards of 50-80 pound monofilament line. This heavy equipment is needed to quickly land the first fish so that chumming and drift fishing can begin before the school disappears.

3. For drift fishing, a light to medium action, fast-tapered, 7 foot rod mated to a conventional reel capable of holding 300 yards of 25-30 pound test line is suggested.

Lure and Bait

The most productive albacore jigs:

Description—Chrome-plated or abalone-pearl head and a natural feather or vinyl skirt.

Colors—Dark colors (like black, purple, green and yellow) during darker periods. Light colors (like red and white, red and yellow) in bright periods.

Size—4-10 ounces.

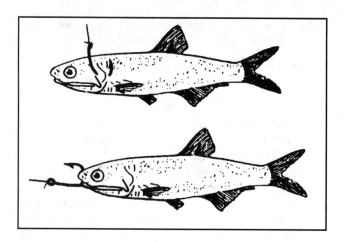

The preferred bait is live anchovies. The best are 3-4 inches long, green backed (they seem friskier), with no scale loss or other signs of deterioration. For surface fishing, hook the anchovy through a gill cover. For deeper action, nose hook the anchovies and use a 1 or 2 ounce rubber-core sinker about 30 inches up the line. Use the sharpest hooks money can buy. Nickel-plated Gamakatsu hooks in #4 and #6 are a good choice.

Where and When to Fish

It varies. Two of the better albacore grounds are Soap Run and Pioneer Sea Mount. These are both 35-55 miles out off the coast of Davenport. Albacore season from year to year is unpredictable. In some years there may not even be a sport season because the fish are too far offshore. Check often with party boat operators, tackle shops and fishing publications, starting in August.

Cleaning and Cooking

Albacore is most often steaked. Make sure the dark flesh is removed from each piece. Like salmon, albacore has a relatively high fat content. Also like salmon, the most popular way to prepare it is barbecuing. The smoke seems to add to the flavor. Poached albacore tastes like canned tuna, but even better. Poached albacore may be stored in the refrigerator for several days or frozen for a short time. Sauteing albacore is also popular. These strong tasting fish work well in recipes with spicy or tomato-based sauces.

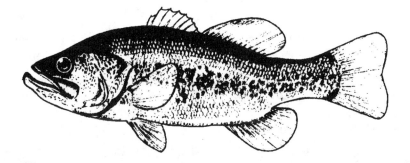

How to Catch . . . Largemouth Bass

The largemouth bass is one of Northern California's most popular warm water game fish. It's found in nearly all suitable lakes, sloughs, farm ponds and most of the lakes featured in this book. But these fish are not native to California. It is believed that the Northern-strain largemouths were first planted in California in 1879. The locale was Crystal Springs Reservoir in San Mateo Co.

In 1959 Florida-strain largemouths were first planted in some Southern California lakes. This strain reaches much greater weight than the Northern-strain largemouths. World class Floridas are in the 20 pound-plus range, whereas the trophy-sized Northern-strain bass are 10 to 12 pounds. But now, Northern-strain, Florida-strain and hybridized populations are found in many Northern California lakes. Experts say that it is almost impossible to tell the strain of a caught fish since the young can exhibit the features of either parent's strain.

It's certain that Florida-strain fish are making an impact on NorCal bass fishing records. The state's record (22 lbs) was taken at Lake Castaic in Southern California in March 1991. But Northern California anglers are gaining. In December 1984 Harold Nakutsu caught a 15 lb - 13 1/2 oz bass in Lake Amador to break the NorCal record. Then in April 1986, Tim Kimura set a new NorCal record with a 17 lb - 1 1/2 oz fish, again at Amador. The current NorCal record, set in April 1988 at Clear Lake by Delbert Abrams, stands at 17 lbs - 8 oz. By the way, the Florida-strain bass grow faster, live longer and spawn earlier, but are more difficult to hook.

If you want to know more about California bass fishing than is presented here, see *Bass Fishing in California* (Marketscope Books, 2000).

Fishing Techniques

Bass fishing is best during the spring and fall. But ironically, probably most people fish for bass in the warm summer months. Why not? Family vacations fit best when kids are out of school. And the weather is comfortable "out on the lake." Don't get me wrong. Bass are caught in the summer, but it takes more effort since the fish are usually down deeper.

The basic technique used in bass fishing is casting and retrieving a plug, spoon, spinnerbait, jig, plastic worm or live bait. Of course, the retrieve approach must match the lure. All types of casting equipment can and is used including bait casting, spinning, spin casting and fly casting. More on this in the Tackle and Equipment section.

Successful bass fishing centers around the answer to three questions: Where to cast? How to cast? What to cast? Here are some guidelines:

- Bass are almost always on or near the bottom, or near underwater cover like a fallen tree. The "bottom" could be near shore in 2 feet of water, or it might be in 40 feet of water on the slope of a sunken island.

- Largemouth prefer to be near structures, whether it be a rocky fall-off, a sunken log, a weed bed, standing timber, a rocky point, etc.

- Largemouth bass prefer a water temperature of about 70°F. This means that in the spring and fall bass are likely to be nearer shore, in shallow "seventyish" water. When the surface temperature is well above 70°F, bass hold out deeper, but do make feeding forays into shallower water, primarily at night.

- At an unfamiliar lake, seek information about "good spots" from other anglers, bait shops, marinas, etc.

- If you (or someone else) catch a bass at a particular spot, and the lake temperature conditions don't change, the spot will probably produce more bass.

- Cast your offering so it lands or is retrieved near structures. For example, put it next to a pile of boulders that are partially submerged, or place it right by a fallen tree. Retrieve parallel to submerged log, not across it. Try inlets where streams flow into lakes.

- Retrieve slowly. Seventy to eighty percent of the time a slow retrieve is best. But if it's not working, don't hesitate to try a rapid retrieve. A combination may also be in order—for example, a few quick turns of the reel handle just after the offering lands (to get the bass's attention) followed by a slow retrieve.

- Retrieve everything, except surface plugs, near or on the bottom. Since the bass are on the bottom, you've got to put your offering on the bottom. After all, we live and eat on the "bottom" of the atmosphere, so doesn't it seem natural for some fish (particularly bass) to live and eat on the bottom of their "atmosphere."

- With plastic worms and jigs "feel" the bottom during your retrieve. No doubt this practice will result in some lost rigs, but it will also result in more bass. Using snagless, or near snagless offerings as described later, will minimize loss.

- Cast quietly. In fact, fish quietly. Minimize engine noise, oar lock noise, "scraping tackle box along the floor of the boat" noise, and so on. Bass fishing is akin to stalking.

- Catchable-sized bass feed mostly on smaller fish (like shad, minnows, bluegill, etc.), crawdads and worms. This means that offerings that are successful look and act like swimming fish, moving crawdads or worms.

- At times, bass strike out of a reflex action. Sometimes they attack an offering the instant it hits the water. At these times, you could be casting anything and it would work.

- Many professional bass anglers feel that bigger bass come on bigger bait.

Lures and Bait

Many an otherwise sane person is driven absolutely crazy by the immense selection of bass plugs, jigs, spoons, spinner-baits, plastic worms, etc. And professional bass-tournament fishermen seem to own at least one of everything, based on the size of the tackle boxes in their boats!

Don't despair. You don't need one of everything to take bass. Largemouth bass offerings fall into seven categories:

- Crankbaits
- Surface Plugs
- Spinnerbaits
- Spoon Jigs
- Jigs
- Plastic Worms
- Live Bait

It's probably a good idea for a serious bass angler to have a sampling of the basic offerings in each category, but that isn't even necessary. For example, some bass fishing experts say that one or two types account for more bass than all the others combined. These two are plastic worms and spinner-baits.

Crankbaits

Crankbaits are a broad category of lures, mostly plugs, that get their name because the reeling speed determines how much the lure dives, vibrates and wobbles. Most of these lures have plastic, fish-shaped bodies. They also have a plastic lip, the size, shape and angle of which imparts action to the reeled lure. Many have two sets of treble hooks which provide a good chance to hook a striking bass. But this also increases the chance of snags, so crankbaits are best used in open water.

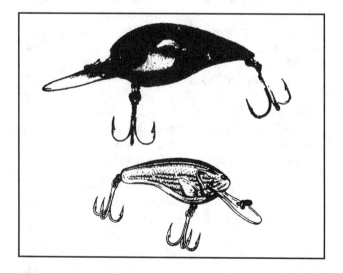

Crankbaits work, to one degree or another, almost all year long at sloping points, along shorelines, in shallow flats, etc.

Crankbaits either float at rest, sink slowly or sink rapidly. The most common way to fish this lure is to first jig it for a moment before beginning the return. Then reel fast to get the lure to the bottom. Now slow down enough to either drag the lure along the sloping bottom or bump it along, or return steadily right over the bottom. Crankbaits are designed to be fished parallel to the shoreline so you can keep the lure near the bass, and at the prescribed depth for the longest time.

Popular bass crankbaits include Bomber Model A's, Rapala Fat Rap and Storm Wiggle Wart. Shad and crawdad styles are popular.

Surface Plugs (and Stickbaits)

Surface plugs are top-water lures that simulate a sick or injured bait fish, frog or other creature. They float both when still and when retrieved. Most surface plugs have an action designed into them using blunt ends, propellers, dished-faces, etc. The proper retrieve for most of these is slow, erratic and stop-and-go. But before retrieving many anglers will just let it sit in the target area for up to a minute or two, just twitching it, to send out vibrations and small ripples around it. Popular surface plugs include Rip-N-Minnow, Chug Bug and Devil's Horses.

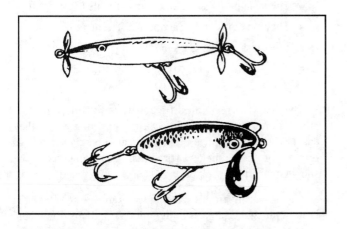

There is another class of surface plugs called stickbaits that are unique because they don't have any action built into them. Probably the most famous of these is the Zara Spook. The action needed to make a stickbait work must come from the skill of the angler. This takes several hours of practice to develop. Articles and bass books can be found at your local library to show you how to do it. The reading and the practice may be worth it because stickbaits have one profound advantage over other surface plugs. They can be kept in the target area longer because very little forward motion is required to give them the action needed. A stickbait in skilled hands may catch more fish than other surface plugs. The prime season for surface plugs is in the springtime spawning season when bass are in shallow water, especially in early mornings and late evenings. They are also good in summertime in shallow water after dark.

Spinnerbaits

Spinnerbaits are one of the most productive of all bass catching lures and are simple to cast and retrieve. They are good all year, especially in water up to 10 feet deep. Use them along brushy structures, in flooded trees or fallen trees. Most spinnerbait designs are semi-weedless so hang-ups are not a constant concern. Veteran anglers vary the return to change depth and action, but in most cases, the slower the retrieve the better.

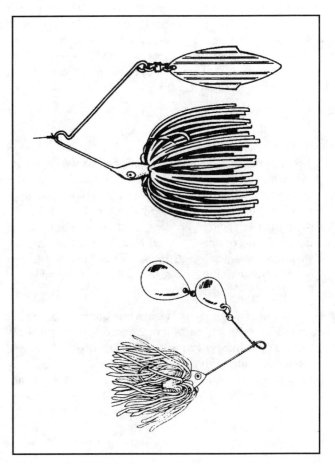

Here are some tips. The best all around colors are probably white or chartreuse (yellowish). Spinnerbaits can be hopped along the bottom like a jig. In this style of fishing, blades that flutter freely on the downfall bring strikes. The size of spinnerbaits should approximate the length of the bait fish in the area. Skirts can be trimmed to accomplish this.

The best tip of all: Add a plastic worm or pork rind on the hook of the spinnerbait. It produces more strikes from bigger bass. Probably because it keeps the lure up in the water, even with a slower retrieve.

Spoons

Jigging a spoon is a little-practiced largemouth technique that is easy and effective. It's a great method to take bass from late autumn through early spring. That's when largemouths seek warm water down deep in Southern California reservoirs. It can also work in midsummer when bass go deep to find water cooler than surface temperatures.

A wobbling spoon is dropped down over the side of the boat and then raised up and fluttered down at whatever depth the bass are at. The more flutter the better on the down drift. Work the jig in about a 3-5 foot, up and down range. Hopkin's 75 and Haddock Structure Spoons in about the one-half to three-quarter ounce range are about right. Fish can be taken in depths between 30-60 ft. with this approach.

Jigs

Jigging, typically with a skirted lead-head jig, is somewhat more complicated than spoon jigging, but it is a very productive technique. The jig is cast out or flipped out (more on this later) and then allowed to drop to the bottom. The most common retrieve is to skip the jig along the bottom in short, sharp jerks. Imagine you're dragging the jig along the bottom from a drifting or steadily trolled boat. That's about how you want your jig to act. Most strikes occur on the initial drop or on the ensuing flutter downs. Garland Spider Jigs and Haddock Kreepy Crawlers are popular.

The most famous jig rig in Southern California bass waters is the "Pig 'n Jig." It's a 3/8 to 1/2 ounce skirted jig (usually dark colored, like brown) with a weedless hook. A pork rind (or plastic trailer) is put on the hook. The rind makes it look more like a crawdad and also slows the rig's descent. When you move the Pig 'n Jig off the bottom, don't just let it drop,

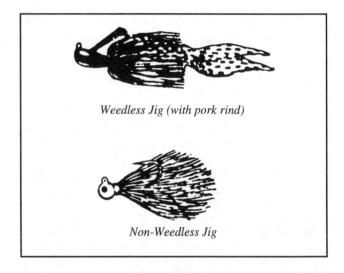

Weedless Jig (with pork rind)

Non-Weedless Jig

let it down and be alert for a take. Keep slack out of your line to feel the strike and watch your line for unnatural movement.

Plastic Worms

Some people claim that each year more largemouth bass are taken on plastic worms than on all other artificial lures combined. This could well be true. Plastic worms do have several special advantages over other lures:

- They can be fished at all depths of water.
- They have outstanding action at different retrieve speeds.
- Weedless rigging is a snap.
- They're inexpensive so anglers don't mind risking them in heavy cover.

They can be rigged in different ways for different situations. For example, in shallow spring spawning waters they can be fished weightless. They can also be rigged with a dropper or sliding sinker. Three popular rigging styles are shown on the following page.

Plastic worms (from 4-6 inches long) are worked along the bottom much the same as in jigging. Work them slowly and erratically, like a nightcrawler twisting and drifting in the current. Dark colors like purple and brown are most productive. Plastic worms can also be used for vertical jigging, like spooning.

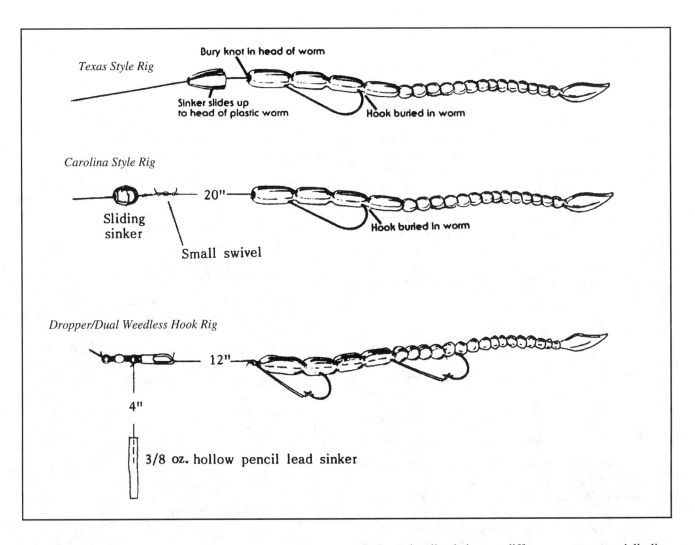

Texas Style Rig

Bury knot in head of worm

Sinker slides up
to head of plastic worm

Hook buried in worm

Carolina Style Rig

20"

Sliding
sinker

Small swivel

Hook buried in worm

Dropper/Dual Weedless Hook Rig

12"

4"

3/8 oz. hollow pencil lead sinker

Live Bait

Live bait bass fishing isn't all that common anymore. That's strange, in a way, because live bait was the only way bass were caught before plugs, spinnerbaits and all the other artificials came along. For instance, I have several live frog harnesses in my collectibles. It holds the little guy in a swimming posture and would be great for casting and retrieving a frog without putting a hook through it. I've never even thought of using it.

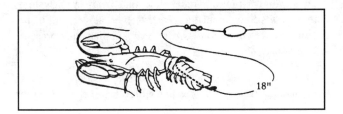

18"

But other live bait are a different matter, especially live crawdads. These critters are the way to go if you want to catch a really big bass. Here's one way to rig them:

Some anglers prefer to just put some split shot up the line about a foot or two from the hook. Others use no sinker at all. Use a #6, 8 or 10 bait hook, depending on the size of the crawdad. When you see a twitch, that is the largemouth picking up the crawdad. As the fish moves off with the bait, the belly will come out of your line. Let the bass run a few feet and then set the hook hard. Don't allow any slack in your line when playing the bass. Fish rocky points, drop-offs and ledges. Spring is the best time to catch the lunkers on live crawdads.

Casting and Flipping

Accuracy is the measure of a good cast. Consistently accurate bass casters will hook more fish. Besides the traditional overhand cast, often a sidearm or even an underhand cast is called for to reach the target (when casting under an overhanging branch, for example) and to gently put the offering on the water. The three keys to accurate casting are practice, practice and practice.

Flipping (or Flippin') is a specialized casting technique. It's used to delicately put a jig or plastic worm on the water, especially near or in heavy cover. Springtime shallow water bassing is the prime flipping time. In elementary terms, the standing angler strips line off the reel, much like a fly angler, as the offering swings from the rod tip like a pendulum. On a forward swing the jig is flipped out and gently "put" on the water. Accuracy is critical as is an almost ripple-free landing. Weedless offerings are a rule. And in order to fight the bass in close and keep it out of cover, heavy equipment is used. A specialized flipping rod (about 7 feet) is matched with 15-25 pound test line.

Tackle and Equipment

Today, many bass anglers use what is known in the trade as a bass boat. These boats were popularized in bass tournaments. They are about 16-20 feet long, with pedestal seats, large outboard motors, an electric trolling motor (used for maneuvering, not trolling), several depth finders, a fish box, a flashy sparkling finish, and on and on . . .

Bass boats are fun and functional, but the good news is that you don't need one to catch your share of bass. The bad news is that successful bass fishing probably does require some kind of boat that can be maneuvered along an irregular shoreline. Many kinds of boats will do: an inflatable, a canoe, a dingy, a row boat, an aluminum boat, or a small stern-drive cruiser. Shore fishing for bass is also possible. And some lakes like Lower Otay have good shore bass angling. But at most lakes, covering a number of promising structures on foot is difficult.

To find promising bass territory during all seasons, you'd best be equipped with maps of the lake, a thermometer that works well under water and an electronic fish finder. A flasher type will do, but a graph recorder or liquid crystal style is preferred.

Now for the tackle itself. Here, there is a great deal of latitude. The possibilities include the following:

- Spinning equipment—6 to 7 foot, light to medium action spinning rod, open-faced reel with 8 to 12 pound monofilament line.

- Spin casting equipment—5 to 6 foot pistol-grip, light to medium rod, closed-faced spinning reel with 8 to 12 pound monofilament line.

- Bait casting equipment—5 to 6 foot pistol-grip, light to medium rod (can be used with spin casting reel), bait casting reel (some have magnetic anti-backlash mechanisms) with level-wind feature, star drag and 8 to 12 pound monofilament line.

What lures to use with these rods and reels? Beginners and once-in-awhile anglers should probably have a good selection of spinnerbaits, crankbaits and a surface plug or two. These are the easiest to retrieve with good action, and they catch a lot of fish. A few wobbly spoons for spoon jigging in deep water are also handy. More experienced anglers wouldn't be without a good selection of plastic worms and lead-head jigs.

Professional bass anglers often put scent formulas on all their lures. Berkley has a whole line of scented products, from Power Worms to Power Spinnerbaits, and all are scented to attract bass. It adds attracting odors and covers up human odors. Next to vibration, bass probably respond most to odor. This is an inexpensive way to improve your chances. Tests indicate that the color of one's lure is also important in producing strikes, depending upon water clarity. There's an electronic instrument called a Color-C-Lector on the market that tells anglers which color offerings to use at a given depth in a particular water clarity. Results have been promising. It's worth looking into.

Ultralight Bass Angling

Want to put more hook-ups and more excitement into your bass fishing? Here's the way: Use ultralight spinning tackle, 2-4 pound monofilament and "forage-sized" lures. With this setup, you're sure to get more strikes because the bass can't see the line, and your offerings duplicate the size of bucketmouths' regular food—threadfin shad and crawdads. And the sheer joy of fighting bass on this light tackle can't be beat. You'll want a rod in the 5'6" to 5'9" range with a fast taper (i.e. a rod that bends under a load only in the upper third of its length). The solid backbone provides good hook setting in the hard mouth structure of the black bass. Match this with an ultralight spinning reel. Note that front drag systems, though less convenient than rear drag models, offer more drag surface over which to dissipate heat and distribute pressure. Use high quality line.

A wide variety of baits are available. There are ultralight crankbaits from companies like Cordell, Rebel and Heddon.

Small spoons (about 1/8 ounce) like Kastmaster and Krocodile are good. Another good bet is soft plastics. Small plastic worms, 2-inch feather-like reapers, tube baits like Fat Git Zit and little curl-tail grubs are all excellent bass takers. Some rigs are best on a 1/16-1/8 ounce p-head jig hook, while others are best on a Texas-style rig. Replace the sliding sinker with a small split shot about 18 inches up the line. Even tournament bass anglers are finding that ultralight bassing can give them that competitive edge.

Cleaning and Cooking

Bass can be scaled, gutted and beheaded, but many prefer to fillet them. This is the easiest way to remove the scales and skin. Any muddy flavor is in the skin. Bass is mild and flaky.

It can be cooked in a variety of ways including sauteing, broiling, poaching, baking and frying. But in any method of preparation, remove the skin before cooking.

Of course, tournament bass anglers release all caught fish by utilizing a live-well in their boats. More recreational bass anglers should probably follow the catch and release ethic. And nobody should keep more bass than they can properly use.

Where to Fish

The top largemouth lakes in Northern California are highlighted in the "Freshwater Fishing" chapters of this book. But don't overlook farm ponds, irrigation ditches and sloughs near home.

Special: Alabama Spotted Bass

Today there is another bass, other than largemouths and smallmouths, in selected California impoundments. The introduction of Alabama spotted bass in the early 1980s has created a fishery second to none on lakes like Shasta, Whiskeytown, Camanche, Berryessa, Folsom, and Oroville. The world record spotted bass, 9 pounds 4 ounces, was caught be Gilbert Rowe at Lake Perris, in southern California, the only place with spots south of the Tehachapi Mountains.

But why spotted bass, anyway? Wasn't there enough variety in the reservoirs already? Perhaps, but the fisheries, especially for largemouths, also had problems in some locations. Most of the impoundments, after all, are multipurpose developments that produce power, store water for cities and towns and provide water for irrigation. In times of scarcity the water level in some of the reservoirs goes down daily. When that happens many of the nests of largemouth bass are left high and dry before their eggs hatch.

Smallmouths do spawn deeper than largemouths but spotted bass may nest down as far as 20 feet. They occasionally hybridize with smallmouths but rarely do they mix with largemouths which are generally finished spawning before the water warms enough for spots at the depths they prefer.

Although there is some color variation and the lateral band is somewhat different, spots are easily dismissed as largemouths unless you look closely. The easiest way to tell the three species apart is to look at the maxillary bone on the upper jaw. On largemouths this bone extends past the eye, on spots, it's even with the end of the eye, and on smallmouths it extends only to the middle of the eye.

Because they are getting so numerous, spots are apt to be found almost anywhere on a given lake, but early in the year they show a preference for vertical structure such as rock walls where they sometimes suspend over deep water. A good tactic is to fish parallel to such structure rather than casting toward it because your offering stays in the strike zone longer that way. On calm days you can go light for spots and have a ball. Try a 4 or 5 inch brown worm rigged with a split shot for weight, a 1/8 or 1/4 ounce brown jig with a purple pork frog, or a Fat Gitzit. Later in the spring you might find spots grubbing on the bottom for crayfish around points or in creek channels. At that time a Texas rigged worm on a leader behind a swivel with a sliding sinker in front is good. Occasionally spots, which are aggressive and hard fighting, will grab a spinnerbait or crankbait.

Most anglers think spotted bass are a great addition to their local fisheries. On some lakes all three species of bass can be caught nearly everyday. Chances are good, though, that spots will outnumber the rest in the impoundments where they have really taken hold.

44

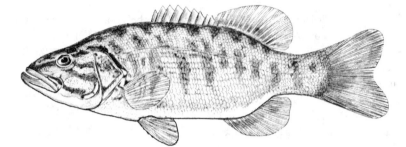

How to Catch . . . Smallmouth Bass

Smallmouth bass are plentiful in some Southern California reservoirs. According to the best historical information, they were planted in the Napa River and Alameda Creek in 1874. Following this introduction to California waters, smallmouths were soon released in many other streams and rivers. They flourished. The addition of dams on these free-flowing waterways restricted the movement of smallmouths, but did not inhibit their successful adaptation. In fact, as canyon-type reservoirs aged, they favored the smallmouth over the largemouth. Smallmouths prefer open, rocky shoreline areas and clear water, which is just what's left after the brush, trees and other organic matter decomposed in a newly flooded reservoir.

The California record smallmouth was caught in 1979 at Trinity Lake. It weighed 9 pounds 1 ounce. This is monster size for a smallmouth. Anything over 4 pounds is bragging size. Many smallmouth anglers insist that they're better fighters, pound for pound, than largemouths. And for those who prefer stream fishing for trout, smallmouth provide another flowing-water fishing alternative. The smallmouth, or "bronzeback," is easily identified by its brownish, almost bronze cast, with vertical dark bars. And in contrast with the largemouth, the upper jaw does not extend beyond the eye, and the dorsal fin has a very shallow notch.

Fishing Techniques

The approaches used for smallmouth fishing have much in common with largemouth angling, but there are critically important differences. It's these differences that this section highlights.

Tackle. Most smallmouth bass anglers scale down their line and lures to match the smaller size of the bronzeback. 6 and 8 pound test monofilament is typical, but largemouth rods and reels are used with several exceptions. For example, fly rodding for smallmouth in rivers and streams with popping bugs and streamers is great sport. And some anglers use ultralight spinning equipment.

River Fishing. The overriding rule is to fish for smallmouth in the same way you would for stream trout. Stream bass prefer undercut banks, tangles and large boulders in midstream. Walk in an upstream direction to fish smaller streams. But you can float larger rivers like the Lower Feather. Cast your offering above the target and allow it to flow to the target area. Try to match the local food supply, be it hellgrammite, crawdad, or even lamprey eels. Small minnow imitation plugs like Rapalas and Rebels that float at rest and shallow-dive on retrieve are good stream producers, as are streamers and poppers.

Habitat. Lake smallmouth are most often found over rocky points, over submerged gravel bars and near sharp bank drop-offs. Coves and waters with stumps showing just above the water can also produce in lakes. Smallmouths prefer water that is somewhat cooler (mid 60's) than largemouths, so they spawn deeper (8 to 15 feet) and sooner than largemouths in the same waters.

Bait and Lures

Baits are proportionally more productive for smallmouth than for largemouth. Department of Fish and Game creel census checks show that minnows are the best overall bait for smallmouths. Anglers often fish them with a small split shot about a foot above the bait hook, using a bobber. Other productive baits include crawdads, nightcrawlers, hellgrammites and crickets. One caution: Crickets are not allowed in some lakes. But the whole array of artificials also produce smallmouths. Cast surface lures early and late in the day. Work plastic worms and jigs along the bottom and use crankbaits, spinners and spinnerbaits at different speeds and depths next to cover. Shad and minnow imitations are good crankbaits. The Git Zit, a small plastic tube bait on a lead-head jig, is a very effective smallmouth lure.

When and Where to Fish

Shasta and Trinity Lakes are probably the premier smallmouth fisheries in the state. These lakes are at their peak for larger fish in February and March. A little farther south, some of the best smallmouth waters are Almanor, Black Butte, Collins, Folsom, Oroville and Pardee. In the Bay Area, Putah Creek, the Russian River and Lake Berryessa are good. Pine Flat, New Melones, Don Pedro and Lake Nacimiento have their spring peak in March and April.

The Lower Feather River, from the Thermolito Afterbay to its mouth at Verona, is probably the top-producing bronzeback river in California. A boat, either a canoe, aluminum boat, or drift boat, is necessary to fish here because of the size of the stream and the difficulty of access to the prime bass spots. Cast offerings parallel to the shore and retrieve them slowly. April and May are particularly good months, especially when flows are low (2500-4000 CFS).

As mentioned above, another good smallmouth stream is the Russian River. Bass are found throughout the drainage, but best results are often between Brown's Pool and Mirabel.

Cleaning and Cooking

For information on the cleaning and cooking of smallmouth, see the Largemouth Bass section.

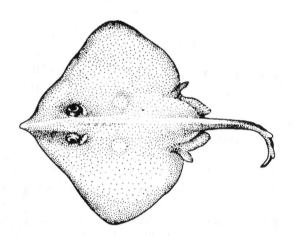

How to Catch . . . Bat Rays

Here is an overlooked sport fishing challenge that will put even the toughest saltwater fishing tackle to the test. Bat rays are big and strong. It's not unusual to hook into 60 to 100 pound fish. And their powerful wings, actually fins, give them an inordinate amount of pull or leverage. Bat rays are found in the open ocean at depths to 150 feet, but most anglers prefer to pursue them in shallower waters like San Francisco Bay, Humboldt Bay and Elkhorn Slough near Moss Landing. In bays and sloughs they feed heavily on clams, oysters, shrimp and crabs.

Bat rays are not considered good eating, which in some respects is probably an advantage. Why bring these flapping, angry guys into the boat if you don't have to? If your skilled and lucky enough to win the fight with a big ray, just release it at the side of the boat. The largest recorded catch in California weighed in at a whopping 181 pounds and measured 4 feet 9 inches across.

Fishing Techniques

During most of the year, bat ray are scattered. But in early summer, often in May, they congregate to spawn. Then larger numbers congregate, usually at high tide along shorelines. Both boat and shore anglers have a shot at them. Bait fished right on the shallow bottom is the method of choice. Fish the incoming water up to high tide. Since bat rays are nocturnal feeders, tides corresponding with dusk or dawn, or even dark if local regulations permit, are probably the best. Hooking rays in water 2 to 4 feet deep is common. Cast your baited rig out as far from the boat or shore as possible, then set a taut line with a loose or free drag and with the reel clicker on. A screaming clicker means it's time to set the hook on the ray as it flees towards deeper water. Often this first run will strip a reel bare and smoke the drag.

Tackle, Bait and Rigging

Medium to heavy saltwater tackle is in order. Equipment used for open ocean rockfishing or cannonball-type salmon trolling will work just fine. See the Rockfish and Salmon sections for specifics. You'll need at least 20 pound monofilament and 5/0 hooks. Flatten the barb on the hook to make releasing the bat ray easier. By the way, if you can't easily remove the hook, just cut the leader to let these big rascals go. The hooks will dissolve. A sliding sinker setup shown on the next page is the rig of choice.

Slide the sinker up the line and then tie on a snap swivel to which you can attack a snelled hook. A very effective bait is frozen whole squid. Boxes are sold at most grocery stores. Some anglers use more exotic bait like chicken parts.

When and Where to Fish

In San Francisco Bay, the far south end is probably the best bet. Elkhorn Slough, a Monterey Bay estuary at Moss

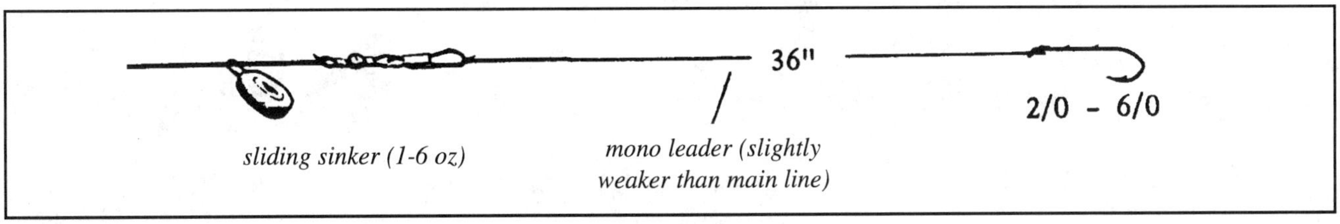

36"

2/0 - 6/0

sliding sinker (1-6 oz)

*mono leader (slightly
weaker than main line)*

Landing, is a big bat ray hangout. A popular ray and shark tournament is held there each year. Humboldt Bay also has an abundance of bat rays. Peak fishing occurs in early summer during spawning on tidal flats. To reiterate: do release these cow-eyed giants so they can continue to cruise the bottoms and provide great fishing pleasure to future anglers.

How to Catch . . . Bluegill (and Redear Sunfish)

Bluegills are the most abundant panfish in California waters. They're in virtually all warm water lakes in Northern California. They were introduced into California in 1908 from Illinois. These fish are fun to catch and are very enjoyable eating. And in many locations they are abundant, so there is no need to feel guilty about taking them. They reproduce with great success, and heavy populations can crowd out large sport fish and stunt bluegills' growth. Bluegill angling is easy and relaxing fishing. And it is especially enjoyable for youngsters. Give them a rod and reel, a can of worms and a little dock, and they're set for hours of fun and adventure.

Redear Sunfish

Redear sunfish are California's bigger and better, modern day bluegill. Let me explain. When nature shaped the landscape of California, warm water lake and stream habitats, and the fishes that occupied them, were limited. Only the Sacramento perch, tule perch and a number of minnow and sucker species were found in warmer sections of streams and the few permanent lakes that existed prior to 1870. But during the decades that followed, large scale reservoir construction greatly expanded warm water lake habitat. Many species (black bass, catfish, crappie, bluegill) were stocked and flourished in these artificial, warm water lakes.

Redear sunfish are native to waters in the southern United States, Rio Grande and Mississippi rivers. But they were observed in the lower Colorado River, in Southern California, in 1940. They've since been stocked in Southern California lakes and reservoirs because they outperform the old standby bluegill. While not as plentiful as bluegills, which they resemble and with which they often hybridize, redear are highly regarded by SoCal anglers because they usually grow faster and larger then bluegills. The listed California record redear is 3 pounds 7 ounces! Fish in the 1/2 to 3/4 pound range are not uncommon. They can be distinguished from other panfish by their bright orange-red margin on the tip of each gill cover, a more slender body than the bluegill, and a typical greenish color blending to pale yellow on the lower body and abdomen.

Finding Fish in a Lake

Fishing habitat and techniques for bluegill and redear sunfish are much alike. If you're catching giant bluegill, they're probably redear! So in the remainder of this section, the word bluegill will be used to refer to both bluegill and redear, except where a distinction is made for redear sunfish.

The easiest time to find bluegills is when they spawn in shallow water in the spring (March-May). They'll be in 2 to 10 feet of water over sand or gravel bottoms. Be careful not to spook them if the water is clear. In summer bluegills behave like bass, moving to submerged channels, under docks, over bars, to weed beds or drop-offs. It's at these times that it may be necessary to fish 10-40 feet down. A drifting, rowed or trolled boat with baits suspended at various depths can often find them. Bluegills are always in schools, so when you find one, you've found a bunch. Any type of fishing tackle (spinning, spin casting, bait casting, cane pole) is fine.

Bait Fishing

This is probably the most popular approach, especially for kids. Some of the best baits are red worms, mealworms, crickets, chunks of nightcrawlers and small grasshoppers. Commercial dough-type baits also work. A bobber is most often used to keep the bait off the bottom and to signal a bite. From shore you can use a bobber rig as illustrated below.

From a boat or dock you can use the same bobber rig, or take the bobber off and fish straight below the pole or rod tip.

Still fishing, or bait fishing for bluegills, might be somewhat of a misnomer. Most experts agree that a slight movement of your bait is desirable. With any rig, flick the rod tip frequently to move your bait. Another principle is to change depths if action is slow. Frequently, large bluegills are down deeper than most bobber anglers suspect.

Fly Fishing, Casting Bobbers, Etc.

Fly casting for bluegills is enjoyable and productive. A medium action, 7 1/2 to 8 1/2 foot rod is suggested, but any will do. A wide variety of offerings will produce depending on the lake, the time of year and the time of day:

- Panfish poppers—swim them slowly along in a stop-and-go fashion
- Rubber or plastic-legged spiders
- Mosquitos, Ants, Wooly Worms, Black Gnats (#10,12)
- Bucktail streamers (size 8)
- Nymphs (black, gray, olive, brown, etc.)
- Indiana spinners (#2 blades, #8 hook)

A casting bobber is a small bobber, usually made of clear plastic, that is attached to monofilament line. Because of its weight, (some allow you to let in water to make it even heavier) it allows anglers to cast poppers, flies, etc., using spinning, spin casting or bait casting equipment. So you can enjoy "fly fishing" without having to use a fly rod and reel.

Another category of offering that works great are soft plastic grubs and small jigs. Jig heads (micro jigs) in the 1/16

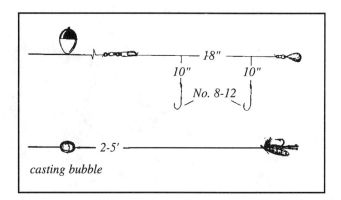

casting bubble

to 1/32 ounce size are about right. For more details, see the Crappie section.

Where to Fish

Bluegills can be found in just about any waters holding bass or other warm water species. (See the "Freshwater Fishing" chapters.) Bullards Bar is known for its large bluegill. Clear Lake is a good place for bank anglers because of abundant docks and brush. Top producers for redear sunfish are Indian Valley, Lake Sonoma, Amador, Stony Gorge, East Park, Folsom, Black Butte, Pardee, Oroville and Collins.

Cleaning and Cooking

Since bluegills are small most people clean them in the traditional way. Scale them by rubbing a knife or scaling tool from the tail of the fish towards the head. Next, cut open the belly, starting from the anus, and remove the guts. Finally, cut off the head. Rinse them off and they're ready for the pan. An alternative is to fillet them, especially for bigger sunfish. This yields small fillets and eliminates skin and bones in the cooked fish. See instructions on filleting in the Fish Cleaning chapter. Sauteing the whole fish or individual fillets is most popular. See the Crappie section for an excellent recipe.

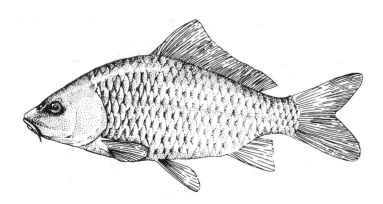

How to Catch . . . Carp

I recently read an article in *Sports Afield* magazine about carp. That's right, carp! The article starts out with the sentence, "In the grand scheme of things, carp are slightly lower than a used doughball." Pretty funny . . . and probably true. But carp fishing is fun, and we here in Northern California have a special historical tie to the lowly carp. It seems that a fellow named Tulius Poppe of Sonoma, California, managed to import about half a dozen small carp from Germany in 1872. Carp, if nothing else, are survivors. And the Sonoma carp did survive and reproduce. Soon offspring were sold to farms throughout California. By the 1890s, carp had settled in all over the United States.

Other interesting facts about carp: They can survive in the murkiest water, so murky that light can't penetrate; water temperatures above 100^0F don't phase them; and life spans reach 50 years. Carp are considered a great game fish in Europe. Anglers practicing catch and release use highly sophisticated tackle to take 20 and 30 pounders. By the way, goldfish, the ones in the aquariums and ponds, are members of the carp family.

When and How to Fish

Carp are all over the place in Northern California—lakes, sloughs, rivers, and farm ponds. They are the mainstay of bow fishermen at places like Clear Lake. The Delta is another carp haunt as are the large NorCal reservoirs. They can provide great sport for those who enjoy big fish on light tackle. Doughball baits are probably the most popular. Carp are also fond of molasses-coated popcorn.

Rigging is simple. You can use a catfish rig, or a sliding sinker rig like that used for striped bass or trout. A #3 hook is about right. For calm, shallow waters little or no weight is needed. Any type of light, freshwater tackle will do. In the fall, when waters reach their warmest temperatures, carp are active and fishing is good.

Keeping and Cooking

There is an excess of carp; therefore, anglers should keep them when caught. That's because carp eat game fish spawn. But cooking carp so that they are enjoyable to eat is a challenge to most people. Anglers with Asian or European cooking prowess can turn carp into a delicacy. These experts say that the flaky, white, mild-flavored flesh is ideal for frying, baking in a sauce or braising.

WHITE CATFISH

CHANNEL CATFISH

How to Catch . . . Catfish

Catfish are widespread and abundant in Southern California lakes, rivers, sloughs, canals and farm ponds. Despite their unappetizing appearance and somewhat negative image, catfish are very good eating. (Catfish are not as difficult to clean as one might suspect, either.) The delicious meals provided by catfish are attested to by the existence of hundreds of catfish farms, primarily in the Southeastern U.S. where these fish are raised and sold to restaurants and food stores. They get large too. California state records for blue and channel catfish are in the 50-80 pound range.

Fishing Techniques

Catfishing means still fishing. And catfish means warm weather fishing since these critters like warm water and are most active when lakes, ponds and rivers warm up in the late spring, summer and early fall. Boats are not needed for catfishing. Simply find a spot on shore where you have enough room to cast out your weighted rig. Let it sink to the bottom. Snug up the line. And wait for the prowling whiskerfish to find your offering. A bank, dock or pier where you can sit on a comfortable chair makes things perfect.

The best catfishing and the largest catfish (they can weigh 5, 10, 20 pounds or more) are often caught after dark. From dark to midnight and the several hours before sunup are particularly good. Early evening can also be good. But many catfish, including big ones, are caught on lazy summer after-noons. Bring several baits along. If one doesn't produce, try something else. Often, this single maneuver can make all the difference. In daylight hours, concentrate on shady spots.

Tackle and Equipment

Any rod and reel combination that can cast out a rig with a 1/2-6 oz. sinker will do just fine. These include specialized bass fishing tackle, light to medium spinning equipment and surf casting equipment. In some situations, you'll probably be better off with a longer rod (7-8 feet), so longer casts are possible. Use at least 10 pound test. But heavier line such as 15-20 pound test is no problem.

Bait and Rigging

Catfish will eat almost anything, and they feed by both sight and by smell. Their smell sensors are on their whiskers. In fact, some catfish baits are often referred to as stink baits because, at times, it seems that catfish prefer smelly offerings such as beef liver, coagulated blood, chicken entrails, etc.

In Northern California some of the most successful baits are less repulsive. These include fresh clams (keep them on ice, pry them open with a knife, thread hook through hard outer edges), nightcrawlers, anchovies, red worms, sardine chunks and chicken livers.

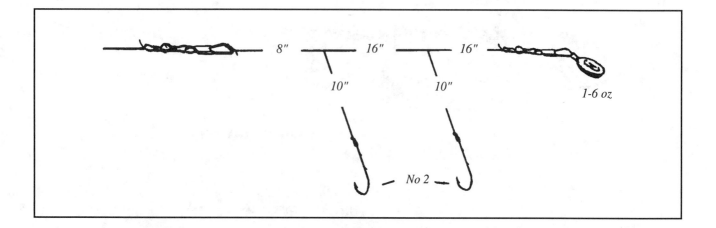

The conventional catfish rig is shown above. A popular alternative is the sliding sinker rig. (For a specific description, see the Striped Bass section.) Some anglers use a treble hook which helps hold on the bait. Use enough weight to get the casting distance you want and to hold the rig on the bottom if there is a current. Some anglers prefer a dipsey sinker. It has a flat metal rim around the edge which makes it flutter up on a quick retrieve, so it's less likely to get caught in rock crevices and roots.

Where to Fish

Some of the best spots are in the lakes and reservoirs described in this book. The Delta and Sacramento Valley rivers are also very good. (See the "Freshwater Fishing," "Delta Fishing" and "Central Valley River" chapters.)

Night fishing is legal in many waters. In the Bay Area some of the best after dark catfish action occurs at Parkway, Chabot, Shadow Cliffs, Del Valle and San Pablo. Check the hours on these waters. Clear Lake, Berryessa, the Delta, Pine Flat, Don Pedro and New Melones can be fished all night. Sacramento area anglers can pursue big whiskerfish at night at Black Butte, East Park, Camp Far West, Bullards Bar, Shasta, and foothill farm ponds.

Cleaning and Cooking

The first step in catfish cleaning is skin removal. To skin a catfish, cut through the skin all around the fish just below the gill cover. Then using a pliers, pull the skin down the fish while holding the fish's gills. Be careful not to be poked by the sharp pectoral and dorsal fin spines. Some people nip these off with wire cutters. For larger fish it is suggested that the fish be nailed (through the head) to a tree trunk or fence post using an adequately sized spike. The skinned catfish can then be filleted or steaked. (See the Fish Cleaning chapter for more details.) Catfish meat is flaky, mild and has a moist texture. It is good sauteed, fried or poached.

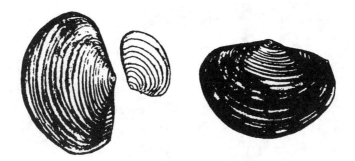

How to Catch . . . Clams

Diggers either wear old tennis shoes and old pants, or waders. If you don't go the waterproof route, be sure to bring along a change of clothing. One of the best ways to get familiar with clam digging is to take a family outing to a popular clamming ground. Wander around. Watch. Ask questions. Observe the equipment and techniques. You'll have a ball.

Clamming Techniques

Clamming is probably the most popular in Northern California in late fall and early winter. During this period a tide chart is all that is needed to tell you when to go. The best time is a minus low tide. This is when the ocean rolls back to expose the prime clam beds. Clams are not found on long stretches of exposed beach. They need protected waters. Good clamming grounds include Humboldt Bay, Tomales Bay, Bodega Bay, Half Moon Bay and Elkhorn Slough (at Moss Landing).

Besides digging equipment, clammers also need a measuring device, fishing license, plastic bucket or burlap sack. The type of clams that are found depend on where you dig. Cockles are especially prolific in Tomales Bay, Half Moon Bay and the Ano Nuevo Area (don't dig in the state reserve here). These small clams (minimum size limit is 1 1/2") are found in rock and sand mix, only about three to four inches below the surface. Washington and horseneck (gapers) are smooth and reach a maximum length of 5 inches. They are found at Elkhorn Slough, Tomales and Bodega Bays.

For horsenecks, diggers are out on the tide flats during minus tides looking for small siphon holes in the sand. These are feeding holes. When a bubbling hole is spotted, dig down.

Somewhere down there is a clam. The favorite tool for these larger and deeper species is a clamer shovel. It can dig a narrow yet deep hole rather easily. Clam hooks can also be used. One caution: Never put clams in a galvanized bucket. An electrolyte action may be set up, ruining the clams.

Where to Dig

Humboldt Bay has Washington, horseneck and cockle clams. The most productive area is the south end of the bay. Cockles are the main quarry at the north end of the bay. Bodega Bay completely drains on a minus tide. The west side is particularly good for clamming. Tomales Bay clammers have immense areas to work, but the western shoreline in Tomales Bay State Park is a favorite. Half Moon Bay is good just inside the north and south ends of the harbor. At Elkhorn Slough clammers can be seen digging in the area east of Hwy. 1. Be aware of clamming regulations. They differ by location and species.

Cleaning and Cooking Clams

The best way to get sand out of clams is to keep them in saltwater for two or three days. Change the water several times during this period. Don't use fresh water. Another way to clean clams is to freeze them. When they thaw they'll gape open and the sand can be quickly rinsed out. Cockles are a favorite for eating. Many people steam them and then dip them in butter sauce (perhaps seasoned with garlic). Washington and horseneck clams are excellent when fried. Overcooking of any clam should be avoided to prevent toughness.

54

BLACK CRAPPIE

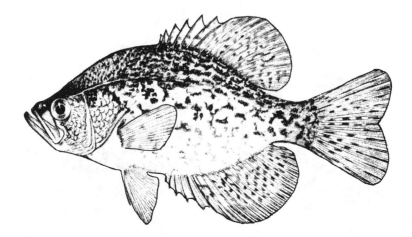

How to Catch . . . Crappie

Crappies (pronounced krop'-i) are the king of the panfish. Both black crappies and white crappies can grow quite large (state records: black crappie—4 pounds 1 ounce; white crappie—4 pounds 8 ounces), but most crappies average a pound or even less. A two-pounder is bragging size. Crappies provide fun and relaxed fishing on light tackle and are excellent eating.

Black crappies are the most widespread of the two types and do the best in clearer water. Adult crappies are fish eaters, so they need an abundant supply of forage, like shad, to do well. Surprising to some, crappies also need a good deal of fishing pressure, otherwise they overpopulate their lake and all are stunted. So enjoy catching and eating crappies, it's good for the fish and good for the angler.

Finding Crappies in a Lake

The key to successful crappie fishing is finding them. These are school fish that cluster in different parts of a lake depending on season, water temperature, reproductive cycles, underwater contours, etc.

Crappies are easiest to find and catch when they move into shallow water to spawn. This happens when the water temperature reaches about 60-65°F. March, April and May are the likely months. These fish like heavy cover to accompany the shallow water. Look for water 3-8 feet deep with sunken trees, tule beds, cattails, lily pads and undercut rocky banks. This is much like the cover used by largemouth bass. Shore anglers do well in spring, as the fish move in close.

In summer and winter crappies are harder to find, so stringers get skimpier or are empty. But they are still there and eating. Here are some ways to find them. Look in deeper water. They're usually down in 10-20 foot water or deeper. Crappies like underwater islands and stream beds, ledges, etc. Often they are in deeper water just adjacent to where they were in the spring. One good way to find them is to troll a jig or minnow across likely spots with lines of various depths. Mark the spot and depth when you get a hit. Troll slowly with oars or electric motor, or drift. Electronic fish finders will also do the job.

In the fall, crappies are not quite as deep as in the summer (8-16 feet). And early and late in the day, crappies, like bass, move into shallower water to feed. So even in the summer, the first angler on the lake, or the last to call it a day, may fill a stringer with crappies in shallow water.

Jig Fishing

This is by far the most popular method of taking crappies all year long. A word of caution before getting into the technique of this approach: It's easy to spook schools of crappies (especially in shallow water), so fish quietly and keep a low profile. And don't, for example, slide an anchor or tackle box along the bottom of your boat. Approach likely spots slowly and carefully.

Crappie jigs, or mini-jigs, are in the 1/32 to 1/8 ounce size range. Most are little lead-head jigs with a bright colored feather covering the hook end. Eyes are often painted on the head end. Some like Sassy Shad Jigs have rubber bodies that imitate swimming shad.

Tie these jigs directly on about a 4, or even a 2 pound test line. Light line gives the jig better action. Short, accurate casts are called for from boat or shore. But since you'll be casting into cover, expect snags and expect to lose some jigs. Allow the jig to sink to the desired depth, and then retrieve either smoothly and slowly, or impart a twitching action with the rod tip.

A small, clear casting bobber can be added up the line from the jig if it's too light to cast the desired distance. The bobber will also prevent the jig from going deeper than it is set below the bobber. See the Bluegill section for illustration of a casting bobber. Boat anglers, when directly over a school of crappie, can drop a jig straight down and then twitch it around.

Crappie jigs come in many colors. Here are some guidelines. Light colors, like white, work well on clear days in clear water. Yellow is better on overcast days and at dawn and dusk. In off-colored water try dark colors like brown and blacks. Experiment with different styles and colors. These jigs are inexpensive. Sometimes color doesn't even seem to matter.

Bait Fishing

Crappies love minnows, so if you prefer live minnow fishing, this is the way to go, but be sure minnows are a legal bait where you are fishing. Bait can be fished from shore, dock or boat. Most anglers use a bobber. A typical rig is shown below.

Minnows are best hooked up through both lips.

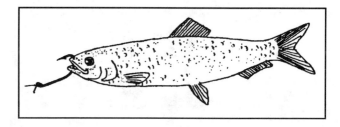

Most experts agree that a slight movement of your bait is desirable. Flick the rod tip frequently to move your bait. Another basic principle is to change depths if the action is slow.

Frequently, larger crappies are deeper down than most bobber anglers suspect. These anglers use a sliding bobber rig to get their bait deeper while still being able to cast and retrieve the crappie to back near the rod tip. The main line slides through the slip bobber. This rig can be reeled in all the way until the bobber is up against the swivel. That's because the rubber band bobber-stop is small enough to pass smoothly through the rod line guides. After casting out, the sinker will pull the rig through the bobber until the rubber band bobber-

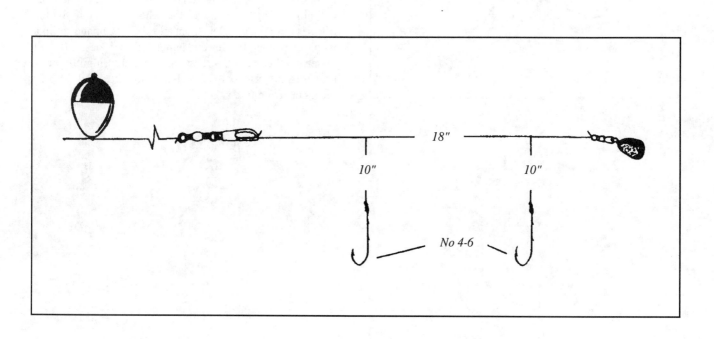

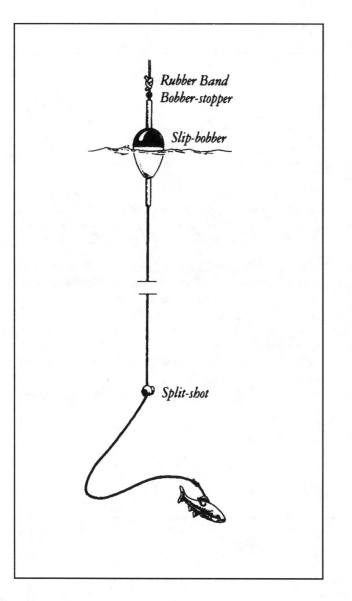

Rubber Band
Bobber-stopper

Slip-bobber

Split-shot

stop gets to the bobber. By changing the location of the bobber-stop on the line, you can change fishing depth.

Tackle and Equipment

Just about any light freshwater tackle will do such as light spinning, spin casting, bamboo poles and long fly rods. Actually, the lighter the tackle the better, since it will help cast out the light jigs and baits. Ultralight spinning tackle is popular. The only other thing you'll need is a stringer or a collapsible fish basket.

Where to Fish

Crappies are found in abundant supply in many Northern California lakes. Some of the lakes that are known for fine crappie fishing are Clear Lake, Camanche, Berryessa and Black Butte. Back sloughs and ditches in the Delta are also good. See the "Freshwater Fishing" chapters.

Cleaning and Cooking

Many people clean crappie in the traditional way. Scale them by rubbing a knife or scaling tool from the tail of the fish to the head. Cut open the belly and remove the guts. Finally, cut off the head. Rinse them off and they're ready for the pan.

An alternative for good-sized fish is to fillet them. This yields a little less meat, but filleting eliminates skin and bone in the cooked fish. See instructions on filleting in the "Fish Cleaning" chapter. Sauteing the whole fish or individual fillets is most popular. Dip them into sifted flour and sprinkle with salt, pepper, parsley and lemon flakes (if desired). Melt butter in a hot skillet, toss in the fish and turn until golden brown. Another delicious method is to batter and deep-fry pieces cut from fillets.

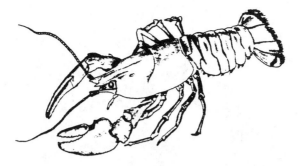

How to Catch . . . Crawdads

And besides, they're easy to catch and a snap to prepare. California crawdads can reach about 6 inches long and vary in color from brownish, to reddish or greenish. Although there is no minimum size limit, most anglers return smaller crawdads (less than 2 to 3 inches) since the amount of edible meat on these is slight.

Fishing Techniques

The easiest way to catch a batch of crawdads is to use one or more wire traps. These traps have funnel-shaped openings that allow the crawdad to get in but not out. Crawdad traps are available in many bait and tackle shops. They go for about $15 to $20, but can be purchased on sale for as little as $10.

These traps are baited with a piece of chicken or liver, or a can of dog food (fish flavored is good). Perforate the dog food can with a can opener. Secure the can or other bait in the middle of the trap with a line or string. All you do is lower the trap to the bottom on a rope and wait. Crawdads are most active at night and prefer rocky areas (provides a place to hide). Undercut river banks in shady areas are also good. If evening or night fishing is not convenient, try it in the daytime. I've seen many crawdads caught when the sun is up.

Another technique popular with kids is to lower a strip of bacon or piece of liver into the water using a string or fishing line. Lower it to the bottom and wait. Once in awhile, slowly raise up the bait and ease a landing net under it, right near the surface. Usually the crawdad will hang on to the bait long enough to be caught in the net. A boat dock or tied-up houseboat is a great place to catch crawdads using this technique.

Caught crawdads can be stored alive for up to a day in a bucket that is covered with a damp towel or gunnysack. This is important because crawdads are cooked alive (like lobster), at least they are alive when cooking starts.

Tackle and Equipment

You'll need the following to catch crawdads:

- A bucket (to keep your catch in)
- A crawdad trap or two, or...
- A pole and line (or rod, reel and line)
- Bait (dog food, chicken leg, bacon, liver)

Where to Fish

The Delta is very good. Many lakes, ponds and streams are also good. See the "Freshwater Fishing" chapters for more details.

Cleaning and Cooking

Crawdads don't need to be cleaned. Most people cook them whole—the edible meat is in the tail and pinchers. But some people just remove the tails and cook them. If you do this, you can remove the tail by twisting and pulling it off where it meets the body. Then grasp the middle of the three flippers at the end of the tail. Twisting and pulling it will pull out the black entrail string that runs along the top of the meat under the tail side. If it doesn't come out, don't worry. You can easily remove it after cooking when the shell is removed.

The first step in most crawdad recipes is cooking them for about 10 minutes in boiling, salted water. The shell is bright red when crawdads are done. A whole crawdad can then be eaten like small lobster. Or you can clean out the meat (use a nutcracker and nut pick) and saute it in your favorite Newburg sauce.

A popular recipe is to heat a little butter in a skillet and add fresh pressed garlic, sweet basil, finely chopped fresh parsley, a touch of olive oil and pepper. Now add about a fourth cup of white wine, a bowl of boiled and shelled crawdad claws and tail meat, and saute for a few minutes. Serve over rice for a gourmet treat!

How to Catch . . . Flounder and Sanddabs

Here are two great saltwater species that don't get the attention they deserve. Both of these junior-sized members of the flatfish family are lots of fun to catch, and rank among the best eating of all Southern California sport fish. The flounder caught in Southern California, both commercially and by sport anglers, is the starry flounder. It is sometimes sold in fish markets as sole. The pan-sided sanddab, served in some of the finest fish restaurants, is not available at most fish markets.

Catching Starry Flounder

Each winter thousands of starry flounder migrate from Pacific Ocean waters (at a depth of as much as 900 feet) into bays, lagoons, and to some extent even into the fresh water of coastal streams, where they then spawn. Fishing is usually good from mid-December through March with a peak in February. The average catch is 1 to 3 pounds and 12 to 18 inches in length. But 6 to 7 pounders about 2 feet long are caught. Starry flounder are dark brown on the top side, white on the bottom side, and have a very distinctive checkerboard orange and black alternating color pattern on both the upper and lower fin lines.

San Francisco, Richardson, San Pablo, Grizzly, and Honker Bays are all good, as is Elkhorn Slough, at Moss Landing on Monterey Bay. Fish shallow water with sandy or mud bottoms. One key to success is to seek out areas around the bays where fresh water runs in. River inlets, sloughs, creeks or even storm drains are all likely spots. Here are some specifics:

South San Francisco Bay—the west shoreline at Point San Bruno, Folger's Point, south of San Francisco Airport along the Millbrae and Burlingame Flats to Coyote Point.

Richardson Bay—beneath the Highway 101 bridge where Mill Creek comes in.

San Pablo Bay—the mouth of the Napa River between Mare Island and Vallejo, the mouth of Napa Slough, the mouth of Petaluma River, Novato River and Gallinas Creek.

Suisun Bay—the South Hampton Flats; the Middle Ground by the Mothball Fleet.

Any freshwater or light saltwater tackle and line will do. Tie or snap on a surf rig as shown in the Surf Fishing section of Chapter 2. Two #6 baitholder hooks and a 1 to 2 ounce pyramid sinker are about right. Sliding sinker rigs also work. Top baits for starry flounder are pile worms, blood worms, mussels, and shrimp. Bring along several different baits and experiment. Best fishing is before, during and after a substantial high tide (5 feet or so). Remember to keep your rig on the bottom—that's where flatfish feed.

Catching Sanddabs

Some seasoned fish eaters consider sanddabs the best tasting of all ocean fish—including salmon, halibut and albacore tuna. These little guys are commonly caught commercially, and served in many fine restaurants. But not many sport anglers pursue them, perhaps because they're small, only about 6 to 12 inches long. Although sanddab inhabit water that is from 30 to 1800 feet deep, they are most abundant at depths of 120 to 300 feet. As their name suggests, they live on sandy bottoms.

Some Monterey Bay rockfish anglers, who work the Monterey canyon drop-offs, will "stop off" at about 20 fathoms to catch a mess of sanddabs on their way back to the harbor, if time and weather permits. Salmon trollers who are getting "skunked" also switch over to sanddabs at times.

Off the coast of Northern California if the depth is correct (120-250 feet) and the bottom suitable, it is extremely difficult to keep sanddabs off the hook. Rock cod rigs work. Surf rigs work. Use cut pieces of squid, pile worms, grass shrimp or ghost shrimp for bait. In years when ocean waters are warmer than usual, sanddabs are also plentiful in San Francisco Bay.

Cleaning and Cooking

Starry flounder are usually large enough to fillet. Remember there are 4 fillets on flatfish. Use a sharp, flexible fillet knife. See the five steps in the diagram below.

Starry flounder have a delicate, but distinctive flavor and nice texture. You can use them in any sole recipe. Skinless fillets are suitable for sauteing, poaching or broiling (if on the longer side).

Sanddabs are very easy to clean. The shape of their body is such that you can remove their head and their intestinal cavity in one cut taken diagonally over the head and the top of the pectoral fin. No need to scale or skin them. Just rinse them in cold running water after cutting. This fish is sweet, nut-like and moist. It's great charcoal grilled or pan fried. Breaded dabs pan fry quickly in about 2 minutes per side. They can be easily de-boned at the table, just like pan-sized trout or sunfish. Insert a butter knife or fork (or two) beneath the upper fillet and lift it off. The skeleton is now exposed on top of the bottom fillet. Just lift these bones off in one piece and you have a second de-boned fillet.

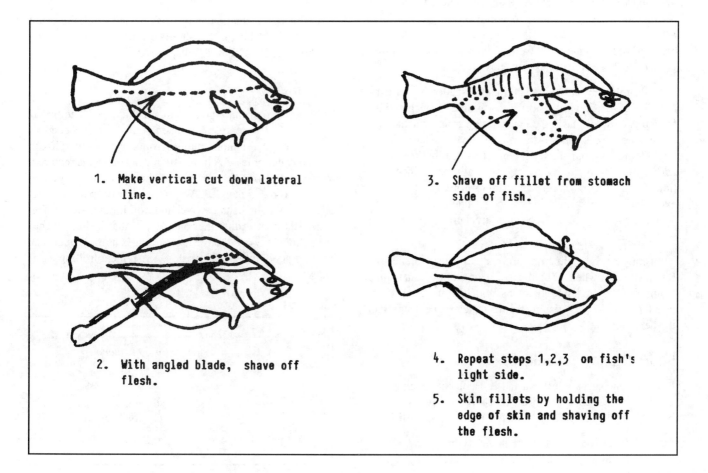

1. Make vertical cut down lateral line.
2. With angled blade, shave off flesh.
3. Shave off fillet from stomach side of fish.
4. Repeat steps 1,2,3 on fish's light side.
5. Skin fillets by holding the edge of skin and shaving off the flesh.

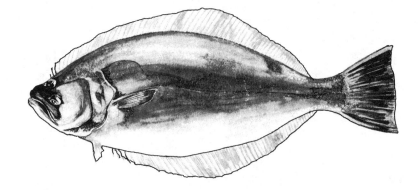

How to Catch . . . Halibut

A California halibut is a flatfish and can range in size up to 50-75 pounds. The typical keeper is from 10-20 pounds. Adult halibut move into shallower water in the late spring and summer to spawn. Young fish swim upright, but during their first year, one eye migrates to the other side of the head and they begin to swim in a horizontal position. Also, the side with the two eyes (the top) turns dark or sand-colored, while the bottom side turns light. Halibut live right on the sandy bottom. A ruffling of fins and tail kicks up a cloud of sand that settles back on the fish and hides it from both its predators and prey. Only its two eyes are noticeable above the sand.

California halibut fishing is primarily shallow water fishing. Because of this situation, it is possible to catch halibut from piers, by surf casting on beaches, or from a boat. In all these cases the basic idea is the same: Get your offering down on the sandy bottom and keep it moving. Halibut feed most actively during moving current, especially on an incoming tide. The 2 or 3 hours before a high tide are often the best. And even slack water at high tide can be productive. Halibut do school, so if one is hooked, chances are there are more in the same location.

Fishing at the right time of year is critical to success. Summertime is when the halibut are in the shallow water. June is not too early in some locations, and July and August are usually good. Weekly fishing reports in newspapers highlight the best time.

Shore Fishing Techniques

Both pier and surf anglers can and do catch halibut although, admittedly, the vast majority are taken from party and private boats. Two elements are essential for successful shore fishing:

1. Be there when the fish are there. Halibut move depending upon the whereabouts of anchovy schools and spawning patterns. The key is to keep up on local action.

2. Keep your offering moving. Halibut ambush moving forage fish. So your offering must do the same. This requires a constant cast and retrieve pattern. Slow retrieves are usually the most productive.

For more information on pier fishing and surf fishing, not only for halibut, but for all inshore saltwater game fish, see the "Fishing . . . NorCal Style" chapter.

Trolling

There are two primary boat fishing techniques. The first is trolling. Most trollers use equipment similar to that needed for non-downrigger salmon trolling. Trollers work the surf line in 20 foot water or less. A large landing net or gaff is required. You should also have a fish billy. A sharp blow midway down the body is recommended. When trolling a deep diving lure, attach it to a good snap swivel and troll it out about 50 feet behind the boat. Adjust the boat speed so that the lure touches the bottom now and then. Slow trolling is best. Trollers can cover a good amount of territory. A typical trolling rig is shown below:

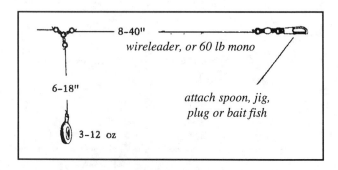

Drift Fishing

Many anglers prefer boat drift fishing. This technique is used extensively for halibut and striped bass in San Francisco Bay. Because of its popularity, a separate section has been set aside to describe drift fishing. See the "Fishing . . . NorCal Style" chapter.

Lures and Bait

Common bait and lures used for halibut are . . .

- Anchovies, shiners, small perch—live, hooked through the lips for drifting; hooked on a salmon rig when trolling.

- Hair Raisers

- Pet Spoons

- Kastmasters

- Rebel minnow-type plug—about 6 to 7 inches

- Bagley Bango-B deep diving plug—6 to 9 inches (blue back, silver belly, bleeding gills); model has been "hot" in San Francisco Bay.

- Scampi-type twin tail soft plastics—about 5 inches (in rootbeer)

Where to Fish

There are many good fishing locations along the Pacific coast which are described in the "Pacific Ocean Fishing" chapter. Here are some hot spots:

- Bodega Bay—the entrance along the rocky breakwater

- Tomales Bay—near entrance at Lawson's Landing just south of Dillon's Beach

- Marin coast—Stinson, Muir and Tennessee beaches

- Golden Gate—just outside the bridge between the Cliff House and Seal Rock area, inshore to Baker Beach

- San Francisco and Pacifica shoreline—South Bar, Mussel Rock and the coves inside Lindamar and Devil Slide

- Half Moon Bay—Pillar Point Harbor

- Monterey Bay

In San Francisco Bay, some of the best places to fish for halibut on an incoming tide are listed below.

- Crissy Field—Fishing is best in June, July and August. Drift parallel to shore in about 10-20 feet of water.

- Alcatraz Island—Using anchovies, fish the shoal on the west side July through September in 20-45 feet of water. On incoming tides boats drift towards the island.

- Treasure Island—Fish the flats north and west of the island. Use anchovies or shiners in 20-40 feet of water.

- Angel Island—There are two spots here: Point Knox Shoal on the southwest side of the island at 20-50 feet and Raccoon Strait between the island and the Tiburon Peninsula.

Farther south, a good area is the flat between Oyster Point and San Francisco International Airport.

Cleaning and Cooking

Smaller halibut can be filleted. Larger ones are steaked. Even when filleting, the tail section can be steaked. When filleting, first make a vertical cut (the fish is laying flat) along the lateral line down to the spine. This allows you to "lift off" two manageable-sized fillets from each side of the fish.

Halibut is dense, mild, somewhat sweet, and low in fat. Popular cooking methods include broiling, barbecuing, poaching, frying and baking. The fillets can be sauteed.

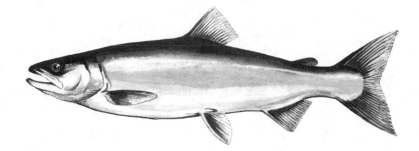

How to Catch . . . Kokanee

Kokanee are a land-locked sockeye salmon. They were originally planted in Western reservoirs in the late 1940's. Today, the kokanee fisheries are quite active in selected Northern California locations. Kokanee reach adulthood in about 4 years, the same as for other salmon. They spawn in late summer or fall in lake tributaries. Kokanee can reach a length of 16 to 20 inches or more, but the overcrowding of the species (and resulting need to share a limited food resource) generally results in mature kokanee in the 8 to 14 inch range. Even at this modest size they are a desirable catch because they taste great.

Plankton is the main food source of kokanee, so fishing for them requires an offering that provides color and movement to get their attention. They are a school fish, so once one is located, the chances of catching more are good.

Fishing Techniques

The almost universal technique for catching kokanee is trolling. Like other salmon, kokanee prefer cold water (about 50⁰F, in fact). This means that when a lake is stratified the kokanee are down deep. However, in spring and late fall, kokanee can be trolled for near the surface.

The approaches used for kokanee trolling have much more in common with lake trolling for trout. In fact, identical equipment and rigging is used. Lake trolling is described in detail in the Trout (in Lakes) section of this chapter. Rather than repeating all of this information, here are some highlights of the few differences and the key points to success:

- The most popular lures are nickel/red head, fire/pearl, rainbow and pearl/red head. Small spoons are most popular; Needlefish and Super-duper, size #1. A Wedding Ring lure tipped with corn is also great.

- In very cold, clear water it is possible to troll near the surface using the type of rig shown on the next page.

- However, when kokanee are down more than 10 feet (the usual situation), the rig illustrated on the next page is typical.

- A rubber snubber is necessary because kokanee have soft, delicate mouths. The snubber absorbs the shock of the strike.

- A diving plane or lead core line can be trolled down to about 40 feet. Downriggers are well suited to kokanee trolling at 20 to 40 feet, or even deeper. A typical downrigger setup is shown on the next page.

- Use the same trolling techniques as used for trout; troll slow, work in an S pattern and vary your speed often.

- An electronic fish finder can locate the school of kokanee and tell you what depth to troll.

- Many kokanee anglers add a single kernel of white corn, a small pinch of worm, a salmon egg, or a short piece of red or white yarn to the hook of their lure. Try it if action is slow.

Where to Fish

Lake Tahoe, Donner and Bullard's Bar can produce kokanee in the 14 to 20 inch size bracket. Mature, smaller fish (8 to 12 inches) are the rule in lakes like Whiskeytown, Pardee, Bucks, Ice House, Camanche, Echo and Stampede.

Cleaning and Cooking

Most anglers clean and prepare kokanee the same as they would smaller trout—see the Trout (in Streams) section. Kokanee have a very mild, salmon-type meat.

Surface Rig

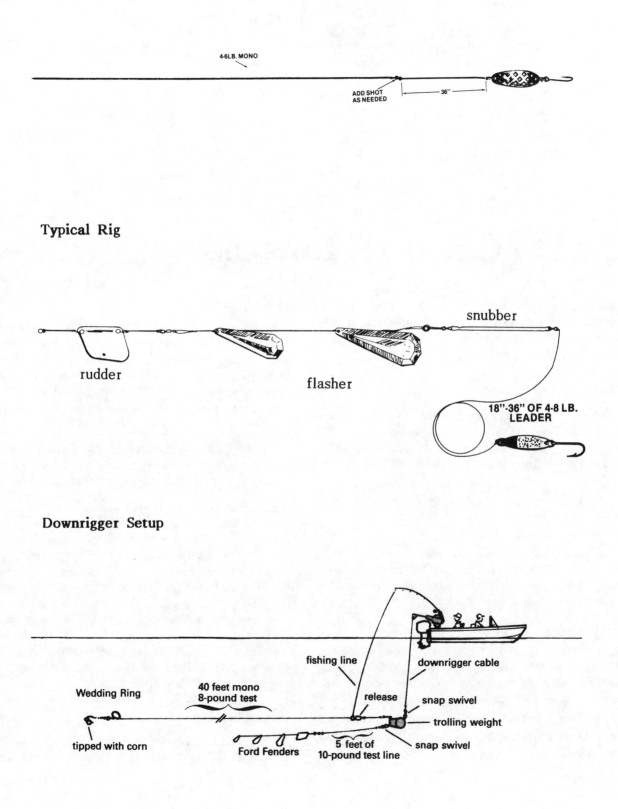

4-6LB. MONO

ADD SHOT
AS NEEDED

36"

Typical Rig

snubber

rudder

flasher

18"-36" OF 4-8 LB.
LEADER

Downrigger Setup

fishing line

downrigger cable

release

snap swivel

trolling weight

snap swivel

Wedding Ring

40 feet mono
8-pound test

tipped with corn

Ford Fenders

5 feet of
10-pound test line

How to Catch . . . Lingcod

Guess what? Lingcod aren't a cod. Lingcod are actually greenling which are rockfish. But they're much larger and tougher than other rockfish. Lings can reach upwards of 5 feet and weight up to 70 pounds.

Fishing Techniques

Lingcod can be caught at any time of the year. And many are caught by rock cod fishermen, particularly while fishing in deep water (200-400 feet). In fact, at times a large ling will strike a small rockfish that has just been hooked.

Dedicated lingcod pursuers, however, choose to fish in fall and winter. Three of the best months are December, January and February. During this period lings are more active and move to shallower water to spawn.

Lingcod fishing, like rock cod fishing, is bottom, drift fishing. It is done over rocks or reefs. Once the rig has been lowered to the bottom, it should be jigged up and down. Try to stay off the bottom to prevent snags.

Tackle and Equipment

You'll need a gaff (lings will tear up a landing net), a fish billy (to subdue this fish that has sharp teeth and fins), and a needlenose pliers (to take out the hook). The tackle you'll need is the same as needed for deep-water rockfishing:

- Medium heavy to heavy roller-tipped, 6-7 foot rod
- A 6/0 or 4/0 ocean reel
- 30-50 pound monofilament line

Lures and Bait

The most commonly used lure for lingcod is the chrome hex bar with treble hook. The appropriate lures range from 6-15 ounces depending on ocean conditions and lings' preference. Some fishermen remove the strong treble hook that comes on this lure and replace it with light wire treble hooks. When hung up in the rocks, the light hook bends and gives before the line breaks, thus saving the expensive hex bar.

Another good offering is a lead-head bucktail jig with a pork trailer. About a 5-inch pork rind is good. The pork looks like the tentacles of small octopus, a favorite food of big lings.

Many lingcod fishermen prefer bait fishing. The best bait is whole fish. Good choices include sanddabs, rockfish or squid. Some anglers cut the dorsal fin off rockfish when using it as bait. They say it makes the bait more appetizing. It's best if the bait is alive, or at least freshly caught. Seven to 10 inches is a good size. Use a two hook rig like the one shown on the following page. The end hook goes through the bait fish's upper lip (or through both lips) and the other hook goes into the side of the fish near the tail. A secret, sleeper bait is octopus. Sometimes lingcod spit them up after being caught. Or you might find one in a ling's stomach. In either case, use this gift bait to catch another ling.

Where to Fish

Lingcod seem to congregate on high rock pinnacles and along the irregular edges of reefs that drop off rapidly to deeper

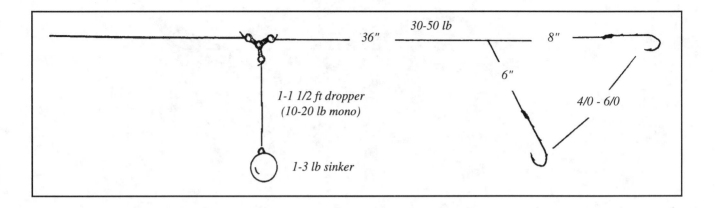

water. Key on such structured bottom characteristics with your electronic fish finder. Then position the boat to drift over likely holding spots. The Northern California coast from Monterey to the Oregon border has many lingcod-rich reefs. Off the Golden Gate, the Farallon Island chain, Fanny Shoals and Cordell Beach are the most likely producers of big lings. See the "Pacific Ocean Fishing" chapter for detailed location information.

Cleaning and Cooking

Lingcod are most often filleted. Larger ones can be streaked. Lingcod fillets or steaks are lean and mild tasting. Lingcod meat (depending on the age of the fish where it is caught) is often green, but turns white upon cooking. Thick fillets or steaks can be barbecued or broiled. They are also suitable for poaching or frying. Thinner fillets can be sauteed. Lingcod is rather dense, so it takes somewhat longer to cook.

Barred Surfperch

How to Catch . . . Saltwater Perch

In the "Fishing . . . NorCal Style" chapter there is an entire section on surf fish—everything you need to know about catching perch in the surf is detailed. But there are a lot of other places where surfperch or saltwater panfish can be caught, like in bays and harbors. And the fishing is great because the tackle is light, the waters are relatively calm, and the action fast and furious. So if you want to catch and eat saltwater perch, which are very tasty, but don't want to surf fish, here's the place for you.

Variety is the name of the game. Pile perch are the largest and best fighters. They weigh up to several pounds and are 14-16 inches in length. There are also perch with names like rubberlip, walleye, white, black, silver, etc. What these fish have in common is that they all bear their young alive, and they can be found around structures like wharfs, piers, docks, pilings, boat slips, sunken barges, rock retaining walls and rocky banks, especially in wintertime.

Fishing Techniques

Current and structure are the keys to finding saltwater perch. Try to think of structure in the same way freshwater black bass anglers do. This is where the perch congregate for protection and food. Most experts agree that a fairly substantial incoming tide is the best time to fish. A 3 to 4 foot difference between low tide and high tide is good. Remember, much of saltwater perch fishing takes place in bays, harbors and coves where tidal movements can make or break fishing success. Days with less wind are also best. Wind-driven waves can muddy up the shallows. In coastal areas, some experts say that fishing is best just after a minus low tide. The perch go on a feeding binge as the incoming tide starts.

Savvy perch chasers enhance their chances of success by chumming. At low tide, anglers use a hatchet or strong knife to gather soft-shelled mussels from beneath boat slips, docks and wharf pilings. The large mussels are saved for bait, and the smaller ones are crushed under foot and tossed into the current. Often in 5 minutes or less, an entire school of perch is biting baited hooks at a furious pace.

Saltwater perch angling can be done from a boat or shore. But most perch fishing is probably done from shore, and with excellent success.

Tackle, Rigging and Bait

Tackle for saltwater perch is easy. Most anglers use freshwater trout gear. It is perfect from boat, dock or pier. Sometimes a longer stick, like a 9 foot steelhead rod, is better from piers and rocky walls.

Two types of rigs are used. The first is the traditional surf rig with #6 hooks. Use enough sinker at the end to take it down where the perch are feeding. If you want, fish it at mid-depth under a float or straight-line right down from the rod tip. Another good setup is to tie a #6 hook right onto the main line. Put a small split shot or two about 18 inches above the hook. Bait can then be drifted with the current to perch hangouts under piers or along pilings, etc. Of course, this rig can also be fished under a bobber.

Sand crabs, mussels, clams, pile worms, squid strips, grass shrimp and cut anchovy pieces are all used successfully as perch bait. Take at least two different baits on each trip. Sand crabs are probably the premier perch bait along the coast, and grass shrimp and fresh mussels are tops in the bays.

Some anglers take along an extra outfit rigged with a favorite crappie jig or small Kastmaster spoon. When a school of perch are hitting, you can "get back into the water" faster when fishing artificials.

Where and When to Fish

Many good spots are described in the "Pacific Ocean Fishing" and the "San Francisco Bay Fishing" chapters. Along the coast it is best to fish wherever you can find a small stream flowing in. Harbors, jetties, pilings, docks, wharfs and piers are all good. Spots on Monterey, San Francisco, Tomales and Humboldt Bays offer good "calmer-water" perch fishing. Here are some perch spots on San Francisco Bay for boat and shore anglers:

From Boat	From Shore
Sausalito, western shoreline	Ft. Point Headlands
Richmond, San Rafael bridges, western side	Marina Green rock wall
Berkeley and Emeryville waterfront	Ft. Mason Pier
Fort Baker area, around piers and breakwaters	Pier #7 (foot of Broadway)
Treasure Island Shoreline	Warm Water Cove (foot of 24th St.)
Belvedere boat slips	San Mateo Pier
Berkeley Pier, old pilings	Fruitvale Bridge
San Francisco waterfront, Fisherman's Wharf to Hunters Point	Berkeley Pier
	Muni Pier (Aquatic Park)
Hunters Point to Candlestick Point	Alameda Estuary (piers and park)
Oyster Point and Oyster Cove Marina	Emeryville Marina (rock wall)
San Francisco Airport pilings	Red Rock Marina
Coyote Point Harbor	Point Pinole
	Richmond (breakwater and piers)
	East Fort Baker (u-shaped pier)
	Sausalito (seawall)

Wintertime is probably the best bay and harbor saltwater perch fishing period, with January and February being the peak months. But perch can be taken year around.

Cleaning and Cooking

Saltwater perch are cleaned just like crappie or bluegill. See these sections for details. With saltwater perch it is best to ice down your catch at once. Cook them quickly, since the delicate meat dries out if cooked too long. They are excellent when breaded and pan fried.

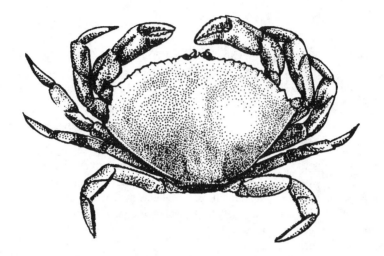

How to Catch . . . Rock Crab

Anglers who fish in the shallow Pacific waters near breakwaters and wharfs are often frustrated by rock crabs stealing their bait. Rather than getting mad at these plentiful pirates, why not get even by catching and eating them? Crabbers work harbors, bays and rocky inlets where good numbers of red, rock, yellow and slender crabs scurry about the bottom in search of food. All of these crabs offer eating in the same league as the famous Dungeness crab.

Fishing Techniques

Rock crab fishing is simple and leisurely. All you need is a hoop net and about 75-100 feet of rope (nylon or clothesline will do). Rock crab nets are sold in many fishing tackle shops for less than $20. Ask the shop how to attach the rope to the particular net you purchase. The most common bait is a fish carcass . . . or what's left after a large rockfish has had its fillets removed. They come either fresh or frozen at bait shops (especially those on or near popular public wharfs) and fish markets. Frozen squid are also a good bait.

One rule of thumb holds true: The more bait in the net, the more rock crabs you'll catch. Crabs find the bait by smelling it. So more bait gets more smell into the water. The fish carcasses are tied to the bottom of the net. Once out on a jetty or a wharf, simply lower the baited net into the water, all the way to the bottom. With a little experience you'll realize how often the net should be raised up to the water surface for checking. When a rock crab is spotted in the net, quickly raise it up all the way. Remove it from the net (but avoid the pincers) and place it in a bucket of sea water. Lower the net and haul up some more.

Timing will improve your catch. Crabbing is often best just before and after the peak of high tide. A three-hour period centered around high tide is recommended. Winter months are most popular for sport crabbing.

Rigging and Equipment

You'll need a hoop net, 100 feet of rope or line (strong enough to lower and raise the net) and a large bucket. Also take a measuring device and fishing regulations. Pay particular attention to the regulations regarding size limitations and possession limits for the individual species.

Where to Fish

Piers, wharfs and rocky breakwaters or jetties along the Pacific coastline are most popular. Good spots include Moss Landing, Pillar Point Harbor, San Francisco Bay near Fort Baker, Bodega Bay and Humboldt Bay.

Cleaning and Cooking

Rock crabs are cooked and eaten like lobster. Most of the meat is in the pincers. Cook crabs in boiling water until shells turn red (about 10 minutes).

How to Catch . . . Rockfish

Rockfish are a group of ocean-dwelling bottom fish, often called rock cod. They are fun to catch and delicious to eat. Varieties of rockfish go by names such as blues, reds, yellowtail, cabezon and browns. Rockfish run up to 7-10 pounds, but average 2-4 pounds. These fish are quite ugly, with large mouths and pointed fins, but they produce delicious fillets.

Fishing Techniques

Rockfishing for most anglers means drift fishing from a boat. It can be done as close as 1/2 mile from shore to as far out as 25 miles or more over offshore reef and bank areas. The technique is quite simple. With the use of an electronic fish finder, locate the boat over a rocky bottom. Often the best location is one where a depth is changing, either on the upslope of a canyon or on the changing slope of a reef. Position the boat so it will drift towards promising territory. Now just lower your rig over the side until you feel the weight hit the bottom. Put the reel into gear and crank up a foot or two. Check for the bottom by lowering your line frequently to avoid drifting into snags or letting your bait move too far from the bottom. Jigging (moving your offering up and down a few feet) is also a good idea. The motion catches the eye of the rockfish.

Sometimes rockfish are also caught alongside kelp beds in the shallows near shore. Again, fish near the bottom and reel in fast to keep the fish from snagging in the kelp.

Traditional Tackle, Equipment, Rigging, Bait and Lures

The heft or weight of the tackle needed for rockfishing depends primarily on the depth of water you're fishing in. See the chart accompanying this section.

At the end of your line fasten a heavy swivel snap. To this, attach a rock cod rig or shrimp fly rig with about 6/0 size hooks. Many anglers prefer the shrimp fly rig since they have feathers that add to the attractiveness of the offering. Shrimp fly rigs can be purchased in most ocean-oriented bait and tackle shops for less than a dollar each. They typically have 3 hooks and a snap swivel at the end to attach the sinker, as shown on the next page.

Component	50-100 Feet	300-400 Feet
Rod:		
length	6-7 feet	6-7 feet
stiffness	med.-med. heavy	med. heavy- heavy
guide	(roller tip helpful)	(roller tip)
Reel:	med. ocean baitcasting	Penn Senator 114 6/0
Line:	25-40 lb. mono	40-80 lb. mono
Sinker:	4 oz. to 1 lb.	1/2 to 2 lb.

The most common bait for rockfishing is cut-up squid pieces. Cut the pieces large enough to cover the hook. Other common baits are pieces of small rockfish or anchovies. At times, fish can be hooked using bare shrimp fly rigs. But bait adds an odor that is often helpful in enticing a bite.

Rockfish are also taken on lures, especially metal jigs and soft plastics. Diamond hex bar jigs and Tady, Salsa and Sea Strike metal yo-yo type jigs are all producers. Jigs in the 4 to 6 ounce range will work in shallow water, or even up to 200 feet of water when the boat drift speed is slow.

Light Tackle Rockfishing

The Southern California trend to lighten fishing tackle is apparent in rockfishing. Depending on wind and current conditions, water depth and rockfish species, anglers are taking fish on freshwater spinning tackle, black bass tackle and even on ultralight rigs. It makes rockfishing much more challenging and exciting. And it surely beats cranking up a two or three pound weight and several bucketmouth rockfish from a depth of 300 feet or more.

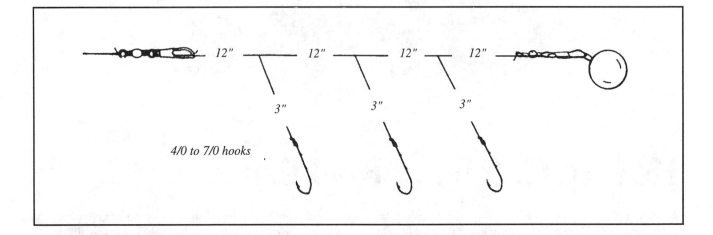

Best light tackle opportunities occur in water that is 30-120 feet in depth. Light wind and current is also desirable because then less weight is needed to take the offering down to the fish. And with less weight, you can use lighter tackle and line. One approach is to use this lighter tackle with a rock cod rig or shrimp fly rig. Casting out one or two ounce jigs in the direction of the drift is also a good approach. If your main line is less than 10 pound test, consider using about a 10 pound, 2 foot leader. If the jig stops sinking, put the reel in gear and set the hook. If there is no hit, retrieve in short, quick hops by pumping the rod tip, or jig it up and down near the bottom. Bucktail jigs and soft plastic lead-head jigs work well. At times, you can fish suspended rockfish in shallow water. Yellow rockfish are the most likely candidates. It's great fun to cast to these 2 to 5 pound fighters.

Where to Fish

Rockfishing locales all along the Northern California coast are highlighted in the "Pacific Ocean Fishing" chapter. Some of the best shallow water opportunities are in Monterey Bay off Santa Cruz and Capitola, north from there along the coast in kelp beds and over reefs, and at the Farallon Islands.

Cleaning and Cooking

There are almost 50 varieties of rockfish along our coast. Commercially caught rockfish are most often sold in fish markets as snapper. All varieties are almost always filleted. Since most varieties of rockfish have very large heads, the yield of fillets can be as low as 20-30% of fish weight. Rockfish meat is lean, has low fat content and is mild tasting. These fillets lend themselves to the cooking method of choice including sauteing, broiling, poaching, frying or baking.

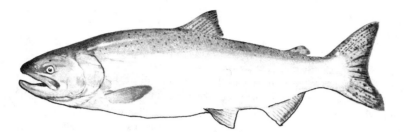

How to Catch . . . Salmon (in the Ocean)

Both king (chinook) and silver (coho) salmon are caught in Northern California ocean waters. But kings are by far the most common. The salmon in California salt water were spawned naturally (or in hatcheries) in tributaries of coastal rivers like the Klamath, Trinity and Sacramento. About 60% of California ocean-caught salmon originate in the Sacramento River system including the Feather and American Rivers.

Only one single, barbless hook (either manufactured that way, or with the barb flattened by pliers) is allowed per rod. Undersize fish (called shakers) should be released without netting or handling. A needle-nose pliers is needed. This prevents the fragile, protective membrane on the body of the fish from being broken. Grasp the leader about a foot up from the hook. Next, grasp the hook shank with the pliers (or slide a rod or stiff wire into the curve of the hook). Now raise and rotate the hook upside down. The salmon will drop off into the ocean.

It's obviously easier for a salmon to throw a barbless hook, so a slack line condition must be avoided when playing a fish. Once a keeper salmon is netted, it should be clubbed between the eyes with a hammer handle or fish club to subdue it. Most seasoned fishermen gill and gut salmon when caught, and then store them in an iced fish box or cooler. The tail is clipped to distinguish it from a commercially caught salmon.

Fishing Techniques

There are four primary techniques for taking salmon in salt water:

1. Trolling with a diving plane.

2. Trolling with a cannonball sinker with sinker release.

3. Trolling with a downrigger.

4. Mooching—basically drift fishing with bait. This method is growing in popularity. Position the boat so as to drift over the top or along the side of a school of bait fish.

Trolling

The most common method for taking ocean salmon in California waters is trolling—pulling a lure or bait through the water using boat movement. Since salmon (especially kings) are often found 10 to 100 feet below the surface, methods must be employed to take bait or lures to these depths. That's where diving planes, cannonballs with sinker releases and downriggers come in.

Diving Plane—A weighted, air foil device that used the motion of the water to dive and takes the terminal tackle with it. After a salmon strike, the diving plane neutralizes its position allowing the rig and fish to rise up to the surface.

Cannonball-Sinker Release—This approach relies on the heft of a steel or lead cannonball of 1, 2, or 3 pounds to take the rigging down. The cannonballs are attached to a sinker release mechanism which released the weight when a salmon hits, allowing the fish to rise and fight.

Downrigger—A pulley and boom (manually or electrically activated) which lowers about a 10 pound weight on a steel cable. A clip holds the rod's fishing line and releases it when a salmon strikes.

Trolling with a diving plane or cannonball-sinker release works like this. With the boat at trolling speed (2-4 knots) lower the terminal tackle into the water, check the lure action, then let out about 24-40 pulls of line. (This puts the hook at about 15-20 feet deep.) Other rods should be deeper or shallower until fish are located. Put on the reel clicker and then set the drag just tight enough to hold the line. Put the rod in a holder. The singing drag will signal a strike, and the pull of the salmon will drop the weight or open the diving plane, allowing the fish to rise and fight. Some anglers maintain trolling speed while fighting the fish. This minimizes the chance of slack line and a thrown hook. The landing net should always be placed from the front, forward and under the fish.

Trolling with a downrigger has several advantages. It allows deep trolling (50-100 feet) without the use of heavy rods/reels and line. And the downrigger "tells you" exactly how deep you're trolling, so successes can be duplicated. Downriggers cost between $100-300 and probably are not necessary, or some say, desirable, if the fish are at 10 to 20 feet. Beyond 30 feet they are very useful. Downriggers are also very useful for trolling for trout and salmon in lakes during the summertime when these fish are 50-100 feet down. So once purchased, they have multiple uses.

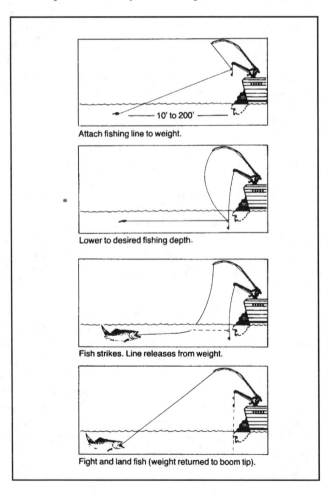

Attach fishing line to weight.

Lower to desired fishing depth.

Fish strikes. Line releases from weight.

Fight and land fish (weight returned to boom tip).

Mooching

Mooching, or drift fishing, for salmon can be very effective and quite exciting, if you can locate the fish. Feeding birds are one clue, as are a "boil" of bait fish on the surface. Electronic fish finders are also helpful to select the proper depth to fish. Often, mooching is done just off the bottom with a whole anchovy rigged on a 1/0 or 2/0 hook. At other times, moochers are successful nearer the surface. Mooching is generally more effective in the summer, while trolling is usually best in spring when salmon are more scattered. Pre-tied, two-hook mooching rigs are available at coastal tackle outlets. In the Pacific Northwest, where mooching has been honed to a real science, the Banana mooching rig illustrated on the following page is used.

Some moochers, especially in Monterey Bay, prefer to use a sliding sinker mooching rig. A large, about #5 Slydo is used so that the amount of weight can be changed conveniently. This rig which is also shown on the next page can be used with either a single or double hook setup.

How to hook bait for mooching is a matter of preference; anglers often hook the end hook through the tail and the upper hook through the back. But here's how they bait the mooching rig in the Pacific Northwest. Start by pushing the end hook through the roof of the mouth to just behind the head of the bait. Push the second hook through the same hole. Hook the end hook through the bait just in front of the dorsal fin underneath the backbone. Pull the line tight so that the top hook is secure in the head and the end hook is secure in the back.

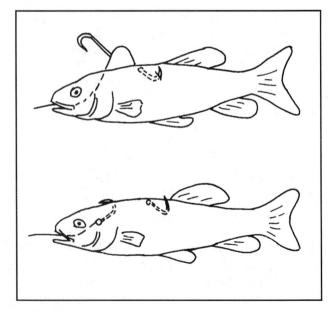

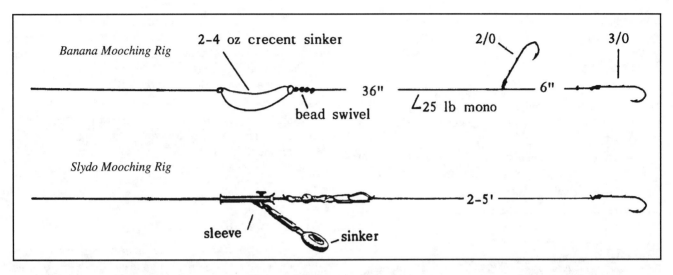

Use only enough weight to hold the bait down at a 50-60 angle. Dangle the offering. Lift the rod tip, come up a few cranks, wait. Lower it and repeat the process. Often the salmon will "bump" the bait a few times before striking solidly. Don't set the hook until a substantial strike is felt.

Another mooching rig that works is to tie about a 1/2 ounce jig (like a Hair Raiser or Fat Git Zit) directly to your main line. You can bait the jig with a whole anchovy or anchovy fillet. Work it along the bottom. A crescent or banana sinker placed up the line a ways may be needed to get the jig down.

Tackle and Equipment

No matter which approach you use, you should have a large cooler with ice, fish club or hammer, needle-nose pliers and a large landing net.

For trolling with a diving plane or weight you'll need a medium to medium heavy boat rod with roller tip (about 6 feet) and a saltwater trolling or casting reel that can hold 300 yards of 25 pound test monofilament line. Spinning reels or level wind reels are not generally used.

The diving plane terminal tackle includes a dodger to attract salmon. Vibration put out by the dodger is especially important when water clarity is poor in the spring. Both the diving plane and Cannonball-sinker release terminal tackle are illustrated below.

For trolling with a downrigger you'll need the downrigger, bait casting or spinning rod of 6-8 feet and a bait casting or spinning reel that can hold 200 yards of 10-20 pound monofilament line. For mooching you'll need about the same types of rod/reel combinations used for downrigging. Specialized

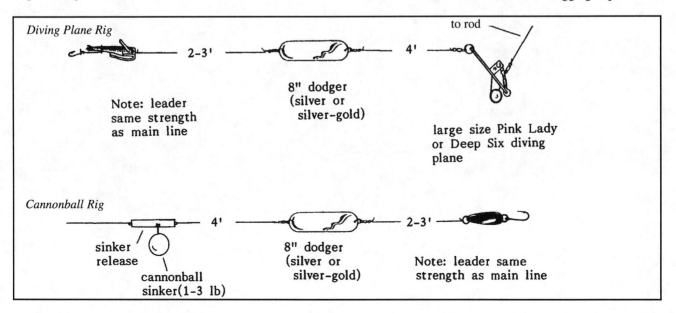

downrigger and mooching rods are made by leading rod manufacturers. Levelwind bait casting reels are popular.

Lures and Bait

The most popular bait for ocean salmon are anchovies. They are purchased frozen, laying flat on a plastic tray, from bait shops. For trolling, the anchovy is either rigged on a crowbar hook or on a plastic bait holding rig.

When trolled, it's crucial that the anchovies roll or wobble like a wounded bait fish. Without practice or specific experience, this is difficult when using the crowbar hook. But with

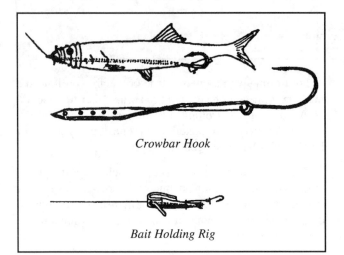

Crowbar Hook

Bait Holding Rig

the plastic bait holding rig (common brand names—Rotary Salmon Killer, Herring Aid), a rolling action is guaranteed because of the fin shape molded into the plastic. Also, putting the anchovy into either of these rigs takes only a few seconds. Commercial salmon fishermen typically rig crowbar hooks in advance because it requires patience and a steady hand.

Some Silver Spoons and lures that imitate squid can also be effective. These include Krocodile and Hopkins (1 and 2 ounce), McMahon (#4), and Apex (4 1/2 - 5 1/2 inches). Hoochies (a hula skirt jig) of about 3-4 inches in assorted colors are also popular.

Where to Fish

See the "Pacific Ocean Fishing" and "San Francisco Bay Fishing" chapters. It's always best to call the day before you intend to go fishing. Ocean-oriented bait and tackle shops know exactly where the salmon are and how deep to fish them.

Cleaning and Cooking

Scale salmon with the jet of a water hose nozzle. Salmon are usually filleted. Large ones are steaked. Fresh salmon and properly frozen salmon, as anyone knows who has eaten it, is out of this world. Many anglers prefer to barbecue this rich, relatively fatty meat. It is also very good poached (served hot with a sauce or chilled), broiled, baked or smoked.

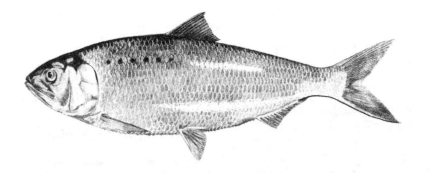

How to Catch . . . Shad

Veteran shad anglers consider this fish the best fighter, pound for pound, of all sport fish in Northern California waters. Shad spawn in the Sacramento River and its tributaries (American, Feather, Yuba) in late spring and early summer. Fishermen usually begin their shad quest in late April or early May. A typical American shad weighs in at 2 to 5 pounds.

Fishing Techniques

Casting is the predominant technique for taking shad. Shad strikes very aggressively at small, silver objects that show bright colors such as red, orange, green, white and yellow. Shad are more protective of their territory than hungry (during the spawning period) so they are difficult to hook. They fight savagely, so a hook-up doesn't necessarily result in a fish in hand.

Casting is done both from shore and from anchored boats depending upon local river conditions. Shore fishing is done mostly where there is a shoal in the bend of a river. Deeper water and the availability of launch ramp facilities provides the opportunity for boat fishing.

One shad fishing technique which is commonly used, particularly at the mouth of the American River, involves fishing from an anchored boat in a relatively strong current, using a spinning or bait casting rod. A small lead sinker is placed at the end of the line, and a weighted fly is tied on a 24 inch dropper about 18 inches above the sinker. The line is played out until the sinker just clears the bottom. It is necessary for the current to be strong enough to give the fly the proper action. This method of fishing has so many followers that space to anchor at the mouth of the American River is often at a premium. Shore anglers at the mouth of the American River successfully use spinning gear and a floating plastic bubble attached about three feet above the offering.

You can buy many types of shad lures and flies in Sacramento Valley sporting goods stores. On a weekend during a good run, late arriving shore anglers may find it difficult to locate a place to fish. Nevertheless, the most popular method of shad angling in California, and perhaps the most rewarding, is to fish from shore with a fly or spinning rod. The fly rod is used with a fast-sinking line or a shooting head. A tippet with about a 6 pound test breaking strength is desirable since the shad can be quite large. Some will exceed 5 or 6 pounds. In addition, there is always the possibility of hooking a striped bass or a large steelhead.

Let's assume you have found a likely spot on a river, just below a riffle where the fast water breaks and slows down at the head of a long pool. You wade out into the water and cast across toward the opposite bank, allowing the current to swing your line downstream. You wait a few moments as the fly at the end of your line makes its way downstream and toward the bank below you. As you are ready to pick up and cast again, you hook your first shad and are in for a delightful surprise. Before long, on a typical day, you may repeat this experience again and again until you have caught and released or kept a considerable number of fish.

If you use a spinning outfit, the shad fly is tied to the end of the line and a split shot is pinched on from 18 to 24 inches above the fly. Just enough weight is used to enable you to cast easily. Cast out across the water as you would with a fly rod, but immediately after completing your cast, reel in just fast enough to prevent the split shot from snagging the bottom. But do use enough weight to keep your offering down. Shad usually follow the contour of the river bottom on their way upstream.

Tackle and Equipment

Shad fishing means light tackle fishing. Equipment must be light enough and flexible enough to toss small offerings. Anyway, the light tackle makes for more challenge. Spinning, fly fishing and bait casting setups are all used. Popular lures include Shad Darts, Fly-Fly and T-Killers (in white or yellow with red heads) and 1/16 - 1/8 ounce Crappie Jigs and Teeny Rounders in chartreuse, yellow, orange and white.

Where to Fish

Good areas are described in the "Central Valley River Fishing" chapter. Selected locations are the Yuba River from the mouth upstream to Daguerre Point Dam, the Feather River from the mouth to fish barrier at Oroville, and the American River from the mouth to Nimbus Dam. There is also good shad action along the Russian River.

Cooking and Cleaning

Many anglers release shad because they are so bony. And filleting a shad is no easy task, even after you've seen it done by an expert. The Department of Fish and Game tried a number of years ago to encourage the eating of shad. They did this by publishing a booklet that describes *How to Fillet a Shad—In 32 Steps!* Step 32 concludes, "In a little while, with some patience, you will be able to trim a shad into two boneless fillets in about 15 to 20 minutes."

Shad is mild, quite firm, with a meatlike flavor and a moderate fat level. It is good baked, poached, pickled, or smoked. Some anglers prefer the shad roe.

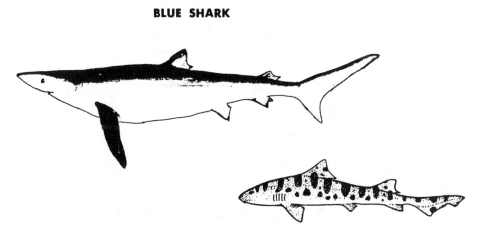

BLUE SHARK

LEOPARD SHARK

How to Catch . . . Sharks

Sharks are misrepresented fish. All the media ever talks about are great white sharks. But there are other varieties of shark in Northern California waters. These include leopard shark, seven gill, soupfin and blue shark. What's more, the media never mentions that these sharks are becoming more and more popular among sports anglers—popular to fish for and popular to eat.

Seven gill sharks can get quite large. The largest seven gill shark caught was over 500 pounds! It's quite possible to hook fish in the 200 pound range. However, the most common shark caught in Northern California waters is the leopard shark. These can weigh up to about 30 pounds and are about 4 feet in length. The average fish is between 10 and 20 pounds. Blue sharks are often caught in the 80-150 pound range. Soupfin are in the same size range. Here is a rundown on the best fishing techniques for each shark.

Leopard Shark

Leopard sharks are the most plentiful and easiest to catch of all Northern California sharks. They're found throughout San Francisco and San Pablo Bays. They are also caught, incidentally, by bottom anglers in the open ocean. Leopard shark fishing is good all year, but the best action is from April through August. Some noteworthy leopard shark haunts are around the San Mateo Bridge, the area off Pt. Richmond, Hunter's Point off San Francisco, the channel near Dumbarton

Bridge, the ship channel opposite the Cow Palace, outside the Alameda rockwall, the deep-water channel near the San Rafael and the San Francisco Bay bridges. Larger fish are usually taken in the deeper channel areas away from shore.

Leopards have distinctive black spots and crossbars on their backs. They are excellent eating and fun to catch on lighter tackle. A variety of baits will work including anchovies, squid, salmon bellies, grass shrimp, midshipman and mudsuckers. Midshipman and mudsuckers are used whole. Within this wide array, the best baits are probably whole squid, pieces of salmon belly and midshipman. Squid are readily available, but attract nuisance fish (small rays, too small sharks and crabs). The hook should be run through the squid several times, and check your bait frequently. Pieces of salmon belly are difficult to come by, but work well. Midshipman are caught as a by-product of shrimping. They work well because smaller nuisance fish don't seem interested in them. Party boat captains often use midshipman as bait. A typical leopard shark rig is shown on the next page.

Most leopard shark fishing is done from an anchored boat using a sliding sinker rig and fishing on the bottom. It's the same approach used when still fishing for striped bass. The rig is baited up and tossed out. Depressions in the bottom or deep holes are prime spots. An incoming tide, a couple of hours before top, is a good time to fish. Leopards also hit on outgoing tides. Always keep an eye on your rod tip (or hold

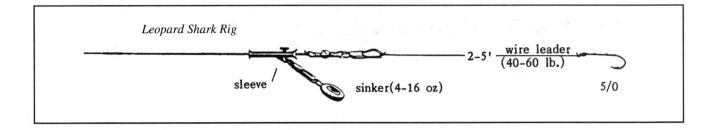

Leopard Shark Rig

sleeve

sinker(4-16 oz)

2-5' wire leader (40-60 lb.)

5/0

your rod). When the tip moves, point the rod at the fish and then set the hook hard.

Many leopard shark anglers use sturgeon fishing tackle, striped bass fishing tackle, rock cod fishing tackle or even salmon fishing tackle. Any tackle that can handle 20 or 30 pound test monofilament line and an 8 ounce sinker will do for most shark fishing. The two essentials, however, are wire leaders and a fish club. A gaff is useful for landing leopards. They have a way of putting holes in landing nets.

Seven Gill Sharks

Seven gill shark fishing is concentrated in San Francisco Bay. It is best during the spring to fall months. Seven gill sharks, sometimes called cow sharks, have gray or brown backs with small dark spots and an all white belly. These big guys eat most anything including sturgeons, rats, smaller sharks, any small fish, etc. Good baits include whole or portions of stickleback shark, leopard sharks, salmon, squid, saltwater perch and rockfish. Fish these baits from an anchored boat near the edges of the main ship channels. Use a depth finder to probe the bottom for holes or shelves. Prime spots include the south and east sides of Angel Island, "Big Hole" just west of Angel Island, near the Harding Rock buoy, the "Green House" just off the Marine Shoreline south of Sausalito (look for the green building at the bottom of the cliff), and the channel from the Bay Bridge to the San Mateo Bridge. Seven gills, according to veteran shark chasers, seem to prefer to feed at slack tide, either high or low.

Heavy tackle is needed for chasing these monsters in relatively deep water. A 6 1/2 foot medium action rod with heavy roller guides matched with a 4/0 reel and 90 pound wire line is typical. Rigging is similar to the leopard shark rig, only heavier. A 1 1/2 pound sinker might be needed. Use a 250 pound plastic coated lead and about a 13/0 hook. The bite is subtle so stay alert. Keep slack out of your line. Some pros use a rod belt to protect the lower back.

Soupfin and Six Gills

Soupfins are also San Francisco Bay regulars. Their backs are light brown to gray and they have white bellies. Specimens up to 90 pounds and 6 feet long can be taken. Most shark hunters consider the soupfin to be a faster and harder fighter than the seven gill. At times, they will jump clear out of the water. Soupfins are taken on the same tackle and with the same techniques as used with seven gill. But when soupfins invade the shallower ship channels in the south bay, "leopard shark tackle" and monofilament line can be successful.

Six gill sharks are also taken in San Francisco Bay, but with less frequency than the other two big sharks. They are noted by their emerald green eyes and jet black bodies.

Blue Sharks

How about some open ocean shark action? Stretching out below Monterey Bay starting at Moss Landing is a canyon deeper than the Grand Canyon. Action begins just a mile or two out in the ocean. Head southeast out of the harbor until you're over 150-200 feet of water. Here is the edge of this massive, nutrient-rich trench. Life is good for blue sharks here because there is so much to eat. In the fall when ocean water temperatures are warmest is the best time to go after blues in the 50-150 pound class. The technique of choice is to chum with a basket full of ground up frozen fish. Anchovies are good and can be caught with a crab net off a wharf. Carcasses from filleted rockfish, stripers or salmon are also good, as are shad. Carcasses are available in quantity from commercial fish processing operations or some fish markets. Call around. You'll be surprised how easy it is to find dead fish or fish carcasses. Frozen fish are easiest to grind. You'll want enough to fill 2 or 3 half gallon milk cartons. Fill these with the processed chum and freeze them solid (2 days or more). A floating panfish basket makes an excellent chum block holder. Once at sea take off the carton, drape the block in the basket and drop the whole thing off the back of the boat on a short rope. A dead drift will lay down an oily, enticing chum slick.

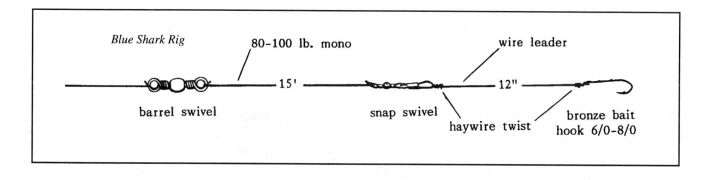

Blue Shark Rig 80-100 lb. mono wire leader barrel swivel 15' snap swivel 12" haywire twist bronze bait hook 6/0-8/0

With some luck you'll see blue sharks cruising behind your boat soon. But, be patient. It may take up to an hour. Don't be surprised to see up to a dozen blues mulling around. Pick out the one you want to wrestle with and cast to him. For the fight of your life, go with light tackle—12 to 15 pound monofilament or medium freshwater bait casting or spinning equipment. You'll need good butt strength in the rod, superb reel drag capability and line capacity of 250 yards. If necessary, put down a float marker (block of styrofoam, colored plastic milk carton) to hold the shark location and then follow a running fish with the boat. Terminal tackle is simple as shown below.

An anchovy, small rockfish, jacksmelt, mackerel or frozen squid are all good baits. Don't retrieve them. Drifting bait is best. Blue sharks are good eating if bled immediately after landing. But most anglers release the graceful fighters. It is easiest by just cutting the wire leader. The bronze hooks will dissolve much faster than stainless steel hook material.

Safety, Cleaning and Cooking

All sharks can do a great deal of damage to fingers, hands, arms and other body parts that come within their range. And large sharks are extremely dangerous. If you plan on keeping a big shark, it should be killed while still in the water. Experts use a bang stick, available at dive shops, to accomplish this. Make sure the fish's head is under water. Cautious anglers will not bring aboard any shark over 5 feet in length. They tie it off in the water.

Good eating requires immediate cutting in the tail area to bleed the fish. Smaller specimens are filleted, while the larger ones are steaked. Remove the tough skin and any red meat. Soaking in a mild solution of vinegar, lemon juice or milk will remove any ammonia smell or flavor. Shark meat is very firm, mild to moderate in flavor and has very little fat. It can be grilled, broiled, barbecued, deep fried or smoked. Add it to soups, stews or casseroles.

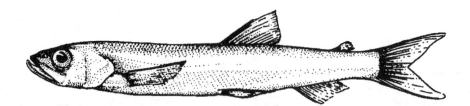

How to Catch . . . Surf Smelt

Southern Californians have their grunion which they snatch off the beach by moonlight. These romantic little fish have come ashore to spawn. Well, Northern Californians have little fish making spawning runs on their beach also. And NorCal anglers have an advantage—they can take their quarry, slender 4 to 10 inch surf smelt, using nets, whereas grunion, by regulation, can only be taken by hand. Surf smelt fishing is great fun among friends or with the entire family. There are runs in the daytime and nighttime throughout the peak summer season. And many smelt anglers will tell you that there isn't any fish that matches the delicate flavor of fried or smoked smelt.

Fishing Technique and Equipment

Smelt run onto the beach in breaking waves near the peak of an incoming tide, lay their eggs in the sand, then return out to sea on the next wave. Experienced surf anglers stand back from the breakers and watch for fish in the face of waves as they come into the beach. Bird and sea lion activity can also tip off smelt school locations. Smelt are usually found in lazy rolling waves rather than in big breakers that lead a set of waves. Horizontal, dark lines of smelt can be spotted in the good waves as they run into shore. Smelt are often caught in several successive waves. Then the catch can taper off or disappear for minutes or hours, only to reappear without warning. Anglers move in and gather smelt with either an A-frame surf dip net or a Hawaiian throw net. A-frame nets have rigid triangular frames of aluminum or wood. They cost around $100-125. The net is worked into the wave as it rolls onto the beach. Lower cost ($25-50) throw nets are circular with lead weights around the perimeter and a draw string to close the net around the fish. The A-frames take less practice and can be used in several waves before emptying. Throw nets must be retrieved, emptied, if necessary, and reset before each throw. Whichever net you use don't just stand in the surf and "net" waves. All the commotion may actually discourage smelt from coming in. Experienced surf netters wear wet suits or waders. Bring along blankets, folding chairs, jackets, food, and flashlights or lanterns for night fishing. Bonfires round

out the scene. You'll also need buckets to hold your silvery catch.

When and Where to Fish

Smelt run from April through October, with the best action in June through August. Though surf smelt run somewhere just about every day in the summertime, the runs are very localized and, at times, inconsistent. So it is a good idea when planning a trip to the north coast to call ahead. Tackle shops, bait shops, state beaches, and private campgrounds near traditionally productive waters are all good sources of information.

There are actually two species of smelt spawning on NorCal beaches. Daytime spawners, which are called "surf fish" by locals, run about 6 to 10 inches long. Nighttime spawners, or "night smelt," run 4 to 6 inches long. Spawning smelt prefer coarse, black sand beaches. Some of the best spots are where freshwater streams enter the Pacific.

Smelt are caught as far south as the Russian River, but the best producing areas are probably from Manchester near Point Arena, all the way up north past Arcata and on to Crescent City. Some of the best beaches are listed below and are shown on ocean fishing maps in the "Pacific Ocean Fishing" chapter.

> Manchester Beach near Point Arena
> Mac Kerricher State Beach (Ft. Bragg)
> Ten Mile River Beach (Inglenook)
> Wages Creek Beach (Westport)
> Juan Creek Beach (Leggett)
> Centerville Beach (Ferndale)
> Luffenholtz Beach (Trinidad)
> Freshwater Lagoon Ocean Beach at Orick
> South Beach (Crescent City)

Cleaning and Cooking

Smelt are frequently cooked whole, or they can be gutted and be-headed. Deep frying or pan frying of lightly floured smelt is a delicious treat.

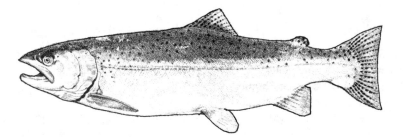

How to Catch . . . Steelhead and Salmon (in Rivers)

Steelhead and salmon fishing in coastal rivers and streams and in the Sacramento River system is one of the most pleasurable and rewarding of all fishing experiences. Many veteran anglers, who have fished all over the world, insist that steelhead and salmon fishing is the ultimate fishing experience, despite the wind, rain and cold. Anglers endure and overcome wet and cold because the fall and winter months are when most ocean-toughened, acrobatic steelhead trout (actually a variety of rainbow trout) and large king (chinook) salmon migrate into fresh water to spawn.

But early fall migrating steelhead are often juvenile fish that don't spawn. These are called "half-pounders" even though they run from 1/2 to 2 pounds. Mature spawning steelhead that migrate later in fall and in winter average 5 to 10 pounds, with fish in some streams reaching up to 15-20 pounds.

The migrating king salmon (some streams also have runs of smaller silver, or coho salmon) are larger fish, on average, than those caught in the ocean during spring and summer. This is because only the mature adult fish join the spawning run. They move up river to their spawning beds, spawn and die, their life cycle complete. Steelhead, on the other hand, will spawn and return to the ocean several times. King salmon catches are in the 10-20 pound range with occasional fish weighing as much as 40 pounds. The record caught on the Sacramento River near Red Bluff in 1979 weighed in at 88 pounds! Fresh-run salmon are bright, much like ocean-caught salmon. As spawning time comes closer, salmon turn dark and are not good eating. These should probably be released to spawn. A fresh-run steelhead has a bright red stripe along its side and is gourmet eating. However, as the season progresses, they turn steel blue and the meat is soft and inedible. Release these to spawn and return to the ocean.

Sometimes it is difficult to distinguish between king salmon, silver salmon and steelhead trout. Here are some basic keys:

King Salmon—On the lower jaw, the crown of the gums where the teeth project is dark, as is the rest of the mouth. There are usually large, angular black spots on the back and both lobes of the tail.

Silver Salmon—The crown of the gums where the teeth project (lower jaw) is whitish, the rest of the mouth lining is darker. There are usually spots on the back and upper lobe of the tail, but none on the lower lobe.

Steelhead Trout—The inside of the mouth is whitish. There are teeth on the tip, but not on the back of the tongue.

Steelhead and salmon that are migrating in fresh water are not particularly interested in eating. In fact, all agree that salmon don't eat at all. And steelhead eat little or nothing. This situation means that anglers can't rely on a fish's appetite to induce a strike. Most experts feel that steelhead and salmon strike out of instinct, curiosity, or most likely, to protect their territory. They will not move far to take an offering, most stray only a few inches to either side of their hold.

In some coastal streams, particularly the Klamath and Trinity, there are summer-run steelhead. These steelhead eat, behave and often take on the appearance of rainbow trout (because they are in fresh water 6-10 months before spawning in the spring). Summer-run steelhead are caught using stream trout fishing techniques. See the Trout (in Streams) section of this chapter.

Some steelhead salmon anglers use boats. Others fish from shore or use waders. Boats are useful in some streams when private property limits access, or where a boat can provide access to an area too steep to climb down to from a road or trail. Boat anglers can cover much more potentially good fishing spots in a day than the shore anglers can. One highly specialized and highly successful steelhead and salmon fishing technique called backtrolling requires a boat. (More on this later.)

The fishing techniques, bait, lures, tackle and equipment are the same or similar for both steelhead and salmon fishing. There are several exceptions, and these will be noted and explained in the sections that follow.

Some Fundamentals

All steelhead and salmon fishing techniques have one common denominator. They are designed to get a lure or bait right down on the bottom of the stream. This is the only place the fish are, and in the winter when they're not eating, they won't move up to take an offering. A lure or bait that's not within several inches of the bottom has almost as little chance of catching a fish as one still sitting on a shelf at the tackle shop. An old saying goes like this, "If you're not losing terminal tackle, you're not fishing deep enough." Unfortunately for our pocketbooks, but fortunately for tackle manufacturers, this statement is all too true. Happily, there are rigs and approaches that minimize the loss due to hang-ups and these are emphasized here.

We know that salmon and steelhead are on the bottom of the stream or river. The next question is where along all that bottom are we most likely to find them? Here are the choice spots for steelhead:

- At a tributary stream mouth. (In fact, some of these are so productive that they are closed to fishing for a certain period each year. See individual river regulations.)

- Just off the main current of a river in water 3-8 feet deep. Not in the very fast water, but not in backwater either.

- At the head or tail end of a deep hole.

- Along a deep side channel.

- Just above or below a riffle.

- A few feet behind a slick formed by the current breaking around a boulder. (This includes submerged boulders and bridge pilings and abutments that are "artificial" boulders.)

- The tidal basin of the river or stream and the upper limit of high tide in any stream. Pools and holes in these sections are also good for salmon.

- In small streams steelhead hold along and under sweeps of overhanging bush and foliage.

- Along underwater ledges, cliffs or undercuts.

- In the fall, early-run steelhead are frequently in riffles themselves. In small coastal streams steelhead will often hold in shallow water (a foot or so) above or within a riffle.

While steelhead anglers work broken waters, tailouts, etc., salmon chasers concentrate on the deep holes in each river system. For example, in the Sacramento River, salmon are pursued in holes deeper than 10 feet. The deepest areas in tidal waters are also usually the most productive.

There are a number of approaches used to catch steelhead and salmon. Here is a rundown of each.

Drift Fishing

For those readers not familiar with coastal river fishing terminology, a brief explanation is in order. Drift fishing in this usage has nothing to do with a boat. It refers to drifting a bait or lure along in the current of a river. Most anglers do this from shore or while wading out, but it sometimes is done from an anchored boat. It is actually very similar to the bait fishing approach used for trout in streams in the summertime, except the terminal tackle is heavier because the water is faster and deeper, and because the fish are larger and stronger.

The lure or bait is cast upstream at about a 45 angle and then allowed to drift downstream into likely holding areas. Slack line is taken up as the drift proceeds. A key is to use the proper weight so that the offering moves freely, yet stays on or near the bottom. A weight that is too heavy will freeze or even hang up, while one that is too light will move off the bottom. The perfect amount of weight is that which will result in a tap-tap-skip action as it make frequent contact with the bottom and then bounces up a bit before hitting it again.

Strikes are often soft in this type of fishing. The fish just mouth the offering, but don't hit it or run with it. Often, fish are lost because the angler can't differentiate between a bite and the feel of the bottom. Any momentary slowing or stopping of a drifting lure or bait should be assumed to be a take. Respond by setting the hook hard.

There are several different weight systems that drift anglers use depending on personal preference. Commercial weights designed to minimize snags are available. Brand names include Slinky Drifter and Bouncing Betty. In all systems the weight is 18-24 inches up from the lure or bait. Leaders are the same weight as the main line. These are the popular alternatives:

Lead Cinch—These are basically 3-way swivels with rubber tubing attached to the middle swivel. They are available in stores. A pencil lead weight (3/16" diameter is most popular) of varying length is inserted into the tubing. It slips out to free the rig from a snag.

Hollow Pencil Lead — Fastened (crimped) to the knot dropper at the swivel. If hung up, it will pull away from the lead if not crimped too tight.

3-way Swivel with Dropper—Use when larger weight is needed.

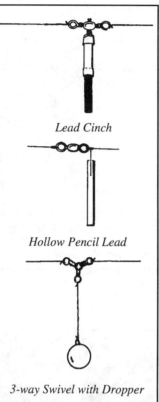

Lead Cinch

Hollow Pencil Lead

3-way Swivel with Dropper

For smaller streams a simple choice is to use a rubber core sinker. Tie the hook to the main line and put the sinker on about 18" up the line. Have a selection of sinker sizes with you.

Lures and Bait for Drift Fishing

The choice of bait and lures is very wide in drift fishing. Here are the most popular:

Salmon Roe—Tie in dime to quarter sized red Maline bags with thread. These are put on a special steelhead baitholding hook. Hook size #1 is good. Bags can also be put right on a regular hook.

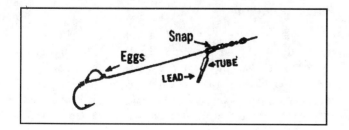

Nightcrawlers—Thread on the hook. Let an inch or so at the end dangle free.

Drift Bobbers—These are not regular bobbers but buoyant lures usually in bright colors, and they often rotate in the water to send off vibrations. Some slide on the leader of the hook, in front of a bead, to enhance rotation. Others come with metal shafts and their own treble hook. These are very productive and have replaced roe as the main offering of many anglers. Popular ones are Okie Drifters, Spin-N-Glo and Glo-Glo.

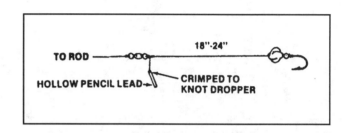

Yarn—Yarn can be fished along, but usually it is added to roe or drift bobber rigs. Good colors are red, orange and cerise. It enhances the offering's appearance, and gets tangled in the fish's teeth (preventing deep hooking and helping to signal bites). Some can also be tied to the line above the drift bobber.

Single Salmon Egg Rig—For small coastal streams use a hook size that is entirely engulfed by the egg. Large white eggs are good. Fish with as little weight as possible (a few split shot or small rubber core sinker a foot up from the hook). This system can often catch big fish.

Plunking

Here we have another "steelhead" word that simply means still fishing. Here the anglers intentionally put enough weight on their terminal tackle so it will not drift. Bait or floating lures are used. The rod is then propped up into a rod holder and coffee is poured. Actually, many plunkers have another rod for casting to pass the idle time. Some plunkers use a sliding sinker rig (see Trout in Lakes), while others use the same rig as drift anglers. Bait and lures are also the same as for drift fishing. A good plunking spot is the margin between fast and slow moving current.

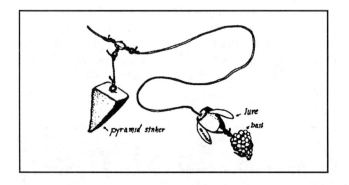

Casting

Casting is simply that. Weighted spinners or spoons are cast up and across the stream and then returned. This is an active approach, but since retrieves are by necessity near the bottom, they result in frequent hang-ups and loss of lures. Of course, drift fishing also results in hang-ups, but typically less costly offerings are used and rigs are used that often result in only partial loss of terminal tackle.

A small snap swivel should be used at the end of your main line to attach casting spoons and spinners. Wobbling spoons of about 1-3 inches long (e.g. Kastmaster, Daredevil) that are striped, dotted or have solid bright fluorescent hues, or spoons of nickel, bronze or copper are favorites. Mepps or Mounti-type spinners in nickel, brass or copper are good in sizes 4 and 5.

Choose the size to meet water conditions, so that the retrieve is natural and near the bottom. Heavy spoons are best in fast water. Light and narrower ones are best in quieter water. In roiled waters or at low light levels, spinners are preferred.

Backtrolling

Backtrolling is probably the most productive method of taking steelhead and salmon. It necessitates a boat. Here the anglers face the boat upstream and apply just enough power to allow the boat to slowly move downstream. A deep-diving plug, weighted plug or weighted bait is trolled off the back of the boat. Since the current is moving much faster than the boat, it takes the offering deep down in the current. The backtroller slowly works the boat back and forth across a

promising hole, then drops downstream a few feet and works across again. This approach is not recommended for anglers who are not experienced at river current boat handling.

Steelhead backtrollers use Hotshot (size 10, 20 or 30) or similar lures tied directly to the line.

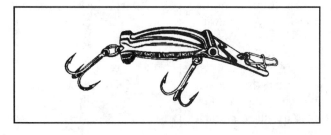

Salmon backtroller use Flatfish (M-2, T-50 and T-55, or similar lures). Often bags of salmon roe are tied to treble hooks and a sardine fillet is tied to the underside of the lure.

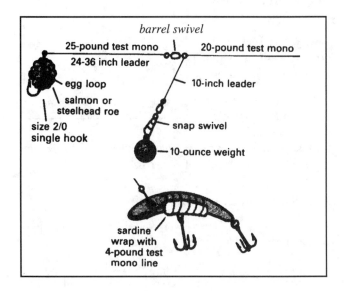

Back-Bouncing

Back-bouncing is a river boat fishing technique that is similar to backtrolling, but it is done from a boat held stationary in the current. Offerings like large egg clusters behind a winged bobber weighted to get them down are played out a foot or two at a time behind the boat. When it becomes difficult to find bottom, the rig is reeled in and the process is repeated. Several changes in boat position allows complete coverage of a hole. This is a popular method for large king salmon. They tend to hold up in the deepest and slowest water in a deep hole.

Float Fishing

Drift fishing requires experience and skill in getting the offering right on the bottom and in detecting subtle bites. Some anglers, if they're not too self-conscious, add a float or bobber to their rigs to minimize these difficulties. A float set at the right distance holds the terminal tackle off the bottom, but right near it. Take up slack line as the bobber floats downstream, and set the hook if the bobber pauses or dips.

Fly Fishing

Fly fishing equipment and techniques can be used for fall and winter-run steelhead and salmon. But, it is the exception rather than the rule. Specialized knowledge and skill are needed. If you intend to pursue this area, check out some steelhead and fly fishing books from your public library, or rent some videos at a large tackle dealer. Hiring a guide might also be instructive.

Water Conditions

Water conditions have an effect on your lure selection and fishing technique.

Muddy Water—Use roe, salmon eggs or nightcrawlers, anything with a scent. Use larger, more garish-colored drift bobbers and use drift bobbers that spin fast to make vibrations.

Off-Colored Water—Use drift bobbers and artificial eggs. Ideal steelhead and salmon water is milky-green color, dropping and clearing after a freshet. Fish during a new rain—fish are stimulated.

Clear Water—Use small offerings and more subdued colors. Spoons and spinners work well.

Estuary Fishing

Often early in the salmon run the best place to take large salmon is right in, or near the river mouth. The salmon are getting acclimated to fresh water and waiting for the rainy season to fill the river beds. Expert guides find that salmon move in and out of the estuary with the tides. They come in with the high tide, get acclimated, then head back out with the outgoing tide. The method of choice is trolling and one of the most popular offerings is the Bear Valley #3 brass spinner. A cannonball sinker about 36 inches up from the spinner is used to hold the rig down. Success depends upon using enough weight to stay on the bottom and on ensuring that the spinner blade is always rotating. A stout rod of about 6 feet, 25 to 30 pound test line and a levelwind reel complete the package.

Tackle and Equipment

Tackle used in steelhead and salmon fishing can be quite specialized, but for most situations, basic equipment is sufficient. The following is a rundown:

Rod—Most drift and plunker anglers use a 8-9 foot, medium action (or medium-light action) spinning or bait casting rod with a two-hand grip. A sensitive tip is essential. For fishing wide tidal areas from shore, some anglers use surf casting equipment. Backtrollers generally use about a 6 foot bait casting boat rod with medium-heavy action and sensitive tip.

Reels—Spinning reels need to be large enough to hold 200 yards of 10 pound monofilament line and have a good drag system. The same is true for bait casting reels. Bait casting reels are typically level winds with free spool and star drag.

Line—Monofilament is almost universal. A 10 pound test is most common for steelhead and smaller salmon. For larger salmon, 20 pound line is common.

Other equipment and riggings that are needed are as follows:

- Substantial landing net (for boat anglers); shore anglers beach their fish.

- File—to continually re-sharpen hooks—they get dulled on rocks, gravel, etc.

- Needle-nose pliers—to remove hooks

- Knife—to gut and gill fish

- Chest high waders

- Warm clothing, a waterproof jacket and hat, and polarized sun glasses

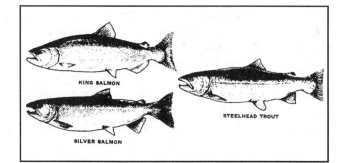

Where to Fish

See the "Coastal River and Stream Fishing" and "Central Valley River Fishing" chapters.

Cleaning and Cooking

Smaller fish are filleted. Larger ones are steaked. For cooking instructions, see the Salmon (in the Ocean) and Trout (in Streams) sections of this chapter.

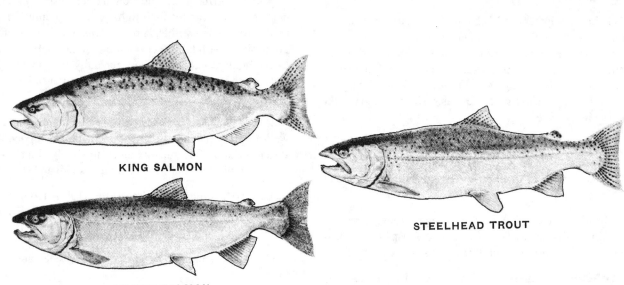

KING SALMON

SILVER SALMON

STEELHEAD TROUT

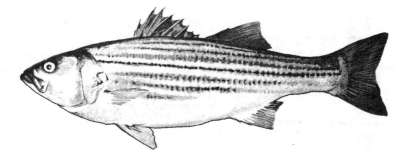

How to Catch . . . Striped Bass

One could write a book, and several people have, on the subject of striper fishing. This is the case because many techniques are used to catch stripers, depending upon the location, the season of the year and the preferences in approach of different anglers. Our purpose here is to present the basics of the most successful approaches.

Striped bass were first introduced to California from the East Coast in 1897 near Martinez. Twenty years later, the commercial catch alone was averaging well over one million pounds per year. In 1935, commercial fishing was stopped because of the dwindling population. Currently, the striper population is declining, and not nearly as good as it was 20 years ago. Sport anglers should release all ocean, bay and river caught stripers.

The life cycle of the striper is important to be aware of because it has much to do with when and where to fish. Stripers spawn in the fresh waters of the Sacramento (from Sacramento to Colusa) and San Joaquin Rivers (between the Antioch Bridge and the Middle River) from about April to mid-June. After spawning, these fish move back down into salt water, or the brackish waters of the San Pablo and San Francisco Bays. Stripers move back up into the Delta starting in September and these early arrivals winter over for the spring spawn. Striped bass range in size up to 40 pounds or more. The average catch is probably 6-10 pounds. What this all means, as far as where the stripers are at any given season, is summarized in the accompanying table.

The striper's habits and life cycle, of course, are all separate from the striper fishing that exists in several reservoirs (e.g. San Luis, New Hogan). Impoundment populations exist because of planting programs of young stripers, or through young fish migrations through aqueducts.

⧄ Prime Fishing Locations For Striped Bass	J	F	M	A	M	J	J	A	S	O	N	D
Ocean						⧄	⧄	⧄				
S.F. Bay							⧄	⧄	⧄			
Delta		⧄	⧄	⧄	⧄					⧄	⧄	⧄

Trolling

Trolling for stripers is probably the most popular technique. It allows you to cover a fairly wide area, if you're not sure where the fish are. Trolling is also suggested if the tides are not favorable. That is, the best striper fishing usually occurs on a large (greater than 5.0 feet) incoming tide, after a low, low tide (2-3 feet, or even minus). If these tide conditions don't exist, trolling may be the best bet.

The key to successful striper trolling is to keep your offering near the bottom. Most often the bass are laying close to the bottom. The most notable exception to this is probably lake striper, where surface trolling is often productive. Of course, the main problem with trolling on or near the bottom is snags. But many experienced striper trollers look at losing lures to snags as part of the cost of successful fishing. The truth is that if the stripers are on the bottom, that's where you've got to troll or else you'll just be wasting fuel.

Often in the Delta and bays the stripers are in 8-25 feet of water. In these depths, it's important to get your offering well back behind the boat. The engine noise and wake spooks the fish, but if you're out far enough from the boat (50-140 yards), the bass have time to return before the lure passes through their area.

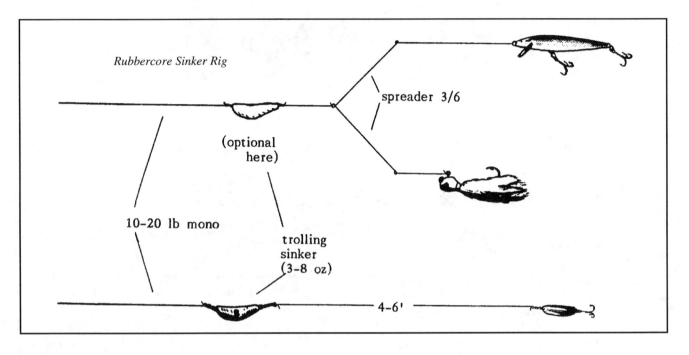

Rubbercore Sinker Rig

spreader 3/6

(optional here)

10-20 lb mono

trolling sinker (3-8 oz)

4-6'

The best trolling speed is 3-4 mph. Once your rig is out, check the tip of your rod. It should be twitching constantly. This is the action from your lure. Adjust the boat speed to get this effect.

The rig you troll depends a lot on the depth of water you're trolling in. Use the rig that keeps your offering near the bottom. In shallow water (8-10 feet), a deep diving plug, spoon or jig can be tied directly to the line, or attached using a snap swivel. In deeper water (10-20 feet), use one of the two rigs shown above.

Deep Troll

For this type of trolling (e.g. deep water channel of the Sacramento or San Joaquin Rivers), if this is where your sonar tells you the fish are, you'll need to use diving planes, leadcore line or downriggers. This type of equipment and approach is described in the Salmon (in Ocean) and Trout and Salmon (in Lakes) sections of this book.

The most popular trolling offerings for shallow or deep work are as follows:

- Rebel, Rapala and Bomber lures (5-6 inches, 3 treble hooks, jointed, deep-diving, minnow-type plugs)

- Spoons (Pet, Hopkins, Kastmaster, size 3-4 inches)

- Bug Eye Jigs (2-3 ounces)—used on short leader of spreader to provide depth

Set the drag on your reel just firm enough to prevent line from being taken out. Set the clicker in the "on" position. A singing clicker means a strike. The trolling action will have set the hook. Tighten down slightly on the drag before playing the fish.

Bait Fishing

Bait fishing can be done from a boat or shore, although it is probably more productive from a boat (because more prom-

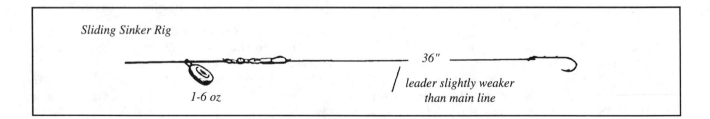

Sliding Sinker Rig

36"

leader slightly weaker than main line

1-6 oz

ising areas can be reached). As with trolling, bait fishing is best on a big changing tide. Fish often feed on the edge of drop-offs at these times. Fish the upstream edge of an incoming tide and the downstream edge on an outgoing tide. The edge of a shallow flat or sandbar is often good.

Boat anglers usually anchor and then cast out a sliding sinker rig with a big bait hook. Stripers aren't shy, so a partially visible hook is no problem. The reel is left in the free spool position. Watch the tip of your rod at all times. Point your rod at the fish and play out 5-10 feet of line on the slightest nibble. Next, the fish will hit hard. Set the hook solidly by raising the rod to a vertical position quickly. Both shore and boat anglers should use enough lead on the rig to prevent the current from drifting it.

Popular striped bass baits include threadfin shad, anchovies, sardines, shiners, blood worms, mudsuckers, bullheads, ghost shrimp and grass shrimp. Local bait shops will know which are most effective depending upon location and season. Live bait fish are hooked just below the dorsal fin, with the hook entering on one side and exiting on the other side of the fish. Once a live bait fish dies, the hook may be put in more securely, often with the leader secured to the tail by a half-hitch knot. Dead bait fish are often mutilated, or butterflied (opened vertically from throat to tail, folded over and then threaded through the curve of the hook several times) to put blood and oil into the water. For large sardines, fillet off a side flank. Cut it in half for enough bait for 2 hooks. For blood worms, some experts suggest always keeping the hook tip covered with worm.

Casting

Casting for striped bass can be done from shore, a boat or in the surf. In tidal waters like San Francisco Bay, casting is most productive on rapid, incoming tides. And like largemouth bass casting, it is often best to cast around and about structures such as bridge columns. One-half ounce Hair-Raisers, Cordell Spots and Lucky 13's are good.

In lakes, feeding birds are a key to stripers feeding on shad near the surface. Surface plugs (shad patterns) and 1/2 ounce Krocodiles or Kastmasters are effective.

Surf casters also depend on the feeding birds to tip off the location of the stripers. Common offerings are Rebel and Rapala lures.

Surf, Drift and Pier Fishing

Surf fishing is a popular approach for taking stripers along the Pacific coast, especially from the Golden Gate Bridge south to Half Moon Bay. Drift fishing is used to catch striped bass in San Francisco and San Pablo Bays. Pier fishing at several San Francisco and San Pablo Bay piers, and particularly at Pacifica Pier, can be productive for stripers.

Each of these three techniques is described in detail in the second chapter of this book, Fishing . . . NorCal Style.

Tackle and Equipment

Striper fishing can be done with a wide variety of tackle. Lightweight black bass tackle can be used for casting or bait fishing. Medium-weight spinning equipment or free spool/star drag conventional reel-light action rods are used for trolling. Light spinning equipment can also be used for trolling. Some feel this is the most exciting way to take stripers in the 4-12 pound range.

Where to Fish

See the "San Francisco Bay Fishing," "Central Valley River Fishing," "Delta Fishing," and "Freshwater Fishing" chapters of this book.

Cleaning and Cooking

Smaller stripers are usually filleted. Large ones (above 10 pounds) can be steaked. Striped bass fillets or steaks are white, mild in flavor, low in fat and especially good eating. Barbecuing, broiling, poaching, baking and frying are all good approaches.

WHITE STURGEON

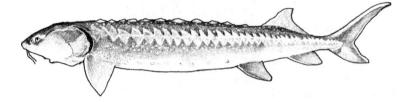

How to Catch . . . Sturgeon

Of the 16 species of sturgeon, two live in local waters (San Francisco Bay, San Pablo Bay, Suisun Bay, the Delta, Sacramento River). Green sturgeon (sometimes locally referred to as yellow) are the least prevalent. Greens have long slender snouts and grow to about 7 feet in length and 350 pounds. White sturgeon (actually grey) have a more blunt nose and can grow even larger! The white sturgeon is the largest fish found in North America fresh waters. And this prehistoric species has a life span of over 100 years. Sturgeons are bottom feeders with a diet consisting of clams, grass shrimp, craps and herring roe.

Fishing Techniques

Sturgeon fishing is done almost always from a boat at anchor. And the exclusive approach is still fishing. Because of this, it's important to drop your bait in a promising location. There are prime sturgeon fishing spots throughout the bays and Delta.

Sturgeon fishing is best on a strong, incoming tide and at the turning of this tide. Most sturgeon are caught in 10-20 feet of water, often at drop-offs. Electronic fish finders are very helpful in locating these contours and actually "seeing" the sturgeon themselves. But many sturgeon are caught by anglers who don't have depth finders. Try a location. Move on in half an hour if there is no action.

Sturgeons are bottom feeders. In fact, their mouths hover over the bottom and literally suction or vacuum in the food, so bait must be right on the bottom. A sturgeon's initial "bite" is very soft, which dictates two things:

1. A sliding sinker rig.
2. A rod tip that is sensitive enough to detect the light movement as the sturgeon picks up the bait and moves slightly as it suctions it in.

Many sturgeon anglers cast out or lower in their offering, tighten up the line after the bait sinks to the bottom, and then lean the rod against the transom of the boat (the rod butt on the floor). Then, when a tap is detected, the angler lifts the rod up and points the tip directly at the fish. A big pull means to set the hook hard. Several pumps are probably in order. Sturgeons have tough mouths.

Tackle and Equipment

As mentioned above, a rod with a sensitive tip is recommended. But some anglers prefer heavy-action rods. These also work fine, especially if the angler likes to hold the rod and sense the bite by keeping the line between the thumb and index finger. The rod should be 6 1/2 to 8 feet long and have a long butt below the reel mount to lend leverage while playing the fish.

Most sturgeon anglers use conventional ocean-weight fishing reels. But relatively heavy spinning reels, with a good drag and the capability to hold 250 yards or so of 30 pound line, will also work. A landing net will work for sturgeon that are only a foot or more over the legal limit (40 inches). Beyond this, a gaff or snare is probably required.

Bait and Rigging

Two or three hook sturgeon rigs can be purchased at many Bay Area bait shops. 6/0 size hooks are recommended. These leaders use wire line. Attach the rig to your line with a strong snap swivel as shown in the diagram on the next page.

Grass shrimp are the most common bait. Mud and ghost shrimp are also used. Two people need about one pound of bait. Load up each hook with bait. 4 or 5 shrimps may be needed. The bigger the wad the better. Live or fresh bait is most desirable. You can slide shrimp up the hook leader.

sliding sinker
2-12 oz, or more

3'

Some suggest putting shrimp on the hook, tail first. Anchovies and clams can also be used for bait. Some use a small hair net to hold their baits in a glob.

Where to Fish

See the "San Francisco Bay Fishing," "Delta Fishing," and "Freshwater Fishing" chapters.

Cleaning and Cooking

Many anglers put caught sturgeon on a heavy rope stringer and then bleed them while still in the water. Cut the fish deeply behind each gill.

The first item on the cleaning agenda is to gut the fish. Next, slice off the sharp spines along the sides, top and bottom. Slice through the skin on the back and belly, and along the rear or the gill cage. By hand, or with a pair of pliers, pull the skin off each side. Now, cut off the head and make a deep cut around the fish right in front of the tail. You can now remove the spinal column in one piece. Finally, steak the fish and fillet the tail section. Trim off the red meat along the sides and next to the spinal column.

RAINBOW TROUT

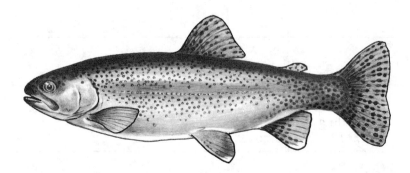

How to Catch . . . Trout (in Streams)

We are blessed by the numerous, fine trout streams in Northern California (these are described in the "Freshwater Fishing" chapters). Stream trout fishing is appealing because it can be the type of experience you personally want it to be. It can be accessible or remote, challenging or relaxing, simple or complicated.

Many people have a stereotype in their minds of the typical trout angler. It includes a fly rod, hip-high waders, a vest decorated with multi-colored flies, a hat with more multi-colored flies, a landing net hanging from the waist, all topped off with a Norman Rockwell-like wicker creel. This, of course, exactly describes some trout fishermen. But, forget this stereotype. Stream trout fishing can be productive and enjoyable, not only for the avid, well-equipped fly fisherman, but for everyone. You don't even need to use a fly rod if you don't want to.

The purpose of this section is to describe, in detail, several of the basic ways to catch stream trout, regardless of the type of fishing you prefer and the type of tackle you have.

There are several different types of trout in Southern California streams. The most common are rainbow. Most of these are planted, but some are wild. Others include the German brown trout, the brook trout and the golden trout.

Marketscope Books publishes the bestseller, *Trout Fishing in California*, for those who want to know more about stream trout fishing.

Some Fundamentals

Stream trout fishing, no matter what equipment is used, focuses on casting a fly, spinner, spoon or bait into a likely place in the stream and then retrieving it in as natural a manner as possible. Other fundamentals:

- Trout always face upstream, watching for food to be delivered to them by the moving water. So your offering should be presented in the same manner—moving from upstream to downstream.

- Trout are very leary and easily spooked. Since they're facing upstream and smelling the water that comes from upstream, always move upstream as you fish. This way you're less likely to be detected. Move quietly and stay out of the line of sight of likely trout hangouts. Keep your shadow off the water. Wear dark clothing. When wading, move slowly and try not to dislodge rocks.

- In the same vane, fish on the shady side of the stream, especially in the hours after sunrise and just before sunset.

- Casts in an upstream direction or up and across the stream are preferred over downstream casts. Down stream casts require a retrieve that is against the current, and therefore unnatural in appearances.

- Trout stay near the bottom of the stream. So your offering must move along near the bottom. The exception to this rule is when dry fly fishing. Dry flies (floating flies) imitate floating insects being carried along by the current. Trout will rise up to take these flies. Dry fly fishing is evening fishing.

- As with most fishing, early morning and evening are best fishing periods. But trout can be caught at any time of the day.

- Keep hooks sharp. Banging rocks and pebbles can dull them quickly.

- If you're not succeeding in whatever approach you're using (flies, spinners, bait), try other offerings until you find the one that works.

● Trout hang out behind boulders that break the current, in deep holes, in slower water near the undercut edge of a stream (especially in shaded areas), and at the head and tail of pools. Concentrate your efforts on these areas.

● When you spot an obviously expert trout angler, watch where he or she casts from, where he or she put the offering and how it is retrieved.

● Often the best places to cast from are in the water. Don't let that stop you. Just be careful and carry a wading staff to probe the bottom and improve balance. Waders may or may not be necessary.

Fly Fishing

Flies, both dry (floating) and wet (sinking), are very small and light—too light to cast any distance. In fly fishing this difficulty is overcome by using fly line that has enough weight so *it* can be cast. The fly, connected by a light leader to the end of the fly line, "just goes along for a ride" as the line is played out and finally set on its final trajectory. The purpose of the fly reel is simply to store line that is not being used at the moment, and to retrieve line when necessary.

Fly fishing is an art and a science. Some say it is the ultimate fishing experience. Some people only fly fish. Many entire volumes have been written on fly fishing. In our limited space we cannot compete. But here are some insights that produce fish in Northern California.

Most experts agree that stream trout feed primarily below the surface. In fact, they probably spend 90% or more of their eating time feeding on aquatic life or terrestrial life that does not float (e.g. worms that fall off banks). Sure, if there is a good batch of mayflies, caddis or stoneflies, trout will come up to feed. And this is the time for dry fly fishing. But if trout spend most of their time feeding below the surface, then that's where you should put your fly most of the time.

So trout fly fishing is roughly divided into two categories. The first is dry fly fishing. Dry flies are designed to emulate adult forms of terrestrial and aquatic insects.

● Dry flies must float. Floating solution, tapered leaders and good floating fly line make this possible.

● Present the dry fly beyond the suspected feeding fish and let it float naturally through that feeding area, free on the current.

● Dry fly fishing is an evening affair. The several hours before dark are best. As the truism goes, "match the hatch," dry flies should match nature as closely as possible. To accomplish this, catch a flying insect and then use a similar fly. A premier SoCal outdoor writer, Rex Gerlach, carries these dry flies: Adams (sizes 18, 16, 14, 12, 10), Royal Wulff (sizes 16, 14, 12, 10), Black Ant (sizes 18, 16, 10), Blue Wing Olive (sizes 18, 16), Blonde Goofus Bug (sizes 16, 14), Elk Hair Caddis (sizes 18, 16, 14), Joe's Hopper (sizes 12, 10, 8), and Bird's Stone Fly (sizes 8, 6, 4).

The second major category of trout fly fishing is wet fly fishing. Wet flies imitate underwater creatures such as the larva or pupae state of aquatic insects, nymphs, grubs, etc. The traditional winged wet flies are meant to suggest drowned adult insects. Streamer wet flies imitate bait fish.

● The whole idea behind successful wet fly fishing is to present the fly and allow the current to sweep it along close to the bottom at the exact same speed as the surrounding currents.

● As the fly drifts back towards you, keep the fly line from becoming too slack, so you can respond promptly should the line pause or stop, indicating a take.

● It is often difficult to detect underwater strikes. It is sometimes helpful to attach a strike indicator (a small, bright-colored float) to your leader and watch closely for any slight hesitation. The strike indicator should be set to correspond with the depth of the water.

● Sometimes two wet flies of various colors are better than a single fly. Use a standard nine foot tapered leader with a dark pattern fly at the tip, and 12 inches up from the tip, use another lighter colored wet fly on a six inch dropper leader.

● There are literally thousands of wet flies. But the late Larry Green, the expert angler and NorCal outdoor writer, recommended you start with a half dozen standard wet fly patterns (preferably lightly weighted) in sizes 6 and 8. The six basic colors should incorporate (1) yellow and black to resemble a yellow jacket or bee; (2) light brown with spent wings; (3) all black wet fly with grey hackle spent wings; (4) cream-colored wet fly to represent a caddis larva; (5) peacock tail wet fly for multiple colors; and (6) green wet fly to represent moss.

● Popular streamers (which imitate bait fish) are the matuka (in olive), the marabou streamer and the muddler minnow.

There is a great deal of variety in fly fishing equipment. One can spend hundreds of dollars, or you can buy a rod/reel

Dual Fly Rig

combination that is quite decent for less than $50. For starters, a 7 1/2 to 8 1/2 foot rod matched with #6 line is good. An automatic reel costs a few dollars more, but makes taking up excessive line so much easier.

If you're having trouble handling fly fishing equipment, consider a fly fishing class, watch others do it, read up on the subject in specialized books, and check out some videos.

One last, yet very important point, that applies to both dry and wet fly fishing: Casting skill is not as important to fly fishing success as it often seems. In fact, long, accurate casts are not necessary or desirable on most Southern California mountain trout streams. Long casts just put flies in the branches and waste valuable fishing time. Instead use stealth as you move upstream. And then just flip your fly 10 to 20 feet out to likely territory. Use a short, precise flip of a cast. That's all that is needed in most situations. Flip casting and "dapping" (or just dropping your fly over brush, beyond a boulder or next to an undercut bank) are great when wading up the center of smaller streams. This approach puts emphasis where it should be, on fly fishing, not fly casting.

Spinning

Spin fishing means stream trout fishing using spinning or even spin casting equipment. The most popular setups include light or ultralight spinning tackle. Ultralight tackle is the easiest to handle and probably the most appropriate. It's capable of casting even small offerings with a 4 pound test line to sufficient distances. Here are the fundamentals of stream trout fishing with spinning tackle:

- The most common lures are very small spinners. Since retrieves are with the current (you're still casting up stream), a spinner whose blade rotates freely with little more motion than current speed is more desirable. These spinners imitate swimming bait fish. A popular example of a spinner of this caliber is the Panther Marten #2, 1/16 ounce black-bodied spinner. Gold blades are good for low light or overcast periods, chrome blades are recommended for sunny periods, and copper is good for not-so-clear water. Try several.

- Besides spinners, spoons are also good, like the Kastmaster. Retrieval speed is critical for the success of both spinners and spoons. Test both in quiet pools. Both types put out a vibration that can be sensed in the motion at the tip of the rod. Watch for this and adjust retrieval speed accordingly. Also, frequently change retrieve speed to give the offerings a more natural swimming pattern.

- Spinners and other lures need to be worked near the bottom. Adjust your retrieval speed to achieve this. You'll hang up some lures, but you'll catch more fish.

- Drifting spinners and spoons is also a good approach. Instead of retrieving, drift these little lures (like you would drift bait) in riffles and in fast moving water of the head and tail of pools, etc.

- Some lures are best tied directly to the main line. Others may twist the line if a small snap swivel is not used. Experiment, but if using a swivel, make sure it is in good working order and has a rounded connector at the lure end. This will insure proper action in the water.

Bait Fishing for Trout

Stream trout fishing with bait is the most flexible of all approaches. It's flexible because of the wide choice of baits that produce fish. And it's flexible because it can be done with either fly fishing equipment or spinning equipment. Some devotees even combine the two by using monofilament line on a fly rod and reel. All these possibilities are fine. Here are the fundamentals of trout stream bait fishing:

- Red worms are probably the most popular bait followed by bottled salmon eggs. Cheese and marshmallows are also popular, as are moldable manufactured baits like Berkley Power Bait. Then there is a whole category of natural live baits including crickets, beetles, grubs,

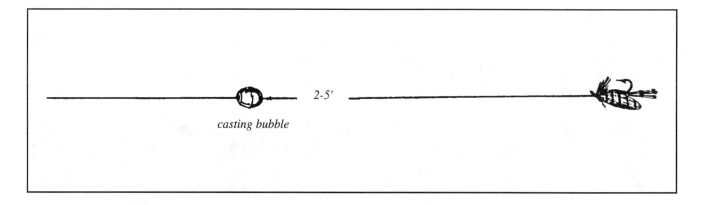

casting bubble   2-5'

larvae and pupae. Some anglers collect bait right out of the stream by using a fine mesh screen to trap bait dislodged by moving large rocks in the stream beds.

● If you're using live bait, it should be alive. So store and transport them carefully and hook them so as not to inflict fatal damage (at least not instant fatal damage).

● A short shank #8 or #10 hook is good. Try to conceal the entire hook into the bait.

● You want the bait to drift along with the current near the bottom of the stream. Unweighted drifting is best. If you need weight to get near the bottom, use as little split shot as possible, about 8-10 inches from the hook.

Since your bait is under water and drifting, it's not all that easy to detect bites. It helps to keep slack out of the line (while still allowing drift) and to set the hook on any sign of hesitation or pause in drift.

Using Casting Bobber for Trout

Purest fly fishermen may cringe at this approach, but here it goes anyway. Some people would like to be able to cast flies or small baits without mastering a fly rod. And some can't afford fly fishing equipment. For this group a casting bobber is the answer.

A casting bobber is a small, clear plastic float that adds enough weight to a fly or a small bait to allow casting with a spinning or spin casting reel and monofilament line. Thread the main line through the bobber and then tie on a swivel to keep it in place. Now add a leader and fly.

Casting bobbers are available in several sizes and configurations. Cast-a-Bubble in sizes FS25 or FS35 are good. Some even allow you to vary weight by allowing water inside the bobber. A bobber about half full of water provides a good casting weight. Most casting bobbers sink when filled with water.

Fish a casting bobber rig just as you would a dry fly. If you use a wet fly or bait, allow enough distance between the bobber and the hook so your offering gets down to near the bottom. In rapidly flowing water, some split shot about 8 inches from the hook may be added. A casting bobber/fly rig can also work in trout lakes in the evening when a hatch is on. Use a slow retrieve and twitch the fly from time to time.

Tackle and Equipment

Besides your choice of rod, reel, line and enticements to put at the end of it, trout anglers need several other items. Essential are both a creel (canvas ones can be purchased for as little as $5.00) or a fishing vest and an inexpensive landing net. A needle-nose pliers or other hook removing device like a hemostat is also essential. Small trout should be released with as little hook damage as possible. In fact, some trout fishermen flatten the barbs on their hooks to facilitate catch and release. Releasing large trout is possibly even more important. It takes large ones to produce small ones.

Optional equipment for trout fishing includes polarized sun glasses, waders and a wading staff. The sun glasses help take the glare off the water and improve underwater visibility. The use of waders depends on air temperature, water temperature, the number of stepping stones in a stream and one's desire to stay dry. Wading staffs (a proper length, light tree limb) are great to help maintain balance.

Cleaning and Cooking

Small trout (pan size) are generally just gutted and gilled (field cleaned). Larger trout are often filleted. Trout is mild, lean and sweet. It is suitable for just about any cooking approach. Sauteing is probably the most popular. The flesh of trout is tender, delicately flavored and can range in color from white to a pinkish we associate with salmon.

California Trout

Rainbow Trout—Native of California, found in nearly all lakes and streams where water temperatures do not exceed 70°F for any length of time. Dark, bluish-green back, black spots on back and tail, red stripe on sides, silvery belly. Spawns on gravel bars in fast, clear water. Most suitable of all trout for artificial propagation and highly regarded as a game fish for its fighting qualities.

Brook—Native of Atlantic coastal area, found in many mountain lakes and spring-fed streams throughout the state. Dark olive, worm-like lines on back and sides, red spots along sides, belly reddish-orange to lemon, lower fins red tipped with white. Unlike other species, it may spawn in shallow areas of lakes having spring seepage.

Brown—A native of Europe, generally the hardest of California inland trouts to catch. Plentiful in many Sierra streams and scattered elsewhere throughout the State. The record fish in California weighed 26 pounds. Dark brown on back with black spots, shading to light brown with red spots on sides. The only trout with both black and red spots on its body.

Golden—State fish of California, the golden trout is native to the high country of the Kern River watershed, and now is found in many lakes and streams in the Sierra from Mt. Whitney north to Alpine County. Medium olive back, shading down the sides to brilliant golden belly and reddish-orange stripes from head to tail, crossed with olive vertical bars. Lower fins golden-orange.

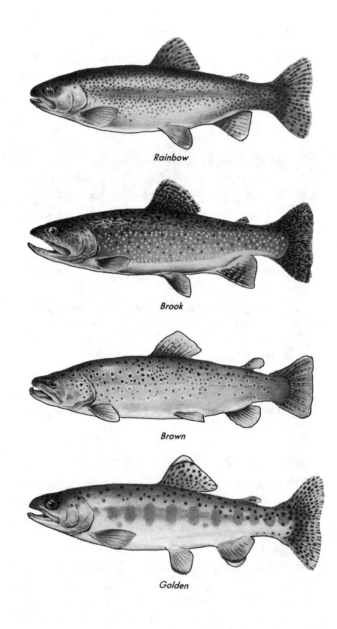

Rainbow

Brook

Brown

Golden

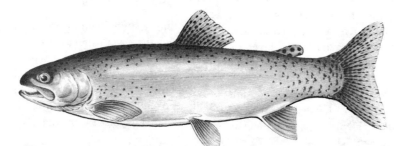

EAGLE LAKE RAINBOW TROUT

How to Catch...Trout and Salmon (in Lakes)

Fishing for trout in lakes is very different from stream trout fishing. This is true because the lake environment changes the behavior of trout. Stream trout are always facing upstream, confined to shallow waters, on or near the bottom, and near or behind structures like boulders, undercuts, etc. The stream determines the location and habits of trout.

Trout in lakes have different ground rules dictating their lives. Food doesn't necessarily "flow" to them, they must find it. Lake water temperatures vary by season and depth, so trout will change depth to find oxygen rich water of a comfortable temperature for them. At times they may be near the surface, and at other times they may be down 80 feet or more.

Several Northern California trout lakes also had kokanee and/or silver salmon planted in them. Salmon and trout in lakes behave and are caught using the same techniques, lures and bait. Usually, anglers pursuing trout will catch an occasional salmon if they are present.

If you're catching trout in a trout and salmon lake, especially in the summertime, and you'd like some salmon, it sometimes helps to fish a little deeper. Research has shown that rainbow and brown trout favor water temperatures of between 55 and 60°F. But, the same research determined that salmon favor 55°F water, which will be down deeper.

Marketscope Books publishes the bestseller, *Trout Fishing in California*, for those who want to know more about lake trout fishing.

Reading a Lake

The specifics of a lake says a lot about the location of trout, and as many anglers have discovered, you've got to find them before you can catch them. As a matter of fact, catching trout in lakes is quite easy, once they are located. Here are the fundamentals:

- Trout, even in lakes, relate to structures. Trout use structures to shelter themselves from predators and to keep out of direct sun. Depending upon the time of year, overhanging trees, cliff areas, submerged points, coves and submerged river channels are good starting points.

- Trout move to locate food and oxygen. The primary inlet to a lake is always a prime location. It washes in food and cool, oxygen-rich water. In cooler months, shoreline weed beds may also provide insects and bait fish. The windward shoreline is also a good possibility. Drifting food will concentrate here. Finally, newly planted trout usually hang around the planting site for several days or more.

- An electronic fish finder can be an important tool. It not only will locate structure-like underwater islands and submerged drop-offs, but it will also locate schools of bait fish and the trout themselves.

- Trout are found down deeper in lakes in the summer months. Some Southern California lakes stratify (or divide) into three layers during the warming months and can remain in this condition until fall. The top layer is too warm and too low in oxygen for trout and salmon. They concentrate near the top of the second layer, or thermocline. In this layer there is plenty of oxygen and forage fish. This layer may be from 15-50 feet down depending upon lake depth and size. Water temperature will be in the 55-60 degree range. A fish finder, underwater temperature gauge or locals can all help you to determine the proper depth to fish.

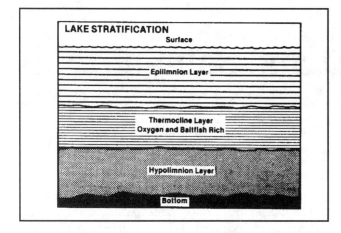

Fishing Techniques

There are three primary methods of catching trout in lakes:

1. **Trolling**—In one form or another, this is probably the most productive method of catching trout in lakes.

2. **Bait Fishing**—A very good method, especially for shore fishing. Can also be done from a boat; for example, at a stream inlet of a lake.

3. **Casting**—Also a very productive shore fishing method. Can also be done from a boat.

It is also possible to catch trout in lakes by fly fishing. But even avid fly fishermen will admit it is difficult. Dry flies will only work, for example, when an insect hatch is taking place. Even then, they may not work because they don't move with the current as they do in streams. Wet flies, streamers, etc. can be used in lakes, and can produce at times if you're either very skillful or very lucky. When there are hungry trout and little angling pressure, remote, high altitude mountain lakes are the best candidates for lake fly fishing success. If you're interested in more information on lake fly fishing, check out several fly fishing books from your local public library, or rent a specialized video.

Trolling for Trout

Trolling is simply pulling an offering at the end of your line through the water using a boat. It can and is done with boats ranging from a canoe, to a rowboat, to an inboard/outboard. There are also several different trolling approaches ranging from trolling a fly on spinning tackle to downrigger trolling. But no matter what depth you're trolling, or what techniques or equipment you're using, these tips will help produce fish:

● Troll slowly. The best trolling is slow trolling. For example, some highly successful trollers use only oar power.

● Change trolling speed often. Every minute or two isn't too frequent. Sometimes it even helps to over speed for just a few seconds and then slow down. This gives added up and down action to the flasher and lure.

● Change depth. If you're not sure of the depth you're trolling at (it can vary depending upon boat speed and amount of line out for all approaches except downrigging) or the depth the trout are at, vary depth until you get a strike. Then stick at this depth.

● Troll an "S" pattern. Trolling experts suggest this approach because (1) it covers more territory than straight line trolling, and (2) it causes speed, direction and depth changes to occur in the flasher and lure. These movements and resulting vibrations attract trout.

When trout are feeding near a lake's surface (i.e. when surface temperatures are low), light tackle trolling is in order. Just about any light spinning or spin casting rod and reel combo will do. Conventional bait casting tackle is also appropriate. Use 6 to 10 pound monofilament line depending upon the size of the trout you're expecting to catch and the type of rig you're trolling.

A full-blown trolling rig consists of several components which are listed below in order of placement on the line.

1. Rudder—A blade to prevent line twist. It also has a hole in it where a weight can be attached to take the trolling rig deeper.

2. Flasher—An attractant that imitates a school of bait fish. It's highly visible and also sends out vibrations.

3. Swivel—Useful in preventing line twist.

4. Snubber—A rubber tube ensemble that absorbs the shock of the strike, sometimes helping to prevent the hook from pulling out of the trout's mouth.

5. About 18 inches of monofilament that is often lighter and less visible than the main line.

6. Offering—A spoon, plug, spinner or baited hook. The best choice for each lake and season is detailed in the "Freshwater Fishing" chapters.

The flasher and rudder are usually sold in a packaged unit. Use larger units for murky water or deep trolling. Then you just attach on the snubber, tie on a leader and attach your offering. See the diagram below.

It's not always necessary, or even desirable, to use a complete trolling rig. Sometimes just a minnow plug is the best choice. If line twist is a problem with the offering you're pulling, add a good quality swivel, or even a trolling rudder between two swivels. Flashers, at times, really do help attract trout to strike.

When putting your rig into the water behind the moving boat, pull the line off your reel, in strokes, with your free hand. By counting these "pulls" you can return fairly accurately to a specified depth, or be able to increase or decrease depth.

Deep Trolling

Trout are often down quite deep, especially in warmer weather months. Pulling a trout rig, as described above, at this time will not produce fish. What should you do? Here are several options:

- Use leadcore trolling line on a good-sized conventional reel. Medium Penn freshwater reels with levelwind are popular. With a slow trolling speed, leadcore line sinks at about a 45 angle, so for example, 50 feet of line will produce a 25 foot trolling depth. Most anglers use a full trolling rig (i.e. rudder, flasher, etc.) when leadcore trolling. The flasher helps attract fish in the low visibility light condition of deeper water, and it also adds a weight to the already weighted line.

- Use a downrigger—this is by far the most desirable approach, especially if you need to go down to 30 or 40 feet or more. A downrigger will take your trolling rig down to a known depth (they're equipped with depth counters), and allow you to play and land the fish on light tackle (see illustration below). The trolling rig can be made even lighter by removing the flasher from the trolling rig setup. Instead, attach it to the downrigger weight (see illustration on next page).

- Use a diving plane—a weighted, airfoil device that uses the motion of the boat to dive and take the terminal tackle with it.

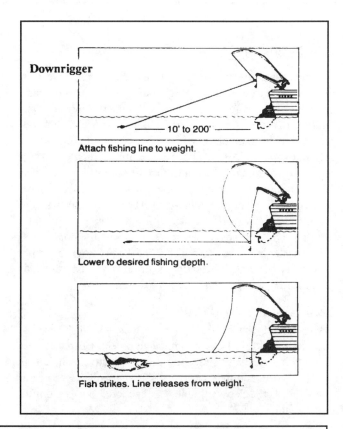

Downrigger

— 10' to 200' —

Attach fishing line to weight.

Lower to desired fishing depth.

Fish strikes. Line releases from weight.

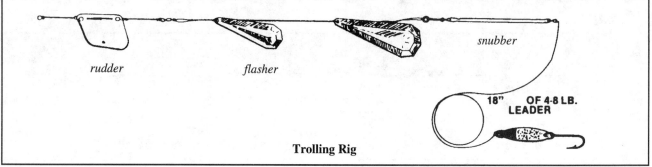

rudder   *flasher*   *snubber*

18" OF 4-8 LB. LEADER

Trolling Rig

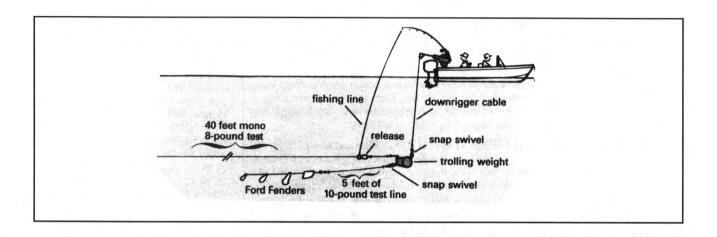

Trolling a Fly

Sometimes trout will rise up in a lake in the evening to feed on insects. The trout will jump right out of the water producing raindrop-like rings on the surface. Summertime from 6 pm until dark is the time to be alert for this show. And here's how to catch your share of these insect-chasing trout. Simply tie a fly onto the end of 4-6 pound monofilament rigged on a spinning rod and reel. Let out about 40 yards of line and slow troll through the feeding activity, usually near shore. An electric trolling motor is ideal. You'll be very pleased with the results. By the way, if you see evening hatch activity on a lake but are without a boat, try this. Tie a small spoon, like a Kastmaster, on your spinning outfit. Then remove the treble hook, put on a 2 1/2 foot leader and tie on a fly. Cast softly into the feeding activity and be ready to set the hook.

Bait Fishing for Trout

Bait fishing can be done from shore or boat. The most common tackle is light spinning equipment. Despite all the variety in trout bait fishing, the most productive technique is probably the sliding sinker rig. It is most often used from shore, but it's also well suited to anchored boat fishing in coves and inlets.

The purpose of the sliding sinker rig is to allow the bait to move freely when a trout picks it up. With a fixed sinker rig, the trout would notice the drag on the offering and drop it.

The process begins by casting out the baited rig to a likely spot. Let it sink all the way to the bottom and then slowly crank in any slack. Now, sit down, get comfortable and open the bail on your spinning reel. Personally, I don't believe in putting a rod down or propping it up on a stick. I believe in holding the rod. Then you can feel the slightest tug on your bait. In fact, I like to have my line in front of the reel go between the thumb and index finger of my non-reeling hand.

When the trout picks up the bait, play off line from the spool so no resistance is felt by the fish. A pause may be detected after the first movement of line. Wait until it starts moving out again (this means the trout has swallowed the bait, literally swallowed the bait). Close the bail and set the hook. You've got yourself a fish.

A wide variety of baits are used such as salmon eggs, cheese, minnows, shad, worms, commercial baits, and crickets. A combination of baits is also popular. Some use a small marshmallow/salmon egg/nightcrawler combination. The egg provides visual attraction and the marshmallow provides

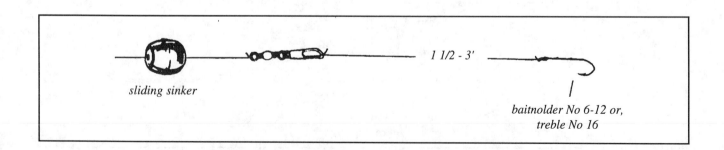

buoyancy, so the whole offering floats slightly off the bottom. Another way to accomplish this buoyant effect using night-crawlers is to inflate them with air. Crawler inflaters are available to accomplish this task. Many large trout are caught on both combination baits and inflated nightcrawlers.

Bobber fishing can also be quite effective for trout. This is an especially effective method in winter and early spring when lake surface temperatures are cool and trout are often feeding near the surface. Simply tie your hook to the line, put a split shot a foot or so up from the hook, and snap on a bobber up the line. Six feet is a good distance to try first. Cast it out and watch your bobber closely. By the way, up to 3 hooks are allowed on one rod. So two or three hook rigs like crappie rigs can also be good trout getters. With his type of setup you can try several baits at multiple depths.

Sometimes trout are holding at mid-range in a lake, they're too deep for regular bobber fishing, but they're not on the

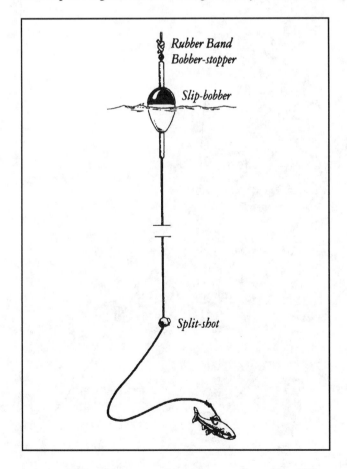

Rubber Band
Bobber-stopper

Slip-bobber

Split-shot

bottom. When this occurs, it's time to pull out the sliding bobber rig. With this rig you can fish at 20, 30 or even 50 feet, while still being able to cast a short rig and retrieve the hooked

trout right up to near the rod tip. This rig allows the split shot weighted bait to pull line through the slip bobber until the bobber stop gets to the bobber. When reeling in, the stop-knot slides through the rod guides so you can bring in line all the way to the split shot. Stop-knots and sliding bobbers are available in packaged kits, or stop-knots can be tied. Some anglers use thread to tie a knot larger than the hole in the bead, while others use a piece of rubberband to tie the stop-knot.

Casting for Trout

Casting for trout is a popular shore option, especially among younger anglers. And it can be effective. The most popular tackle is again light spinning or spin casting.

Lures can be tied directly to the end of the main line or attached with a snap swivel. I prefer the snap swivel. It prevents any line twist and provides a way to change lures easily. Most trout lures imitate small bait fish. Silver and gold colors are good in 1/16 to 1/4 ounce sizes. Some popular trout casting lures are Kastmasters, Roostertails, Phoebes, and Mepps Spinners.

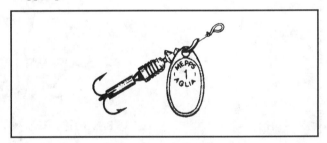

Cast out as far as possible, let the lure settle to the desired retrieve depth, and return at the speed that provides the most natural action. Slower is probably better. And vary the pace of your retrieve. The small bait you're trying to duplicate don't swim as fast, and they don't swim at a steady pace. Sometimes it's best to let the lure sink for some time before starting your retrieve. A problem with this approach is the frequent snags (on sunken branches, etc.) and lost lures. Some anglers minimize this difficulty by replacing the original treble hook with a weedless hook. It's even possible to cast a fly from shore using spinning tackle. See the Trolling A Fly discussion earlier in this section.

Cleaning and Cooking

See the Trout (in Streams) section for cleaning instructions. Smaller trout are best when sauteed or oven-fried, or when baked, either plain or with a light sauce. The larger, whole trout are excellent when baked or poached. Trout is at its best when prepared simply.

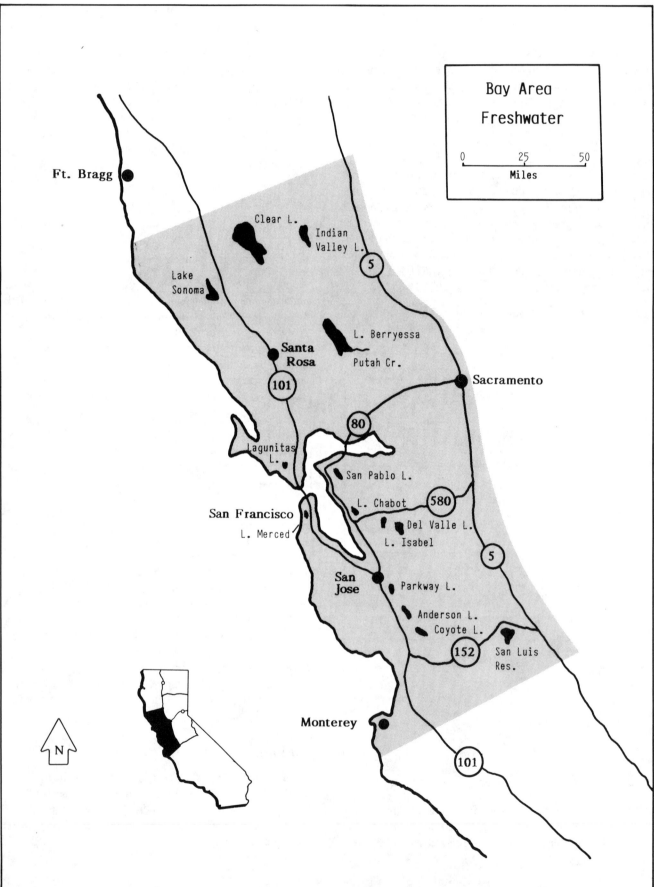

Bay Area Freshwater Fishing

This is the first of five freshwater fishing chapters. This chapter as well as the four succeeding chapters covers a specific zone of Northern California. These regions are illustrated on the map below.

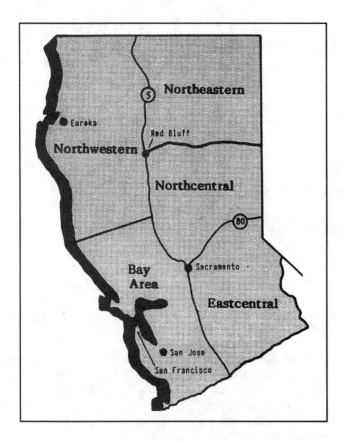

The Bay Area freshwater territory is bordered on the east by I-5 and on the west by the Pacific Ocean. The northern border passes just above Clear Lake, while the southern border passes below San Luis Reservoir, east of Gilroy. There are about ten major fishing lakes in this area, scores of smaller lakes, and even a surprisingly good all season trout stream. All these Bay Area freshwater hot spots are featured in this chapter. See the Bay Area freshwater map on the previous page for the specific locations.

Almost all Bay Area anglers like getting away for a weekend or week-long fishing trip to one of the many great fishing areas in Northern California. But it is also nice, at times, to take advantage of the great freshwater fishing opportunities close to home. Look at the map and see how convenient most of the lakes are to Bay Area residents. They offer great fishing only a short drive from home. They're fantastic for day trips, or even half-day or evening outings.

Read up on these lakes, and then plan a "close-to-home" fishing adventure with a friend, or the entire family.

Lake Anderson (map - p. 104)

Lake Anderson is one of several lakes that offer good fishing within easy reach of South Bay residents. It is primarily a bass, panfish and catfish lake. Facilities at Anderson include a full-service marina off Cochran Rd., launch ramps and picnicking. Camping and night boating are not permitted at this 7 mile long lake. Power-boating and waterskiing are popular on weekends, so angling is best on weekdays and early in the day.

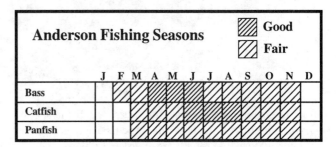

Anderson Fishing Seasons		Good
		Fair
	J	F	M	A	M	J	J	A	S	O	N	D
Bass		░	░	░	░	░	░	░	░	░	░	
Catfish			░	░	░	░	░	░	░	░	░	
Panfish			░	░	░	░	░	░	░	░	░	

Anderson Fishing Tips

At Anderson, bass fishing is best near the rocky points by the dam, in the coves on the north shore of the lake, and in the narrows at each end of the lake. Catfishing is good at the E. Dunne Avenue bridge, near the marina and at the dam. Clams, anchovies and chicken livers work well for catfish. Bass are deep in summer, from 35-50 feet. One good way to get down to bass at these depths is to jig a spoon vertically. Drop it straight down to the bottom, lift it up a few feet, and let it flutter down. Bass strike on the initial drop and on the flutter drop. There is trout action in Coyote Creek below Anderson dam. Information: Santa Clara County Parks and Recreation, (408) 358-3741

Lake Berryessa (map - p. 105)

Lake Berryessa is one of California's premier recreation areas, combining fine fishing with resorts, camping, water and jet skiing, and sailing. And it's right near Napa Valley's wine country. Traditionally, trout (rainbow and browns) fishing has been the main draw for anglers at Berryessa. Many trout in the 2 to 3 pound class are taken, and 5 pounders are not that unusual. But Lake Berryessa also boasts Florida-

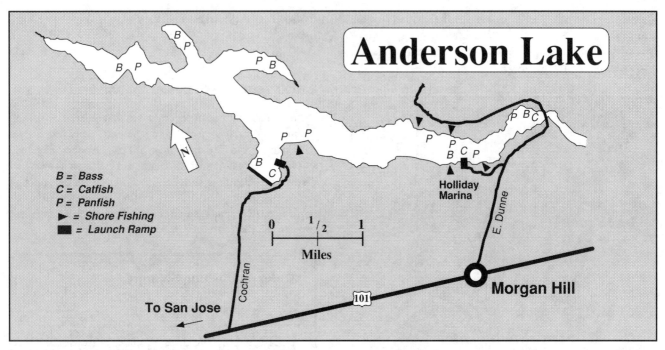

strain largemouth bass, smallmouth bass, Alabama spotted bass, crappie, catfish and bluegill. The lake and its facilities are open all year. In total there are over 1200 campsites in the vicinity, and houseboats are available at some resorts. Berryessa is nestled in a low and hidden valley between two spurs of the Coastal Range. It has more miles of shoreline than massive Lake Tahoe.

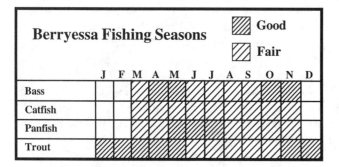

Berryessa Fishing Seasons	J	F	M	A	M	J	J	A	S	O	N	D
Bass			▨	▨	▨	▨	▨	▨	▨	▨	▨	▨
Catfish				▨	▨	▨	▨	▨	▨	▨	▨	
Panfish			▨	▨	▨	▨	▨	▨	▨	▨		
Trout	▨	▨	▨	▨	▨	▨	▨	▨	▨	▨	▨	▨

▨ Good ▨ Fair

Berryessa Fishing Tips

The Monticello Dam on Putah Creek which created Lake Berryessa was completed in 1957. Part of the recreational plan for this lake was to create an outstanding largemouth fishery. But as things turned out, the bucketmouth fishing at Berryessa has not been as consistent year to year as the smallmouth fishing. That's not to say that largemouth fishing can't be good—or even outstanding. For example, in April 1988, Delbert Abrams caught a 17 pound 8 ounce largemouth while shore fishing a plastic worm at Oak Shore Park! This is the largest black bass ever caught in Northern California.

Smallmouth action begins at the points on the south end of the lake about mid-February—this end of the lake warms up first. Crankbaits are an early favorite. Smallmouth action is in full swing in April. Anglers score on 4 inch plastic worms, Git Zits and grubs as the fish school up in brushy coves.

Largemouths follow their littler cousins on up to the spawning beds in about early May. Plastic worms and crankbaits are major takers. Next comes Alabama spotted bass action in late May and June. Wragg Cove and Skiers Cove are the best for "spots."

Crappie fishing is at the peak at Berryessa in May and June. Some anglers find schools of these 1 to 2 pounders by trolling live minnows. Then they switch to yellow, or white and red crappie jigs to work the school. Some good spots include upper Putah Creek, around the islands, Portuguese Cove, Steel Canyon, Skiers Cove and Pope Creek. Crappies may be in open water or near brush. Panfish action continues with a good bluegill bite in June and July. Successful anglers work the rock piles in the coves, around submerged trees and docks, and in the brush at the back of the coves.

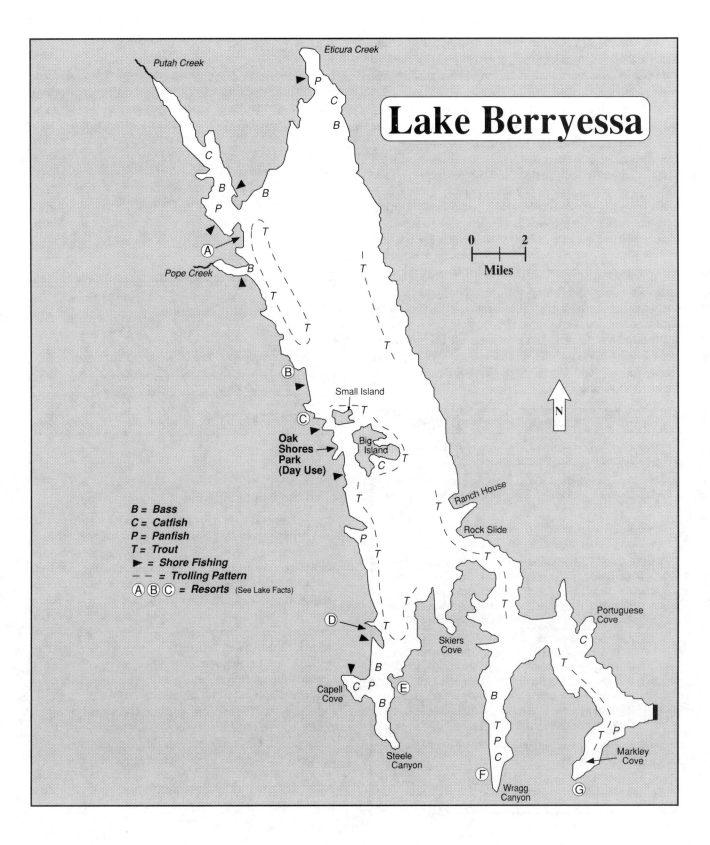

Putah Creek

Eticura Creek

P

C

B

Lake Berryessa

C

B

B

P

T

0   2

Miles

Pope Creek

B

T

T

T

B

N

T

T

T

Ⓐ

Ⓑ

Small Island

T

Ⓒ

Oak Shores Park (Day Use)

Big Island

C

T

Ranch House

T

Rock Slide

T

B = Bass
C = Catfish
P = Panfish
T = Trout
► = Shore Fishing
− − = Trolling Pattern
ⒶⒷⒸ = Resorts (See Lake Facts)

P

T

T

T

Portuguese Cove

Ⓓ

T

Skiers Cove

C

B

B

Capell Cove

C P

Ⓔ

B

T

Steele Canyon

B

T P C

Ⓕ

Wragg Canyon

T P

Markley Cove

Ⓖ

Hot weather in the summertime brings out the catfishermen. Some of the best spots are the very north end of the lake around Putah Creek, and at the south end of the lake in Capell, Wragg and Portuguese Coves.

Because of the depth of Berryessa and the resulting cold water, trout is the king of all the Berryessa fisheries. And with the advent of downrigger deep trolling technology, trout are taken all year at Berryessa. Trout are down deep in the summer and early fall months. 30 to 40 feet is often a good depth. The Kastmaster is the most popular trolling lure. Other spoons and spinners also produce. Once the lake turns over and cooler water returns to the surface, the trout action moves up top. Surface trolling, bait under a bobber, and casting all work then. Many trout are caught from shore during this period from about November through spring.

Speaking of shore fishing, there are good spots all along the west and north shores. Bank anglers take trout, bass, catfish and panfish, depending on the season. Good spots are scattered along the west shore from Capell Cove on up to Pope Creek. The Putah Creek area and on over to Eticura Creek is also good. The entire east side of Berryessa is off limits to shore anglers.

Lake Berryessa Facts

Location: Berryessa is about 65 miles north of San Francisco and about 50 miles west of Sacramento.

Size: This is a big lake. It's 25 miles long and 1 to 3 miles wide. There are 168 miles of shoreline. Maximum depth is 275 feet.

Species: Rainbow and brown trout, largemouth, spotted and smallmouth bass, crappie, bluegill and catfish

Facilities and Campgrounds: There are a number of facilities at Berryessa. Most offer a complete range of services including camping, launching, marinas, stores, boat rental, restaurants, etc. Here is a list with phone numbers and map key letters. There is a free public launch ramp at Capell Cove.

A	Putah Creek Park	(707) 966-2116
B	Rancho Monticello	(707) 966-2188
C	Berryessa Marina Resort	(707) 966-2161
D	Spanish Flat Resort	(707) 966-7700
E	Steel Park Resort	(707) 966-2123
F	Pleasure Cove Resort	(707) 966-2172
G	Markley Cove Resort	(707) 966-2134

Boating: All boating is permitted. Launching and marinas are at resorts listed above.

Information: Napa Chamber of Commerce, P.O. Box 9164, Spanish Flat Station, Napa, CA 94558, (707) 226-7455

Lake Chabot (map - p. 107)

Lake Chabot rates among the best Northern California urban lakes. This 315 acre lake is in the almost 5,000 acre Anthony Chabot Regional Park. Located just east of San Leandro, Chabot boasts big channel cats and Florida-strain largemouth bass, as well as a good and steady supply of stocked rainbow trout. This lake has good stretches of shore fishing access, lots of large fish and a year-round schedule. To get to Chabot take Lake Chabot Road from Castro Valley or Fairmont Drive east from San Leandro.

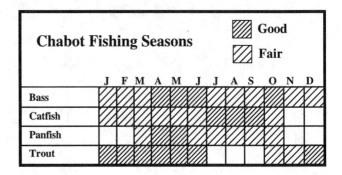

Chabot Fishing Seasons — Good / Fair

	J	F	M	A	M	J	J	A	S	O	N	D
Bass												
Catfish												
Panfish												
Trout												

Chabot Fishing Tips

Bass fishing is at its best in early spring. Fish up to 5 pounds are not uncommon. Purple and brown plastic worms are local favorites as are plugs like the Rebel Deep Wee R. Rebel and Rapala minnow-type plugs also produce as do spinnerbaits and jigs. Bass Cove is productive as is the north shore of Honker Bay. Channel cats at Chabot are in the 1-4 pound class, but the marina reports some much larger catches. Chicken livers are one of the best baits here. Nightcrawlers produce catfish as well as some bass. Summer is the best time for catfishing, but they are taken all year-round. Chabot also has some top-notch crappie activity in the spring. They range up to a foot long and are mostly taken on artificial crappie jigs like Fle Flys. Experienced anglers recommend using the smallest jigs available. Trout are the standby species at Chabot. Trolling is a popular angling technique as is anchored and shore fishing with a sliding sinker rig. Garlic marshmallows and salmon eggs are top baits. Spinners and trout spoons (like Kastmasters in 1/8 ounce gold) are good at lake inflows or when fish are near shore.

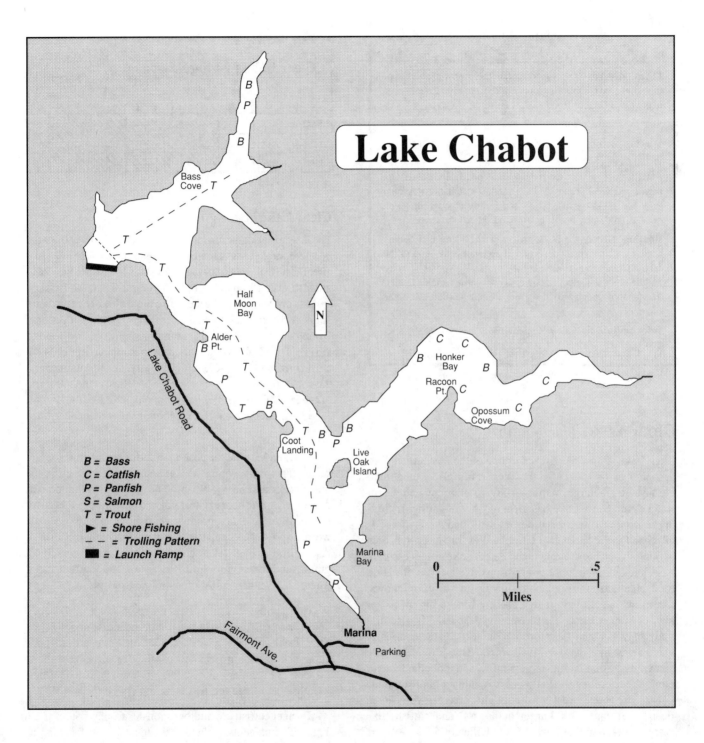

Lake Chabot

Bass Cove

Half Moon Bay

Alder Pt.

Honker Bay

Racoon Pt.

Opossum Cove

Coot Landing

Live Oak Island

Marina Bay

N

B = Bass
C = Catfish
P = Panfish
S = Salmon
T = Trout
► = Shore Fishing
– – = Trolling Pattern
■ = Launch Ramp

Lake Chabot Road

Fairmont Ave.

Marina

Parking

0   .5
Miles

Lake Chabot Facts

Location: Lake Chabot is located in the southwest corner of the 5000 acre Chabot Regional Park. Entrance to the marina is off Lake Chabot Road east of Fairmont Avenue.

Size: 315 surface acres

Species: Rainbow trout, channel catfish, largemouth bass, panfish

Facilities: The lake itself has rental boats, a coffee shop, picnic areas, and other day-use facilities. Chabot Regional Park has hiking trails, group and family campgrounds, an equestrian center, a golf course and other facilities.

Boating: No private boats are allowed. There is a fishing access trail that provides good shore access all around the lake. There are also nine fishing piers. Rowboats, canoes, paddle boats and electric powered boats are available to rent. The Chabot Queen provides a tour around the shoreline of the lake.

Information: East Bay Regional Park District, (510) 562-7275

Clear Lake (map - p. 109)

Clear Lake is now recognized as one of the best largemouth bass and catfish lakes in the West. It's also exceptional because it's a large, natural body of nutrient-rich warm water. And Clear Lake has great on-shore facilities including resorts, marinas, restaurants, towns, and much more. It bills itself as the "Bass Capital of the West" and it hosts scores of major black bass tournaments. Clear Lake produces many large bucketmouth for several reasons. It all starts with a rich food chain, from zooplankton on up to native minnows, threadfin shad and crayfish. These all make big meals for always hungry bass. Furthermore, Clear Lake is a natural body of water and therefore not subject to fluctuations in water level like dammed reservoirs. This provides stable spawning grounds for largemouths and abundant cover along the shorelines. Shallowness is another almost unique Clear Lake asset. Most Northern California reservoirs are in deep, cold canyons. Largemouth bass (and catfish) like warm water, and that's what Clear Lake provides. Anglers catch more bass and bigger bass at Clear Lake than any other lake in the West. Average largemouths run anywhere from 3 to 5 pounds, and monsters up to 10 pounds are caught frequently. Commercial carp operators at Clear Lake have netted and released bass in the 16 to 17 pound range.

Clear Lake Fishing Seasons

	J	F	M	A	M	J	J	A	S	O	N	D
Bass			Good	Good	Good	Good	Good	Good	Good	Good		
Catfish		Fair	Good	Good	Good	Good	Good	Good	Good	Good		
Panfish		Fair	Good	Good	Good	Good	Good	Good	Good	Good		

Good: ▨ Good Fair: ▨ Fair

Clear Lake Fishing Tips

The larger Florida-strain largemouth are taking over from the northern-strain bass that were first planted in Clear Lake just after the turn of the century. Florida bass have been known to grow to over 15 pounds in just 5 years. When the bass are "turned on" at Clear Lake they are caught almost everywhere. Anglers report catching and releasing 30 to 40 fish per day. During the spring and early summer months, the north end of the lake from Lakeport on up north to Rodman Slough is the most consistent bass producing territory. In late summer and the winter months, anglers seem to score best at the south end of the lake. Good winter bass spots include Konoti Harbor, Jago Bay, Glen Haven Reef, Monitor Point and Clear Lake Keys.

April and May are the peak months for bass action at Clear Lake. This is spawning season and big bass are up in the tules, rocks and heavy brush. The flipping technique was developed in tule beds at Clear Lake. Tule beds provide cover for the bass and are productive fishing locales. Plastic worms, spinnerbaits and Pig 'n Jigs are productive offerings. As California bass lakes go, Clear Lake has a variety of grasses and cover more similar to eastern and southern lakes. There are over 100 miles of shoreline to work.

After spring spawning, bass move back out into deeper, cooler water. They also hang out in the shade under docks. Shag Rock, Soda Bay and Henderson Point are all good summer bass fishing areas because they're fairly deep—15 to 20 feet. September and October are usually excellent bass months—and there are less bass anglers on the water.

Channel catfish are another monster trophy fish of Clear Lake. Tournaments are held here regularly. Catfish ranging from 10-20 pounds are not uncommon. The best catfish bite is in the evening from about 9 p.m. to 1 a.m. Another good bite is from 4 to 7 a.m. The largest catfish are caught at night. The best catfishing areas are near sloughs, or where you can find bottom depressions. Rodman Slough, at the north end

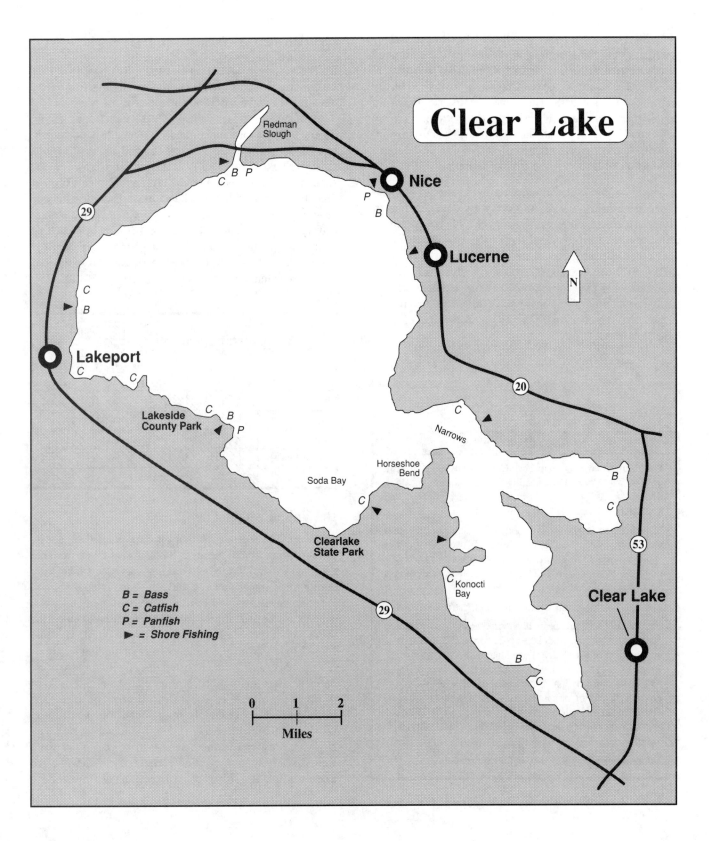

Clear Lake

Redman
Slough

29

C B P

C

B

Lakeport

C

C C

Lakeside
County Park

C B
P

Soda Bay

Clearlake
State Park

C

▶ Nice
P
B

▲ Lucerne

N

20

C

Narrows

Horseshoe
Bend

C

B

C

53

C Konocti
Bay

Clear Lake

B
C

B = Bass
C = Catfish
P = Panfish
▶ = Shore Fishing

29

0   1   2
Miles

of the lake, Cache Creek at the south end, Kesley Creek at the state park, and the slough at the county park are all good spots. Holes near Monitor Island, Rattlesnake Island and at Jago Bay are also productive. Clams, anchovies and turkey livers are all good bait. But some anglers use live water dogs-either under a bobber or on the bottom. Trophy largemouth have been "mistakenly" caught using this approach. Another popular method is to fish minnows about 5 to 8 feet under a bobber along rocky shorelines.

Black crappie is the dominate crappie species at Clear Lake. And this is being reinforced with large plantings of Florida-strain black crappie. Catches of 2 or 3 pound fish are now common, maybe because these fish are active feeders all year-round. These guys are known to hang out as far down as 25 feet. Bluegill can be taken along the shoreline virtually anywhere when the water warms up in the summer. Another fishing "opportunity" at Clear Lake, particularly for archers, is the carp. The National Bowfishing Tournament is held here each May.

Clear Lake Facts

Location: Clear Lake is in Lake County between Hwy. 101 and I-5, with Hwy. 20 connecting the two and running along the lake's north shore. It's about 110 miles north of San Francisco.

Size: It is the largest natural body of water entirely within California. It is about 20 miles long, has over 100 miles of shoreline and 43,800 surface acres of water. It's deepest point is 60 feet with an average of 28 feet. Lake elevation is 1300 feet.

Species: Florida-strain largemouth bass, catfish, panfish

Facilities: There are probably more facilities surrounding Clear Lake than any other lake in California. The only public camping facility is at Clear Lake State Park, (707) 279-4293. Reservations are suggested during the summer months, (800) 444-7275. Information on the scores of other resorts, campgrounds, launching ramps, marinas, etc. is available from the Greater Lakeport Chamber of Commerce, (707) 263-5092 and from the Clear Lake Chamber of Commerce, (707) 994-3600.

Information: See the phone numbers listed above.

Del Valle Lake (map - p. 111)

Del Valle Lake is located in Del Valle Regional Park near Livermore. This park offers year-round camping, fishing and day use. The lake has 1000 surface acres of water and 16 miles of shoreline. Del Valle provides a varied and exciting fishery. Trout, largemouth and smallmouth bass, catfish, bluegill and striped bass all provide good action at various times during the year. Del Valle attracts large crowds in the summer, but September through May provides plenty of quiet time for fishing, hiking and boating. Facilities include developed campsites, snack bars, day use areas, complete bait and tackle sales, boat rentals and a 4-lane boat launching ramp. Swimming is allowed, and a 10 mph speed limit is enforced on the lake. A tour boat operates in the summer as well as scheduled naturalists programs.

Del Valle Fishing Seasons	J	F	M	A	M	J	J	A	S	O	N	D
Bass												
Bluegill												
Catfish												
Striped Bass												
Trout												

Good / Fair

Del Valle Fishing Tips

Trout provide the most action and are planted regularly. Trout ranging from 6 inches to 8 pounds are taken from the lake year-round. Anglers working very deep take trout during the summer months. Favorite baits include salmon eggs, nightcrawlers and cheese. The dam area and creek channel are the two top producers. Where the creek enters the south end of the lake is very productive in April, May and June. Trollers score on a variety of lures including Kastmasters, Panther Martins and Roostertails. Trolling flashers are optional. Bass go for rubber worms, crankbaits and crickets. A Rapala or Rebel is also often effective on bass, and sometimes works well on the trout population. Catfish can provide anglers with steady action if you can locate them. Nightcrawlers, red worms, clams and stinkbaits all work well. Usually anglers who find a school of catfish will catch a stringer full. Big striped bass surprise anglers from time to

surprise anglers from time to time. Although not common, they do cruise the Del Valle waters. Most are taken by fishermen working for trout or bass.

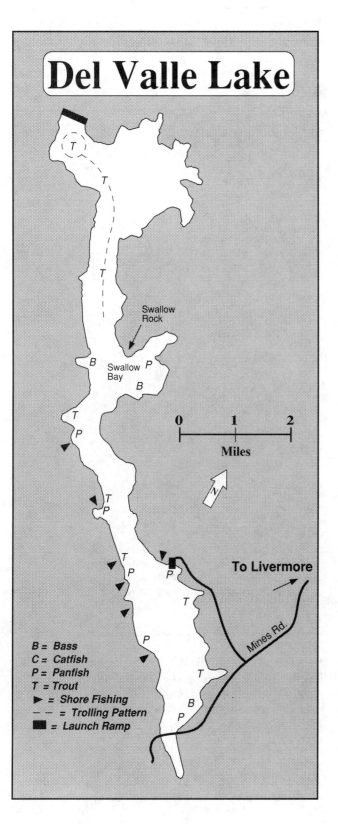

Del Valle Lake Facts

Location: Del Valle Lake is in the Del Valle Regional Park, 10 miles south of Livermore.

Size: The lake has almost 1000 surface acres of water and about 16 miles of shoreline.

Species: There is an active planting program. Species include trout, largemouth bass, catfish, bluegill and striped bass.

Facilities: The lake itself has two swimming beaches, four-lane boat ramp, tour boats and rental boats. Del Valle Regional Park, at 3445 acres, has picnicking, camping, hiking trails and an equestrian center.

Information: Del Valle Park, 6999 Del Valle Rd., Livermore, CA 94550, (925) 373-0332; East Bay Regional Parks, 7000 Del Valle Rd., Livermore, CA 94550, (510) 562-7275

Indian Valley Lake (map - p. 112)

Indian Valley Reservoir has a different personality from many other Northern California major fishing lakes. It's somewhat off the beaten path and often overshadowed by Clear Lake, it's big neighbor 15 miles to the west. This means that the fishing pressure is lighter than at most other lakes. And none of the brush and trees in the lake canyons and valleys were cleared before filling began in 1974; therefore, there is excellent fish habitat. Indian Valley has lots of largemouths (some smallmouths) in the 3-5 pound range, and both Eagle Lake and rainbow trout up to 25 inches. There are also good populations of catfish, crappie and bluegill. At 1,475 feet elevation, most of the lake is about 120 feet deep, and up to 200 feet at the dam.

Indian Valley Fishing Seasons														Good
														Fair
	J	F	M	A	M	J	J	A	S	O	N	D	
Bass														
Catfish														
Panfish														
Trout														

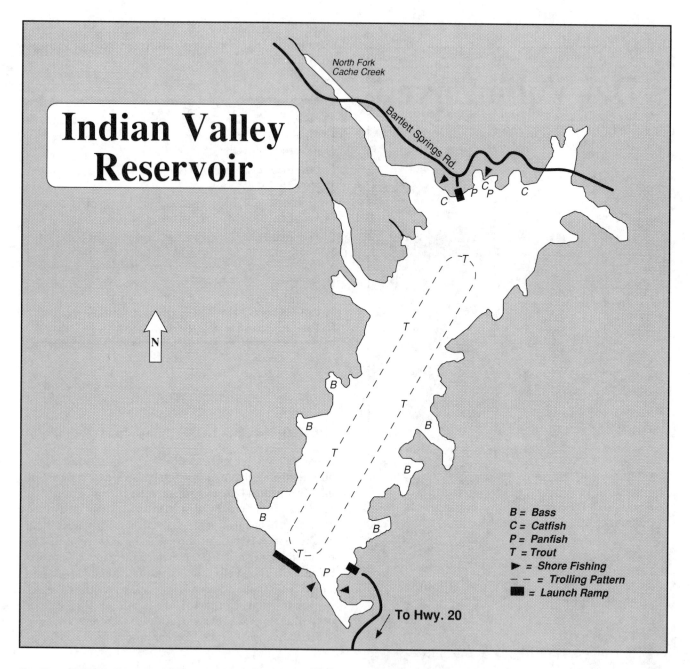

Indian Valley Reservoir

North Fork Cache Creek

Bartlett Springs Rd.

N

To Hwy. 20

B = Bass
C = Catfish
P = Panfish
T = Trout
► = Shore Fishing
– – = Trolling Pattern
■ = Launch Ramp

Indian Valley Fishing Tips

Shallow trolling produces trout in the winter. Summer trollers move deeper and closer to the dam. Try to stay above the old Cache Creek Channel to avoid snags, especially when the water level is down. Good offerings include Flatfish, Triple Teasers, Needlefish and nightcrawlers behind flashers. Best trolling action is usually from first light through midmorning and again from late afternoon to dark. Flashers like Dave Davis or Ford Fenders are good but no added weight is needed in off-light hours. But even in cooler months, midday trolling success may require getting down to about 25 feet. Surprisingly, locals also find success when casting to exposed tree tops that appear when water levels fall. Rooster Tails and Mepps produce this way, even out in deep water.

May is the peak of the largemouth spring season at Indian Valley. Look for them right along the edge of deep underwater ridges and at the ends of brushy arms and inlets just off main lake. On the west shore, work the rocky coves and points. On the steeper eastern shore, work the shoreline brush that marks the drop to deeper water. Most fish, even in spring, are taken in the 8 to 12 foot range—maybe because the water is very clear.

Dark plastic worms (black and motor oil) are the most consistent producers for bass. And spinnerbaits and crankbaits work when offered at the right depth. Flipping is an especially good technique at Indian Valley because of the great cover. And heavier than normal line (say 10-14 pounds) is used by most bass anglers because of the abundance of submerged brush.

The far north end of Indian Valley is prime crappie territory. Look for them to congregate here, especially in midsummer. Anglers work the trees with crappie jigs until a school is located. Casting and vertical jigging at the right depth both work. Most action takes place 10 to 15 feet below the surface. Bluegill fishing is also strong in July and into August. And these Indian Valley panfish are big. Don't be surprised to catch them in the 10 to 12 inch range. Red worms under a bobber in 1 to 5 feet of water is the way to go. And do use small hooks (about #8)—even big bluegill have small mouths.

```
┌──────────────────────────────────────────────────┐
│              Indian Valley Lake Facts             │
├──────────────────────────────────────────────────┤
│                                                    │
│ Location: In eastern Lake County, off Hwy. 20      │
│ between Clear Lake and Williams.                   │
│                                                    │
│ Size: About 6 miles long and 1 to 2 miles wide.    │
│ There are 3800 surface acres of water and 39 miles │
│ of shoreline.                                      │
│                                                    │
│ Species: Rainbow trout, largemouth and smallmouth  │
│ bass, catfish and panfish                          │
│                                                    │
│ Facilities: At the south end there is a store,     │
│ paved launch ramp and campgrounds. The north end   │
│ has paved launching and a primitive campground.    │
│ The warm, clear water is ideal for swimming.       │
│                                                    │
│ Boating: There is a 10 mph speed limit.            │
│                                                    │
│ Information: Indian Valley Store and Campground     │
│ (at the lake's south end), (530) 662-0607          │
│                                                    │
└──────────────────────────────────────────────────┘
```

Los Banos Creek Reservoir

While most anglers read about the O'Neill Forebay or the San Louis Reservoir, there is a small lake just south of those impounds that lies in their shadows. It not only offers a variety of fishing, but provides a variety of other recreational opportunities as well. It's called Los Banos Creek Reservoir.

Los Banos Creek Reservoir is located nine miles from the town of Los Banos. It is 54 miles from Hollister and 77 miles from Stockton. It is south of Santa Nella just off Interstate I-5. To get to the lake, anglers will have to get off at the Los Banos exit along State Highways 152 or 165 since there is no direct freeway access. Pioneer Road will take visitors to Canyon Road which will lead to the lake. Pioneer Road runs into Highway 165 and can be accessed by Volta Road off Highway 154.

The reservoir is the host to trout, bluegill, catfish, and large and smallmouth bass. This small lake offers 410 surface acres and 12 miles of shoreline. It has a paved launch ramp on the northwest side near the dam. Powerboats, sailboats, rowboats, canoes, and inflatables are allowed. A 5 m.p.h. speed limit is enforced.

There are 20 primitive camp sites in the rolling grassy hills that surround Los Banos Creek Reservoir. The sites offer only area water and chemical toilets. There are often good winds for sailing and wind surfing. Swimming and water fowl hunting are also popular, in season.

Los Banos Fishing Seasons	Good (shaded) / Fair (hatched)

Species	J	F	M	A	M	J	J	A	S	O	N	D
Bass			Fair	Fair	Good	Good				Fair	Fair	
Bluegill	Fair	Fair			Good	Good	Good	Good	Good			
Crappie			Fair	Fair	Good	Good	Good					
Trout	Fair	Fair	Fair								Fair	Fair

Los Banos Fishing Tips

Catfish are king at Los Banos. And some of them are quite large. Locals often fish at night in the hot summer months. Spring is the peak of the bass fishery. Most of the catches are in the 1 1/2 to 2 1/2 pound range. A stocking program of mostly 10 to 12 inch rainbow trout makes for a popular attraction in the winter and early spring. Good areas include the dam and launch ramp areas. Power Bait and floating nightcrawlers are proven winners.

```
┌──────────────────────────────────────────────────┐
│                  Los Banos Facts                   │
├──────────────────────────────────────────────────┤
│                                                    │
│ Location: This lake is at an elevation of 328 feet │
│ in the foothills of the grasslands west of Los     │
│ Banos.                                             │
│                                                    │
│ Size: Surface area covers 410 acres.               │
│                                                    │
│ Species: Trout fishing for planters during the     │
│ cooler months, but most warm-water species. Bass,  │
│ catfish, and bluegill are prevelant.               │
│                                                    │
│ Facilities: There are 20 primitive sites around    │
│ the lake with shade ramadas and some trees. No     │
│ water at the sites. Launch ramp. Full facilities   │
│ nearby at Los Banos.                               │
│                                                    │
│ Information: California Parks and Recreation, Four  │
│ Rivers Area, (209) 826-1196                        │
│                                                    │
└──────────────────────────────────────────────────┘
```

Lake Merced (map - p. 114)

San Francisco's Lake Merced is actually two lakes separated by a narrow strip of land. Merced provides very good trout fishing all year-round. So there is no need for anglers on the Peninsula to drive for hours to reach good trout waters. And Merced, surrounded by tules and sitting amid rolling green hills, hardly seems like its in the midst of a major city. Trout fishing tends to be best in the spring and fall but the coastal weather keeps water conditions good throughout the summer. Because of limited runoff, the water remains clear in the winter, also providing good fishing conditions. Black bass, catfish and carp compliment the trout fishery. Rainbow trout range from 6 inches to 10 pounds. 2 pound trout from the North Lake are very common. A state fishing license is required. In addition, a $2.50 daily permit is required on the North Lake and a $0.50 permit on the South Lake. The North Lake is planted once a week with trout ranging 3/4 pound to 10 pounds. California Fish and Game plant approximately 7500 fish in each lake monthly. Lake Merced offers fishing derbies, trout of the month contest, trout of the day contest, limit buttons and whopper buttons.

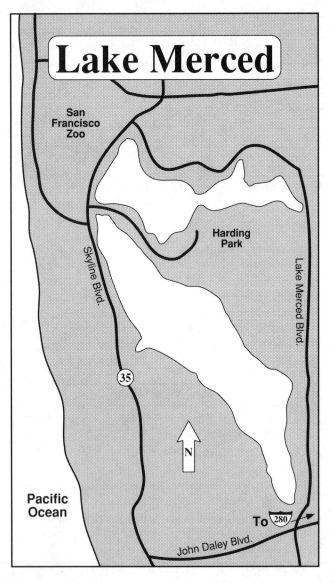

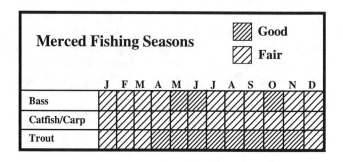

Merced Fishing Seasons		J	F	M	A	M	J	J	A	S	O	N	D
Bass													
Catfish/Carp													
Trout													

Good / Fair

Merced Fishing Tips

Some patterns are apparent at Merced. The North Lake provides larger trout, but results are unpredictable. Also, a consistent stream of smaller trout come from the South Lake. And finally, boat anglers outscore shore anglers on both lakes. So anglers who want to be assured of fish work the South Lake in a boat, and anglers who want the best chance at a lunker, work the North Lake from a boat. Boat anglers are advised to work the tule-lined shoreline; 10 to 30 feet out from the tules is a good bet. Some of the most productive shore fishing spots include the beach on the North Lake, and the bridge and fishing pier on the South Lake. Basic trout fishing methods work here. Bait fishermen score with cheese, nightcrawlers, salmon eggs and marshmallows. Fish with as little weight as possible and 4 to 6 pound test line. Size 6 to 10 hooks work well. Fish from a boat, if possible, because it provides better mobility. Move until you find a fish. Shore fishermen do well, but often need to wait the fish out. Try a variety of baits until you score. Trollers and lure casters also take their share of fish. Mepps, Rooster Tails, Panther Martins and Z-Rays all produce fish. Some trollers often use small flashers in front of nightcrawlers. Black bass fishermen score on spinnerbaits and nightcrawlers. Carp are taken on corn and dough baits.

Lake Merced Facts

Location: In San Francisco, just 1/2 mile from the Pacific Ocean, adjacent to the Harding Golf Course and the San Francisco Zoo. From I-280, take John Daley Blvd. west, turn right on Skyline Blvd and continue to the lake.

Size: The North and South lakes combined are a total of about 386 surface acres.

Species: Primarily a rainbow trout fishery, but there are bass, catfish, panfish and carp

Facilities: Concession stand, boat rental, boat ramps on both lakes, fishing pier

Boating: Row boats, electric power boats and canoes can be rented. Canoes, prams and electric power boats can be launched. No gasoline engines allowed.

Information: Lake Merced Boating & Fishing Co., 1 Harding Rd., San Francisco, CA 94132, (415) 753-1101

Parkway Lake

Parkway Lake is a very good, urban trophy trout fishery. During trout season, a dozen or more trout weighing 10 pounds and up are caught each month. The average fish catch per rod is better than 3 pounds. And all this fine fishing is only about a 30 minute drive for most anglers in the South Bay. Parkway Lake is small—only about 35 acres. But it is deep (about 40 feet) and the water is relatively clear. Parkway plants about 15,000 trout per month, including many larger than 8 pounds. In the summer months, there are catfish (also stocked), bass and panfish to pursue. No license is required, but there is a fishing fee.

Parkway Fishing Seasons   ☒ Good   ☒ Fair

	J	F	M	A	M	J	J	A	S	O	N	D
Bass				☒	☒	☒						
Catfish						☒	☒	☒	☒			
Panfish					☒	☒	☒	☒	☒			
Trout		☒	☒	☒	☒	☒				☒	☒	☒

Parkway Fishing Tips

Bait fishing for trout is popular. Use a sliding sinker rig and bait such as salmon eggs or small garlic marshmallows.

Many larger fish are caught on lures like Mepps Lightin', Rooster Tails and Panther Martins. Wolly worm flies also work. Even though the fish can be big, light tackle is in order. Spinning tackle with 4 or 6 pound line, with patience and skill, will land even a 10 pounder. Trout fishing is good at the northwest corner of the lake and at the south end. Catfishing is best on the east shore. Work the brushy areas for Florida-strain largemouth bass. This type of facility is a great place to teach a kid about fishing. Some days it's hard not to catch fish!

Parkway Lake Facts

Location: About 5 miles south of San Jose via Hwy. 101. Take the Bernal exit west and then head south on Monterey Rd. (Rte. 52). Then go west on Metcaff to the lake entrance.

Size: Parkway has 35 surface acres of water.

Species: Planted rainbow trout and catfish, bass, panfish

Facilities: Parkway is a popular day-use fishing destination. There is a store, picnic area and rental row boats. No private boats are allowed.

Information: Parkway Lake, (408) 629-9111; Coyote Discount Bait & Tackle, (408) 463-0711

Putah Creek

There are many wonderful trout streams in Northern California. But almost all of them are so far away from the Bay Area that a multiday trip is required to fish them. Not so with Putah Creek. It's located just below Lake Berryessa a few miles out of the town of Winters. This is a comfortable drive for Bay Area and Sacramento area anglers.

In the late 1950's, Monticello Dam was constructed in a narrow canyon stretch of Putah Creek, forming Lake Berryessa. Prior to this, Putah was one of the finer smallmouth bass fisheries in the state. But the cold outflow from Berryessa changed all that. Planted rainbow trout flourished, and the trout fishing is still good today. One more attraction—Putah Creek can be fished in winter when most Sierra streams are closed. Putah is a wide, flat stream that is ideal for fly fishing as well as for bait and lure angling. Access is very good via Hwy. 128 and camping is available. Regulations and limits vary by season, so be informed. The good trouting fishing section extends for about five miles below Lake Berryessa.

San Luis Reservoir/O'Neill Forebay
(map - p. 117)

San Luis Reservoir and the adjoining O'Neill Forebay offer some of the best freshwater striped bass fishing anywhere. This includes consistent trophy-sized fish opportunities as well as fast-paced action on bass in the 2 to 8 pound range. The primary purpose of most people who visit San Luis is to catch striped bass. Maybe that's because facilities are limited, and in this rolling but arid setting on the southern slopes of Pacheco Pass, it can get hot and it can get windy. But if you're looking for a place for some dedicated, first class striper angling, San Luis should be your choice. There is no managed fishery program at San Luis. Rather, the great striper fishing is a result of the millions of gallons of Delta water that is pumped into O'Neill and San Luis. Small fry and fingerling stripers that are hatched in the Delta's sloughs come along in the pumping process. Once in the forebay and reservoir, stripers grow and thrive.

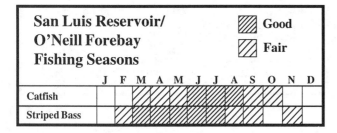

San Luis Reservoir/ O'Neill Forebay Fishing Seasons												▨ Good ▨ Fair
	J	F	M	A	M	J	J	A	S	O	N	D
Catfish			▨	▨	▨	▨	▨	▨	▨	▨		
Striped Bass		▨	▨	▨	▨	▨	▨	▨	▨		▨	

San Luis Reservoir/O'Neill Forebay Fishing Tips

Striped bass in the 30-pound class are not uncommon, and a good number of 40 to 50 pounders have been taken in the lake's 20-plus year history. The largest San Luis striper, actually caught in the forebay in June 1988 by Ted Furnish, weighed in at a whopping 66 pounds (50 inches in length). It is the current IGFA landlocked striped bass world record. Trolling a plug on 15 pound test line hooked this giant.

Trolling probably produces more stripers at San Luis than any other approach. Most fish are taken from 15 to 40 feet down. The basic strategy is to pull a threadfin shad (the primary forage fish) imitation lure along the edge of a break line, channel, or over the top of submerged hills. Rebels and Rapalas, 6 or 7 inch broken-back plugs, are among the most productive offerings. Some anglers use a spreader so they can pull two lures at the same time. Hair Raisers (1/2 or 3/8 ounce in yellow or white) are often used in conjunction with the minnow-style plug. Other good trolling offerings include 1/2 ounce Kastmasters and Krocodiles. Fourteen-pound test line is about right, but some anglers looking for lunkers move up to the mid-twenties. A good trolling speed is around 3 mph, depending on lure action.

The key is to find fish, and electronic fish finders are very helpful on these big lakes. Leadcore trolling line can be used to get the lures to the proper depth. Downriggers also work. But at times all that is needed is a deep-diving plug.

Vertical jigging using spoons and jigs is another method that produces once a school has been located. Surface feeding stripers, tipped off by bird action, can be taken by casting plugs or spoons. Stripers are school fish. So anglers repeat successful tactics in the same locale. Casting the shoreline structure from a boat also works at San Luis and O'Neill. Rocky points, banks, shallow mounts, and along the boulder-lined dam are all good prospects. Most agree that stripers can be taken year-round. But March through July is a prime period. Early mornings and late evenings are the best times to chase stripers.

Bank fishing can be quite successful in both San Luis and O'Neill. One tried and true method is to bait cut anchovies on a sliding sinker rig. Stripers move up into the shallows to forage on threadfin shad, and will take these anchovies...just like their cousins in the Delta. Casting plugs and spoons from shore is another good approach.

Some of the top producing areas in the main lake are the eastern shoreline of Portuguese Creek and Lone Oak Bay (troll about 500 yards off shore), Willow Springs Bay, Romero Point (underwater islands), and the dam face. Casting the flats on the south and southeastern shorelines of the forebay is often productive. A good trolling route in the forebay is at the deep canal just inside the levee. Work the buoy line, then turn and come back along the face of the dam.

San Luis Reservoir/O'Neill Forebay Facts
Location: It lies about 150 miles southeast of San Francisco, 75 miles northeast of Fresno and 12 miles west of Los Banos, on Hwy. 152.
Size: San Luis—13,000 surface acres of water with 65 miles of shoreline. Maximum water depth is 304 feet. O'Neill—2700 surface acres of water with 12 miles of shoreline. Maximum depth is 61 feet.
Species: Primary attraction is striped bass, including many trophy-sized fish. There are also largemouth bass, catfish and panfish.
Facilities: San Luis—camping (79 developed sites) at the Bosalt Area; launching at Bosalt and at Dinosaur Point. O'Neill—camping (undeveloped) at Medeiros; launching at Medeiros and San Luis Creek Area.
Boating: All boating permitted, but there is no boat rental, fuel or marina.
Information: San Luis Reservoir and O'Neill Forebay Camping, (209) 826-1196

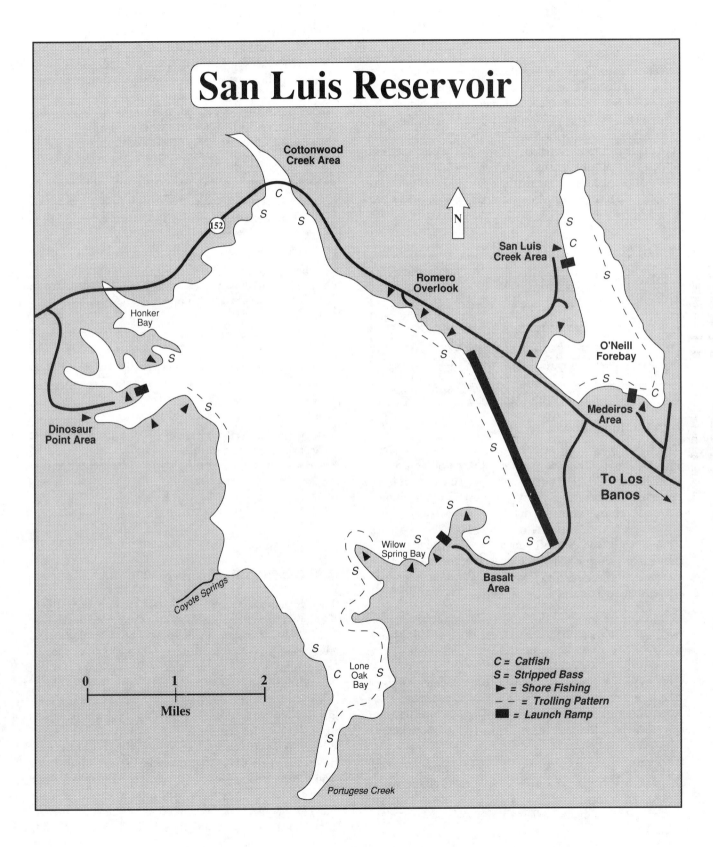

San Luis Reservoir

Cottonwood
Creek Area

152

San Luis
Creek Area

Romero
Overlook

O'Neill
Forebay

Honker
Bay

Medeiros
Area

Dinosaur
Point Area

To Los
Banos

Coyote Springs

Wilow
Spring Bay

Basalt
Area

Lone
Oak
Bay

| 0 | 1 | 2 |

Miles

C = Catfish
S = Stripped Bass
► = Shore Fishing
– – = Trolling Pattern
■ = Launch Ramp

Portugese Creek

San Pablo Lake (map - p. 119)

Excellent fishing is available at this day-use reservoir located just east of the San Francisco Bay near Berkeley. The lake's record rainbow is 15 pounds, and many are caught in the 3-6 pound range. Trout plants, done weekly, average about 1 pound per fish. Anglers at San Pablo frequently average 2 to 3 trout per rod, from both boat and shore. The only live bait allowed at San Pablo are red worms and nightcrawlers. San Pablo offers many good shore fishing locations for trout and catfish. For boaters, a topographical map showing the holes to fish is for sale at the lake for less than $1.00.

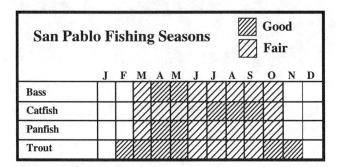

San Pablo Fishing Seasons		J	F	M	A	M	J	J	A	S	O	N	D
Bass				▨	▨	▨	▨	▨	▨	▨	▨		
Catfish				▨	▨	▨	▨	▨	▨	▨	▨		
Panfish				▨	▨	▨	▨	▨	▨	▨	▨		
Trout			▨	▨	▨	▨	▨	▨	▨	▨	▨	▨	

Good ▨ Fair ▨

San Pablo Fishing Tips

Trout fishing is good at San Pedro throughout its open months. From opening day until about June trollers take fish right near the surface. During spring when the water is high, fish closer to shore for warmer water. Best fishing at this time is from shore to about 30 feet out. In summer as water warms, try starting from 35 feet out from shore. Look for deep holes close to shore and drop-off structures. From June through July trollers score at about 15 feet. Best depth in August and September is from 25 to 35 feet. Late season trollers work up closer to the surface.

Most of the shoreline on the west side of the reservoir is well suited for shore angling. Trout shore fishing at San Pablo is best using a sliding sinker rig and salmon eggs, marshmallows, nightcrawlers and cheese. Inflate nightcrawlers or use marshmallows to float eggs, nightcrawlers or cheese up off the bottom. Casting spinners and spoons also works from shore. Boat trout anglers troll (behind flashers) nightcrawlers, Rooster Tails, Triple Teasers, Kastmasters and Panther Martins.

April and May are usually the peak largemouth bass months. In spring, plastic grubs, tube baits and plastic worms are top producers. Crankbaits and spinnerbaits work in the warm weather months. Inflated nightcrawlers also produce bass.

Catfish in the 5 to 12 pound range are common at San Pablo. They can be taken all the time, but peak action occurs in the late afternoon and early evening from July through October. Nightcrawlers, cheese, chicken livers and even salmon eggs all produce. Crappie fishing is best from March until early June. Two of the top spots are the back end of Scow Canyon and off the Berkeley Tower shore.

San Pablo Lake Facts
Location: In the hills northeast of Berkeley and east of El Cerrito, off San Pablo Dam Road
Size: 860 surface acres of water. Length is about 4 miles. Depth is 173 feet at the dam.
Species: Planted and holdover rainbow trout including some trophy fish, planted catfish, resident bass, crappie and blue-gill
Facilities: Launch ramp (4 lane), boat rental, store, picnic area
Boating: Row, electric and gasoline power boats are rented. The southeastern end of the lake (the Waterfowl Preserve) is restricted to non-gasoline powered boats.
Season: Mid-February to mid-November
Information: San Pablo Reservoir, 7301 San Pablo Dr., El Sobrante, CA 94803, (510) 223-1661

Lake Sonoma (map - p. 120)

Lake Sonoma is the newest major reservoir in Northern California, and it's only a 90 minute drive from the Golden Gate Bridge. On-shore facilities have been developed, and everything is in place for fishing and boating fun. Sonoma was formed with the construction of Warm Springs Dam at the confluence of Dry Creek and Warm Springs Creek. Filling began in 1982 and finished in 1985. The lake is really divided into two sections. In the main body, water skiing and speed boating are permitted. But up in the Dry Creek and Warm Springs Creek arms, very little of the brush and trees were cleared, so the bass habitat is ideal. This fact combined with a 10 mph boat speed limit makes bass fishing a pleasure. Here the shoreline is thick with submerged and partially submerged vegetation. Sonoma offers largemouth and small-mouth bass, rainbow trout (actually landlocked steelhead),

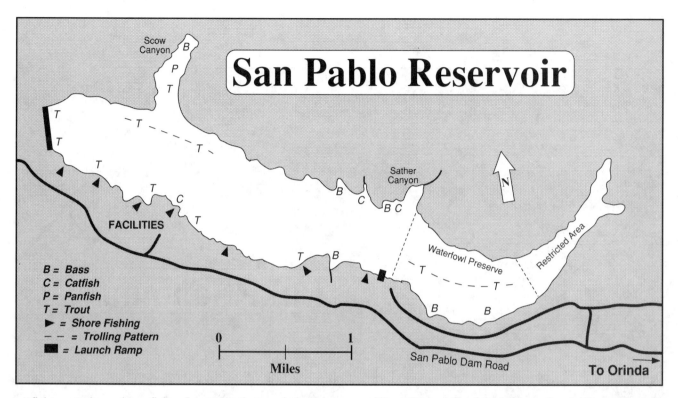

catfish, crappie and sunfish. Largemouths are hybrids (northern strain and Florida), and fish approaching 10 pounds have been caught. And Lake Sonoma has one of the best and biggest redear sunfish populations in the state. Average fish run from 3/4 to 1 pound with 1 1/2 pounders not that uncommon.

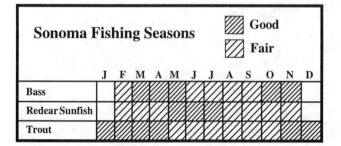

Sonoma Fishing Tips

The Department of Fish and Game is managing Lake Sonoma as a warm water fishery. So emphasis has been placed on largemouth bass and redear sunfish. Trout are not planted, and the holdover population of steelhead trout originally trapped behind the dam is dwindling. Bass action is good at Sonoma, but most of the fish are still small—less than the 12 inch legal limit. But 7-8 pounders are caught each year. Because of the vegetation, almost the entire lake, except the waterski area, offers good fishing. Two top producer areas

are Warm Springs Creek and Cherry Creek. Twin-tail grubs are effective at Sonoma as are plastic worms and Pig 'n Jigs.

Because of the lack of trout plants and the somewhat stunted nature of the bass population, the fantastic redear action stands out at Sonoma. Find the brush at Sonoma and you'll find schools of delightfully tasting redear. They're back up in the cover where limbs are sticking out of the water. Some of the best redear fishing takes place in the Upper Dry Creek, Cherry Creek, and Yorty Creek. Brush Creek and Warm Springs Creek are also good. Bait anglers use red worms and mealworms. Mini-jigs, cast and worked in the cover, also work.

Lake Sonoma Facts
Location: In Sonoma County between Cloverdale and Geyersville off Hwy. 101
Size: 3600 surface acres of water with 73 miles of shoreline. Lake elevation is 495 feet.
Species: Largemouth bass, smallmouth bass, redear sunfish, steelhead trout, catfish, bluegill
Facilities: There is a marina, store, boat rental, and launch ramp (fee) on the south end. Across the bridge at the south end is a public, free launch ramp which requires some walking to its boat parking area. Public launching is also available at the north end off Hot Springs Rd. Public camping (110 sites) is available around the lake. There are also 113 hike-in and boat-in public campsites at Sonoma.
Information: Lake Sonoma Recreation Area, (707) 433-9483; Lake Sonoma Marina, (707) 433-2200

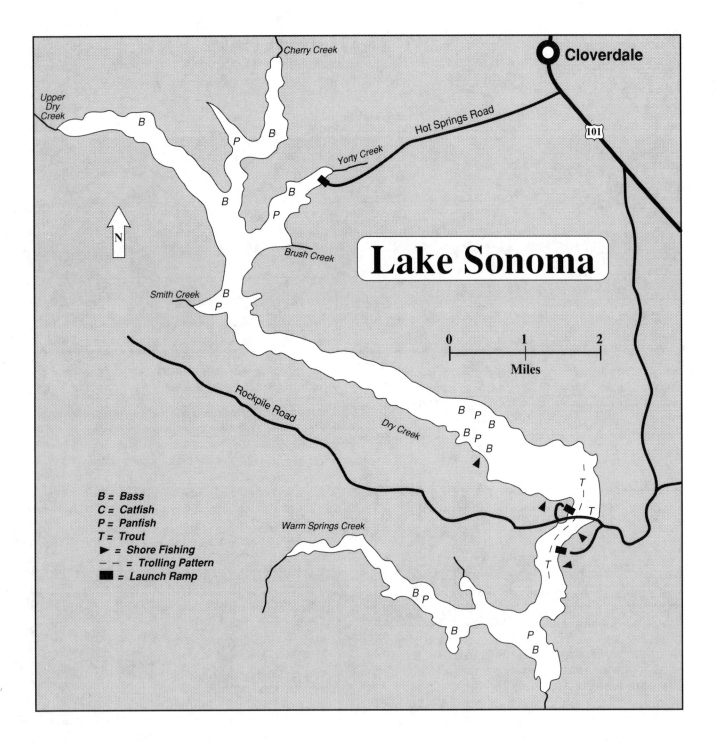

Los Vaqueros Reservoir

A big, new fishing opportunity has sprung up in the East Bay. And some experts believe it could become the best freshwater fishing among all of the 45 Bay Area lakes. Plus, Los Vaqueros Reservoir is set in beautiful, picturesque rolling hills that cover about 18,000 acres of wildlands. The lake itself is 1,500 acres, making it by far the largest East Bay lake. A marina with boat rental is now open, providing access to rainbow trout, large-mouth bass, and catfish. Close-in drop-offs are also expected to make for excellent shore fishing.

The south gate, off Vasco Road, out of Livermore provides access to the marina and to a hiking trail that extends about half way around the lake and yields some excellent views. The north entrance, on Walnut Avenue, out of Brentwood is great for long distance bike rides. Currently, no private boats or dogs are allowed at Los Vaqueros. The south entrance is about 3 miles north of the Vasco Road-580 interchange near Livermore. Information: Los Vaqueros Marina, (925) 371-2628.

Other Bay Area Freshwater Hot Spots

North Bay: There are seven Marin Water District Lakes in the County. Lagunitas and Bon Tempe Lakes have been planted with trout in recent years. Lake Lagunitas, in 1989, was converted to Wild Trout status by DFG. Special regulations apply, but fishing should improve. No boats are allowed on any of these lakes. Other fish producing Marin lakes include Alpine, Kent, Soulajule and Nacasio. Anglers hike to Kent and Alpine Lakes for trout, some quite large. Soulajule offers black bass and bluegills, but is not conveniently located. More accessible Nacasio has an overpopulation of carp as well as bass, panfish and catfish. In winter, the mouths of Lagunitas and Walker Creeks, downstream of the Hwy. 1 bridge, offer steelhead and silver salmon prospects.

East Bay: The East Bay has a wonderful collection of lake fishing opportunities. Chabot, Del Valle, Isabel and San Pablo are featured in this section. Here are some more. Lafayette Reservoir, with three miles of shoreline for boat and bank anglers, is located just south of Lafayette off Tunnel Road. Rainbows, catfish and largemouths are there for the catching. Cartop boats are allowed (with electric motor only) and boat rentals are available.

Lake Terneseal, at 10 acres, can be reached by going east on Hwy. 24 to the Broadway/Hwy. 13 exit. Go left on the access road to the Terneseal entrance. This little lake offers year-round anglers largemouth bass, rainbow trout, panfish, catfish and carp.

Contra Loma Reservoir in Antioch measures 71 acres. Take the Lone Tree exit off Hwy. 4, then south on Lone Tree Way to Fredrickson Lane, then right on Fredrickson Lane to the park entrance. Attractions include largemouth bass, striped bass, crappie, sunfish, channel catfish and American shad.

Cull Canyon Lake offers largemouth, crappie, bluegill and bullhead in its 19 acres. It is located in a 360 acre park off Cull Canyon Road near Castro Valley.

Don Castro Reservoir is a 25 acre lake in Hayward. Take the Center Street exit off Hwy. 580, right on Center to Kelly Street, then left on Kelly to Woodroe. Offerings include rainbow, largemouth, bluegill, crappie, sunfish, channel catfish and bullhead.

Shadow Cliffs Reservoir, a 75 acre lake near Pleasanton, has some extremely good trout fishing. There are also largemouth bass, bluegill, channel and white catfish and black crappie. Boats are restricted to 17 feet and there is a launching fee. Take 580 to the Santa Rita Road exit. Go south on Santa Rita to Main Street to Stanley Boulevard. Turn left on Stanley to the park entrance.

Shiner Pond, a 90 acre lake in the Niles area of Fremont, offers a wide variety of fishing. It has striper, trout, bass, catfish, carp, sucker, perch and bluegill. From the Niles area of Fremont enter the Niles Community Park at the foot of H Street. Hike along the Alameda Creek trail to the pond.

The East Bay Regional Park District (510-562-7275) can answer questions on most of these lakes. They also publish a weekly anglers' newsletter which is available for a small subscription fee.

South Bay: Besides Anderson and Parkway Lakes, there are some other good South Bay fishing waters. Coyote Lake, South of Anderson Reservoir, is planted with trout regularly and trout fishing can be good in Coyote Creek below the reservoir. Santa Clara Reservoir System contains 11 lakes in all. One of these, Lexington Reservoir, along Hwy. 17, offers good trout fishing when the water level is adequate. Two smaller reservoirs (Chesbro and Uvas), both west of Morgan Hill, are fished regularly by local anglers for catfish, bass and panfish. In Santa Cruz County, Loch Lomond offers good fishing prospects. This is a beautiful, secluded mountain lake with angling for trout, bass and panfish. Loch Lomond is supervised by the City of Santa Cruz water department.

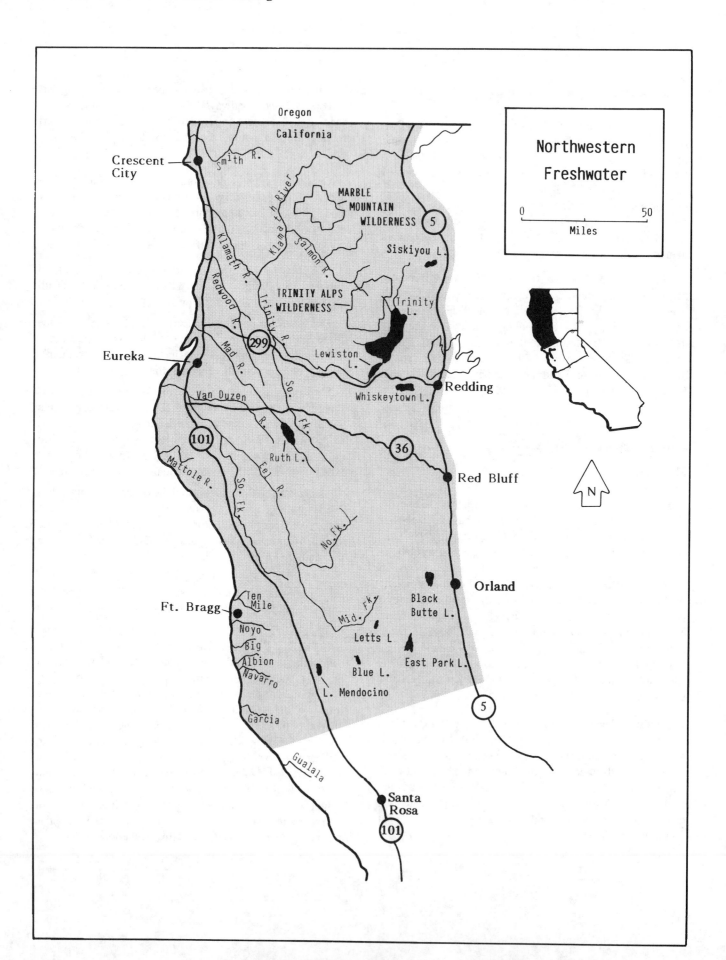

Northwestern Freshwater Fishing

The northwestern section of Northern California is probably best known for its fabulous salmon and steelhead river fishing. Rivers like the Klamath, the Eel and the Smith are legendary. These and others provide wonderful salmon and steelhead action even today. In fact, these rivers are so special that there is a separate chapter, "Coastal River and Stream Fishing," that focuses on these gold mines.

This chapter is concentrated on all of the other fine freshwater fishing opportunities in the California area bounded by the Pacific Ocean to the west, the Oregon border to the north, I-5 to the east, and the northern shore of Clear Lake to the south. The waters in the Northwest are many and varied, encompassing large and small lakes, wilderness areas, cold water and warm water lakes, and trout streams. See map on previous page.

Black Butte Lake (map - p. 124)

Black Butte is a large, warm water reservoir that has good fishing and well-maintained onshore facilities. It is a popular summertime destination for both day-use and over-night visitors. And because it is located in the foothill country of the Sacramento Valley, summertime temperatures do get quite high. But, of course, all this warmth is good for largemouth bass, crappie, catfish and bluegill. There are no fees for fishing, day use, launching or parking—probably because Black Butte is a U.S. Army Corps of Engineers facility.

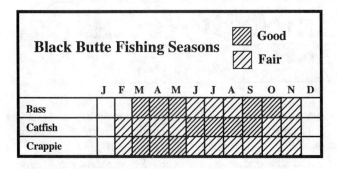

Black Butte Fishing Tips

Black Butte has a decent population of largemouth bass, as well as some smallmouths. Bass in the 5 to 6 pound range,

and larger, are taken each year. Action usually starts with a bang in March. Three good spring areas are Squaw Point, Wackerman's Point and the rocky areas around the dam. Rapalas, Bombers and Rebels in crawdad color are local favorites. September and October, after most of the visitors have disappeared, is another good time for serious bassers at Black Butte. Hot spots include the Eagle Pass day-use area, the launch ramp area, and the island right off the marina. Tossing crankbaits in the early morning or late evening could produce a trophy fish.

Crappie are a major attraction of Black Butte. They grow big (up to 2 pounds) and taste great. March, April and May are prime months. In the spring when the crappie are spawning, look for them in 3 to 4 feet of water around Fisherman's Cove and shallows elsewhere. Also, the extreme end of the main arms of Black Butte plus the dam area are some of the best places to find crappie, especially in the summertime. There are submerged willows in areas of both arms and inside the buoy line at the dam. These will be partially uncovered in the lower-water, summer months. Fish in about 10 feet of water, or even 15 feet. Most successful crappie hunters use live minnows below a bobber on a #4 or #6 baitholder hook. A split shot about a foot above the hook keeps the dorsal fin-hooked bait down. Bass and catfish also hit these rigs so use 4 or 6 pound line.

Summertime brings great catfish action to Black Butte. There are channels, blues, whites and bullheads, ranging from pan-sized to 12 pounds and larger. A local favorite bait rig is to put 4 or 5 dead minnows on a 1/0 or 2/0 hook. About 1 ounce of weight will keep it on the bottom. Nighttime fishing with lanterns is popular.

Black Butte Fishing Seasons													Good / Fair
	J	F	M	A	M	J	J	A	S	O	N	D	
Bass													
Catfish													
Crappie													

Black Butte Lake Facts
Location: About 12 miles west of I-5 at Orland
Size: There are 4500 surface acres of water with 40 miles of shoreline. Elevation is 470 feet.
Species: Largemouth bass, smallmouth bass, crappie, catfish, bluegill
Facilities: There is a full-service marina, store, 3 launch ramps, 2 campgrounds and a day-use area
Information: Black Butte Park Manager, (530) 865-4781; Black Butte Marina, (530) 865-2665

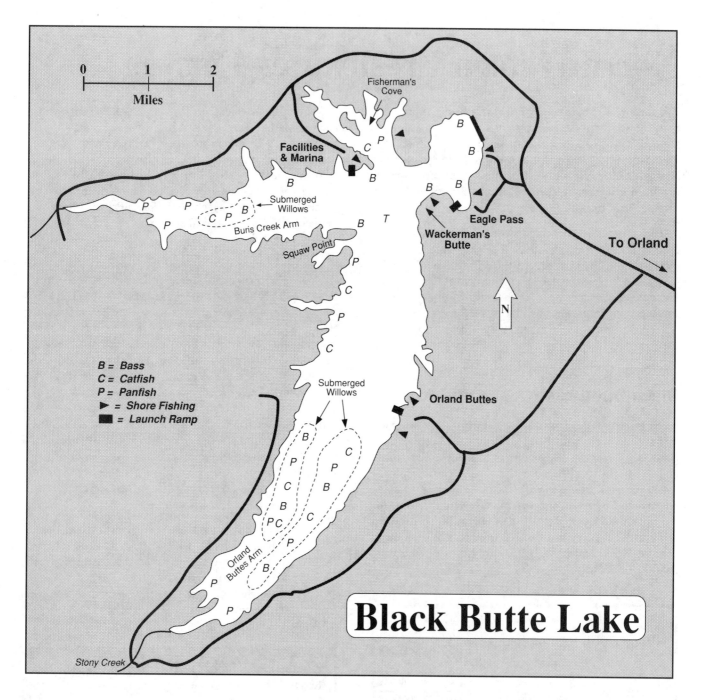

Black Butte Lake

Legend:
B = Bass
C = Catfish
P = Panfish
► = Shore Fishing
■ = Launch Ramp

East Park Reservoir and Letts Lake

East Park Reservoir, known as Logoda Lake by many locals, sits among oak-studded foothills on the west side of the Sacramento Valley. Despite the fact that it's been around for a long time (since 1910) it is still relatively undeveloped as a recreation area. There are unimproved campsites and a gravel launch ramp at this popular destination for boaters, campers and anglers. Warm water species, including large-mouth and spotted bass, crappie, red-ear sunfish, and channel catfish dominate this impoundment with 25 miles of shoreline. Bucketmouths up to 12 pounds and channel cats in the 20 pound class have been taken in recent years. East Park, like its neighbor to the north Black Butte, has fabulous spring crappie action.

The little town of Stonyford is just northwest of East Park. The road going west from there heads up along Stony Creek into the Mendocino National Forest and eventually to Letts Lake. Along this road the north and south forks of Stony Creek hold some nice, mostly small, native rainbow. Letts Lake, at 4500 feet, is about 30 acres. The Forest Service maintains the campgrounds here. The lake is stocked with trout in the colder months, while bass and panfish provide the summertime action. Boating is restricted to canoes, prams and float tubes. Information: Mendocino National Forest, Stonyford Ranger District, Lodoga Rd., Stonyford, CA 95979, (530) 963-3128

Blue Lakes

There are two tiny jewels lying in the coastal range between famous Lake Mendocino and giant Clear Lake. Upper Blue Lake and Lower Blue Lake are spring fed, natural, and filled with clear, cold water. Trout are the main quarry, although there is some good fishing for bass, bluegill and catfish. The lakes are planted by the Department of Fish and Game with free fishing access anywhere around the lakes. A feature that distinguishes Blue Lake from many other NorCal destinations is the onshore facilities. There are four fully developed, privately run resorts on the two adjoining lakes. Amenities include cabins, restaurants, lounges, campgrounds, boat rentals, swimming beaches, launch ramps, stores, etc. Information: Narrows Lodge, (707) 275-2178; Pine Acres Resort, (707) 275-2811; Blue Lakes Lodge, (707) 275-2178; LeTrianon Resort (707) 275-2262

Lewiston Lake

Lewiston Lake, the forebay of massive Trinity Lake, covers 610 acres, is about 6 miles long and has about 16 miles of scenic shoreline. It boasts a healthy population of rainbow, brown and brook trout, including some trophies. Cold, constantly flowing water from Trinity provides an ideal, all season fishing environment. Its small size and protected valley setting makes it ideal for small skiffs, prams and float tubes. Lewiston is a designated fishing lake with a 10 mph boat speed limit. All types of angling are productive. And fishing is good from both boat and shore. This rich tailwater lake system has become extremely popular with fly anglers. Some work its clear waters in the winter when storms rile nearby salmon and steelhead streams. Facilities at Lewiston

include 3 USFS campgrounds, two resorts, a marina, and two launch ramps. Information: Shasta Trinity National Forest, Weaverville, CA 96093, (530) 623-2121; Trinity County Chamber of Commerce, P.O. Box 517, Weaverville, CA 96093, (530) 623-6101; Pine Cove Marina (530) 778-3770

Marble Mountain Wildnerness

The Marble Mountain Wilderness (242,000 acres) is within the boundaries of the Klamath National Forest in Siskiyou County. The area where the Marble Mountains now exist was once part of the flat bottom of an ancient, shallow ocean. Millions of years ago, violent volcanic upheaving and the erosive cutting action of rivers and glaciers combined to form the present day landscape. Almost all of the lakes of the Marble Mountains (there are over 90) were formed by ancient glacial activity. The colors of this wilderness area, from the majestic white of Marble Mountain, to the lush green of Morehouse Meadow, to the deep blue of Cliff Lake, interspersed with various hues of sheer rock cliffs and densely timbered mountainsides, provide a spectacle not soon to be forgotten. These mountains are relatively low—scarcely a peak among them exceeds 7000 feet—but they have an alpine flavor.

Mother nature usually doesn't open the Marble Mountains much before June. Angling for rainbow, brook and brown trout is probably best in September and October, but is rated good earlier in the season. At times, during warm spells in late July and August, fly fishing is apt to be slow as the fish move to the cooler depths. Horse pack trips are popular here and in the Trinity Alps. This is a popular alternative to backpacking. There are a number of pack guides in the area. Wildlife in the wilderness includes black bear, deer and osprey. The extensive trail system is served by nine trailheads, five of which are open to pack animals. Maps of the wilderness area and of the surrounding national forest are available from the Klamath National Forest, 1312 Fairlane Rd., Yreka, CA 96097, (530) 842-6131.

Lake Mendocino

Lake Mendocino offers anglers in the northwestern portion of this wondrous state a unique fishing alternative—striped bass in the 5 to 10 pound range. This 1740 acre reservoir surrounded by woods is just north of Ukiah and just east of Hwy. 101. Army Corp of Engineers maintained facilities includes campgrounds, two launch ramps, two marinas, a swim beach and a hiking trail.

Striper action peaks most years in March and April. May can also be a prime month. Trolling is the method of choice because you can cover lots of water. Most popular offerings include lip-hooked live minnows, blue-backed, shallow-running, silver Rebel or Rapala minnow plugs in the 4 to 6 inch range, and lead-head jigs with red and white tail feathers. Summertime trollers set downriggers at 40 to 50 feet. Best trolling areas vary depending on the season and time of day. Check on current hot spots at one of the marinas. If stripers aren't your cup of tea, Mendocino also harbors small and largemouth bass, trout, panfish and some monster catfish. Information: Lake Mendocino Park Manager, 1160 Mendocino Dr., Ukiah, CA 95482, (707) 462-7581

Migratory Waters

The fact that migratory fish like salmon and steelhead trout share the flowing waters of the northeast with rainbows and browns makes fishing regulations designed to protect juvenile ocean-bound fish somewhat complicated! There are waters open to fishing all year with a three trout or salmon limit, but no more than two salmon. Then there are a few streams open during the normal trout season (last Saturday in April through November 15) with a ten trout limit. There are waters that are closed to fishing completely. And finally, there is an "all other streams" category regulation that runs from the Saturday preceding Memorial Day to November 15 with a limit of five trout. The last category is usually referred to as the north coast stream trout season.

The "Saturday preceding Memorial Day" opener allows trout anglers to explore literally hundreds of miles of smaller, mountain tributary streams that are the permanent homes of resident wild trout. Many of the mountain stream fish are in the 6 to 8 inch range, but 10 to 12 inchers are caught. U.S. Forest Service Maps and topographical maps are recommended. Complete fishing information on the steelhead and salmon aspects of coastal runs can be found in the "Coastal River and Stream" chapter.

Ruth Lake (map - p. 127)

Ruth Lake is a wonderful fishing lake. The only problem is mustering enough energy and determination to decide to make the drive. So most people who do go to Ruth plan on staying for awhile. Of course, one wonderful aspect of the "off-the-beaten-path" nature of this lake is that it's hardly ever crowded. Ruth is a cold water reservoir, built on the upper Mad River in the 1960's, so rainbow trout are the main target of Ruth Lake anglers. But decent black bass fishing has also taken hold.

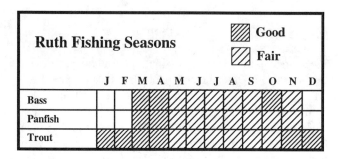

Ruth Fishing Seasons													
	J	F	M	A	M	J	J	A	S	O	N	D
Bass			▨	▨	▨	▨	▨	▨	▨	▨		
Panfish			▨	▨	▨	▨	▨	▨	▨	▨		
Trout	▨	▨	▨	▨	▨	▨	▨	▨	▨	▨	▨	▨

Good / Fair

Ruth Fishing Tips

As is true in many Northern California lakes, late fall, winter and early spring are the easiest times to take trout. The temperature of the surface water is cooler so the trout aren't down deep. Ruth Lake trout move to the shallower, south end of the lake during this period. It is at this time that bank anglers, on both the east and west shores of the extreme south end, do very well. Murky water makes bait a good choice. But one advantage of Ruth is that its water usually returns to a fishable condition within a day of heavy winter rains. Trolling near the surface also produces deep, fat Ruth Lake trout in the cooler months. After April, most trout are found farther and farther north, toward the deeper end of the lake. As the surface water warms up, trollers move farther north to fish deeper waters. The Mad River, below the Ruth Lake dam, provides some fine summertime stream trout action.

Bass spawn in Ruth in the March and April period, producing top action. Most are little guys, but there is an occasional lunker bucketmouth. The shallow end of the lake near the Mad River inflow seems to produce most consistently. Anglers concentrate on rocky points and outcroppings on the west side. Spinnerbaits are local springtime favorites. Crappie fishing is also good especially in the spring.

Ruth Lake Facts

Location: South of Hwy. 36 and near the town of Mad River

Size: 1200 surface acres of water and about 8 miles long; elevation is 2800 feet.

Species: Rainbow trout, largemouth and smallmouth bass, catfish and panfish

Facilities: There is a full-service marina with boat rental and 3 free launch ramps. USFS maintains several campgrounds along the east side of Ruth Lake.

Information: Ruth Lake Marina, (707) 574-6524; Ruth Lake Community Services, (707) 574-6332

Lake Siskiyou (map - p.129)

Lake Siskiyou is a relatively small lake surrounded by beautiful scenery, the most spectacular of which is the great views of 14,162 foot, snow-capped Mt. Shasta. Combine this with trophy-sized trout fishing, good bass fishing, excellent onshore facilities, and no water skiing, and you've got an angler's dream. Trout in the 16 to 22 inch range are commonplace at Siskiyou and they can weigh up to 6 to 8 pounds. The largemouth bass fishing has long been recognized, but now the smallmouth (to 3 1/2 pounds) and spotted bass fisheries are coming on.

Siskiyou Fishing Seasons

▨ Good
▨ Fair

	J	F	M	A	M	J	J	A	S	O	N	D
Bass			▨	▨	▨	▨	▨	▨	▨	▨	▨	▨
Catfish			▨	▨	▨	▨	▨	▨	▨	▨		
Panfish			▨	▨	▨	▨	▨	▨	▨	▨		
Trout	▨	▨	▨	▨	▨	▨	▨	▨	▨	▨	▨	▨

Siskiyou Fishing Tips

In the colder months all kinds of approaches produce trout. That's when cold surface water attracts big browns and rainbows that cruise in the upper several feet of water looking

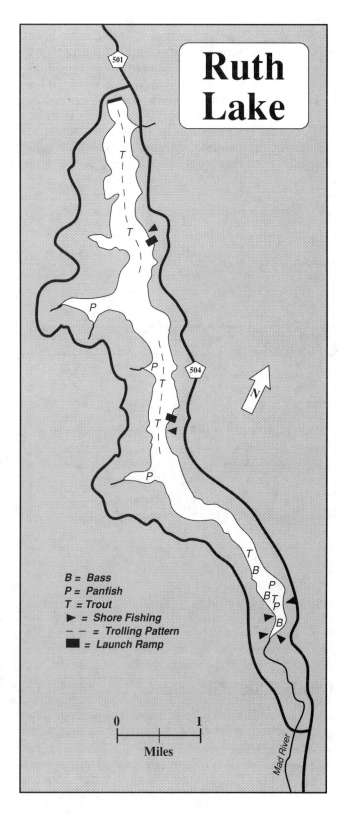

B = Bass
P = Panfish
T = Trout
► = Shore Fishing
– – = Trolling Pattern
■ = Launch Ramp

0   1
Miles

for food. Nightcrawlers below bobbers take fish, as do sliding sinker rigs fished in the shallows. Tossing spoons and spinners, or shallow trolling is also good. Most trophy trout are taken at Siskiyou during the February through April period. Downrigger trolling is excellent in the summertime for mostly 9 to 15 inch trout. Largemouths and smallmouths provide some action in the spring. Particularly good spots are the coves south of the launch ramp. It's possible, at times, to catch and release a dozen or more of these beauties. Crawfish-pattern crankbaits, plastic worms, spinnerbaits and small jigs are usually the best. Fat Git Zits and Green Weenies are also tops. Overall, because of water temperature and altitude, Lake Siskiyou is much better for trout than bass.

Lake Siskiyou Facts

Location: North of Lake Shasta, off I-5, east of the town of Mt. Shasta

Size: 437 surface acres with 5 inches of shoreline; lake elevation is 3181 feet.

Species: Rainbow and brown trout, largemouth, smallmouth, catfish, panfish

Facilities: Over 300 campsites, full-service marina, store, launch ramp, boat rental, swimming beach

Boating: Boat speed limit of 10 mph, no water skiing

Information: Lake Siskiyou, P.O. Box 276, Mt. Shasta, CA 96067, (530) 926-2618

Trinity Alps Wilderness

Trout fishing is very good in the Trinity Mountains that are north and west of Trinity Lake. Several types of outings are possible here. If you're fishing and camping on Trinity Lake and have a desire to do some stream fishing for trout, then you're in the right place. Here are some choices:

Upper Trinity River—This river runs along Hwy. 3, north of the lake. Both this and the Little Trinity River farther upstream provide good fishing, especially in late spring and fall.

Coffee Creek—This creek is a tributary of the Upper Trinity River. Access is good via Coffee Creek Road which parallels it. Coffee Creek provides some of the best all season trout fishing in the area.

East Fork of Upper Trinity—This stream runs north out of the northwest section of Trinity Lake. It has a generous caddis fly hatch. Some of the best fishing is in the riffles and pools downstream of the access where East Side Road crosses the river.

If you'd rather hike than drive to your trout fishing stream, the Salmon-Trinity Alps Wilderness Area is close by. There is some wonderful stream and lake fishing in this area. You'll find 500,000 acres of jagged granite mountains, deep valleys, 400 miles of trails and 81 alpine lakes. Two convenient access points are Stuart Fork near Trinity Alp Resort (Hwy. 3) and Big Flat (end of Coffee Creek Road).

Maps of the wilderness area and of the surrounding national forest are available from Shasta-Trinity National Forest, 2400 Washington Ave., Redding, CA 96001, (530) 246-5222.

Trinity Lake (map - p. 130)

Trinity Lake is a beautiful, alpine-type lake located on the Southern fringe of the Trinity Alps. In fishing circles, Trinity is best known for its smallmouth bass fishing. The state record smallmouth (9 pounds 1 ounce) was caught here and 4 to 5 pound trophy-sized bronzebacks are taken each year. Trout fishing is also very good. There is a regular spring planting program of catchable-size fish, and holdovers and some brown up to 20 inches are taken. There is also a steady kokanee salmon fishery. Trinity Lake, also known as Clair Engle Lake, has extensive camping and launching facilities as well as a number of privately run full-service resorts right on the lake. One appeal of Trinity is that it never really seems that crowded. Maybe it's because its better known and more accessible sister, Lake Shasta, draws so many people. Or maybe it's because trout anglers concentrate on Lewiston Lake, just south of Trinity. Being 22 miles from end-to-end also helps spread out Trinity's anglers and boaters.

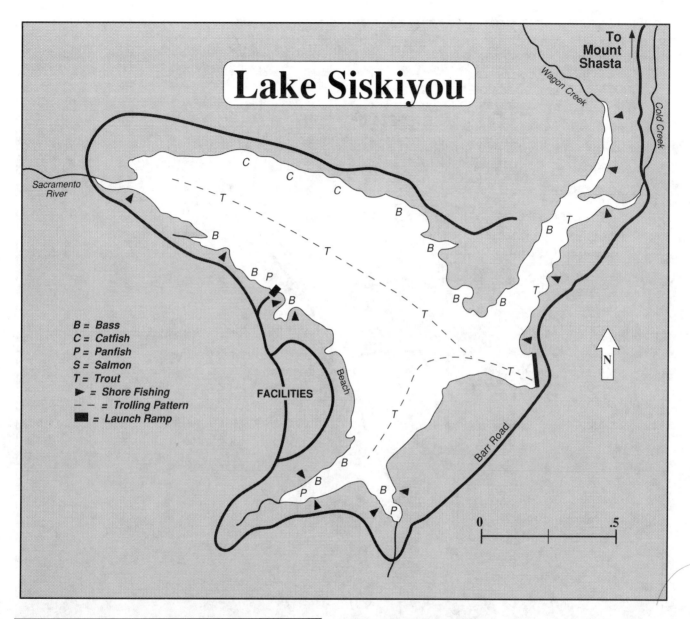

Lake Siskiyou

To
Mount
Shasta

Wagon Creek

Cold Creek

Sacramento
River

C   C   C
B
T
B   B
B   T
T
B   P
B   B   B   T
B
T
B
FACILITIES
Beach
T
B
B
B
P   B
P

Barr Road

B = Bass
C = Catfish
P = Panfish
S = Salmon
T = Trout
► = Shore Fishing
– – – = Trolling Pattern
■ = Launch Ramp

N

0   .5

Trinity Fishing Seasons

Good

Fair

	J	F	M	A	M	J	J	A	S	O	N	D
Bass												
Kokanee												
Panfish												
Trout												

Trinity Fishing Tips

Smallmouth bass fishing in Trinity is concentrated at rocky points and outcroppings. Another good bass structure to look for is the underwater, shallow water plateaus or shelves that are most often found off shore of relatively level campgrounds. An example of an area like this is the gentle slope from Wyntoon Camp north, near Trinity Center. This area which goes on for a mile or more also has some stumps, so it can be productive for largemouth Smaller offerings are better in this lake. Two to three inch grubs, four inch worms and

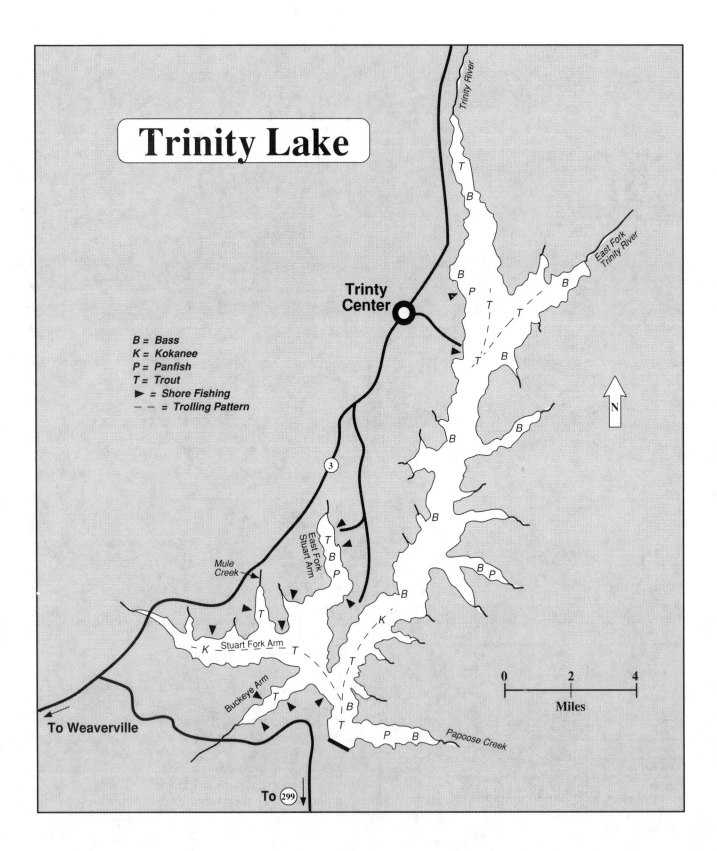

Trinity Lake

B = Bass
K = Kokanee
P = Panfish
T = Trout
► = Shore Fishing
— — = Trolling Pattern

Trinty Center

Trinity River

East Fork Trinity River

N

3

East Fork Stuart Arm

Mule Creek

Stuart Fork Arm

Buckeye Arm

To Weaverville

Papoose Creek

0   2   4
Miles

To 299

1/16 to 1/8 ounce jigs are good choices. Local favorites are the Git Zit, Rebel Wee R and Teeny R, Storm's Wiggle Wart and Rapala's mini Fat Rap. Six pound test line is standard. At the north end, good spots are the rock piles near Squirrel Flat and Hay Gulches near Trinity Center. At the south end, Chicken Flat and stump beds on the Stuart's Fork arm are consistent producers.

In early spring, trout can be found most often near, or in the major feeder streams of the lake. In late spring and early summer, trout are often near the drop-offs of the shallow shelves. When Trinity stratifies, the trout go deeper with the band of about 55 water. By August trout anglers need to work down about 40 feet below the surface. A thermometer is a good way to find the 55 region. In spring Trinity trout like bait or trolled nightcrawlers. Later in the season, spinners and spoons seem to work best. An excellent warm weather deep trolling area is near Trinity Dam. The deep water here provides cool temperatures for the trout. Trinity Lake kokanee are most often caught deep-trolling with downriggers.

Trinity Lake Facts

Location: About 45 miles northwest of Redding via Hwy. 299

Size: 17,000 surface acres with 145 miles of shoreline. Elevation is 2400 feet.

Species: Smallmouth and largemouth bass, rainbow trout, kokanee salmon, panfish

Facilities: There are over 400 U.S. Forest Service campsites in the vicinity plus about 36 boat-in campsites. Also, there are about 8 resorts on Trinity that have marinas, camp-grounds, stores, launch ramps, cabins, etc.

Information: Trinity County Chamber of Commerce, P.O. Box 517, Weaverville, CA 96093, (530) 623-6101; Brady's Sports Shop (530) 623-3121

Whiskeytown Lake

Whiskeytown, a large lake east of Redding on Hwy. 299, is best known as a great place for power boating and sailing. The National Park Service maintains extensive facilities here. On most good weather days, there is a great deal of boating activity in the main waters of the lake. But, if you're looking for an excellent place to take kids for some fast-paced bluegill action, try the back coves of Whiskeytown. Warm water coves like the Whiskey Creek arm, off Hwy. 299, and the Brandy Creek area on the south side of the lake, are excellent choices. These and other coves are fine shore fishing locales. Boat anglers can do well by concentrating near the rocks along the dam. Anglers at Whiskeytown who are looking for more action can also wet a line for rainbow trout, kokanee, bass, crappie and catfish. Information: Whiskeytown Ranger District, (530) 241-6584; Oak Bottom Marina (530) 359-2269

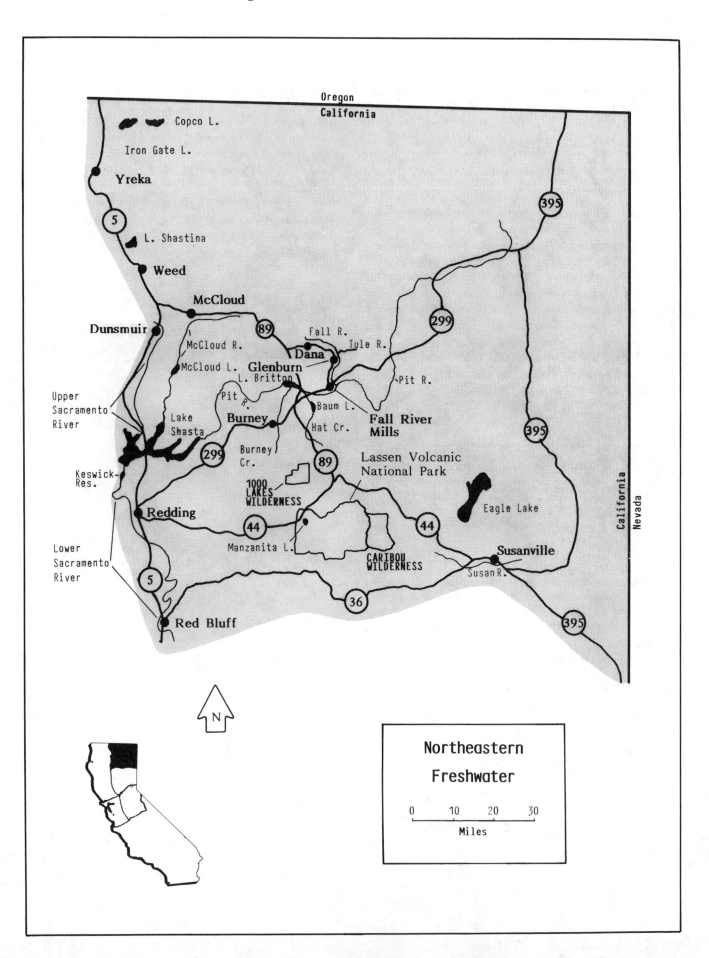

Northeastern
Freshwater

0   10   20   30
Miles

Northeastern Freshwater Fishing

Mount Shasta and Mount Lassen must have some special effect on trout. Some of the best trout fishing in California, in fact, some of the best trout fishing in the Western United States can be found in the territory stretching out between these twin volcanic peaks. Four great trout streams flow within sight of Shasta and Lassen—the Upper Sacramento, the McCloud, Hat Creek and the Fall River. Each of these are featured in this section. And then there are the Shasta-Lassen lakes like Lake Shasta, McCloud, Baum, Manzanita, Keswick, Britton and Shastina. These, as well as the more eastern and ever special Eagle Lake, are covered in this chapter.

The northeastern freshwater fishing region is bounded by the Oregon border on the north, the Nevada border on the east, I-5 on the west and Hwy. 36 on the south. See the accompanying map for specifics.

An excellent source of information on the Shasta-Lassen area is the Shasta-Cascade Wonderland Association, 1699 Hwy. 273, Anderson, CA 96007 (530) 365-7500 or (800) 474-2782.

Eagle Lake (map - p. 135)

Eagle Lake is the home of the famous Eagle Lake rainbow trout. Eagle Lake trout are said by many to fight like steelhead and taste like coho salmon. Eagle Lake is a large (16 miles long), natural body of water located at a high altitude (5100 feet) in the northern Sierras. Its waters are so alkaline that only the Eagle Lake trout and a small minnow called the tui chub can survive there. Eagle Lake trout are good-sized fish. The lake record is almost 11 pounds, 4-6 pounders are frequently caught, and 1-2 pound fish are common. Facilities include a full-service marina, camping and several resorts. Eagle Lake is the second largest natural body of water contained entirely within California. (The largest is Clear Lake.) Its irregular shape covers 22,000 surface acres. Maximum depth is only 92 feet. And most of the lake is less than 50 feet day deep, with the majority of the deeper water at the south end. The upper two-thirds is mostly less than 15 to 20 feet deep. Eagle Lake's west and south

shores are heavily forested, while the north and east shores are more open.

In the 1950s, the population of native rainbow trout in Eagle Lake was badly diminished because of poor spawning conditions in adjoining streams. To counter this, the Department of Fish and Game now traps fish in Pine Creek near Spaulding, takes their eggs and milt, and raises the fish until they are large enough to be safely returned to the lake. A total of 150,000 are put into Eagle Lake each year. They weigh 1 to 2 pounds by the time the season opens. The program has been so successful that Eagle Lake is now the premier trophy rainbow trout lake in all of California. And surplus Eagle Lake hatchery fry are planted in other Northern California lakes.

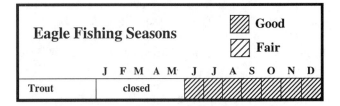

Eagle Fishing Tips

As is true in many trout lakes, trolling is the surest way to catch Eagle Lake trout. Offerings (behind flashers) include Speedy Shiners, Needlefish, Z-rays, Triple Teasers, Kastmasters and Rapalas (#5, 7, and 9 sinking). When trolling leadcore line, use a long leader (30 feet of 6-8 pound) since the fish can see the leadcore. Electronic fish finders are helpful in locating the ledges and drop-offs where the trout congregate. Another good trolling bait is nightcrawlers threaded on a long shank bait hook. Flashers can be used but are not essential early in the season when fish are still in the top 15 feet of water. Good water visibility runs until late summer when algae develops. During warmer months trollers use lead core or downriggers to get to about 40 feet in the deeper waters at the south end of the lake.

Another tried and true approach to hooking Eagle Lake trout is to boat fish in deep water using a sliding bobber rig and a nightcrawler. This setup allows anglers to get their bait down 15 to 25 feet or more. A key to successfully fishing this lake is to find the schools of chub bait fish. Fish finders will show them as Christmas tree-shaped clouds. Another clue is bird action on the surface. The trout herd the bait schools to the surface which attracts hungry terns and grebes.

When the mercury drops, Eagle Lake trout move to the shallows around the lake's edge and at the north end. During November and December, shore anglers toss out nightcrawlers on small brown or black crappie jigs hung about 5 feet below a bobber, or they inflate nightcrawlers and use a sliding sinker rig. This is also a good time for fly anglers who concentrate at the north end and at the tules on the west shore south of Spaulding. They use float tubes, waders, or even small boats. Trolling flies produces some big fish, but leadcore line or a split shot on monofilament is needed to get the flies down 5 to 30 feet, depending on how deep the fish are. In the fall, many boat anglers still fish, using nightcrawlers, over the springs. Look for the boats—that's where the springs are. One is at Eagle's Nest and another is at Wildcat. One last hint: Fish early—the bite usually ends by 8 or 9 a.m. And a word of caution: Winds come up very fast and hard at Eagle Lake. So bring along proper clothing and follow safe boating practices.

Eagle Lake Facts

Location: Eagle Lake is in northeastern Lassen County about 17 miles north of Susanville off county road A1.

Size: 22,000 surface acres of water

Species: Eagle Lake rainbow trout

Season: End of May through December 31

Facilities: Launch ramps are at the south end of the lake at Eagle Lake Marina, on the west shore at Spaulding Track, and at the north end at Stones Landing. Boat rentals are available at several locations. There are a total of six BLM and Lassen National Forest campgrounds around the lake, plus RV parking, cabins and motels.

Information: Spaulding Marina and Resort, (530) 825-2118; Eagle Lake Marina, Box 128, Susanville, CA 96130; Eagle Lake General Store, Spaulding Tract, Susanville, CA 96103, (530) 825-2191; U.S. Forest Service, 477-050 Eagle Lake Rd., Susanville, CA 96103, (530) 257-4188

Fall River (map - p. 134)

Fall River like nearby Hat Creek is a great trout stream. In fact, some experts rank these two streams among the top ten trout streams in America. This is a deep, 21 mile long stream with widths ranging from 150 feet to 250 yards. It is spring fed, so runoff has little effect on flow.

Upper Fall River is a wild trout stream like Lower Hat Creek. But since it runs mostly through private property, it is fished using float tubes or electric powered small boats. The fish are big here, many weighing from 5 to 8 pounds. Fly fishing is most popular. There are two lodges that provide access if you stay with them—Lava Creek Lodge and Rick's Hunting and Fishing Lodge. And there is public access at the Cal Trout Boat Launch at the Island Drive Bridge for cartop boats. The DF & G now has a $25,000 five-year lease on a site on Pacific Gas and Electric Company land near Glenburn, which is about 8 river miles upstream from Fall River Mills. The site, which has a paved parking area, a small dock, and a restroom, is suitable for launching cartop boats. Only two other public access sites are on the river, the one managed by California Trout, Inc., five miles upstream from the Glenburn site, and another at Big Lake on the Tule River.

Below, where Tule River meets Fall River, there are no tackle restrictions. There is a put-in for boats off McArthur Road near Glenburn. Good fishing for rainbow, up to 7 pounds, can be had on nightcrawlers, Rebels, Kastmasters and Mepps, as well as flies. For information on Fall River contact Shasta Angler, Fall River Mills, CA, (530) 336-6600, the Fall River Chamber of Commerce, (530) 336-5840, and the Fly Shop (530) 222-3555.

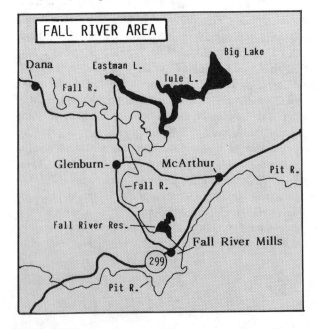

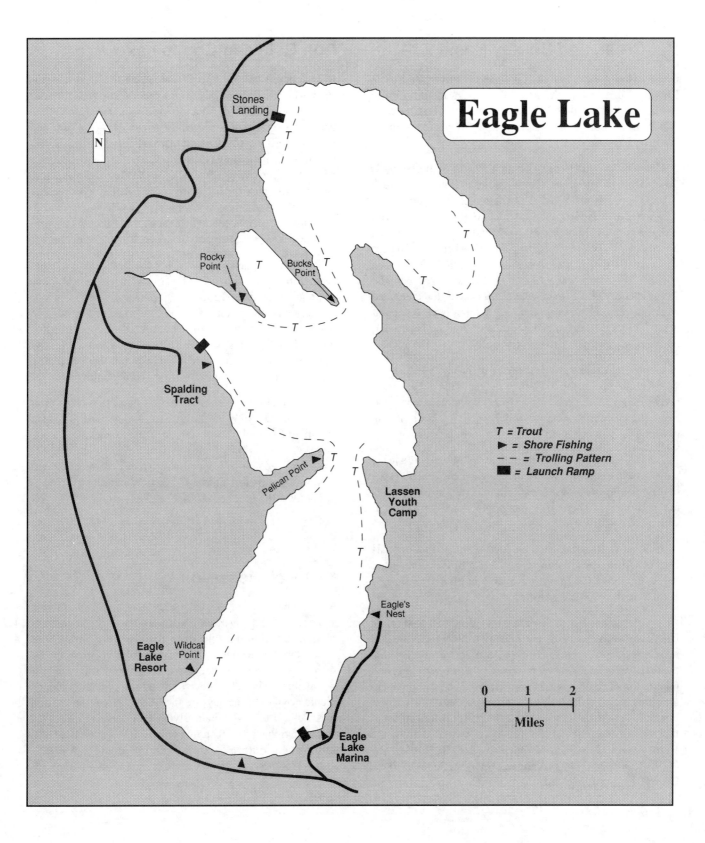

Eagle Lake

Stones Landing

Rocky Point

Bucks Point

Spalding Tract

Pelican Point

Lassen Youth Camp

Eagle's Nest

Eagle Lake Resort

Wildcat Point

Eagle Lake Marina

N

T = Trout
▶ = Shore Fishing
– – – = Trolling Pattern
■ = Launch Ramp

0   1   2
Miles

Hat Creek and Burney Basin

Burney Basin, the home of Hat Creek, is located in Shasta Country, surrounding the town of Burney, about 50 miles east of Redding on Hwy. 299. In this area, both Hat Creek and Fall River are considered among the best trout streams in the West.

Hat Creek, which runs through PG & E property, is divided into two portions. The 3.5 miles of Lower Hat Creek (from Power House No. 2 down to Lake Britton) is a designated wild trout stream. Here, only flies and lures with a single barbless hook are allowed, and a two fish, 18 inch minimum size limit is in effect. Trout hooked here average between 10-16 inches with occasional ones in the 20-24 inch range. There are some lunker browns over 10 pounds! Access is very good. Park where 299 crosses the creek and walk upstream or downstream. Fly fishing is very popular here. This is a broad, meadow stream. Wading is popular, but bank anglers can also do very well.

Upper Hat Creek is well stocked with hatchery fish. Most trout caught are in the 8-11 inch range. This stream from above Baum Lake runs along Hwy. 89 and access is good from the 5 campgrounds along Hwy. 89. Bait fishing (worms, salmon eggs and crickets) is most productive.

Baum Lake is a good small trout lake. Actually it's just a wide spot in that creek with a dam at each end, but all types of trout fishing are productive, and small, non-powered boats are permitted. There is a campground at the PG & E supervised facility.

Another well-stocked and productive stream in the area is Burney Creek. Best fishing is near Lake Britton, above and below the falls. Camping is available in McArthur-Burney Falls State Park at Lake Britton.

All of the streams in this area, including Fall River, Hat Creek and Burney Creek, are actually tributaries of the 200 mile long Pit River.* In the Burney Basin above Lake Britton, the Pit River is quite a large, fast river. But it does have a good population of rainbows and browns. Good spots to fish are on either side of the 299 bridge, and at the old Pit No. 1 Powerhouse some four miles from the bridge. More information on this excellent trout fishery is available from the Burney Basin Chamber of Commerce, Box 36, Burney, CA 96013, (530) 335-2111, or Vaughn's Sporting Goods, Burney, CA 96013, (530) 335-2381.

Iron Gate and Copco Lakes

How about a change of pace? So far, all the locales in this section have been trout waters. But there are two lakes almost up at the Oregon border that provide some fantastic yellow perch fishing as well as some nice "freebies." Iron Gate and Copco Lake are easily accessible from I-5, but they are a long way from home for most California anglers. These lakes are being literally overrun by delicious tasting yellow perch, primarily because the lakes are under fished. So to remedy this problem incentives are available to anglers. There is no catch limit on perch, concrete launch ramps at both lakes are free, and there are even free campgrounds at Iron Gate.

Perch can be taken all year, but the best period is from April through October. Most fish run from 4 to 8 inches, bus some go up to about 12 inches. Anglers use red worms or nightcrawler pieces on a #6 hook. Perch mostly hug the bottom and are found all over both lakes. Expect to catch hundreds of fish on a weekend trip. There is no possession limit, so anglers clean them at the lake, put them in plastic bags and then freeze them for future eating enjoyment.

Largemouth bass fishing is best at these two lakes from May through July. Work the coves. Trout angling is good at the upper east end of Iron Gate, near Fall Creek, and at the dam. There is also a good native trout fishery in the upper Klamath River above Copco Lake. Check for special regulations. Information: Shasta-Cascade Wonderland Association, (530) 365-7500 or (800) 474-2782

Keswick Reservoir

Next time you're in the Lake Shasta area, consider doing some trout fishing at Keswick Reservoir. It's just south of Shasta, and all of the cold water outflow from Shasta Dam passes through the 630 acre Keswick, bringing nutrients for the forage fish and a better than average brown and rainbow population. There is a paved launch ramp, boat dock and picnic grounds at the day-use facilities north of the town of Keswick off Iron Mountain Blvd. Water levels in Keswick fluctuate frequently depending on operations at Shasta Dam. Information: Bureau of Reclamation, Redding, CA 96001, (530) 275-1554

*Also see page 143.

McCloud River and Lake (map - p. 138)

The McCloud River runs parallel to Hwy. 89 from Bartle toward the town of McCloud, then south to Lake McCloud, and finally into Lake Shasta. This is an extremely scenic and prolific trout stream. And variety could be its middle name. It offers every type of water that holds trout. The McCloud is a great stream for the connoisseur angler, and for the youngster or beginner. Flies, bait and hardware (spinners and spoons) can all be effective. There are brook, brown, native rainbow and planted rainbow trout, as well as a few Dolly Varden, which must be released alive. And there is a complete spectrum of regulations, from 10 trout limits in one section of the river to a catch-and-release, barbless flies and lures-only section.

The upper portions of the McCloud from Bartle down to about a mile below Fowlers Camp is a planted section of stream (10 fish limit) that is easily accessible from the campgrounds such as Fowlers, Big Springs, Cattle Camp, Algoma and several others. If you want to get away from other anglers and improve your chances of catching native and hold-over fish, walk the barely hikeable path along the stream to areas between camps. Both spinning and fly fishing is good. Top baits are salmon eggs and worms. Mepps spinners produce. Portions of this stream run through meadow for miles. Flow is gentle, and fishermen wade here in summer without waders. Speaking of wading, the McCloud is a wader's stream. To fish it properly, in this stretch and also below McCloud Lake, you've got to get wet.

A second alternative is to fish the stretch just south of the McCloud Dam. It can be reached by taking Squaw Valley Road about 12 miles out of the town of McCloud. In this 6.5 mile stretch only artificial lures and flies may be used, and the limit is two fish per day. Access is via Ash Campground, about a mile downstream from the dam, on a road on the east side of the river. This is a canyon stream with more flow than in the Upper McCloud.

Finally, there is a catch-and-release stretch of the McCloud that begins at the mouth of Ladybug Creek and extends for about 2 miles. Take the road on the west side of the McCloud Lake Dam that leads to the Ah-Di-Na Campground.

Only artificial lures and flies with barbless, single hooks can be used. Here and in the upper part of the river, the best time for dry fly fishing is from 5:30 p.m. to dark. Adams, Western Coachman, Yellow Cahill and Mosquito are popular. Early morning is weighted wet fly time using a two fly rig of Spent Wing and Burlap, Yellow Jacket or Caddis Larva.

If stream anglers want a change of pace, Lake McCloud (520 surface acres) is a super trout lake. Bank fishing on the lake is best up towards Star City Creek where the river feeds into the lake's north end. There is also good bank fishing down around the dam and around the ridges that surround the lake. Heavy forests and rugged terrain make this a very picturesque setting.

Manzanita Lake

Manzanita Lake, located just inside the west entrance of Lassen Volcanic National Park, hosts a large aquatic insect population making it a favorite of fly anglers. Recently introduced trout management programs and special fishing regulations have made Manzanita into a trophy fishery. This small, 53 acre lake, surrounded by pines and firs, is at an elevation of 5,900 feet. Ice can often prevent spring fishing, but in June when surface water temperatures reach the low 50's, the action breaks loose. Midges hatch first, followed by mayflies. Because of thick shoreline growth, it is almost essential to fish with a small boat or float tube. But waders also score. There is a launch ramp, but motors are not permitted. Shallows are concentrated on the east side, and this is where the best early season action takes place. Since insects are the major part of the trout's diet here, flies are the best way to fish. Of course, Manzanita is a fly angler's paradise, but spin anglers can also get in on the fun—they troll flies like leeches or Wolly Buggers, with or without a small split shot up about 18 inches. Let out at least 100 feet of line so as not to spook the trout. Spin casting nymphs or dry flies using a cast-a-bubble is another good approach. There is camping near the lake and many other kinds of activities associated with this spectacular national park. Information: Lassen Volcanic National Park, P.O. Box 100, Mineral, CA 96063, (530) 595-4444

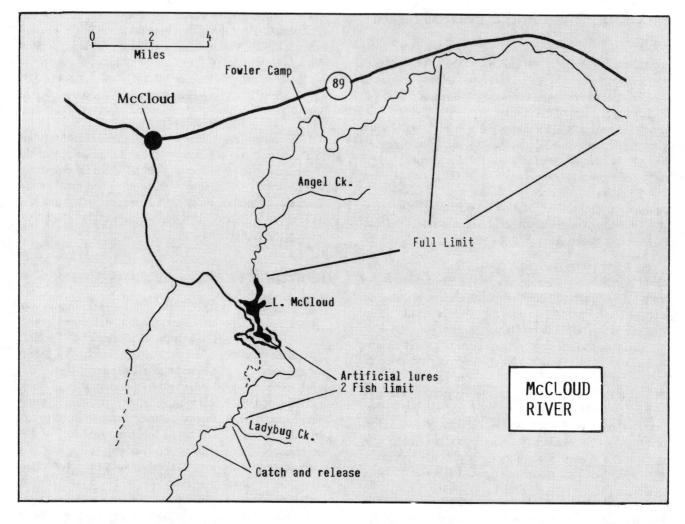

Upper Sacramento River

Many anglers think of the Sacramento River in terms of outstanding salmon, sturgeon, shad and striper fishing. They're correct, but they're thinking of the part of the Sacramento River that runs from Redding to Rio Vista. This is the Lower Sacramento River and it is covered in the "Central Valley River Fishing" chapter. The Upper Sacramento flows more than 45 miles from Box Canyon Dam at the base of Lake Siskiyou all the way down to Lakehead at the upper end of Lake Shasta. This remarkable, trophy trout stream just about parallels I-5 from Lake Siskiyou to Lake Shasta. And the major highway along with the accompanying railroad tracks provides very good access at places like Dunsmuir, Castella, Sweetbrier, Flume Creek, Conant, Sims Pollard Flat, Gibson, La Moine and Delta.

The upper part of the river from Box Canyon Dam downstream through Dunsmuir is a classic pocket water mountain stream. Crystal clear, fast flowing water tumbles over the boulder-strewn stream beds creating holding pockets. From Sims Campground down to Lake Shasta the river flows in long pools divided by short riffles. Spinners and flies both produce. Spinners can be cast out, and retrieved or drifted in the current like bait.

The Upper Sacramento River is truly a special place, but recently it has not been without major troubles. Sadly, on July 14, 1991, all aquatic life in the river between the Cantara Loop Bridge and Shasta Lake was killed following a freight train derailment.

Due to this disaster, the river was closed to all fishing for a period of three years. It was reopened in 1994 to reports of better fishing than ever before, but since then the recovery has slowed somewhat, although the future does, indeed, seem bright. And that's good news to anyone who has ever fished the Upper Sac and especially to the residents of

Dunsmuir who depend on the tourist dollars the river attracts.

To help its recovery, special regulations are now in effect on the Upper Sac. From Box Canyon Dam downstream to the Scarlett Way Bridge in Dunsmuir, only artificial lures with barbless hooks may be used, and the daily limit is zero. From the Scarlett Way Bridge downstream to the mouth of Soda Creek, only barbless hooks may be used and the limit is 5 per day, 10 in possession (the river is stocked in that stretch). From the mouth of Soda Creek to Shasta Lake, the limit is zero, and only artificial lures with barbless hooks may be used.

Some fly fishing devotees compare the Upper Sacramento with the prime fly streams of Montana and Wyoming. It has a very diverse hatch of aquatic insects from July to mid-October. Since the spill and the subsequent recovery that is going on, the Upper Sac has attracted more attention from fly fishers than in the past. The river does produce very well for those who fish dry flies like Humpys or Elk Hair Caddis in the evening and weighted nymphs during the day. Wild rainbows are the mainstay here, and some trophies to 10 inches are taken. The average size is smaller, but beautiful. Camping is available at Castle Crags State Park near Castella and at Sims Campground. Fishing information is available at Ted Fay Fly Shop, Dunsmuir, (530) 235-2969.

Lake Shasta (map - p. 140)

Lake Shasta, a massive reservoir, provides a wide variety of angling, including rainbow and brown trout, smallmouth and largemouth bass, panfish and king salmon. The lake, which is basically 4 flooded river canyons, is 35 miles long and has about 365 miles of shoreline. Maximum lake depth is slightly over 500 feet. There are a number of full-service marinas (many of which rent houseboats) and campgrounds on the lake. Often, one or more families rent a houseboat and "bring along" their fishing boat for angling and waterskiing.

Shasta Fishing Seasons													Good Fair
	J	F	M	A	M	J	J	A	S	O	N	D	
Bass		Fair	Fair	Fair	Good	Good	Good	Good	Good	Fair	Fair	Fair	
Catfish						Fair	Good	Good	Good	Fair			
Panfish				Fair	Fair	Good	Good	Good	Good	Fair			
Trout	Fair	Good	Good	Good	Good	Good	Good	Good	Good	Good	Good	Good	
Salmon		Fair	Good	Good	Good	Good	Good	Good	Good	Good	Fair		

Shasta Fishing Tips

Trolling is the most productive trout and salmon approach. Popular offerings include nightcrawlers, Speedy Shiners, Cripplures, Z-Rays and Kastmasters. Trout anglers often use a combination marshmallow/salmon egg on a sliding sinker rig. The marshmallow "floats" the entire combination. In the cooler months, trout can be caught near the surface with bait and a bobber. Shasta doesn't have a lot of the cover and structures that typifies many largemouth bass lakes. But smallmouth and some largemouth bass can be found in coves and near rocky points throughout the lake. Florida-strain largemouths have been planted in Shasta, and their impact is showing up. Largemouths up to 8 pounds are now being taken by tournament pros. The lake record largemouth, caught in 1992, weighed 15 pounds 9 ounces. Currently, spotted bass make up 65% of the bass catch at Shasta and spots up to 7 pounds have been caught. Live bait, plastic worms, spinnerbaits, crankbaits and jigs all work depending on the time of day, time of year and location. Try a variety of offerings. Local favorites include white spinnerbaits, Git Zit jigs and Zara Spooks. A good largemouth area is the Pit River arm. Work early and late in the day and in shaded coves. Catfishing peaks in the summer months. Fish over deep holes or from shore with clams, chicken livers, etc. Also, in summer, fishing around an anchored houseboat with crickets, red worms or small minnows can produce crappie, bluegill or even trout. The shadow of the boat attracts light sensitive fish. Shore fishing is good in campgrounds and near marinas throughout the lake.

Lake Shasta Facts

Location: Lake Shasta is north of Redding along I-5.

Size: Shasta is the largest man-made lake in California—29,500 surface acres of water. It has more miles of shoreline (365 miles) than San Francisco Bay. It can hold enough water to flood an area the size of Connecticut to a depth of 1 1/2 feet.

Species: Trout (rainbow and brown), bass (largemouth, spotted and smallmouth), king salmon, panfish

Facilities: There are extensive facilities on Lake Shasta. The United States Forest Service (USFS) operates over 20 campgrounds in the vicinity. There are about 10 privately operated resorts on Shasta that feature houseboat rentals, camping, motels, cabins, launch ramps, beaches, marinas, restaurants, etc. There are also several free public launch ramps.

Information: USFS—District Office, 6543 Holiday Rd., Redding, CA 96003, (530) 246-5222; Shasta Recreation Co., (530) 238-2824 or (800) 8-SHASTA; Shasta-Cascade Wonderland Association, (530) 365-7500 or (800) 474-2782

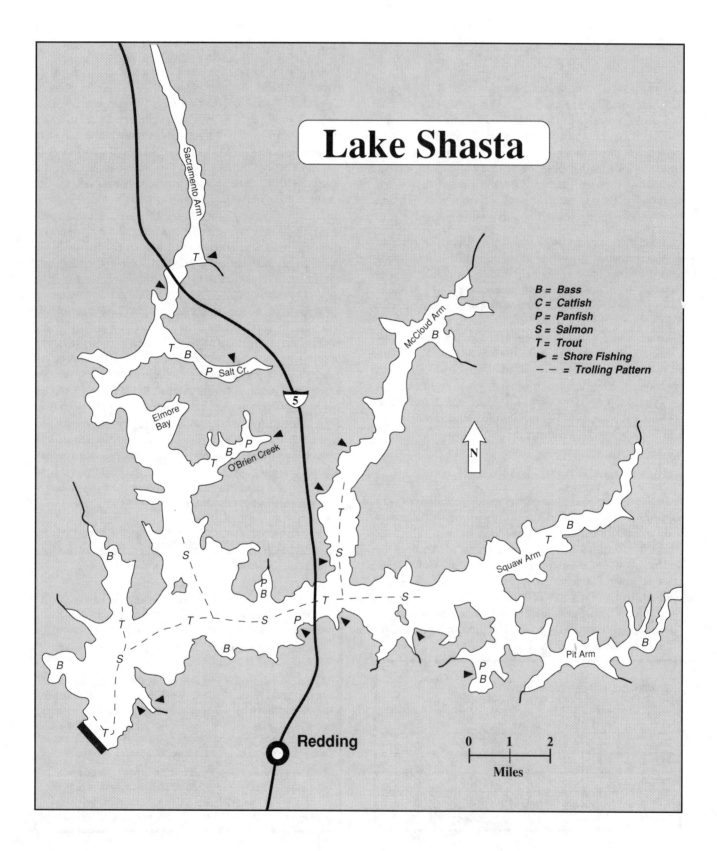

Lake Shasta

Sacramento Arm

McCloud Arm

B = Bass
C = Catfish
P = Panfish
S = Salmon
T = Trout
► = Shore Fishing
– – = Trolling Pattern

N

Salt Cr.

Elmore Bay

O'Brien Creek

Squaw Arm

Pit Arm

Redding

0   1   2
Miles

Lake Shastina (map - p. 142)

Lake Shastina is an excellent trout and bass lake that gets very little fishing pressure. Even at peak fishing seasons there are often only a handful of boats on the water. Limited facilities here make this a great place to enjoy on a day-use basis while you are fishing and camping somewhere in the vicinity—perhaps at Lake Shasta, Lake Siskiyou, the Upper Sacramento or the McCloud. Lake Shastina has over 4 1/2 miles of shoreline plus many productive islands. Rainbows and browns, a few up to 10 pounds, are just one of the appeals. Largemouth bass in the 2 1/2 to 5 pound range are taken consistently. Some anglers report catching and releasing up to 50 of these bucketmouths per boat in a single morning of fishing. Crappie fishing is also fantastic—and they are monsters. 3 pound bruisers are taken regularly.

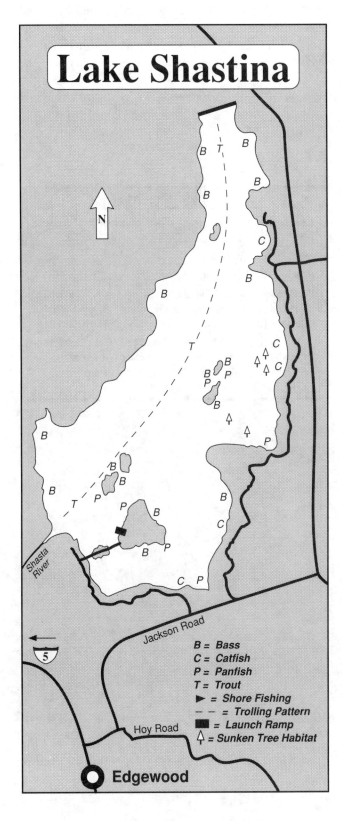

Shastina Fishing Seasons												
	J	F	M	A	M	J	J	A	S	O	N	D
Bass			▨	▨	▨	▨	▨	▨	▨	▨	▨	
Catfish				▨	▨	▨	▨	▨	▨	▨		
Crappie			▨	▨	▨	▨	▨	▨	▨	▨	▨	
Trout	▨	▨	▨	▨	▨	▨	▨	▨	▨	▨	▨	▨

▨ Good
▨ Fair

Shastina Fishing Tips

Trollers probably take the most trout out of Shastina. The midlake channel over the old river bed between the dam and the Shasta River inflow at the south end is the best all-around route. Flashers in front of nightcrawlers work best. Bait works at the inlets in spring.

Shastina's largemouth bass population has been a well-kept secret. Maybe because Shastina's location and character peg it as a trout lake. But the bucketmouths are large and plentiful. Plug fishing is best in the mid-March to mid-April peak. September and October are also exceptional months. The rocky shoreline at the west end and at both ends of the lake are good for deep-diving crankbaits. Don't hesitate to try surface lures in warmer water months.

Crappie are taken in all the rocky, shallow areas near shore and around the new sunken tree habitat placed in the lake in 1988. Peak action is mid-March through mid-April. Catfish up to 15 pounds are caught, but stringers usually have fish in the 12 to 17 inch range. Off the dam, in deep coves, and the south end are good spots. Good baits include nightcrawlers, chicken livers, cut mackerel and clams.

Shastina Creek between I-5 and Lake Shastina produces many brown trout in the 7-10 inch range, but also has some

---

Lake Shastina Facts

Location: In Siskiyou County about 7 miles north of Weed off I-5.

Size: 2700 surface acres

Species: Rainbow trout, largemouth bass, catfish, panfish

Facilities: Public facilities are limited to a newly built launch ramp and trailer parking area administered by Siskiyou County. These are both on Milkhouse Island and are free. Access is via Jackson Road and a causeway to the island.

Information: Shasta-Cascade Wonderland Association, (530) 365-7500 or (800) 474-2782

Wilderness Areas

There are two wilderness areas, both in the Lassen National Forest, that offer good back country trouting. One nice feature of these two areas is that, for the most part, the trails are relatively short and gentle. Beginning backpackers or families with smaller children do well here.

Thousand Lakes Wilderness is small (about 16,000 acres) as wilderness areas go, and doesn't have 1,000 lakes. Its terrain is varied, including rugged rocky areas, pine forests and alpine peaks. Elevations range from 5,000 to 9,000 feet. Although there are several lakes, only 6 offer good fishing. Eiler Lake is the largest lake, and is noted for the largest fish in the area. It is also the most accessible. At about 7,200 feet, Magee Lake and Everett Lake are most difficult to reach, but are rewarding to the determined angler. Other fishing lakes include Barret, Durbin and Hutford. Bait, lures and flies all work at Thousand Lakes. Forest service roads off Hwy. 89, between Burney and Lassen Volcanic National Park, provide access.

Caribou Wilderness (19,080 acres) is on the east side of the Lassen Volcanic National Park, off Hwy. 44. Trail heads are at Silver Lake. Caribou is much like Thousand Lakes in terrain and size, but fishing is not rated as good. Caribou has 20 major lakes.

Special: The Pit River

The Pit River is overshadowed by its own tributaries—Hat Creek and Fall River—and by the Sacramento River of which it is a tributary. It has failed to establish the reputation it deserves—that of a producer of impressive, sizable, energetic, plump rainbows (and a few hefty browns). And not surprisingly, some locals and "in-the-know" angers have even worked hard to keep the Pit a secret. But now the word is out.

The Pit actually begins in Modoc County and flows west through a corner of Lassen County before entering Shasta County. The upper portion of the Pit is considered a warm water fishery with primarily bass and catfish. The Pit River is one of the largest streams in the state, and also one of the most damned, with power houses impeding its progress all the way to Lake Shasta. Despite dams and erratic water flow, food supplies are abundant so rainbows reach 20 inches and four pounds.

In Shasta County, the Pit runs through a series of PG & E hydroelectric plants all the way down to its terminus in the Pit Arm of Lake Shasta. Because of the power houses, the river can rise in a hurry, so anglers should always be on alert. Some say this situation is most apparent between Lake Britton and Pit #1 power house. Here the best fishing often takes place early in the morning when flows are often the lowest.

Trout anglers find many different faces along the Pit. There are wild, roadless stretches that are very strenuous to fish, then are highly accessible roadside locales and there is even a Wild Trout portion.

The section from Lake Britton down to Lake Shasta is one of the most productive for wild rainbow trout. Habitat is excellent and access is good for some 20 river miles. Many anglers drive to Lake Britton dam, park at a turnout and walk down to the river. Trout populations are good and this stretch of water lends itself to fly fishing. The river here parallels Hat Creek Road. Fishing is good all the way down to Big Bend. But some regulars feel that the first four miles below the Lake Britton Dam are the most consistent.

At Big Bend are the Pit #5 and #6 power houses. Access below Big Bend is much more difficult, but efforts to get to the good spots are frequently rewarded. Some anglers will hike for two hours to reach the best waters of the lower Pit. Here the water is very cold and crystal clear. Wild rainbows in the 12 to 15 inch class are common with some going to 18 inches.

The Lake Britton to Lake Shasta section of the Pit is perfect for nymph fishing. It features many riffles, tailouts, pools, rocks, and boulders. Fish can be taken all day long with proper presentation. The Pit has a good population of stoneflies, so anglers often get results drifting black and brown stones. Size 6 is good early in the year and then 10-12 later in the season. Nymph anglers do better using strike indicators. Quick hook setting is a must as are light leaders (about 6x).

Mayflies are also active in early and mid-summer, and on into August and September. There are occasional caddis hatches in the hot summer evenings. Try sparkle pupa and sparkle emergers.

The Pit is not popular with dry fly anglers. Lower Hat Creek and Fall River in the same basin are much better. But there is some surface action from the start of the season through mid-June. Actually, the best action in the whole Burney Basin comes in May and June and then again in September and October. Mid-summer air temperatures are often up in the 90's.

The Wild Trout portion of the lower Pit runs from Pit #3 dam (Lake Britton) downstream to the outlet of the Pit #3 power house. Here only artificial lures with barbless hooks may be used, and the daily and possession limits are now two trout with a minimum size of 18 inches.

Three other good areas in the general regulation waters are noteworthy: 1) the stretch upstream from Pit #5 power house near Big Bend; 2) the section of water from the Pit #4 power house upstream to the Pit #4 dam (Access to this portion of the water is by the road to the dam, the road to the power house, or at the Deep Creek Campground in the middle of the run.); 3) immediately below the Pit #1 power house off Route 299, a few miles east of the town of Burney. Nightcrawlers are a good bait in this area and in some other general regulations waters.

Brown trout cruise in deeper runs and pools. Minnows and trout-imitating Rapalas are good bets.

"Pit anglers" find that good local highway maps and a Shasta-Trinity National Forest map are very helpful. For information on the area, contact the Shasta-Cascade Wonderland Association, (530) 365-7500 or (800) 474-2782. A good source of fishing information is Vaughn's Sporting Goods, Burney, CA, (530) 335-2381.

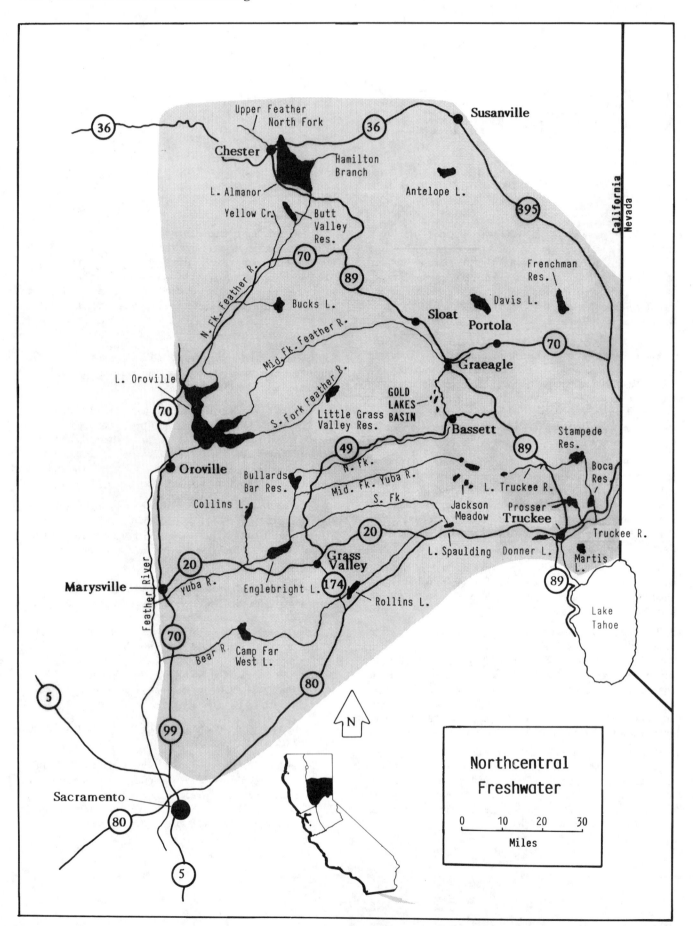

Northcentral
Freshwater

0   10   20   30
Miles

Northcentral Freshwater Fishing

The upper midwestern section of this vast land of ours has its Great Lakes. And they are truly great. But, when I look at the map of the northcentral region that accompanies this chapter, I see a grouping of "great Sierra lakes." In the Feather River drainage you've got Almanor, Bucks, Butt Valley and the giant Oroville. On the eastern slopes there is Davis and Frenchman. In the vast Yuba River drainage there are the Gold Lakes, Bullards Bar, Englebright and Collins. On the Bear River are Camp Far West Reservoir and Rollins Lake. And west and north of Tahoe are the Jackson Meadows Lakes, Stampede, Prosser, Boca, Donner and Martis. All of these marvelous Northern Sierra great lakes are featured in this chapter as are northern Sierra stream and river trout fishing opportunities and some smaller, lesser known lakes.

Many of the waters covered in this chapter are in Plumas County. The Plumas County Chamber of Commerce, in Quincy, is an excellent source of information, (916) 283-6345. See map on previous page.

Lake Almanor (map - p. 147)

Lake Almanor is one of the best trout and salmon fishing lakes in California. Trout include native rainbow, browns and Eagle Lake rainbow. King (chinook) salmon fishing is excellent. Almanor also provides bass (mostly smallmouth), catfish and panfish angling. Although Almanor is at 4500 feet altitude, the lake's surface temperature in summer is about 70.

Lake Almanor, built on the North Fork of the Feather River in 1914 to generate power, was for many years the largest man-made lake in California. Unlike many of the lakes built in the post World War II public works boom, Almanor, which covers 52 square miles, offers a vast array of private and public facilities for visitors. There are campgrounds, lodges and motels, numerous launch ramps, golfing, and much more. But, despite all that is available here, Almanor and its vicinity has maintained a charming, rural character. Guy Earl, one of the owners of the company that built Lake Almanor, named it using parts of the first names of his three daughters—Alice, Martha and Elinore. It is situated where the Sierra Nevada meets the Cascade Range and is surrounded by mountain peaks, pine forests and pleasant meadows.

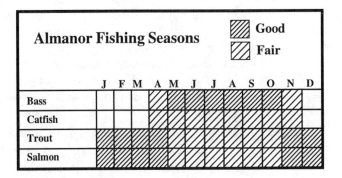

Almanor Fishing Tips

The most productive technique for salmon and trout at Almanor is trolling. Chinook, or king salmon, have continued to grow at a respectable rate since they were first introduced in 1982. Salmon are now taken exceeding 10 pounds. Trout in the two to six pound range are common. When surface water temperatures are cool in the colder months of the year, trout and salmon swim near the surface foraging for food like pond smelt. Trolling near the surface is the best way to take them. But in summer when Almanor stratifies, deeper trolling with leadcore line or downrigger is the way to go. A good starting depth to try is about 30 to 35 feet down. Favorite trolling lures include solid or jointed Rapalas (gold and red fluorescent), Speedy Shiners (silver or gold), Needlefish (bikini or frog pattern) and Flatfish (fluorescent orange).

Some anglers find success by still fishing from a boat. This is an especially effective technique during the warmer months when the trout and salmon congregate around submerged springs. Good spots include the Big Springs Cove, located north of the mouth of the Hamilton Branch, the spring holes off Crawfords Resort on the east shore, and the area that lies to the west of Burnell Point at the tip of the peninsula. Most success comes with nightcrawlers and salmon eggs fished off the bottom using a sliding sinker rig.

Shore angling is good at many locations. Starting at the dam, anglers cast for smallmouth bass from the rocks along the face of the dam. The cove at the west side of the dam is a popular bait fishing spot for salmon and trout. Smallmouths are also taken here. Rocky Point, a PG & E campground location, is another good shore fishing spot for trout and bass. At the north end of the lake, the Chester Causeway crossing of Hwy. 36 is another good locale when the lake level is high enough. Catfish Beach, on the north shore of Gould Swamp, and the lake shore all the way to the mouth of Bailey Creek are good areas during spring and summer. A spring area located a short distance north of the mouth of Bailey Creek hosts both bass and trout. A productive year-round shore fishing spot is in the area where Hamilton Beach enters Almanor. Trout and salmon love this flowing water. Parking and access is provided by PG & E.

Smallmouths of Almanor average between 2 and 3 pounds, but 4 and 5 pounders are taken. They are widely distributed along the miles and miles of shoreline. Anglers score consistently along rocky drop-offs, submerged rocks, tree stumps and other shoreline cover. Most action takes place in 4 to 12 feet of water, but evening action on the surface in the summertime can be fierce.

Lake Almanor Facts

Location: Almanor is located in Plumas County, about 70 miles east of Red Bluff, about 270 miles from San Francisco, and about 120 miles from Reno. Chester, on the northwest shore of the lake, is the major town in this area.

Size: 13 miles long and 6 miles wide, 40 miles of shoreline

Species: King salmon, rainbow trout, brown trout, smallmouth bass, catfish, panfish

Facilities and Campgrounds: There are about 25 facilities on or near Lake Almanor offering a combination of lodges, motels, cabins, campgrounds, marinas, launching, boat rental, etc. Local real estate agents also actively offer private summer homes for rental. In addition, PG & E has about 80 developed campsites, and the U.S. Forest Service has over 100 developed sites.

Boating: There are more than a dozen launch ramps, some in conjunction with full-service marinas. Plumas County regulations state that boats on Lake Almanor can only be docked at night in marinas. Overnighting in boats on Almanor is prohibited.

Information: Chester/Lake Almanor Chamber of Commerce, P.O. Box 1198, Chester, CA 96020, (530) 258-2426; Lassen View Resort (530) 596-3437

Antelope Lake (map - p. 148)

Antelope Lake offers very good fishing, excellent camping facilities and some of the finest scenery in the state without the kinds of crowds that can make summer fishing trips to easier-to-reach lakes a disappointment. At an elevation of 5,000 feet, Antelope is in the Plumas National Forest between Crescent Mills and Susanville. The lake has 15 miles of timbered shoreline with 930 surface acres of water. There are planted rainbow as well as holdover and native rainbow and brown trout that run up to 16 to 17 inches. Trout in the 5 to 10 pound range are caught each year. Largemouths go up to 8 pounds and the biggest smallmouth are in the 3 to 4 pound range. There are over 200 USFS campsites distributed in 3 locations around the lake. A concrete launch ramp is available.

Trout trollers score on flasher/nightcrawler combos and flasher/lure combos. Kastmasters, Super Dupers, Needlefish and Phoebes all work at Antelope. Summertime trollers work down about 30 to 40 feet below the surface. Indian Creek, below the Antelope dam, offers some fine brown trout action. Bass, both largemouth and smallmouth, were introduced into Antelope in the early 1980's to help control the sucker and bullhead populations. Both bass species have prospered. Plastic worms, grubs and spinnerbaits are the most consistent producers. Shore fishing is good at Antelope for both trout and bass chasers. The campgrounds, dam, launching areas, as well as the fishing spots on the north and south shores (served by access trails) are all good. Information: Mt. Hough Ranger District, 39696 State Highway 70, Quincy, (530) 283-0555

Bucks Lake

Bucks Lake is another great summertime vacation and fishing spot high up in the Plumas National Forest. This destination offers excellent trout and kokanee fishing, spectacular scenery and a wide variety of accommodations. It is a pleasant 16 mile drive from Quincy. Bucks Lake is at 5,200 feet and is a good-sized lake at 1820 surface acres. Two prime fishing locations are the major inflows at Mill Creek on the north end of the lake and at Bucks Creek at the east end. Mill Creek produces pan-sized rainbows on sliding sinkers rigs,

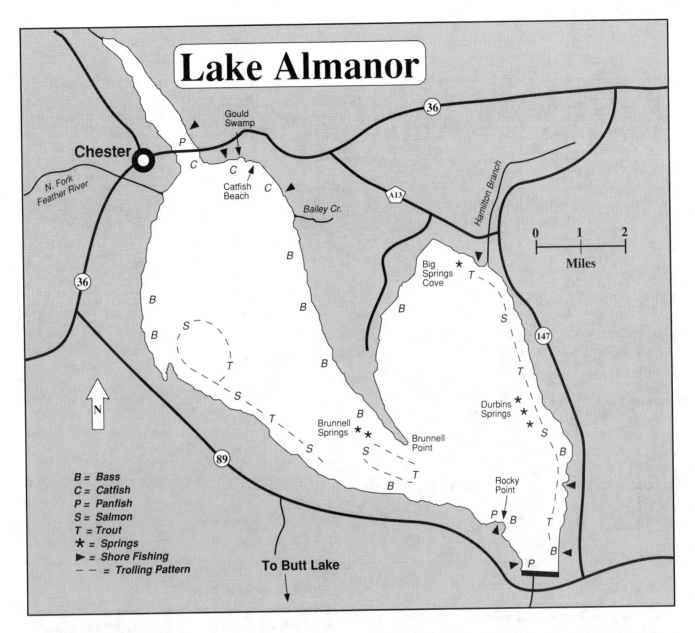

Lake Almanor

B = Bass
C = Catfish
P = Panfish
S = Salmon
T = Trout
* = Springs
► = Shore Fishing
— — = Trolling Pattern

while Bucks Creek has been known to give up some trophy-sized browns. This cold water, summertime trout fishery (the lake is frozen and snowed-in until late spring) is enhanced by kokanee, which are most often taken by leadcore line trollers out in the main lake.

Bucks Lake has both USFS campgrounds and PG & E campgrounds. But a special feature of Bucks that appeals to many visitors are its lakeside resorts. There are three of these that have cabins, as well as boat rentals, beaches, stores, etc. Also, there is a section of summer homes on the lake. Rentals are best arranged through Quincy real estate agents. A note: All this talk of resorts and rentals may make Bucks Lake sound congested and almost urban. That's not

at all the case. Most of the shoreline is still undeveloped forest and the surrounding area includes a wilderness area. Information: Mt. Hough Ranger District, (530) 283-0555

Bullards Bar Reservoir (map - p. 150)

Bullards Bar is one of Northern California's least known and least utilized fishing and recreational lakes. This is true despite its reputation as the best kokanee salmon fishing in the state, a convenient location only an hour and a half from Sacramento and a beautiful locale. A major drawback at Bullards Bar for years has been its lack of facilities. But now there is a complete resort and marina on the lake that even

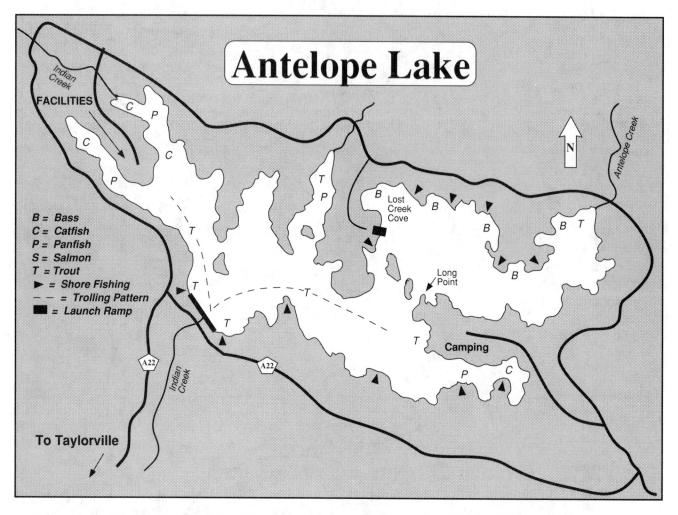

Antelope Lake

Indian Creek

FACILITIES

B = Bass
C = Catfish
P = Panfish
S = Salmon
T = Trout
► = Shore Fishing
– – = Trolling Pattern
■ = Launch Ramp

Lost Creek Cove

Long Point

Camping

N

Antelope Creek

A22

A22

Indian Creek

To Taylorville

rents houseboats. Campgrounds and launching have been available for some time. All types of boating is permitted and this is a popular waterskiing destination in the summertime. Boaters in the run-off months should be alert for floating debris. But because of the steep banks, boat fishing is still the way to go.

Bullards Bar Fishing Seasons													
	J	F	M	A	M	J	J	A	S	O	N	D
Bass		▨	▨	▨	▨	▨	▨	▨	▨	▨	▨	
Catfish		▨	▨	▨	▨	▨	▨	▨	▨	▨	▨	
Kokanee	▨	▨	▨	▨	▨	▨	▨	▨	▨	▨	▨	
Trout	▨	▨	▨	▨	▨	▨	▨	▨	▨	▨	▨	

Good ▨
Fair ▨

Bullards Bar Fishing Tips

Kokanee fishing is at its best from April through July, although they are taken all year. September and October produce the biggest fish (up to 14-18 inches), but overall, action is slower. Trolling is the primary method for taking kokes, and anglers also often hit into rainbows. During the productive spring and summer months, leadcore line or downriggers can do the job. That's when the kokanee are usually found about 20 to 35 feet down. In late summer, trollers need to often work down 40 to 60 feet. The main river channel from mid-lake down to the dam is probably the most consistent kokanee trolling route. A Wedding Ring lure tipped with white or yellow corn is a local favorite. Many anglers swear by Jolly Green Giant's green label. Needlefish (in #1 or #2) in frog, bikini and pearl are also good, as are Lucky Knights. Flashers like the Les Davis Cow Bells or Ford Fenders and a rubber snubber complete the trolling package.

Black bass at Bullards Bar don't get big due to the lack of forage fish and the competition with the kokanee. But there are lots of bass in the 12 to 14 inch range, with some going up to 4 pounds.

Bullards Bar Reservoir Facts

Location: In Yuba County, 5 miles west of Hwy. 49, 10 miles north of Nevada City and 20 miles east of Marysville.

Size: 4600 surface acres with 55 miles of shoreline. Elevation is 2300 feet.

Species: Kokanee salmon, rainbow trout, small and largemouth bass, panfish, catfish

Facilities: Full-service marina and resort including a store, boat rental, houseboat rental, etc. There are campgrounds on the south and east sides of the lake.

Information: Emerald Cove Resort and Marina, (530) 692-3200; USFS, Tahoe National Forest, Comptonville, (530) 265-4531

Butt Valley Reservoir

Northcentral freshwater fishing leads off with a discussion on the great fishing and fantastic facilities at Lake Almanor. But there is a little known lake right next door to Almanor that every serious trout and smallmouth bass angler should experience. Butt Valley is a 1000 acre gem that offers trophy brown and rainbow trout, king salmon and lunker smallmouths. It lies in a picturesque valley which was once a meadow through which Butt Creek tumbled on its way to the North Fork of the Feather River. Now Almanor water, cold and rich in nutrients, reaches Bull Valley via a tunnel. Big fish are commonplace. Smallmouths average 2 to 4 pounds, with 7 to 9 pounders a possibility. In the mid 1980's a 19 pound plus rainbow came out. Browns and salmon in the 10 to 12 pound range are taken. Some locals say it's possible that state record smallmouth, rainbow and brown trout could lurk in Butt Valley.

Elevation is 4,150 feet, so most anglers come in warmer weather months. The lake is about 5 miles long and 1/2 to 3/4 of a mile wide. No waterskiing is permitted. Facilities are limited to a single lane launch ramp, two well-kept PG & E campgrounds and a picnic area, but don't let this keep you from trying Butt Lake when you're in the Almanor area.

You reach Butt Valley by taking the Prattville-Butt Reservoir Road off of Hwy. 89 on the south shore of Lake Almanor.

Camp Far West Lake (map - p. 152)

Camp Far West Lake, located about an hour's drive northeast of Sacramento, is an excellent all around fishing and recreational lake. An added bonus is its fine striped bass fishery. Camp Far West has been stocked with stripers for over 15 years. 10 to 12 pound catches are not unusual, and lunkers go up to 20 pounds. There are also large and smallmouth bass, catfish, crappie, and bluegill. And although this is a warm water lake, it's possible to catch trout up in the extreme ends of both the Rock Creek and Bear River arms. There is camping, picnicking, boat launching and marina facilities.

Camp Far West Fishing Seasons

☒ Good ☒ Fair

	J	F	M	A	M	J	J	A	S	O	N	D
Bass			☒	☒	☒	☒	☒	☒	☒	☒	☒	
Catfish		☒	☒	☒	☒	☒	☒	☒	☒	☒	☒	
Panfish			☒	☒	☒	☒	☒	☒	☒			
Striped Bass	☒	☒	☒							☒	☒	☒
Trout		☒	☒	☒	☒					☒	☒	☒

Camp Far West Fishing Tips

The fishing year at Camp Far West kicks off in the fall with the onset of striped bass action. October through May is usually the best period. Dawn and dusk and after dark are the peak hours to get in on the action. When the lake turns over, large striper hang off points in search of threadfin shad over the submerged channel of the Bear River. Water levels drop in fall. Action improves as the fish are concentrated. Surface action often tips the stripers' location. Stripers are also

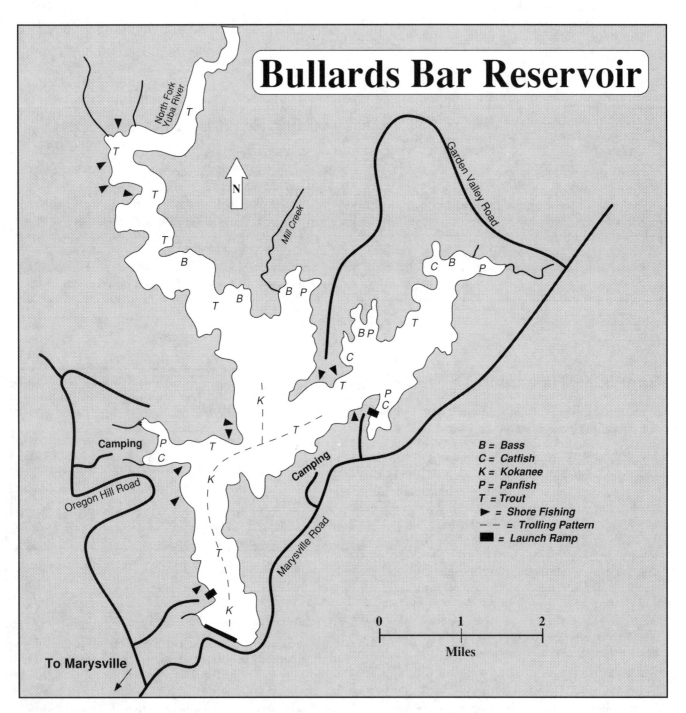

Bullards Bar Reservoir

North Fork Yuba River

Mill Creek

Garden Valley Road

N

Camping

Oregon Hill Road

Marysville Road

Camping

B = Bass
C = Catfish
K = Kokanee
P = Panfish
T = Trout
► = Shore Fishing
- - - = Trolling Pattern
■ = Launch Ramp

0   1   2
Miles

To Marysville

located by trolling large shallow-running, minnow-shaped plugs off the dam and along the main Rock Creek and Bear River channels. Bait anglers take stripers on live threadfin shad about 6 feet below a bobber. Action continues until big storms muddy the water or until the lake cools.

As winter water temperatures drops below 50, stripers often suspend in 20 to 40 feet of water over the Bear River channel. This puts them out of the range of shore anglers. That's when bank anglers pursue channel and blue catfish with frozen catfish instead. Two good areas are at the north and south campgrounds. These are good areas after dark, while the cove between the north campground and the dam are often good both mornings and afternoons.

Boaters at this time go after suspended striper using electronic fish finders. Anglers pursue them with structure spoons or spinnerbait by vertical jigging. Trolling or drifting live minnows also work. In spring, big stripers can be found in 4 to 12 feet of water off long, sloping points. Casting plugs from well off these points often produce. Black bass action starts in spring in the three big coves on the north side of Rock Creek as the shallows warm up. Smallmouth usually start the parade, followed by largemouth and finally crappie. The banks of the Bear usually warm slower than those on the Rock arm, so try these if action has slowed on the Rock Creek arm.

One final note: Trolling probably produces more striper than any other method. Most trollers find success down the middle of the wider part of both the Rock Creek and Bear River arms. The face of the dam and the deeper cover can also be productive. What varies is proper trolling depth. Twenty feet is a good place to test your luck. Then go deeper, or shallower, in increments. A faster trolling speed seems to be best. Two striper plugs are local favorites and seem to be consistently most successful. They are the Rebel and Rapala 7 inchers, in silver with black stripe, or silver with purple stripe. Also, be aware that fishing conditions can very greatly in the cooler months depending on rain, runoff, inflow, etc. It may take several days for the lake to clear after it muddies up. So call in advance.

Camp Far West Facts

Location: Camp Far West is east of Hwy. 65 between Lincoln and Westland.

Size: At 2200 surface acres, Camp Far West is smaller than most other foothill reservoirs. There are about 30 miles of shoreline.

Species: Striped bass to 12 pounds, catfish up to 15 pounds, smallmouth and largemouth bass (up to 6 pounds), crappie and bluegill

Facilities: Camp Far West is a water district reservoir located on state-owned property. The north and south facilities at the lake are operated by the same recreation concession. There are camping and launching facilities on both sides of the lake. The marina and store are on the south shore. The north shore facilities are closed in winter. Gate hours change depending upon the season.

Information: Camp Far West Lake, Box 929, Wheatland, CA 95692, (530) 633-0803

Collins Lake (map - p. 153)

Collins Lake has outstanding camping facilities, excellent fishing, all types of water recreation and it's a pleasant 1 1/4 hour drive northwest of Sacramento. But don't be confused. Some maps label Collins Lake as "Merle Collins Reservoir" or as "Virginia Ranch Reservoir." By any name it's a worthwhile destination. This 1000 acre lake, in a pretty setting in the foothills, has about 12 miles of shoreline. There are fishing only zones posted on the lake in summer and no waterskiing is permitted September 15 to May 15. An intensive trout planting program from February to May each year includes some big fish. Look to fall for trophy trout action. In addition, there are bass (both largemouth and smallmouth) and very large, plentiful catfish (lake record 30 pounds). Facilities include camping, full-service marina, swimming beach, diving raft, etc.

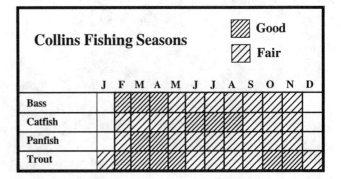

Collins Fishing Seasons		J	F	M	A	M	J	J	A	S	O	N	D
Bass													
Catfish													
Panfish													
Trout													

(Legend: ▨ Good, ▨ Fair)

Collins Fishing Tips

The peak trout action is usually in February and March each year, but it is good through May and again in the fall. Shore anglers using a sliding sinker rig and marshmallow/salmon egg combinations, or inflated nightcrawlers, score on 12-15 inch trout. And lunkers up to the lake record of 9 pounds are caught. A spring surface water temperature of 60 signals peak trout action. Trollers succeed with 1/4 ounce gold Kastmaster and #3 or #4 Rebels and Rapalas in rainbow colors. When the lake warms in May, a thermocline forms and the trout move down to about the 40 foot mark. Flashers in front of shiny lures or nightcrawlers, used with leadcore line or downriggers, produce great summertime action. Collins Lake is 120 feet deep so it sustains a hungry population of trout year-round. By October, the lake "turns over" bringing cold water to the surface along with all the trout.

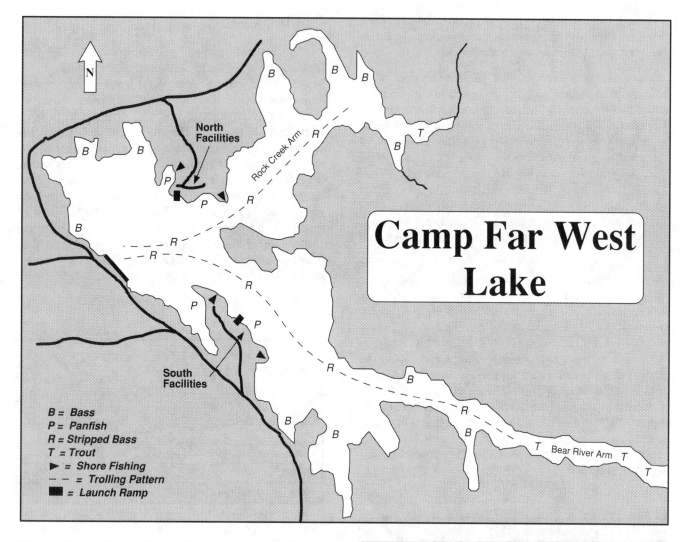

Near-surface tactics and shore fishing are now the ticket to success.

The dominant largemouth variety in Collins is the Florida-strain. Fish up to 10 pounds are caught every year, including lots of 3 to 6 pounders. Probably the best bass fishing at Collins is along the eastern shoreline. Habitat has been improved here with sunken trees and brush piles. Another good spot is near the Oregon House Bridge.

Plastic worms and Bobby Garland jigs (in purple and motor oil) are two good bets. February is the prime month for smallmouths averaging 2 pounds. After storms, the catfishing is best in the water inflows at the north end of the lake. Other times, work the east corner of the dam and the submerged treetops along the east bank. Most catfish hit after dark. By the way, fishing is legal at Collins 24 hours a day.

Collins Lake Facts

Location: In Yuba County between Marysville and Grass Valley. The lake is 42 miles from Yuba City via Hwy. 20 and then Hwy. E-21.

Size: Over 1000 acres with 12 miles of shoreline

Species: Rainbows, browns, northern and Florida largemouths, smallmouths, Alabama spotted bass, catfish, crappie, redear sunfish

Facilities: Full-service campground, boat launching, store and snack bar, swimming beach, marina, picnic area, boat rental. The lake is open all year.

Boating: All boating is allowed, with exceptions. Water skiing is permitted from May 15 to September 15 only. There are also Fishing Only Areas designated on the lake with 5 mph limits.

Information: Collins Lake Recreation Area, P.O. Box 300, Oregon House, CA 95962, (530) 692-1600

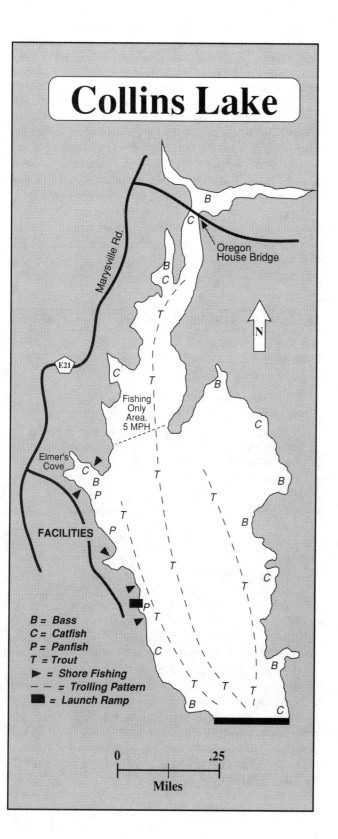

Collins Lake

Marysville Rd.

B

C

Oregon
House Bridge

B

C

N

T

E21

C

T

B

Fishing
Only
Area.
5 MPH

C

Elmer's
Cove

C

B

B

P

C

T

FACILITIES

T

B

P

T

T

C

T

B = Bass
C = Catfish
P = Panfish
T = Trout
► = Shore Fishing
– – = Trolling Pattern
■ = Launch Ramp

P

T

C

T

T

T

B

C

0   .25

Miles

Davis* and Frenchman Lakes

The Western Pacific Railroad passes from the Great Basin and on up to the crest of the Northern Sierra Mountains as it parallels Hwy. 70 in eastern Plumas County. Along this route are Portola and Chilcoot, two famous old railroad towns that are now also stopping-off points to two fine fishing lakes.

Davis is about 7 miles north of Portola. It's a large lake at 4,000 surface acres and 32 miles of shoreline. Trout anglers consistently bring in 2 to 3 pound rainbows, with an occasional brown pushing ten pounds. Trolling is the way to go on this big lake, but lots of shore anglers also score. Try an inflated nightcrawler or other floating bait to keep your offering up off the grassy bottom. Fly-fishing is also popular at Davis. Try areas around Camps, Jenkins Cove and Cow Creek. Damselfly nymphs work well. A surprise to many is the fine largemouth bass fishing that exists at Davis. The extensive weed beds in the north area kick out many 2 to 4 pounders. The island shoreline is also good. Best action is from May through July. Weedless and semi-weedless lures are in order. There are three campgrounds and launch ramps at Davis, all maintained by the Forest Service.

Frenchman is east of Davis and about 5 miles north of Chilcoot. Catchable-size planted rainbow are the order of the day here. Trolling, casting spoons and spinners, and bait all produce at this 1,580 surface acre lake at a 5,600 foot elevation. Frenchman, like Davis, is in Plumas National Forest. The Forest Service maintains a number of campgrounds and a launch ramp. By the way, when you're in the area, don't miss the Portola Railroad Museum. You'll enjoy it, and at the same time, you'll be lending support to the volunteers who are working hard to preserve a bit of railroad history. Information on the area: Plumas County Vistor's Bureau, (530) 283-6345 or (800) 326-2247; Allan Bruzza's Sportsmans Den (530) 283-2733.

Donner Lake (map - p. 155)

Donner Lake has about all the trout angler could ask for, ranging from bruiser Mackinaw trout to hordes of 8 to 12 inch

Someone illegally put northern pike into Lake Davis a few years ago and that action has had dire consequences. The Department of Fish & Game felt the pike posed a threat to the Davis trout fishery and possibly to other species in the waters of the Central Valley, which they could reach via the Feather River system. Consequently, Davis was treated with Nusyn-Noxfish (which contains rotenone) in the fall of 1997 to eradicate all the fish there—pike, trout, and bass alike. The same scenario unfolded at nearby Frenchman Reservoir a few years ago, and the good news is that the trout fishing has recovered there. Davis, which supports a superior trout fishery, should rebound in a couple of years. Meanwhile, the best bet is to inquire about fishing conditions before you visit the lake.

planter rainbows. Throw in trophy-sized brown trout and a good population of kokanee salmon, and you've got a fantastic fishing lake. This seems strange in a way because many associate this locale with the Donner Party or with the hordes of water-skiers, wind surfers and sailors they see on the lake in the summertime. But as is true with many fishing situations, timing, both the right time of day and the right season of the year, is critical to fishing success and enjoyment at Donner. There are all kinds of facilities at Donner including resorts, campgrounds, marinas, swim beaches, picnicking, etc.

Donner Fishing Seasons													
	J	F	M	A	M	J	J	A	S	O	N	D
Brown Trout		▨	▨	▨	▨		▨	▨	▨	▨		
Kokanee					▨	▨	▨	▨	▨			
Mackinaw		▨	▨	▨	▨	▨				▨	▨	
Rainbow Trout		▨	▨	▨	▨	▨	▨	▨	▨	▨		

Legend: ▨ Good, ▨ Fair

Donner Fishing Tips

Some anglers consider Donner as a "manageable-size Lake Tahoe," and it's probably accurate, especially when it comes to monster Mackinaw. The best time to take Donner lakers is February and March. That's the time of year when they're cruising in only 10 to 30 feet of water. Early morning trollers pull very large Rebel and Rapala minnows or J-plugs. Be prepared for some very cold weather. At other times, Mackinaw are much deeper. They're lurking near bottom in as much as 150 feet of water. Because of Donner's irregular contour, wire line and downrigger trollers are often frustrated by snags. But persistence can pay off. Another approach that avoids snag worries is to locate fish with an electronic fish finder and then drop down large spoons (say 3 to 6 ounces) or large minnows. A problem here is that wind can make it difficult to keep the boat over the fish. In spring and fall a compromise approach works. You see, the Department of Fish and Game stocks Donner regularly with catchable-sized rainbows and browns. And the Mackinaw love them! Estimates are that Macks, and lunker browns and rainbows, consume as much as 30% of each fish planting. The afternoon after the plant and the next morning are the prime times to get in on the action. Experts suggest trolling about 20 to 50 feet deep, just outside casting range between the east end boat ramp rip-rap and the next small stream that enters

the lake towards the west. Shore anglers have a chance at big lakers. Nightcrawlers and big plugs cast out near the boat near the boat ramp after stocking often works. Or, if you don't mind snow, this approach can also produce from public access areas in the dead of winter.

Big browns are taken while working the "trout plants" for Mackinaw, either from boat or shore. They are also taken by winter Mackinaw trollers around the boat ramp. Spoons, like Kastmaster in 1/4 ounce size, make good shore casting lures. Use the countdown approach to time your retrieve. Gradually increase the count until you approach bottom. Good spots for pan-sized planted rainbows are the boat ramp, the north shore piers, the lake outlet at the east end, and China Cove. Kokanee are taken by deep trolling in the summer. Best spots are the west end inlet stream area, deep off the boat ramp, and along the drop-off near China Cove.

Donner Lake Facts
Location: 2 miles west of Truckee, just off I-80 along the Donner Pass
Size: Donner is about 3 miles long and about 3/4 miles wide
Species: Mackinaw trout, brown trout, rainbow trout, kokanee salmon
Facilities: On the east end is the Donner Memorial State Park (with campsites), a museum, and a marina with boat rental. The launch ramp is located on the west end.
Information: Truckee Chamber of Commerce, (530) 587-2757

Englebright Lake (map - p. 156)

Englebright Lake offers a special type of camping and fishing experience. All 100 plus campsites are scattered along the 9 mile long, narrow lake, and can only be reached by boat. Granted the campsites are on the primitive side, for example, there are no flush toilets. But in exchange, you get closer to nature. Sites are all near the water, on shelves or sand banks, offering lake views and bank fishing at your doorstep. An added bonus is that the campsites, launching and day use, are free. And in the upper reaches of the lake waterskiing is not permitted, so noise and wakes are not a problem. Surprisingly, for a lake only an hour or so from Sacramento, the facilities are not overrun. Some say it's because of its

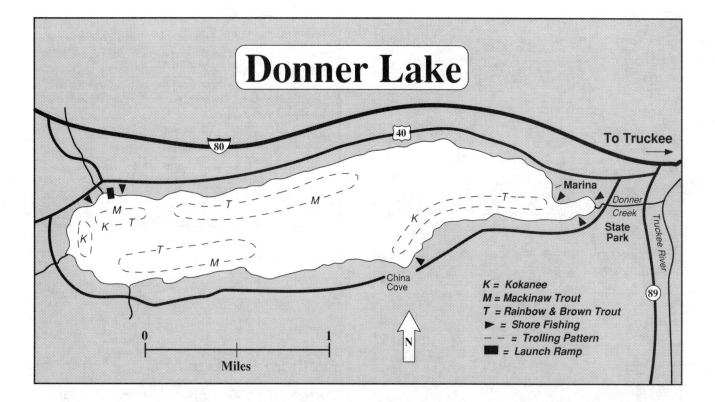

Donner Lake

K = Kokanee
M = Mackinaw Trout
T = Rainbow & Brown Trout
► = Shore Fishing
– – = Trolling Pattern
■ = Launch Ramp

awkward location, off Hwy. 20 between Marysville and Grass Valley. But rest assured, it's not because of the fishing. Trout and bass fishing is good in this clean, green, winding, flooded Yuba River basin. And the water level is usually up near full even in the fall. Facilities include 2 launch ramps, small marina, store and cafe.

Englebright Fishing Seasons

	J	F	M	A	M	J	J	A	S	O	N	D
Bass			▨	▨	▨	▨	▨	▨	▨	▨		
Catfish			▨	▨	▨	▨	▨	▨	▨	▨		
Panfish			▨	▨	▨	▨	▨	▨	▨	▨		
Trout			▨	▨	▨	▨	▨	▨	▨	▨		

▨ Good ▨ Fair

Englebright Fishing Tips

The lake is stocked with rainbow every week or two during the summer. Trolling a small spoon (Needlefish, Z-ray, etc.) can score both trout and kokanee near the dam. There is good shore fishing for picnickers between the marina and the dam. The rainbow are not big in Englebright, but there are some large brown trout. Way up the far extreme of the North Fork of the Yuba, at the remains of the Rice's Crossing Bridge, trout action can be very good. Flies, lures, salmon eggs and worms all produce. Bass anglers do best fishing the many flowing stream coves. In the spring there is a large sandbar where the two forks of the lake join. Bass fishing can be good here. Campsites that are farther up in the lake offer better prospects of fishing from shore, or right in the vicinity of the camp. Think about the sun when picking a campsite. Some warm up early in the morning. Others get warm afternoon sun.

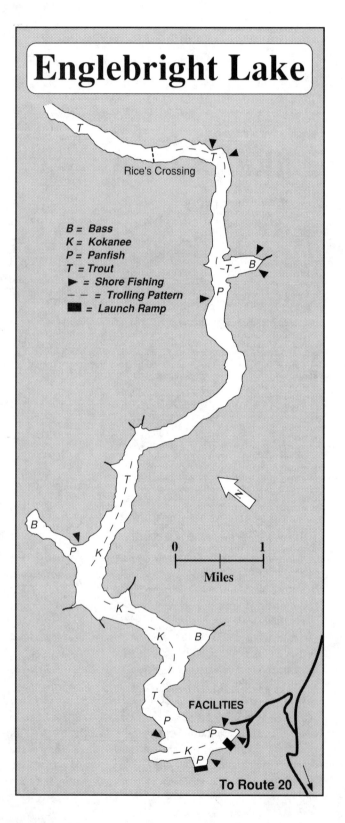

Englebright Lake

Rice's Crossing

B = Bass
K = Kokanee
P = Panfish
T = Trout
► = Shore Fishing
– – = Trolling Pattern
■ = Launch Ramp

0   1
Miles

FACILITIES

To Route 20

Englebright Lake Facts

Location: The lake is between Marysville (20 miles) and Grass Valley (15 miles). From Marysville head east on Hwy. 20 to Smartville. Turn left at Mooney Flat Road and drive 3 miles to the lake.

Size: There are 815 surface acres of water with 24 miles of shoreline stretching nine miles up above the dam in the Yuba River Canyon. Lake elevation is 527 feet.

Species: Many small rainbow (12 to 14 inches) with some larger brown trout, kokanee, smallmouth and largemouth bass, panfish and catfish

Facilities: There are 2 launch ramps, a small marina with boat rental, picnic area, and boat-in campsites.

Information: U.S. Army Corps of Engineers, Box 6, Smartville, CA 95977, (530) 639-2342; Skipper's Cove Marina, 13104 Marina, Smartville, CA 9597-9802, (530) 639-2272

Feather River Basin

The branches and tributaries of the Feather River drain a huge triangular section of the Northwestern Sierras between Oroville, Lake Almanor and Portola. Most of this territory is quite rugged and inaccessible, but because the area is so large, there are still miles and miles of rivers and streams that are quite easy to get to. By the way, the Lower Feather River, which flows south from Lake Oroville, is covered in the "Central Valley River Fishing" chapter.

Let's start our tour at Lake Almanor. The North Fork of the Feather drains into Almanor at Chester. Starting right in town, the North Fork and its streams (Rice Creek, Warner Creek, Hot Springs Creek, Willow Creek, Brenner Creek, Last Chance Creek) have good access, relatively low fishing pressure and native trout. The North Fork itself is a fairly large stream, even in autumn. Most of the streams are spring fed, and run clear and cold throughout the summer. Several types of fishing are offered. Willow Creek is very brushy and is best for bait angling. Some others like Rice Creek are good fly casting waters. There are a number of campgrounds along the creeks providing access and overnight camping.

On the northeast shore of Lake Almanor the Hamilton Branch flows into the lake. It offers good fishing in a series of big pools, separated by white water riffles flowing through a scenic canyon. The Feather River flows out of Lake Almanor at its south end. Senaca Road parallels the river for about 10 miles and leads to Senaca Resort. Lake Almanor dam provides a regulated flow of very cold water to this stretch of water. The best access is where Senaca Road crosses the North Fork. Fish away from this access, either upstream or downstream, for best results.

Between Lake Almanor and Lake Oroville, the North Fork of the Feather River flows along Rte. 70 for much of its course through the Feather River Canyon. Where you can get down to it, the main river is good trout water. A good eight mile stretch is from Nelson Creek to Audie Bar. Perennial hot spots include the confluence of the North Fork and the East Branch of the North Fork, and the mouth of Yellow Creek. These are both just above the town of Belden. The lower section of Yellow Creek near the Feather is fished heavily, but is still productive. Upper Yellow Creek, accessible from Humbug Road off Rte. 89 along the west shore of Lake Almanor, is a fine mountain meadow stream. There is a PG & E campground in the east end of Humbug Valley. The canyon below the valley is also good fishing with flies or bait.

The Middle Fork of the Feather is accessible along Rte. 70/89 between Sloat to Portola. Some of the better areas are Camp Layman, Two Rivers and Carmac Mine.

The Middle Fork from Graeagle and Red Bridge is good bait territory, although fly anglers also succeed in the shallower parts of the stream. Good tributary streams in this area include Mohawk, Frazier, Gray Eagle, Smith, Eureka, Bear and Dear.

For information on the Feather River Basin contact, Plumas National Forest, 875 Mitchell, Oroville, CA 95965, (530) 534-6500; Almanor Ranger District, Box 767, Chester, CA 96010, (530) 258-2141.

Gold Lakes (map - p. 157)

If you enjoy small, high-mountain lake angling while surrounded by spectacular scenery, with the option for nearby stream and river trout action, then you'll instantly fall in love

with the little known Gold Lakes Basin Recreation Area. It is located between Graeagle, on the Middle Fork of the Feather River along Hwy. 89, and Bassett on the North Fork of the Yuba River along Hwy. 49. Most of the more than 30 lakes here lie between 5,000 and 6,000 feet with Eureka Peak at 7,447 feet and the famed Sierra Buttes at 8,587 feet as north and south sentinels overlooking the basin. Access to most lakes, campgrounds, trails to pack-in lakes and to the high-mountain back country is via Gold Lakes Forest Highway at Bassett or Graeagle.

Starting from the south end of the basin a mile or two up from Bassett is the cut-off to Lower and Upper Sardine Lakes. On the way to the lakes are two Plumas National Forest campgrounds and Sand Pond, a favorite for summer swimmers. At Lower Sardine you'll find a lodge with cabins,

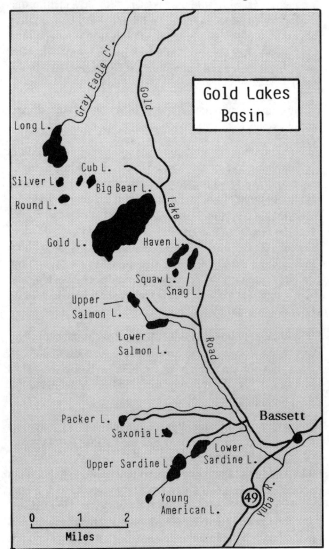

boat rentals and even a restaurant. Trolling for rainbow and some brook trout is good at this gorgeous setting. Bait anglers score at the inlet across the lake. A rough road leads to Upper Sardine Lake where shore angling can be productive. Or you can hike upward along its inlet stream to get to Young American Lake at 7,250 feet elevation for some golden trout possibilities.

A right fork off the road heading into Sardine eventually leads to Packer Lake. This is a nice sized, forested, and well-sheltered lake with cabins and a lodge on the back side. Planted trout in the 12 to 14 inch size range are taken by trollers and bait dunkers.

The next paved crossroad north on Gold Lakes Basin Road leads west to Upper Salmon Lake. Large boulders and wooded banks surround the lake and provide a picturesque setting for the boat-in lodge on the far side. Boat anglers have the best opportunity here. A rough dirt road off Salmon Lake Road leads to Lower Salmon Lake. It is proclaimed by some local experts as being the best fly fishing lake in the basin.

Next up the main road comes a collection of lakes focused around Snag Lake campgrounds. Planted trout and lake-view camping are the order of the day.

The namesake of the basin, Gold Lake, is just north of Snag and can be glimpsed from the main road. Gold is a relatively large, deep lake that offers the angler a chance at Mackinaw lake trout in the 10-16 pound class. They'll hit near the surface in the spring, but be prepared to go down to around 100 feet in the late summer. There is good shore fishing around the north east end, especially near the outflow stream. There is also a campground and boat launching site in this area. On the west side of Gold Lake is Mt. Base Camp Lodge.

A short way up Gold Lakes Basin Road is the cut-off for Gold Lake Lodge. From here anglers take short hikes back into about a dozen small lakes for rainbow, brook and brown trout action. By the way, you can't find any better places for float tubing.

For a change of pace, try fishing some moving water. At the north end, the Middle Fork of the Feather and its feeder streams such as Mohawk, Frazier, Gray Eagle, Smith, Eureka, Bear and Dear have rainbows and browns. At the south end of the basin, good action can be found on the North Fork of the Yuba River and feeder streams like Howard and Salmon Creek. There are also dozens of stream possibilities in the heart of the basin. All the streams that come into and

go out of major lakes such as Long Lake, Gold Lake, the Sardine Lakes and the Salmon Lakes are good. Remote streams that produce include Pauley, Lavezzola and Spencer. Information: Plumas County Chamber of Commerce, Quincy, (530) 283-6345; Allan Bruzza's Sportsman's Den (530) 283-2733

Little Grass Valley Reservoir

Little Grass Valley Reservoir is not easy to get to. But once you arrive, you'll find outstanding cold water fishing, extensive camping and launching facilities, on a good-sized lake high up in the Sierras. Little Grass Valley is located just north of the small town of La Porte. You get to the reservoir by taking Hwy. 20 from Marysville or Grass Valley to the Collins Lake turnoff (12 miles east of Marysville) and then proceed about 50 miles up Quincy-La Porte Road (E-21). Little Grass Valley has 1,600 surface acres of water at an elevation of 5,040 feet. There are over 300 developed campsites in 4 lakeside campgrounds, with a paved launch ramp in the vicinity of each campground.

Big fish are the rule at Little Grass Valley. Brown trout go up to 20 pounds! Rainbows in the 4 to 6 pound class are not unusual. And kokanee salmon run up to 15 to 17 inches. Large browns are most often taken by trollers dragging minnow-style plugs way out behind the boat. Work the shallower points and banks in the spring and then move out into deeper water in the summertime. But bank fishing is also very good, especially in spring and early summer. Bait, spoons and plugs all work. Little Grass Valley Road provides access to good shore fishing locations all around the lake. Stream inlets are particularly good areas to concentrate on. Information: Challenge Vistor Information Service (530) 675-1146 or Feather River Ranger Dist. (530) 534-6500

North of Lake Tahoe

There is some very good lake and stream fishing, just north of Lake Tahoe. Combine this with quality camping, rafting, Reno and the beauty of this area and it all adds up to one terrific spot for a vacation or weekend get-away.

The Truckee River is the premier stream in the area.* It flows along Rte. 89 to the town of Truckee, and then along I-80 all the way to Nevada. There are many good spots in this long and large river. Regulations vary along this river, so be informed. Some of the best fishing is where creeks enter the

*Also see page 163.

main river. Especially noteworthy are the mouths of Donner Creek and Prosser Creek. Another fine stretch is from Hirshdale on down to Farrad. Aggressive wading is required in many stretches of the Truckee. Use a wading staff.

Prosser Lake, just about six miles north of Truckee, is a fine fishing lake. And the 10 mph boat speed limit makes for serene fishing, even in summer. Both rainbow and brown trout of good size are caught in this 750 surface acre mountain lake. The area near the mouth of Prosser Creek is a consistent producer. Late summer deep trolling is good near the dam. There is a good launch ramp, campsites and a picnic area. Prosser Creek which is above the lake is a very good trout stream. The main stream is accessible off Hwy. 89. The north and south forks (near this junction is good fishing) are reached via a Forest Service Road. Prosser Creek flows cold and clear, even in late summer. Small lures and nymph patterns on a light leader are a good bet.

Boca Reservoir, somewhat larger than Prosser Lake, is locate about nine miles northeast of Truckee. Besides a good trout population, there is also an expanding kokanee fishery. Anglers troll for kokanee using a flasher followed by a Kokanee King or Triple Teaser. A white kernel of corn on the hook seems to help. Most kokanee taken are in the 11-13 inch range. All types of boating are allowed and there is a developed campground.

Stampede is last, but not least, in our collection of Truckee area trout lakes. It is by far the largest with 3,500 surface areas of water and 25 miles of shoreline. And, it has some of the best fishing for brown and rainbow trout and kokanee salmon. Stampede is relatively shallow in many areas so food production is outstanding. Kokanee go for the same offerings as at Boca, but run 12-15 inches. Trout trollers often do well with nightcrawlers behind flashers. There are excellent camping and launching facilities at the south side of the lake. Good spots include the Little Truckee inflow area and near the dam. Stream trout anglers often find the Little Truckee River to be a good producer. Access is via Rte. 89 and Jackson Meadows Road, which both parallel the stream. Small spinners are effective. The Little Truckee runs above and below Stampede Reservoir.

Martis Creek Lake is located between Truckee and Lake Tahoe, along Hwy. 267, just north of the Northstar-at-Tahoe ski area. On first sight it doesn't look like much. Sagebrush and, in dry years, a massive mud and gravel ring surround the reservoir. But don't be deceived. Browns in the 5 to 10 pound range are lurking here. Martis (at 700 surface acres when full) was the first locale designated by the California Department of Fish & Game as a wild trout lake. The original idea was to support a population of rare Lahontan cutthroat trout. But now, more aggressive rainbows and browns dominate. Martis is a catch and release, artificial lure and flies-only lake. Most fish from bank, canoe or float tube since motors are not allowed. Adjacent creeks are closed to fishing. Often the best action on Martis is in the channel along the weed beds at the south end of the lake where Martis Creek enters. Trolling is good where there are less weeds along the east side and near the dam. Spin casters use Mepps spinners, Hopkins and Kastmaster spoons. Remember only single, barbless hooks are permitted so change hooks and flatten or file off barbs. Fly anglers use all kinds of things. But dry flies that resemble grasshoppers and moths are good. Wooly Worms and Zug Bugs account for some of the biggest fish. Best months at Martis include May, June, July and October.

For information on the area north of Lake Tahoe, contact the Truckee Chamber of Commerce, Box 361, Truckee, CA 95734, (530) 587-2757, and the Truckee Ranger District, Box 399, Truckee, CA 95734, (530) 587-3558.

Lake Oroville (map - p. 161)

Lake Oroville is a very large, beautiful reservoir that offers excellent fishing. Trout, salmon, bass, catfish and panfish are all plentiful. This canyon reservoir is made up of the branches of the Feather River. Camping is concentrated at the south end of the lake with full-service marinas at both the south and north ends of the lake. Shore fishing is limited because of the steep shoreline and limited access opportunities. The best shore fishing is at campgrounds and marinas, and in the Diversion Pool, Thermalito Forebay and Afterbay. Actually, the Diversion Pool, the two bays and a large area of former gold-dredging flats along the Feather River offer a whole other set of recreation opportunities. This system is called the Oroville Wildlife Area and it is located to the west and south of the city of Oroville. It is a 10-plus mile long recreation zone. Fishing is good in the forebay and afterbay (launch ramps are available) and also in the dozens of small warm water ponds where largemouth bass are prevalent. Explore this complex when in the Oroville area for a pleasant surprise.

Oroville Fishing Seasons

		J	F	M	A	M	J	J	A	S	O	N	D
Bass			Good	Good	Good	Good	Fair	Fair	Fair	Good	Good	Good	
Catfish						Fair	Fair	Fair	Fair				
Panfish				Fair	Good	Good	Good	Good	Good	Good			
Salmon		Good	Good	Good	Good	Good	Fair	Fair	Good	Good	Good	Good	Good
Trout		Fair	Good	Good	Fair	Fair	Fair	Fair	Fair	Fair	Good	Good	Good

Legend: Good (hatched), Fair (hatched)

Oroville Fishing Tips

As a maturing canyon lake, Oroville is probably better for smallmouth than largemouth bass. Oroville is actually 3 separate lakes, from a fishing point of view. The southern forks warm up first in the spring, so bassing turns on first there. The main body warms next with the North Fork warming last. Besides water temperature, keep an eye on your fish finder for the threadfin shad. If they're down, the game fish will also be down. Since Oroville is a very deep (over 500 feet) lake, the fish can go very deep to find food and comfortable water temperatures.

Shore fishing in the lake itself is usually best in the cool temperature months when trout are in shallow water. Boat anglers also score at this time with shallow trolling techniques and with bobber and bait combinations. Salmon are taken as an adjunct to trout fishing. Live minnows are a popular bait at Oroville. Trollers do well in the spring with deep-running Rapalas and Rebels. The dam area and at the mouths of the coves are hot spots. Smallmouth bass fishing is very popular all along the south shore of the South Fork arm. The North Fork arm (especially at Berry and French creeks) is also excellent as are some rocky coves on the east shore of the West Fork arm.

Ponds in the Oroville Wildlife Area vary in size from no more than 100 feet across to one that is a mile long. Rock and earth were removed from this gold-dredging area along the Feather River to help build the Oroville Dam, completed in 1967. Bass anglers work these ponds from shore or from prams, canoes, etc. Some ponds have wide-open shorelines, while others are overgrown. Boat or belly tubes provide access to drop-offs, overhead cover and deep edges of weed beds.

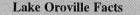

Lake Oroville Facts

Location: Oroville is the farthest north of the Sierra foothills' reservoirs. It's just east of the town of Oroville and about 70 miles north of Sacramento via Hwy. 70.

Size: 15,500 surface acres of water with 167 miles of shoreline. Lake elevation is 900 feet.

Species: Rainbow and brown trout, largemouth, spotted and smallmouth bass, king salmon, catfish and panfish

Facilities: There are two full-service marinas. One at the north end of the lake (Limesaddle) and one at the south end (Bidwell Canyon). Major campgrounds are Bidwell Canyon, Loafer Creek and Foreman. There are also boat-in campsites on the lake, but these are not accessible by vehicle. Houseboats and larger power boats moor overnight in coves all over the lake. Rental houseboats are available at the marinas. Multi-lane launch ramps are available at the dam, the marinas and at Loafer Creek.

Information: Oroville State Recreation Area, 400 Glen Dr., Oroville, CA 95965, (530) 538-2200; Bidwell Canyon Marina, Oroville-Quincy Rd., Oroville, CA, (530) 589-3165; Limesaddle Marina, P.O. Box 1088, Paradise, CA 95969, (530) 877-2414; Huntington's Sportsman's Store, 601 Oro Dam Blvd., Oroville, CA 95965, (530) 534-8000.

Rollins Lake

Rollins Lake is probably too easy to get to. It's only 50 miles from downtown Sacramento via I-80, and only 5 minutes from the Colfax exit. Its locale plus four campgrounds with 250 sites and several launch ramps make it an extremely popular summertime destination for water-skiers, board sailors, swimmers, etc. All of this makes warm weather fishing at Rollins an "iffy" situation. And it has probably prevented Rollins from developing a reputation as a good fishing lake. It's too bad because fishing is good at Rollins, especially in the "off season." Trollers take many brown trout in the 3 to 4 pound range during the peak months of February through May. Local experts suggest using enough leadcore line to get the lure down to about 58-60 water temperature. The irregular bottom contour makes the use of downriggers somewhat risky. Three main areas to work are the Bear River arm, near the dam, and in the Greenhorn Creek inlet. Persistent or lucky anglers take browns up to 10 pounds! Rapala plugs or similar offerings score best. There is also good shore fishing at Rollins for browns and planted rainbows. The smallmouth angling is also good in this rocky canyon reservoir. Work the rocky points and ledges, espe

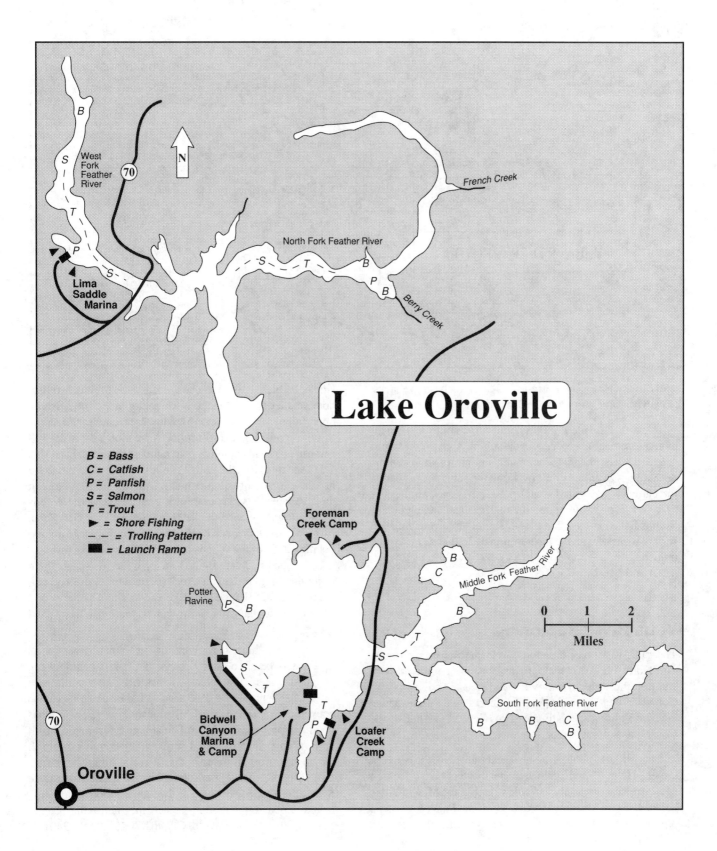

West Fork Feather River

French Creek

North Fork Feather River

Berry Creek

Lima Saddle Marina

Lake Oroville

B = Bass
C = Catfish
P = Panfish
S = Salmon
T = Trout
▶ = Shore Fishing
– – = Trolling Pattern
■ = Launch Ramp

Foreman Creek Camp

Middle Fork Feather River

Potter Ravine

0   1   2
Miles

South Fork Feather River

Bidwell Canyon Marina & Camp

Loafer Creek Camp

Oroville

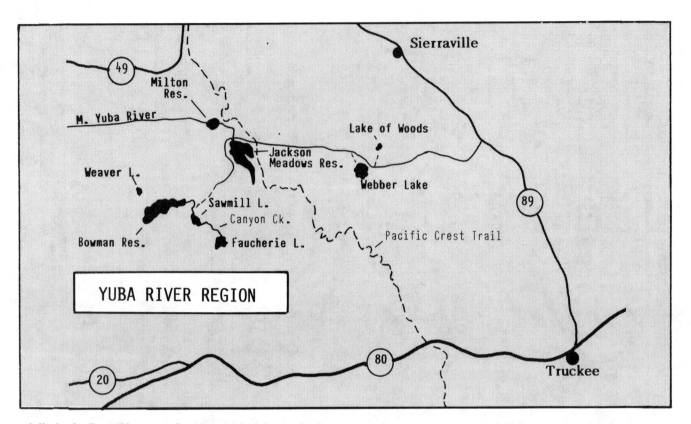

cially in the Bear River arm for 12 to 14 inch bronzebacks. However, some can go up to 2 to 3 pounds.

Actually browns, rainbows, and largemouth and small-mouth bass fishing is decent in the summertime. You've just got to do it early in the morning or late in the evening. Speaking of evening, don't overlook the summertime action for catfish. It's popular and productive on warm, sultry evenings, especially around the marinas and campgrounds. Rollins Lake has over 26 miles of shoreline surrounding 900 surface acres of water at an elevation of 2,100 feet. Information: Peninsula Campground, (530) 477-9413; Long Ravine, (530) 346-6166

Yuba River Region

The Yuba River has three forks—North, Middle and South. The North Fork flows alongside Hwy. 49 from the Sierra summit through Downieville and most of the way to Comptonville. There is good fishing in many places along the North Fork, especially near Downieville, and in Downie Creek and Salmon Creek.

The Middle Yuba is quite inaccessible except where it crosses Hwy. 49 and again at its headwaters below Jackson Meadow Reservoir. The 1.5 mile stretch of the Middle Yuba, below Jackson Meadows as well as Milton Lake, is a special regulation trophy trout fishery. Only artificial lures with

single, barbless hooks may be used, and the limit is two fish, both smaller than 12 inches. There are other good fishing opportunities in the Jackson Meadow area. Jackson Meadow Reservoir itself is a full-service recreation lake with 150 campsites, group camping, boat ramp, picnic area, etc. This 1 1/2 square mile lake with 11 miles of shoreline has good brown and rainbow trout fishing. Other good trout lakes in the area include Bowman (brown trout), Lake of the Woods (brook trout), Webber Lake (browns) and Weaver Lake. Bowman has very steep banks necessitating a boat for good fishing. Lake of the Woods is a gorgeous little lake that also is best fished by boat. In the Canyon Creek drainage, there is good fishing in Canyon Creek (several miles of good bait fishing waters), Faucherie Lake (good shore fishing) and Sawmill Lake (launch near the dam or shore fish in selected spots).

Fishing in the South Fork of the Yuba River in its headwaters between Soda Springs and Lake Spaulding can be good. Here the river switches back and forth with Interstate 80, providing good access. Lake Spaulding can be conveniently reached from I-80 using the Hwy. 20 exit. It has good campgrounds and boat launching. Most anglers troll here. Cooler than expected surface temperatures diminish the need to troll at great depths. Several highway bridges provide good access to the South Fork of the Yuba from Lake Spaulding all the way down to Bridgeport. For information on the Yuba River region contact, the Sierraville Ranger Station, Box 95, Sierraville, CA 96216, (530) 994-3401.

Special: Truckee River and Pyramid Lake

The Truckee River flows between Lake Tahoe and Pyramid Lake in Nevada. An overview of the Truckee River's outstanding fishing potential was presented earlier in this chapter. Now we're going to get down to the nitty-gritty. And as a bonus, we'll also profile the fine fishing in Nevada's Pyramid Lake.

The Truckee River is Lake Tahoe's only outlet. From its beginnings at Tahoe City, it meanders for over 30 miles in a northeasterly direction through mainly pine-studded, open canyon country. Once in Nevada, the Truckee flows through high desert dotted with sagebrush, cattle lands, the town of Reno, and finally terminating 80 miles north in Pyramid Lake.

Most Truckee trout are in the 9 to 12 inch range, but there is also a healthy population of 12 to 14 inchers. Most are rainbow, but some browns are present in both states. Trophy fish are also present, with individual fish going up to 5 to 6 pounds. Stream surveys in both states show a good number of 1 to 3 pounders.

An exciting aspect of the Truckee is that it rewards mostly those who put in the time to learn the river. Spoons are consistently the best producer for hardware tossers. Use the sizes that operate near the bottom. Kastmasters, Little Cleos, Z-Rays, and Daredevils are good in heavy water. In deep holes, plugs like Hot Shots, Wee Warts, and Rebels are winners. Results with spinners are mixed. Baits like worms, nightcrawlers, crickets, salmon eggs, and crawfish tails must be fished deep.

Best fishing on the Truckee often corresponds with the traditional high flow period of early May through mid-June. Fish are scattered through all kinds of water. Fly anglers need to concentrate on getting their offering down quickly and keeping it down in the strike zone. Reading and presentation are the keys to taking fish. Nymphs and streamers used in conjunction with a strike indicator are the way to go.

Both hardware, bait and fly anglers are advised to concentrate on bobbing their offerings. Identify a like hold, wade within range, and then drop it down. Waders and a wading staff are recommended in the Truckee, as is a measure of caution.

The most popular portion of the Truckee is the 15 miles between Tahoe City and Truckee. It is heavily planted by the DF & G. From Truckee downstream past the town of Verdi, Nevada, the river features native trout. There are two Wild Trout sections, one in each state. California's special regulations are in effect from the confluence of Trout Creek in downtown Truckee to Boca Bridge. Nevada's special waters run from the state line on down about four miles to the town of Verdi.

The Nevada Department of Wildlife plants the Truckee with catchables in areas of public access above Reno and in Reno. The park in Reno is one hot spot for planters.

The general trout season applies to the California portion of the Truckee. However, in Nevada, it's an all year stream. Fast water and leery native trout make the Truckee a special challenge.

Let's make it clear by repeating right up front: Pyramid Lake is in Nevada. I know this is Fishing in Northern California, but maybe it's the exception that makes the rule. Besides, since Pyramid Lake is on the Paiute Indian Reservation, California residents can fish it for the same price as Nevada residents. The current price of a daily permit is $6.00, with a season permit priced at $25.00. The season goes from October through June. Boaters are required to pay an additional modest fee. A Nevada fishing license is not required.

Pyramid Lake is one of the last remnants of ancient Lake Lahontan that once covered much of northwestern Nevada. Many consider it the most beautiful desert lake in the world. On top of all this, Pyramid was once, and is again, an outstanding Lahontan cutthroat trout fishery.

Originally, the Paiute Indians fished Pyramid. Later, commercial and sport anglers took a ton of huge cutthroat from Pyramid. At the twilight of this era, in 1925, John Skimmerhorn caught the world record cutthroat trout. It weighed in at 41 pounds! Surely, larger fish were taken and not weighed in prior years.

The Derby Dam, completed in 1905, marked the beginning of the end of huge native Lahontan cutthroats in Pyramid. The dam diverted much of Truckee's water from the lake, lowering its level and inhibiting spawning in Truckee's tributaries.

But Pyramid Lake has now recovered much of its glory. The Paiute's and the U.S. Fish and Wildlife Service have rebuilt the cutthroat fishery. Fishing fees are now a vital part of the tribe's economy. And the cutthroat are big and getting bigger. A few trout over 20 pounds are taken and 15 to 18 pounders come in with a fair amount of regularity. There is a two-fish, 19-inch minimum limit. No live or cured baits are allowed, and only artificial lures can be used.

The Pyramid season begins on October 1 and extends until the last day of June. Fishing can be good at any time, but the prime period is during the March-April spawn. Another good time is when the water temperature starts to dip, usually around Thanksgiving.

Boaters often troll along the western shore of the lake during the fall and winter months, getting off the lake when the winds come up. Use a zig-zag pattern pulling Flatfish, Kwikfish or Tor-P-Do spoons. Electronic fish finders are quite helpful.

Peak Pyramid excitement develops in spring when big "cuts" come from the deeper waters and forage along the shelves just off shore. Then fly anglers and spin anglers can cast from the western banks. Fly anglers use a shooting taper in 9 or 10 weight. Woolly Worms and Woolly Buggers in size 4 or 6 are favorites in black and white. Other colors also score. Spincasters use Tor-P-Dos (in chartreuse and red, white and red, and black and white), Quickfish, and spinners.

Most shorecasters improve their odds by wading out into the lake as far as possible. Some even bring along step ladders so they can even wade out a little farther. Of course, good waders are mandatory, along with other cold weather gear, during this time of year.

Camping is available at the lake. For fishing general information call Pyramid Lake at (661) 295-1245.

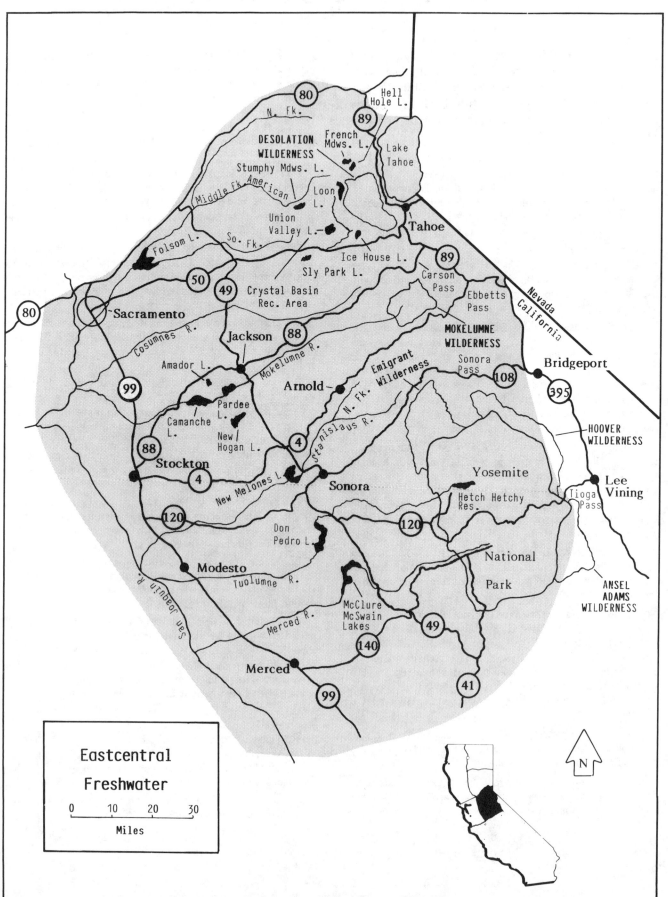

Eastcentral

Freshwater

0   10   20   30
Miles

Eastcentral Freshwater Fishing

The Central Sierra foothills is gold country. But anglers know the territory that parallels Hwy. 49 for something more than the motherlode. They know it for its string of outstanding reservoirs. Starting at the north end there is Folsom Lake. Then in rapid succession comes Amador, Camanche, Pardee, New Hogan, New Melones, Don Pedro, and last but not least, McClure and McSwain. There's some fine trout and bass fishing in this group of lakes. All are featured in this chapter. At higher elevations in the Central Sierras, trouting is very good. Five varied locales are profiled on the ensuing pages. You can spot each on the map that accompanies this chapter.

Lake Amador (map - p. 167)

Lake Amador is a very small lake as NorCal lakes go—only about 400 acres. But it offers just about everything any angler could want. First, it is a dedicated fishing lake. No waterskiing is allowed. And the fishing includes trophy size Florida-strain largemouth bass (lake record, 17 pounds 1 ounce), rainbow trout (about 50,000 are planted each year), catfish (up to 20 pounds) and panfish (crappie, redear sunfish and bluegill). Amador, located about 40 miles east of Stockton, has full facilities including campgrounds, full-service marina, boat rental, cafe, store, water slide, swimming pond, etc. This lake has about 14 miles of shoreline and is open from early February through Thanksgiving. The lake elevation is 485 feet in the small, black oak studded Jackson Creek Valley just below the first ridges of the Sierras.

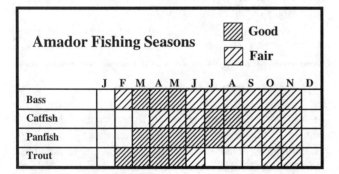

Amador Fishing Seasons	J	F	M	A	M	J	J	A	S	O	N	D
Bass		Fair	Good	Good	Good	Good	Good	Good	Good	Good	Good	Fair
Catfish						Good	Good	Good	Good	Good		
Panfish			Fair	Good	Good	Good	Good	Good	Fair			
Trout		Fair	Good	Good	Fair						Fair	Fair

Amador Fishing Tips

Florida-strain largemouth bass are king at Lake Amador. More big bass per acre of water come from Amador than from any other lake in Northern California. There are many 10 pound-plus fish landed each season. Lake Amador, planted in 1969, was one of the first Northern California lakes to get Florida-strain stock. It is rich in nutrients so the bass thrive and grow rapidly. March, April and May are the prime times for big bass. That's when they come up to the shallows and move into the coves to spawn. Popular lures in spring include spinnerbaits, crankbaits and plastic worms. Salt and pepper grubs and Pig 'n Jigs are also winners. Bass seem to strike worms short, so use a four incher to insure a higher percentage of hook-ups. Live nightcrawlers on a sliding sinker rig also score. Summertime bass action is in deeper water, except late in the evening or under a full moon. Evening top-water action can be fantastic on Zara Spooks, Hula Poppers, Rebel Pop-R's, etc. Bass anglers fish all night when the moon is full in spring and summer. They work the shoreline in coves and off points with surface plugs. Strikes are savage surface explosions.

Rainbow trout up to 5 pounds have been taken at Amador. Most catches are stocked fish in the 12 to 15 inch range, but some larger holdovers are present. Popular spots include the first cove near the dam off the dock and at any lake inlet that is running. Most anglers anchor and fish bait in those inlets in the late winter and spring. Trollers work the surface in the cooler months, but move deeper as June approaches. Trouting at Amador will improve even more as the lake expands its rearing ponds for fish in the 3 to 4 pound range. Winter and spring anglers work the top 15 feet of water, while summertime trollers search deep, cool water in the 30 to 45 foot range by the dams, and up the middle of the lake and the Jackson arm. Salmon egg/marshmallow combos, Rooster Tails and Mepps work well. Trollers use Triple Teasers, Kastmasters, Needlefish and nightcrawlers behind flashers.

In March, crappie start biting, and it gets real good in April, May and June along the shorelines. Fish range up to 2 or 3 pounds. Live minnows work, but mini-jigs in yellow or red and white are the top fish catchers. Keep the jig moving right off the bottom. Hits often occur on the drop. The redear sunfish and bluegill bite come on strong in June and July in the brushy areas of the lake. Anglers take them with red worms or mealworms under a bobber.

While many anglers have concentrated on bass, those going after channel and blue catfish at Amador have also been doing well. Action usually begins as early as April on cats up to 20 pounds. But most of the catfishing activity takes place in the summertime. Chicken livers and anchovies are the bait of choice at Amador. The best action takes place after dark along the face of the dam and in the coves along the campgrounds. Anglers keep their reel bails open, and let the cats take out as much as 20 feet of line before setting the hook.

Lake Amador Facts

Location: In the foothills of the Sierra northeast of Stockton and east of Lodi, off Hwy. 88 in Amador County.

Size: Lake Amador has about 400 surface acres of water with over 13 1/2 miles of shoreline.

Species: Florida-strain largemouth bass, rainbow trout, catfish and panfish

Facilities: Lake Amador is owned by the Jackson Valley Irrigation District. The recreation concession at the lake is quite complete for both day users and overnighters. Facilities include a six-lane concrete ramp, about 200 campsites (many with full hook-up), 12 boat-in campsites, a picnic area, rental boats, a lodge/store, a swimming pond with water slide and a restaurant with bar.

Boating: All boats are allowed, but there is no waterskiing permitted.

Information: Lake Amador Resort, 7500 Amador Dr., Ione, CA 95640, (209) 274-4739

Camanche Lake (map - p. 168)

Camanche is a large East Bay Municipal Utility District reservoir located in the mother lode, about 30 miles northeast of Stockton. It is a fine fishing lake. Offerings include trout (rainbow and Eagle Lake), bass (including Florida and Alabama spotted), king salmon, catfish (channel and white) and panfish. Camanche is a sizeable lake (53 miles of shoreline) and has camping as well as recreation and launching facilities on both the south and north shores. It is open all year.

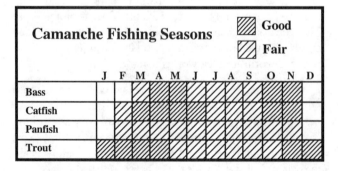

Camanche Fishing Tips

Trout fishing can be productive all year at Camanche. Trout are down 12 to 15 feet in cooler months and as much as 30

to 50 feet in warmer months. Look for them always at 55 water temperature. The night bite for trout is often good. Good trolling lures at Camanche are Krocodile, Needlefish, Triple Teasers and Kastmasters. Nightcrawlers can be trolled or drifted. Bass are caught in spring, summer and fall at Camanche. In fact, some fish are taken in shallow water (less than 10 feet), even during the warm months. But as a rule, the big population in the summer months is down 25 to 45 feet. Plastic worms and lead-head jigs are the top two offerings. Spinnerbaits and the Bobby Garland Spider jig are local favorites. King salmon were first planted in 1982. Some are now caught in the 4-6 pound range. Trolling is the ticket. There are also some kokanee in Camanche. Mini-jigs and minnows produce crappie in the spring in deeper coves. Camanche has a healthy population of catfish (channel, white, blue). Good spots include the creek channel, coves, and off the dikes and spillways of the main lake.

Camanche Lake Facts

Location: Camanche is off Hwy. 12 which runs east from Lodi. Elevation is 275 feet at this foothills lake.

Size: Camanche is a major reservoir. It has 7,700 surface acres when filled to capacity.

Species: Rainbow trout, largemouth bass, spotted bass, catfish and panfish

Facilities: There are two facilities on Camanche Lake—Camanche Northshore Resort, (209) 763-5121 and South Camanche Shore, (209) 763-5178. Both have hundreds of campsites, a full-service marina, a multi-lane launch ramp, stables, swimming beach, boat rental, motel and cottage rental, a restaurant and store, etc.

Information: Contact the numbers listed above or the marina (209) 763-5166.

Carson Pass Trout

Typical of the scores of mountain trout locales in the Sierras that get little or no publicity, yet offer fine fishing, is the Carson Pass Area of Eldorado National Forest. Carson Pass, bisected by Rte. 88, is about 35 miles south of Lake Tahoe's South shore, and is best known as home of Kirkwood Ski Resort. But trout fishing, hiking, camping, and drinking in the alpine scenery reigns in the summertime. The pass is at 8,573 feet elevation, so the summer season is short. Many visitors come in July and August.

There is a wide variety of trout angling opportunities. The most accessible is the planted waters of the Carson River

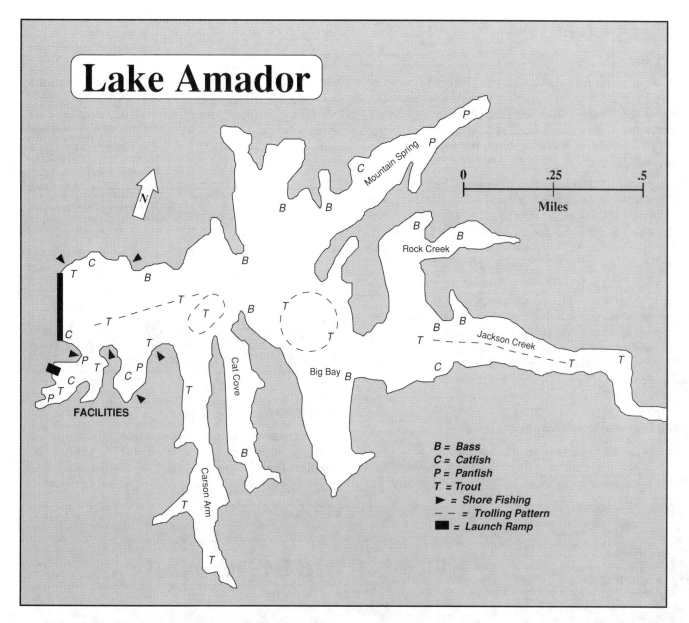

Lake Amador

B = Bass
C = Catfish
P = Panfish
T = Trout
► = Shore Fishing
– – = Trolling Pattern
■ = Launch Ramp

as it flows alongside Rte. 88. Several small lakes are also easily accessible from the highway, including Red Lake, Round-top Lake, Frog Lake and Winnemucca Lake. Blue Lake Road off Rte. 88 leads through Faith Valley to a marvelous collection of small lakes and campgrounds. There are Upper and Lower Blue Lake, Lost Lake, Twin Lake, among others. Blue Creek tumbling down to the Mokelumne from Blue Lake is a rugged but productive stream. And Lost Lake (actually 2 lakes) harbors some large brook trout. Spinners, like the Mepps #2 are good, as are nymphs.

Just west of this collection of lakes is the 50,000 acre Mokelumne Wilderness. One popular destination for backpackers is Fourth of July Lake. The Evergreen Trail to this lake begins on a dirt road north of Upper Blue Lake near Raymond Peak. The trail starts at Wet Meadow near Blue Lake and encompasses part of the Pacific Crest Trail. Raymond Lake offers anglers a chance to catch the fantastically beautiful golden trout. But note, this is a difficult hike. For more information on the Carson Pass area, contact Eldorado National Forest, 100 Forni Road, Placerville, CA 95667 (530) 622-5061 or El Dorado National Forest Information Center (530) 644-6048.

Crystal Basin Recreation Area

There is some fine lake and stream trout fishing in the El Dorado National Forest in El Dorado County. Here, west of Lake Tahoe off Hwy. 50 near the town of Riverton, is the entrance to the heart of the action, the Crystal Basin Recreation Area, and the home of Ice House, Union Valley and Loon Lakes. Each has launching, camping and fine trouting. In close proximity are two more lakes—Sly Park (also known as Jenkinson) and Stumpy Meadow. Variety is the password among these lakes. Sizes range from 300 acres to almost 3000 acres. Kokanee and Mackinaw trout, as well as rainbow and browns, can be had in some waters. Elevations range from 4000 to 6000 ft.

If you want to mix in some stream angling, there are plenty of possibilities, ranging from rivers like the American and Rubicon to small streams. Pilot Creek runs through Slumpy Meadows. Silver Creek and the South Fork of Silver Creek do the same at Union Valley and Ice House, respectively. At Loon Lake try out the nearby Rubicon River.

A good way to hone in on camping and fishing spots that appeal to you is to take an exploratory day trip to the El Dorado Area. You can order an Eldorado National Forest map in advance, and then do some armchair planning followed by some scouting. For information, contact the U.S. Forest Service, 100 Forni Road, Placerville, CA 95667, (530) 622-5061 or El Dorado National Forest Information Center (530) 644-6048.

Don Pedro Lake (map - p. 169)

Don Pedro is an excellent fishing lake, offering a wide variety of fish including rainbow and Eagle lake trout, silver and king salmon, largemouth bass, catfish, crappie and bluegill.

Don Pedro has three major facilities. Each has campsites and launch ramps. Trout range in size up to 6 pounds. Salmon are generally in the 2-4 pound range. Typical bass are 1 1/2 pounds, but range up to 8-10 pounds. The lake has recently been planted with the fast growing Florida largemouth bass. Night fishing is allowed.

Don Pedro Fishing Seasons	J	F	M	A	M	J	J	A	S	O	N	D
Bass			▨	▨	▨	▨	▨	▨	▨	▨		
Catfish			▨	▨	▨	▨	▨	▨	▨	▨		
Panfish			▨	▨	▨	▨	▨	▨	▨	▨		
Salmon	▨	▨	▨	▨	▨	▨	▨	▨	▨	▨	▨	▨
Trout	▨	▨	▨	▨	▨	▨	▨	▨	▨	▨	▨	▨

Good ▨   Fair ▨

Don Pedro Fishing Tips

Trolling is the most productive method for catching trout and salmon. Silver lures, including Needlefish, Kastmasters, Pheobes, Triple Teasers and Z-Rays, are all winners. Casting spinners like Mepps and Rooster Tails can also be productive

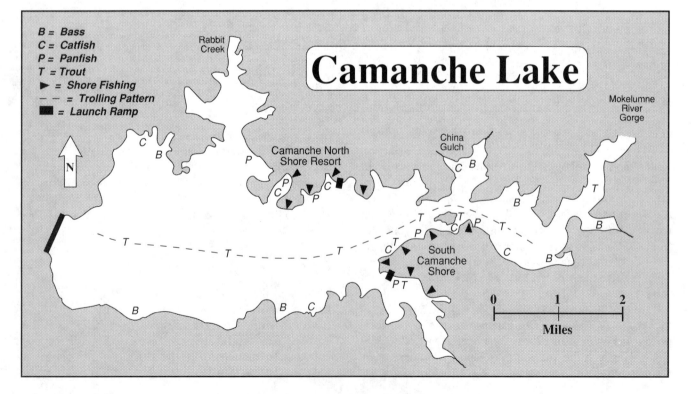

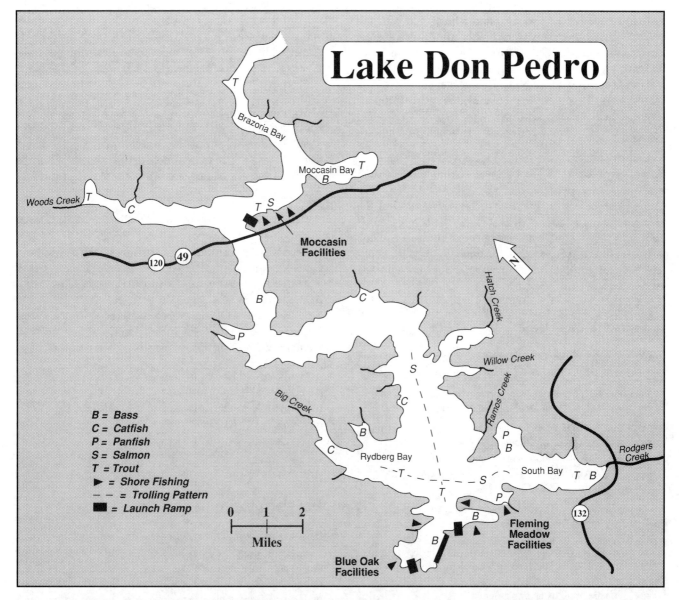

in the spring. Still fishing, using a sliding sinker rig and salmon egg/marshmallow combination bait, works well from shore in the cooler months. Try near or across from the Fleming Meadows Marina. Don Pedro is not only big, but it is also a deep canyon reservoir. So cold-water fish like trout and salmon can go down a long ways in the warmer months. By May, a lot of the trolling action takes place down at the 30-40 foot level. In summer, a productive fishing depth is 40 to 60 feet. The southern end of the lake is probably the most productive trout/salmon area, especially in warmer months. A favorite trolling spot is just north of the Fleming Meadows Marina. Try a zig-zag pattern after locating fish with an

electronic fish finder. Trout fishing is best real early (even before sun-up) and then again in late afternoon and evening.

Rocky points are a year-round hangout for largemouth bass. A sure-fire plug is the 4-inch gold and black floating Rapala. Four-inch black plastic worms are also top producers. Drag them slowly across the bottom. Chartreuse and white spinnerbaits are local favorites. A recent hot item for bassers is the 4-inch Green Weenie. Most anglers toss it out with a split shot crimped on the line about 8 to 10 inches above the deadly worm. Also the salt and pepper 4-inch worm with a chartreuse tail is excellent bait. Don Pedro's waters are often crystal clear. This means fish spook easily.

So knowing anglers keep their distance from the shoreline and work quietly. Long tosses to the brush and structure produce strikes. If there is a little breeze on the water, anglers can move in a little closer. The ripples work to disguise your presence, and then top-water plugs like Rebel Pop-R and Hula Popper bring on the bass. Underwater creek channels are top bass spots. Good prospects include Big Creek, Ramos Creek, Hatch Creek, Willow Creek, Woods Creek and Rodgers Creek. Fish the coves and the mouth of all these.

Crappie anglers score in the back coves where there are trees submerged in 15 feet of water. White mini-jigs and small minnows are the ticket. Use 2 or 4 pound test line. Crappie can be caught in these locales during most of the year. Some anglers work coves at night. A floating crappie light attracts plankton, which attracts threadfin shad, which brings on the crappie. Large, live minnows produce hook-ups. A small split shot up the line from the bait hook may be necessary.

Catfishing is best on summer evenings. Red worms and mealworms produce bluegill in the warmer months.

Don Pedro Lake Facts

Location: In Tuolumne County northeast of La Grange, in the southern motherlode at an elevation of 1500 feet

Size: Don Pedro is huge, in fact, it is the largest California freshwater lake south of Stockton. There are 12,960 surface areas of water and 160 miles of irregular shoreline.

Species: Largemouth and smallmouth bass, rainbow trout, salmon, catfish, panfish

Facilities: The city of San Francisco and several irrigation districts built Don Pedro in 1971. All the recreation facilities are administered by the Don Pedro Recreation Agency, and they are quite extensive. There are three major recreation areas. Amenities include large, full-service marinas, launching ramps, boat rentals, houseboat rentals, campgrounds, stores, picnic grounds and boat-in camping.

Boating: All boating is permitted. Houseboats are available to rent.

Information: Don Pedro Recreation Agency, La Grange, (209) 852-2396; Moccasin Point Marina, (209) 989-2206; Lake Don Pedro Marina (Fleming Meadows), (209) 852-2369

Emigrant Wilderness

Emigrant Wilderness, located south of Hwy. 108 and the Sonora Pass in Tuolumne County, is a beautiful and unique area with breathtaking scenery. It is about 30 miles out of the town of Sonora. There is excellent trout fishing in its many streams and lakes. Terrain is rolling hills, ridges and granite domes with many lakes surrounded by stands of lodgepole pines. High peaks of the Sierras border the east side of the Wilderness.

If you and your family or friends like to combine a backpacking trip with trout fishing, this may be the place for you. But don't plan on a late spring trip. Mother nature usually doesn't open these waters until June, and it may be July before some trails are clear of snow. Most lakes are ice-free by mid-June.

Access to Emigrant is through the Pinecrest Lake-Dodge Ridge area at Strawberry. There are about 5 different trailheads in this area plus a pack station. Crabtree Trailhead is the most popular. Top streams include Summit Creek above Relief Reservoir, Lily Creek and Horsemeadow Creek. A good pristine lake zone (Rosasco, Hyatt, Pingree, Big, Yellowhammer and Lord Meadow Lakes) is in the southwestern portion of the Wilderness. Also the stream between Layton and Yellowhammer Lakes is a good producer.

Emigrant Wilderness is rugged. Only experienced backpackers should explore this area. Information is available from Summit Ranger Station, USFS Star Route, Box 1295, Sonora, CA 95370, (209) 965-3434.

Folsom Lake (map - p. 171)

Folsom Lake combines excellent fishing with an outstanding full-spectrum recreational facility, all within easy reach of the Sacramento metropolitan area. Planted and holdover rainbow trout are numerous at Folsom. In spring, 5,000 half pound or better rainbow are put in per week, and trout are caught up to 5 pounds. King salmon in the 16-20 inch range are also a common catch. There are lots of bass—both largemouth (in the 2-4 pound range, some up to 7 pounds) and smallmouth. And for good measure, catfish, crappie and bluegill fishing is also good. This is an urban lake that is heavily used by all types of boaters and other recreational activities, but the fish don't seem to mind. In fact, for the family who doesn't like long drives, and who wants to combine fishing with sailing, waterskiing, or whatever, Folsom is ideal. Facilities include several campgrounds, a large, full-service marina, hiking, boat-in camping, etc.

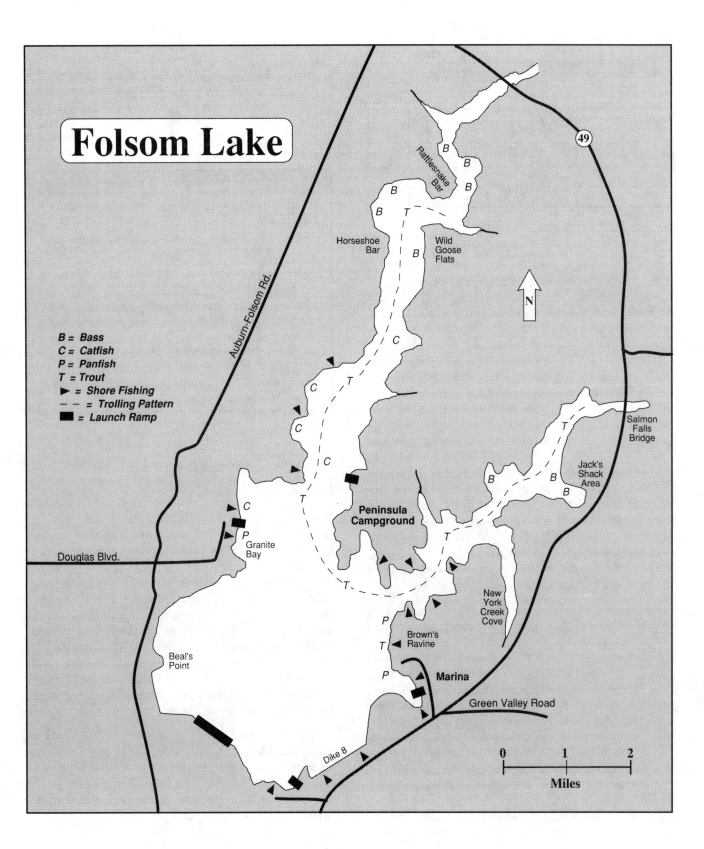

Folsom Lake

B = Bass
C = Catfish
P = Panfish
T = Trout
► = Shore Fishing
– – = Trolling Pattern
■ = Launch Ramp

Auburn-Folsom Rd.

Rattlesnake Bar

B

B

B

B

B

B

Horseshoe Bar

T

B

Wild Goose Flats

N

C

C

C

T

C

T

C

Salmon Falls Bridge

T

T

Peninsula Campground

C

P

Granite Bay

Douglas Blvd.

B

B

Jack's Shack Area

B

T

New York Creek Cove

P

T

Brown's Ravine

Beal's Point

P

Marina

Green Valley Road

Dike 8

0   1   2

Miles

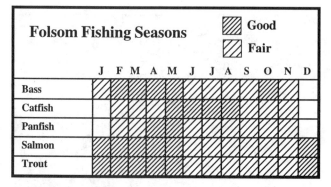

Folsom Fishing Seasons	J	F	M	A	M	J	J	A	S	O	N	D
Bass												
Catfish												
Panfish												
Salmon												
Trout												

Good / Fair

Folsom Fishing Tips

Rainbow trout are the mainstay for Folsom anglers from January through early April. Surface water temperatures are at their coolest so trout are within reach of bank anglers. During the November to March period, about 60 to 70,000 catchable-sized rainbows are planted at Folsom. Holdover and native trout in the 17 to 21 inch range are also taken in many catches. Cool weather shore anglers do particularly well at Dyke 8, Brown's Ravine, the south end of the peninsula, Granite Bay, Beal's Point, Rattlesnake Bar and Salmon Falls. Bait anglers favor inflated nightcrawlers, live minnows, and salmon egg/marshmallow combinations. Both sliding sinker and bobber rigs are productive. Casting spoons and spinners is also popular. Cold weather trollers do well pulling Rapala-type minnows right near the surface. Trollers in spring need only let out 2 or 3 colors of leadcore line. But in the heat of the summer, 15 or more colors are required. Summer trolling with downriggers is increasingly popular. Metallic trolling lures like Super Dupers, Kastmasters, Triple Teasers and Needlefish are most productive. For example, in Needlefish, a #2 size in rainbow trout, bikini, red and pearl are excellent choices. King and kokanee salmon are also taken by trout anglers.

Recent history has shown that most large Folsom bass, up to 9 or 10 pounds, are taken in the months of January, February and March. Smallmouths have fared better at Folsom than largemouths. They tolerate water fluctuations better, and are well suited to Folsom's rocky, boulder-lined shoreline. Most smallmouths are caught in the North Fork, while largemouths are most common in the South Fork. Rattlesnake Bar and up in the coves of the peninsula are two good North Fork areas. In the South Fork, work the coves all the way up to Salmon Falls Bridge. In spring work weed beds with sandy bottoms. Later concentrate on deeper structures. Plastic worms in purple or black with metal flakes are the top producers at Folsom. But all popular bass offerings work including spinnerbaits, crankbaits and grubs. Winter

bassers work their offerings extremely slowly to entice their lethargic quarry. The best crappie concentration is in the structure and rocky areas of Brown's Ravine. Catfishing is best at night in all the back bays throughout the lake. Shore anglers like the west bank of the North Fork. Try clams and chicken livers.

Folsom Lake Facts

Location: Folsom is located about 25 miles northeast of Sacramento.

Size: Folsom is a major reservoir. It has 11,930 surface acres of water with 75 miles of shoreline.

Species: Rainbow trout, king salmon, kokanee, largemouth and smallmouth bass, catfish and panfish

Facilities: Brown's Ravine—marina, store, launch ramp, picnicking, mooring; Dyke 8—launch ramp, picnicking; Beal's Point—camping, swimming, picnicking; Peninsula—camping, launch ramp, mooring; Granite Bay—launching, swimming, picnicking, store

Information: Folsom Park Headquarters, (530) 988-0205; Folsom Marina, (916) 933-1300

French Meadows and Hell Hole Lakes

Here are two wonderful trout lakes that are quite close to civilization as the crow flies, but are so tedious to drive to that they offer a chance to get away from many other lake anglers. Both lakes offer campgrounds, paved access roads, and paved launch ramps in beautiful mountain settings. But note, there are no supplies, food or fuel at the lakes themselves. Auburn is the starting point for a trip to either lake. Count on a 2 to 2 1/2 hour drive eastward from there. French Meadows is reached via Mosquito Ridge Road from the little town of Foresthill (39 miles from the lake). Hell Hole is 40 miles northwest of Georgetown. Use the Feather River and Yuba River Regions Map published by AAA as a resource to find the best route to these lakes.

Once there plan on some fine trouting, especially in spring and fall. Rainbows and browns up to 7 pounds are taken, and 1 to 3 pound fish are common. Experts suggest that the low fishing pressure contributes to the good size of these trout. Trolling is the most productive approach at both lakes.

Lakes McClure and McSwain
(map - p. 174)

McClure and McSwain are adjoining reservoirs on the Merced River that are perfect opposites. McClure is a warm water lake that contains several species (bass, catfish, panfish, trout), is very large (26 miles long), has numerous coves and inlets, and allows all types of boating (including houseboating and waterskiing). McSwain, on the other hand, is a coldwater trout lake, is narrow and relatively small, and has no houseboats or waterskiing. What these lakes do have in common is fine fishing as well as outstanding and complete recreational facilities. McClure and McSwain are located in the Sierra foothills east of Modesto. There are 5 recreation areas on McClure and one on McSwain. Both lakes have camping (565 sites in all), boat launching, full-service marina, laundromats, fish cleaning facilities, boat rentals, swimming lagoons and stores.

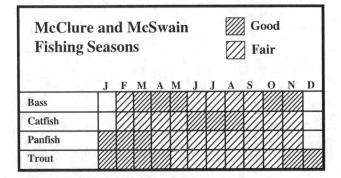

McClure and McSwain Fishing Tips

McSwain is a heavily planted trout lake. Holdover fish get large. The lake record is 10 1/4 pounds and 4 pounders are quite common. Trout fishing is the main on-water activity here. The water is cold, clear and moving through this narrow body of water. Two top trolling lures are the gold-hammered #940 Triple Teaser and the trout-colored Needlefish. A good trolling area is the mile-long stretch between the first and second buoy, about a mile up from the marina. Local anglers advise shore anglers to try water shaded by trees on the south or east side of the lake. One accessible spot is off Exchequer Road near the maintenance area at the lake's north end. Another is near McSwain Dam at the south end of the lake. And near the launch ramp after a trout plant should not be overlooked.

McClure also has rainbow, and some browns and brookies. In the cooler months, schools of shad near the surface signal hot spots. Casting live minnows (put a small split shot about 18 inches up from the hook) into the shad and twitching as the offering sinks brings on strikes. Surface trolling along the shoreline in about 5 feet of water also works when shad are schooling. Good all-season trolling takes place between Mack Island and the dam. Here, in summer, downriggers are used to get down as much as 80 feet, or more, for king salmon up to 10 pounds. This area as well as way up the lake by Bagley are the top two trout and salmon spots at McClure.

Bassing in the spring (about March) begins with smallmouths up to 4 pounds. Anglers concentrate on rocky points. Some good spots include the islands at the south end of McClure Point Recreation Area, Piney Creek Cove, Hunter's Point Recreation Area and on up to the Bagley area. Salt and pepper grubs are a top producer. Cast them toward shore, and work them back along the bottom. Smallmouths are in 5 to 25 feet of water in the spring. April is a top month.

Largemouths and Alabama spotted bass spawn on more gradual slopes usually starting around late April. Crankbaits and spinnerbaits are both good. Look for fish in 5 to 10 feet of water, so casting along the shoreline is often best. Average largemouths are in the 2 to 3 pound range. Grassy, gradual-sloping shorelines are the best bets throughout the lake. "Spots" are taken in the 2 to 5 pound range.

Lake McClure and Lake McSwain Facts

Location: At an elevation of about 870 feet in the Sierra foothills east of Modesto and northeast of Merced

Size: McClure is 26 miles long with 7100 surface acres and 80 miles of shoreline; McSwain is 11 miles long.

Species: McClure—bass (largemouth, smallmouth, Alabama spotted), trout (rainbow, brown, brook), king salmon, panfish, catfish
   McSwain—rainbow trout, panfish and catfish.

Facilities: McClure—5 recreation areas with marinas, camping, boat rental, etc.
   McSwain—1 recreation area with marina, camping, boat rental, etc.

Boating: McClure—all boating including houseboat rental
   McSwain—no houseboats or waterskiing

Information: McSwain—Lake McSwain Rec. Area, (209) 378-2521, Marina, (209) 378-2534

McClure—McClure Pt. Rec. Area, (209) 378-2521; Barrett Cove Rec. Area, (209) 378-2611; Barrett Cove Marina (209) 378-2441; Horseshoe Bend Rec. Area, (209) 878-3452

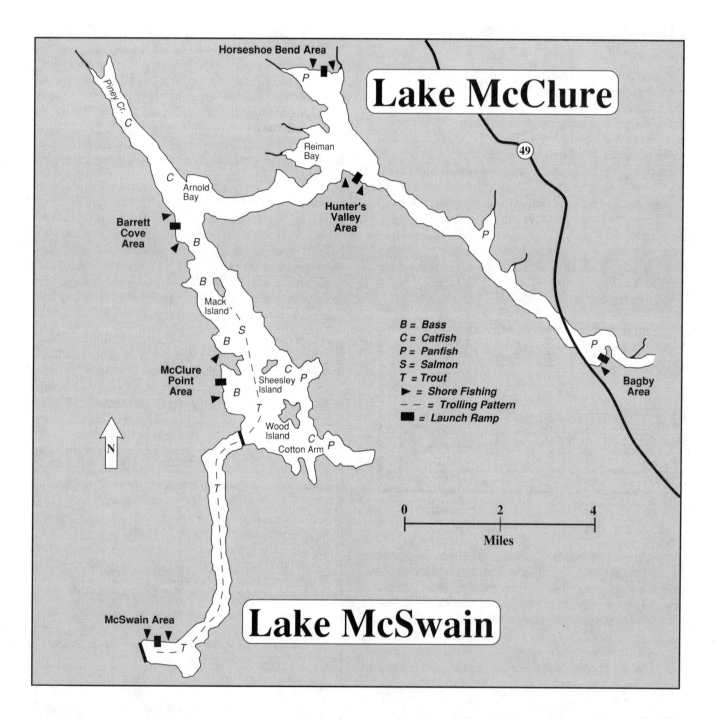

Lake McClure

Horseshoe Bend Area

Piney Cr. *C*

Reiman Bay

C

Arnold Bay

Hunter's Valley Area

Barrett Cove Area

B

B

Mack Island

S

B

McClure Point Area

Sheesley Island

B

C

P

T

Wood Island

Cotton Arm

C

P

B = Bass
C = Catfish
P = Panfish
S = Salmon
T = Trout
► = Shore Fishing
– – = Trolling Pattern
■ = Launch Ramp

Bagby Area

P

N

T

Lake McSwain

McSwain Area

T

0   2   4
Miles

New Hogan Lake (map - p. 176)

New Hogan is one of the motherlode group of lakes. But it is different from all the others because it boasts an excellent striped bass fishery. The Department of Fish and Game first planted stripers in New Hogan around 1980, and they have flourished. Catches in the 8 to 10 pound range are not uncommon. The record New Hogan striper hit the scales at 18 pounds. There is also largemouth bass and catfish action at New Hogan. However, trout, salmon and panfish catches have dwindled with the advent of the striper, which just goes to show that you can't have it all! Trout are no longer planted in New Hogan, but there is some trout action way up in the Calaveras River arm. Facilities at this picturesque lake include camping, swimming, marina, store and launch ramps.

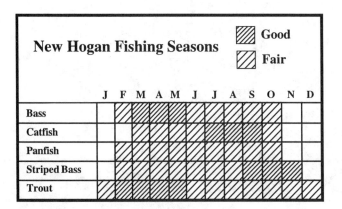

New Hogan Fishing Seasons	J	F	M	A	M	J	J	A	S	O	N	D
Bass		▨	▨	▨	▨	▨	▨	▨	▨	▨	▨	
Catfish			▨	▨	▨	▨	▨	▨	▨	▨		
Panfish		▨	▨	▨	▨	▨	▨	▨	▨	▨		
Striped Bass		▨	▨	▨	▨	▨	▨	▨	▨	▨	▨	
Trout	▨	▨	▨	▨	▨	▨	▨	▨	▨	▨	▨	▨

Good / Fair

New Hogan Fishing Tips

Striper are often scattered throughout the lake. Quick trolling with Kastmasters, Rapalas and Rebels is a popular method of finding and taking them. Boaters also still fish using anchovies or spoons that can be fished vertically. At times, particularly in the spring, the shad and then the stripers come to the surface. Diving gulls tip off the locales. Anglers quickly, but cautiously, motor to the edge of these striped bass feeding frenzies to get in on the action. Casting surface plugs like Zara Spooks or 3/4 ounce Kastmasters bring the striper to hook. One caution: Don't run your boat right into the boiling mass of bait. This drives the striper down fast and angers the collected fishermen. Surprisingly, shore anglers can do well with stripers. Good spots include Wrinkle Cove along the Observation Area, and at the Fiddle Neck day-use area. Bait, like anchovies, as well as cast plugs and spoons both work. Since the water is clean, there should be no hesitation about eating New Hogan stripers.

Best trout fishing is in the upper stretches of the Calaveras arm. Small minnows or salmon eggs score on these browns and rainbows up to 14 inches. Bass structure at New Hogan is limited. Haupt Creek Cove on the upper end of the lake and Bear Creek Cove on the south end have good cover. Several small islands and rocky points (like at Coyote Point) provide good bass prospects. Most bass are largemouth. Plastic worms in purple and shad colors are best. The largemouth record is 15 pounds 8 ounces. It was at the time (1983) the Northern California record.

Catfishermen score using chicken livers, anchovies and clams in the same areas as shore striper anglers. Crappie fishing is not consistent, but can be good using mini-jigs and minnows.

New Hogan Lake Facts
Location: 30 miles east of Stockton, off Hwy. 26 near the town of Valley Springs. Elevation is 700 feet.
Size: 4,400 surface acres of water with 50 miles of shoreline. It's about 8 miles long.
Species: Striped bass, catfish, largemouth and smallmouth bass
Facilities: Camping, marina, several launch ramps, store, day use, boat-in camping and boat rental. Day use and launching are free.
Information: New Hogan Lake, 2713 Hogan Sam Rd., Valley Springs, CA, (209) 772-1343

New Melones Lake (map - p. 178)

New Melones is a relatively new (completed in 1979) and large reservoir that offers excellent fishing. For some time after opening, facilities at New Melones were spartan. But now, on-shore amenities are good. New Melones is one of the largest of the foothills, motherlode lakes, sitting at an elevation of 1088 between New Hogan and Don Pedro. It's in the heart of the gold country. In fact, Hwy. 49 crosses the Stanislaus arm of the lake, and the site of the gold rush town of Melones is now under the lake. Night fishing, waterskiing and swimming are permitted.

New Melones Fishing Seasons	J	F	M	A	M	J	J	A	S	O	N	D
Bass		▨	▨	▨	▨	▨	▨	▨	▨	▨	▨	
Catfish				▨	▨	▨	▨	▨	▨	▨		
Panfish			▨	▨	▨	▨	▨	▨	▨			
Salmon	▨	▨	▨	▨	▨	▨	▨	▨	▨	▨	▨	▨
Trout	▨	▨	▨	▨	▨	▨	▨	▨	▨	▨	▨	▨

Good / Fair

New Melones Fishing Tips

As is true in other locations, at New Melones the larger fish are usually found in deeper water. This is true for trout,

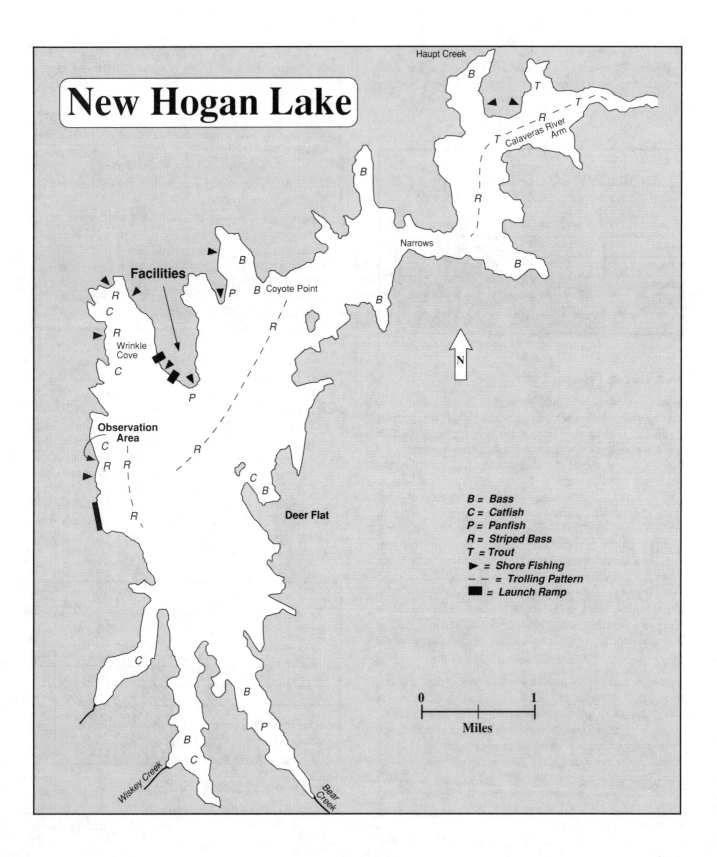

New Hogan Lake

Haupt Creek

Calaveras River Arm

Narrows

Facilities

Coyote Point

Wrinkle Cove

Observation Area

N

Deer Flat

B = Bass
C = Catfish
P = Panfish
R = Striped Bass
T = Trout
► = Shore Fishing
– – = Trolling Pattern
■■ = Launch Ramp

0   1
Miles

Wiskey Creek

Bear Creek

salmon, bass and crappie. So if you're trolling and catching smallish trout, drop it down 5-10 feet and you're likely to pick up some larger fish. Along the same vane, salmon trollers in the summer go down 75-100 feet, whereas trout trollers hit at 35-60 feet. Still fishing, off the dam and spillway, is often good for trout and salmon, especially during the evenings and night.

Trout move into shallow water in the winter looking for warmer water, and into deep water seeking cold in the summer. Big browns and rainbows, 4 to 6 pounds and some up to 10 pounds, are taken in winter by trolling minnow-shaped Rapalas, Rebels, etc. In April and May, many anglers troll with leadcore line at about 10 to 30 feet down using Speedy Shiners, Super Dupers, Kastmasters, etc. Downrigger trolling begins in earnest around Memorial Day. 50 to 80 degree water is the target. In August and September, many anglers night fish with live bait down 60 to 100 feet. Often the trout are feeding right on the bottom at these depths.

When New Melones was filling, bass fishing was extremely good. Everyone was catching limits. Things have changed. Now bass anglers must be a little more savvy to score, especially on larger fish. It is important to follow the seasonal patterns of bass. In winter, from November through February, the bass are living off the deep rocky points or deep, brushy cover. Look for them in 30-45 feet of water. Anglers take them by dropping down large minnows or spoons. Fish near the bottom or around the tops of underwater pine trees. Jig spoons up and down slowly.

When warmer spring rain water starts flowing into New Melones, largemouths become more active. Salt and pepper grubs and Pig 'n Jigs work as the bass move into this muddy inflow. March and April are also good for crankbaits and spinnerbaits. Bass usually spawn in New Melones in May. The largest bass are taken around nesting areas. At this time, lunker seem to strike out at whatever comes near them. Top-water plugs are good in this shallow water. But by July and August, successful bass anglers are working deep again. Plastic worms, Pig 'n Jigs, and deep-running crankbaits all take their share of fish. Work crankbaits parallel to shore just over underwater structures and brush. Letting spinnerbaits tumble down past sunken tree tops is a good summer and early fall technique.

At New Melones, and probably at many other Northern California lakes, crappie are scattered all over the lake. They're down 40 to 60 feet during the period that stretches from summer through early winter. But local New Melones anglers say that in the January to February period, crappie begin to gather in small groups. At this time, night fishing with a crappie light works about one half way up the coves. The best approach is to dangle minnows down about 30 to 40 feet. By March and April, schools of crappie are up in shallow water in coves. Fish them with minnows or crappie jigs. After the shallow water spawn, the crappie scatter and are harder to hook into.

Happily, the bluegill action at New Melones runs for a long period. Look for bluegill down about 35 to 45 feet in early spring and late fall. Fish bait (red worms, mealworms, etc.) down on the bottom to get the largest fish. In late spring and summer, bluegill are taken in 15 feet or less water. When you hook one bluegill, you've usually found an entire school of them.

New Melones Lake Facts

Location: On the Calaveras-Tuolumne County border about 4 miles south of Angels Camp and 8 miles west of Sonora

Size: There are 12,500 surface acres of water (or about 20 square miles) with 100 miles of shoreline. The lake is 25 miles long from the dam to Camp Nine, way up the Stanislaus arm. Maximum depth (near the dam) is 565 feet.

Species: Trout (rainbow and brown), some king salmon, bass (both largemouth and smallmouth), catfish and panfish

Facilities: There are two developed recreation areas: Glory Hole has a marina (with boat and houseboat rental, mooring and gasoline), food service, launch ramp, camping (144 sites) and day use; The Tuttle Town area has launching, camping (45 sites) and day use.

Information: New Melones Lake Marina, (209) 785-3300

Pardee Lake (map - p. 180)

Pardee Lake is one of the motherlode string of Sierra foothill's reservoirs. But although it is one of a group, it is also special in several ways. First, because it offers consistently good rainbow trout and kokanee salmon fishing, and second, because it is a dedicated angler's lake—no waterskiing or swimming is permitted. Large and smallmouth bass and panfish are also available at Pardee. The waters of Pardee are clean and clear. It was built in the 1920's as an East Bay Municipal Utility District reservoir. Facilities include campground, restaurant, store, launch ramp and swimming pool.

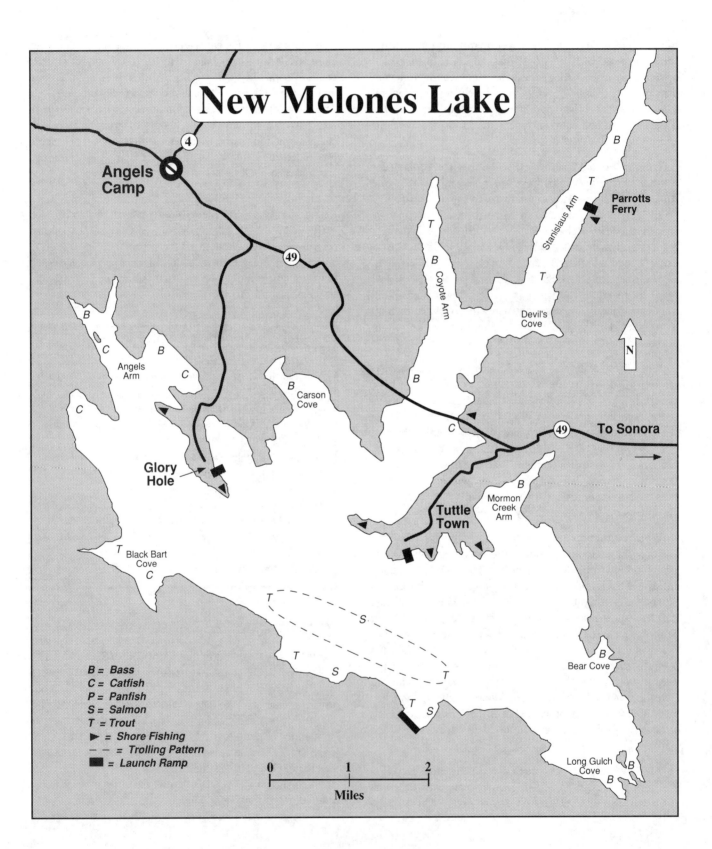

New Melones Lake

4

Angels
Camp

49

B

Coyote
Arm

T
B

Stanislaus Arm

B

T

Parrotts
Ferry

T

Devil's
Cove

N

B

Carson
Cove

B

Angels
Arm

B

C

C

B

C

C

C

Glory
Hole

49

To Sonora

C

Mormon
Creek
Arm

B

Tuttle
Town

T

Black Bart
Cove

C

B

Bear Cove

T

T

S

S

T

T

S

B = Bass
C = Catfish
P = Panfish
S = Salmon
T = Trout
▶ = Shore Fishing
– – = Trolling Pattern
■ = Launch Ramp

Long Gulch
Cove

B

B

0   1   2

Miles

Pardee Fishing Seasons

Legend: Good, Fair

	J	F	M	A	M	J	J	A	S	O	N	D
Bass		▨	▨	▨	▨	▨	▨	▨	▨			
Catfish			▨	▨	▨	▨	▨	▨	▨	▨		
Kokanee		▨	▨	▨	▨	▨	▨	▨	▨			
Panfish		▨	▨	▨	▨	▨	▨	▨	▨	▨	▨	
Trout		▨	▨	▨	▨	▨	▨	▨	▨	▨	▨	▨

Pardee Fishing Tips

Rainbow trout is the number one attraction at Pardee. The lake is planted heavily, including some lunkers. There are also large holdover and native trout. Catches in the 3 to 5 pound class are common with trophies taken ranging up to 10 pounds. Trout action begins on opening day in February. The marina area is heavily fished by both trout trollers and from shore. Trolling is also good by the dam, in the south arm, up in the narrows and even along the shorelines (in colder months). Shore anglers use nightcrawlers (inflated) or salmon eggs (floated with marshmallows), or cast Kastmasters, Phoebes, Krocodiles, Rooster Tails, Mepps, etc. Lures seem to work best early and late in the day. Locals recommend a #8 hook, 30 inch leader (4 pound test) and a 1/4 to 1/2 ounce sliding sinker rig for bait angling. A long leader is also recommended for trolling with leadcore line because the water is so clear. Boat trollers hit with Needlefish, Kokanee King, etc. near the surface in spring and down deeper as surface temperatures rise. When the lake first opens, trollers start at about 10 feet down. By mid-March the depth changes to about 15 feet. During the heat of the summer the best depth is usually around 35 to 40 feet. Leadcore trolling is still more popular at Pardee than downrigging, maybe because the fish never go down really deep, and also because there are shallow spots and sunken islands that can play havoc with downrigger weights and cables. The standard of Pardee regulars is Sunset Line Company's 15 pound test leadcore line. Most put it on a Penn levelwind reel. At the trolling speed setting of most outboard motors, each color of this leadcore line will put the terminal rig down about 5 feet. So during summer, trollers are out about 7 or 8 colors. The slowest trolling speed that still imparts good line action is usually the best. Troll slightly above the desired depth, never below it.

Pardee is one of the most consistent producers of kokanee in California. More than 200,000 kokanee fry are air-drop planted each year. Most kokanee taken by anglers are three years old and run 11 to 12 inches, but 15 inchers are possible. Kokanee are excellent eating and hard fighting. They are most often caught by trout trollers. In late April through June, about half the total catch is kokanee. Kokanee are in schools, so repeat a productive troll. Shore anglers work Pardee at night from the Marina Cove and the other shore angling spot, Woodpile Gulch. Night boat fishing is not permitted.

Black bass fishing at Pardee is not really that popular. Maybe it's because the super clear water calls for patience and hard work, or maybe because bass anglers head to the neighboring famous bass factory, Lake Amador. Largemouth bass anglers at Pardee concentrate on the coves at the south end of the lake. Lunker bass have also been taken by anglers fishing live crawdads off the rocky points. Smallmouth bass chasers also work these same points. Crappie and bluegill fishing at Pardee has been inconsistent in recent years, but catfish up to 16 pounds are taken every year. The best concentrations of catfish are in the channel arm, but the cove at the north end of the lake at the marina is also good.

Pardee Lake Facts

Location: In the motherlode foothills off Hwy. 88, approximately 35 miles from Stockton

Size: There are 2250 surface acres of water with about 43 miles of shoreline. Each of the two lake arms is about 5 miles in length.

Species: Rainbow trout, kokanee salmon, largemouth and smallmouth bass, crappie and bluegill

Facilities: Pardee Lake Resort operates the facilities at the lake which includes a 10-lane launch ramp, full-service marina, boat rental, 2 campgrounds with over 100 sites, a store, and swimming pool.

Season: Open from the second Friday in February until mid-November.

Boating: No waterskiing, no night boat fishing

Information: Pardee Lake Resort, 4900 Stoney Creek Rd., Ione, CA 95640, (209) 772-1472

Stanislaus River Area

The Stanislaus River and surrounding Stanislaus National Forest waters are an often overlooked mountain trout territory. Main access to the area is along Hwy. 4. The North Fork of the Stanislaus River and its tributary, Beaver Creek, are the

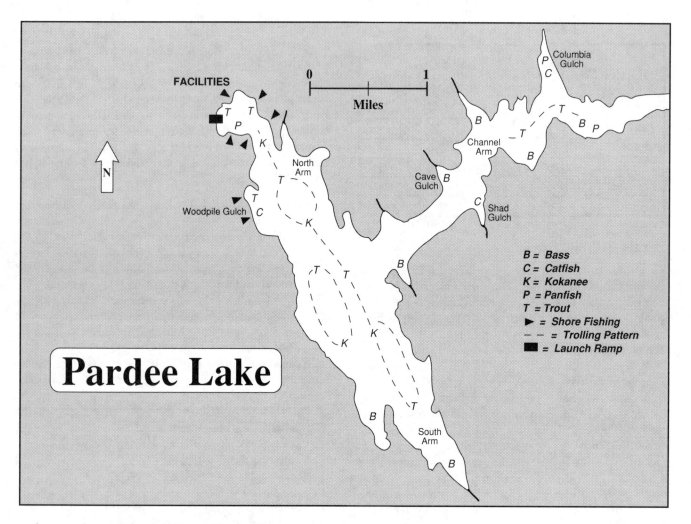

main attractions in the Arnold and Dorrington area. The Stanislaus is a major waterway and offers good trouting throughout the season, but possible high spring runoff could be a negative. A good spring option is Beaver Creek. When it's flow shrinks in summer, the Stanislaus is prime. The first access to these two streams is Parkway Road in the Calaveras Big Trees State Park. Another access to both is out of Dorrington on Boards Crossing Road. The North Fork of the Stanislaus can also be reached by taking Spicer Reservoir Road which is off of Hwy. 4 twelve miles east of Dorrington. Camping is available at each of these access points.

Farther up in the Sierras along Hwy. 4 is Lake Alpine. At 7350 feet, just beyond the Bear Valley/Mt. Reba ski area, fishing is good and the scenery is spectacular. Between Alpine and Ebbetts Pass are several smaller and more remote trout lakes. Check out a Stanislaus National Forest Service map for Mosquito and Highland Lakes. The dirt road leading to Highland Lake parallels the head water of the Mokelumne River for several miles. Fishing here is excellent. Informa-

tion: Stanislaus National Forest, P.O. Box 500, Hathaway Pines, CA 95233, (209) 795-1381

Lake Tahoe (map - p. 181)

As most Northern Californians know, Lake Tahoe and vicinity is a major entertainment and recreation mecca. Gambling, skiing and sightseeing are the dominant attractions. So it's not surprising that very few visitors to the Tahoe area realize that Lake Tahoe is a fantastic trout fishery. Mackinaw trout are the prime catch at Tahoe. They average 2 to 6 pounds, but many are caught in the 6 to 10 pound range, and fish up to 16 pounds aren't that unusual. The lake (and state) record is a 37 pound 6 ounce monster take at the south shore in January 1974. Rainbow trout, and some browns, in the 2 to 6 pound class are also popular catches at Tahoe. And there is a wonderful kokanee salmon fishery. To get in on the action a California or Nevada fishing license is required.

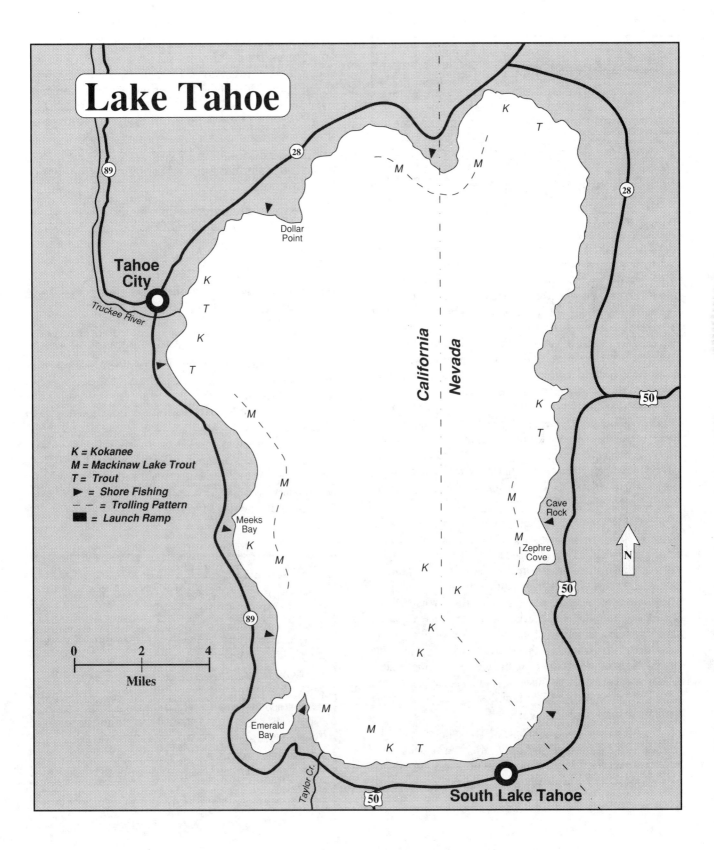

Lake Tahoe

K = Kokanee
M = Mackinaw Lake Trout
T = Trout
► = Shore Fishing
- - - = Trolling Pattern
■ = Launch Ramp

Tahoe City

Dollar Point

Truckee River

Meeks Bay

California
Nevada

Cave Rock

Zephre Cove

Emerald Bay

Taylor Cr.

South Lake Tahoe

N

0   2   4
Miles

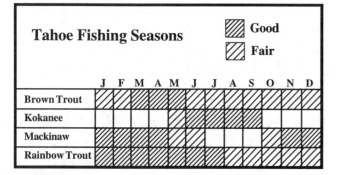

Tahoe Fishing Tips

Mackinaw fishing is predominantly a cold season sport. In fact, it corresponds almost precisely with the snow ski season in the Tahoe region. Surprising to many winter visitors, despite zero degree air temperatures, Lake Tahoe does not freeze over. Fishing for Mackinaw trout is more difficult than most other trout fishing in cold lakes because these guys like to live in deep water, anywhere from 60 to 400 feet is normal. So anglers must get their offerings down deep. The dominate method of accomplishing this is trolling. Downriggers are effective in areas which have a relatively flat sand or mud bottom. But deep-lining with wire or braided stainless steel line, the traditional approach, tends to be quite popular, especially over irregular bottoms where downrigger balls are more likely to snag. Wire lines have the advantage of being heavy enough to take the line down, yet they have no stretch, the classic problem with deep fishing with monofilament line.

Popular trolling lures include plugs like the Lucky 13's, Flatfish, J-plugs and Rapalas. Streamers, such as Mack's Flies, and live Lake Tahoe minnows are also effective. Light-colored plugs, silver or bluish, are most common. Trolling is done right near the bottom over structure or a shelf. A good electronic fish finder, to chart the target rocky ledges that separate bottom-hugging Mackinaw from the uneven structure, is almost a must. Tahoe Mackinaw trolling is an acquired skill. Unpredictable Sierra winter weather adds another variable for boaters on this big lake. Often anglers find that going out on a guided trip or two is the best way to have fun catching Macks and getting an education at the same time.

Another way to catch "Big Macks" (I couldn't resist) is by vertical jigging. In winter and early spring the Mackinaw are often in water from 75 to 150 feet. Anglers tie a 3 to 4 ounce silver spoon, like a Kastmaster or Hopkins, on 12 to 20 pound test monofilament and drop it down. Follow the drop carefully and set the hook on any pause or tap. Once on the bottom, a slow up-and-down action in a 3 to 4 foot zone can produce fish. This approach is best on calm waters so dusk and dawn are prime times. Drift fishing with bait (much like the classic San Francisco Bay drift fishing approach) also works for Mackinaw at Tahoe. Anglers work ledges and sandy holes with live Lake Tahoe minnows on a size 4 or 6 hook. This approach is described in the "Fishing . . . NorCal Style" chapter.

Rainbows and some brown trout are taken in the winter and spring at Tahoe. Fortunately they are up near the surface, unlike the Mackinaw. Trolling deep-running, minnow-style plugs in the 4 to 6 inch range is the most productive approach. Use about 4 pound test line and let it out at least 150 feet behind the boat. In close to shore at creek inlets is a good bet. Best success comes early and late in the day.

Anglers wanting summertime action find kokanee at Tahoe. They run 10 to 14 inches on average, but some measure 16 inches and 1 1/2 pounds. Usually in June kokanee start schooling on the west side of the lake. In July and August they're concentrated in the south end, preparing for a spawning run up Taylor Creek, just south of Emerald Bay, that comes to pass in September. Kokanee are also scattered around in north end locales. Deep trolling is the best ticket for Tahoe kokanee. Action is typically down 40 to 70 feet. Downriggers or leadcore line teamed with flashers are the best producers. Best bite is usually from 5:30 to 9:00 a.m. Good lures are the Red Magic and Needlefish.

Lake Tahoe Facts

Location: On the California-Nevada border, just south of Reno, Nevada

Size: At an elevation of 6228 feet, Tahoe is 25 miles long, 13 miles wide and 1645 feet deep at its deepest point. Surface area is 190 square miles.

Species: Mackinaw lake trout, rainbow and brown trout, kokanee salmon

Facilities: Lake Tahoe has over 20 marinas and launch ramps located all around the shoreline. There are also numerous resorts, motels, public and private campgrounds, etc.

Information: North Lake Tahoe Chamber of Commerce, (530) 583-3494; South Lake Tahoe Chamber of Commerce, (530) 541-5255

Yosemite Area

Some fine wild trout fishing can be found thousands of feet above Yosemite Valley floor, in Tuolumne Meadows along Hwy. 120. Here above Hetch Hetchy Reservoir, the Tuolumne and its branches, the Dana Fork and the Lyell Fork, provide abundant brook, brown and rainbow trout in the 6-18 inch range. The fishing season is short at this 8600 foot elevation. The waters are still high in June. July is usually good fishing and it peaks in August.

The Tuolumne is easily fished in the Meadows itself as it runs along Hwy. 120. A mile or so downstream of the Meadows the Tuolumne quickens its pace as it falls over granite structure. Fish here, and about a mile's walk up from the Meadows in Dana Fork, are larger than those caught right in the Meadows. A short drive east on Hwy. 120 from the Meadows provides access at several points to more of the Dana Fork. Follow the John Muir Trail south from the Meadows to fish the Lyell Fork. Tuolumne Meadows is a popular tourist and camping area. August is the busiest month. Here is a good place to combine family sightseeing, hiking, camping and trout fishing. Fall trouting in the high country of Yosemite is another excellent option. The fish are eager and the tourists are gone.

Coastal Rivers Resource Directory

Campgrounds*

Eel River
1. Huckleberry   2. Madrone
3. Oak Flat
(All at Richardson Grove State Park, 707-247-3319)
4. Hidden Springs
5. Burlington   6. Albee Creek
(All at Humboldt Redwoods State Park, 707-946-2409)

Klamath River
7. Aikens
8. Bluff Creek   9. Pearch Creek
(All Forest Service campgrounds, 707-442-1721)
10. Dillon Creek   14. Sarah Totten
11. Oak Bottom   15. Beaver Creek
12. Fort Goff   16. Trees of Heaven
13. O'Neill Creek
(All Forest Service campgrounds, 530-842-6131)

Mad River
17. Clam Beach County Park, 707-445-7651

Mattole River
18. A.W. Way County Park, 707-445-7651

Salmon River
19. Matthews Creek
20. East Fork
21. Shadow Creek   22. Trail Creek
(All Forest Service campgrounds, 530-842-6131)

Smith River
23. Jedediah Smith Redwoods State Park, 707-464-6101
24. Panther Flat
25. Grassy Flat   27. Cedar Rustic
26. Patrick Creek   28. Big Flat
(All Forest Service campgrounds, 707-442-1721)

Trinity River
29. Tish Tang, Forest Service camp, 707-442-1721
30. Denny
31. Gray's Falls   34. Big Bar
32. Burnt Ranch   35. Big Flat
33. Hayden Flat   36. Pigeon Point
(All Forest Service campgrounds, 530-246-5222)
37. Junction City, Bureau of Land Management, 530-224-2100

Van Duzen River
38. Van Duzen County Park, 707-445-7651
39. Grizzly Creek Redwoods, 707-777-3683

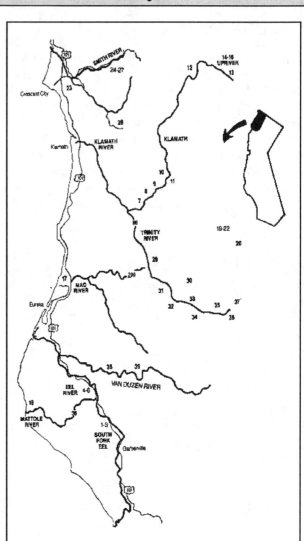

Chambers of Commerce

Arcata Chamber of Commerce, 1062 G St., Arcata, CA 95521, (707) 822-3619

Brookings/Harbor Chamber of Commerce, 97949 Hwy. 101, Brookings, OR 97415, (541) 469-3181

Crescent City-Del Norte County Chamber of Commerce, 1001 Front St., Crescent City, CA 95531, (707) 464-3174

Eureka Chamber of Commerce, 2112 Broadway, Eureka, CA 95501, (707) 442-3738

Ferndale Chamber of Commerce, 451 Main St., Ferndale, CA 95536, (707) 786-4477

Fortuna Chamber of Commerce, 14th & Main St., Fortuna, CA 95540, (707) 725-3959

Gold Beach Chamber of Commerce, 510 S. Ellensburg, Gold Beach, OR 97444, (800) 452-2334

Happy Camp Chamber of Commerce, P.O. Box 1199, Happy Camp, CA 96039, (530) 493-2900

McKinleyville Chamber of Commerce, 2196 Central Ave., McKinleyville, CA 95521, (707) 839-2449

North Klamath Chamber of Commerce, P.O. Box 25, Klamath River, CA 96050, (530) 482-7165

Orick Chamber of Commerce, P.O. Box 234, Orick, CA 95555, (707) 488-3535

Rio Dell/Scotia Chamber of Commerce, 715 Wildwood Ave., Rio Dell, CA 95562, (707) 764-3436

Trinity County Chamber of Commerce, P.O. Box 517, Weaverville, CA 96093, (530) 623-6101

Willow Creek Chamber of Commerce, Corner Hwy. 299 & 96, Willow Creek, CA 95573, (530) 629-2693

*These are favorites of Tom Stienstra, noted outdoor writer and author of *California Camping* and *Pacific Northwest Camping*, both by Foghorn Press.

Coastal River and Stream Fishing

Northern California coastal rivers and streams offer some of California's most enticing fishing. First there are the fish—the hard to hook, fierce fighting steelhead and salmon. But there is also the environment—mountains, river canyons, waterfalls, giant redwoods, wildlife and the sounds and smells of the great Pacific Northwest.

California anglers are blessed with some of the best coastal fishing streams in the world. Sure, fishing in these waters is not what it was 50 years ago, but it is still good and improving because of the efforts of a number of agencies, groups and individuals. The Klamath, Trinity, Smith and Eel, as well as a number of lesser known rivers and streams from the Oregon border south to San Francisco Bay, provide abundant opportunity for steelhead and salmon fishing. In fact, many of these rivers and streams are synonymous with steelhead fishing. Coastal rivers and streams and their tributaries also offer resident wild trout fishing, especially at higher elevations. But in these waters, trout seasons and regulations are special and should be consulted before fishing. These special regulations are designed to protect the young steelhead and salmon.

Certain streams (Klamath, Eel, Trinity, for example) have some steelhead in them all year, and summer fishing is permitted (see regulations) in some. But the major run of large fish (steelhead—8 pounds and up, salmon—average about 20 pounds) takes place in the fall and winter months. This is prime fishing time. Actually, migrating fish begin to show in July and August.

Timing is critical to successful steelhead and salmon fishing. The weather, stream flow, volume and clarity, and many other factors can affect the bite. Knowledgeable fishermen use the telephone to gauge conditions on various streams, and then once fishing, they're flexible enough to move around if fish aren't being caught. Some experienced fishermen, if need be, call ahead for fishing reports and then drive. Two hours driving might be more productive than two hours fishing. One rule seems to hold true: The longer the stream, the longer the run; the shorter the stream, the bigger the fish. In smaller rivers like the Navarro, Garcia and Gualala, the steelhead are able to enter the river only when flows are high. Ideally, fish near the mouth of small rivers some three or four days after a rain, when the river level is raised and a green color is returning to the water. And do it at high tide. Another tip: Many good anglers new

to winter coastal stream fishing or new to a specific river hire a guide. This is often a good idea. The Shasta Cascade Wonderland Association in Redding, (530) 365-7500, maintains a list of guide services. Ads in fishing newspapers and in local Yellow Pages can also be useful. The Northern California Guides Association can be reached at (707) 539-9534.

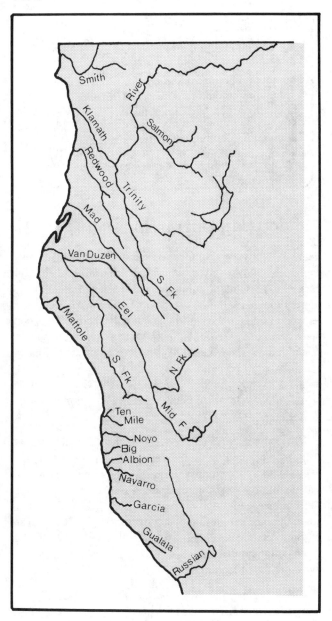

A word about wild versus hatchery fish—stream born wild steelhead are superior to their hatchery bred cousins. Some experienced anglers can I.D. a wild steelhead right after hook up. They are simply superior fighters. Some organizations encourage anglers to release all wild fish—I also strongly suggest this. If we don't release wild metalheads, our kids may never get a chance to feel what it's like to have a truly great fish on the other end of their line. See the illustration below for I.D. details.

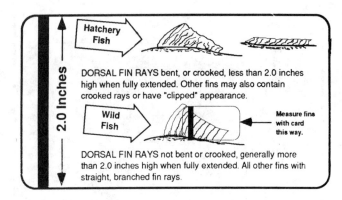

Eel and Van Duzen Rivers (map - p. 186)

Each of Northern California's coast rivers has its own character, its own flavor, its own nature. Take the Eel, for example. This major salmon and steelhead stream flows right through the heart of some of the most spectacular redwood stands in the world, including Humboldt Redwood State Park. And the Eel is famous for both the number and size of its native steelhead. Anglers are just as likely to catch a fish over 10 pounds as they are to catch one under 10 pounds! When the Eel is running right, the water is a beautiful emerald green color, a perfect compliment to the towering redwoods.

King salmon begin to congregate in the Eel tidal waters in August. The run begins in earnest in September and peaks in late October. Most early season salmon activity is concentrated from the Ferndale bridge downstream to the mouth. The majority of Eel River kings range from 8 to 15 pounds, small by standards of some other rivers. But 20, 30 and even 40 pounders are taken. In November, king are still being taken throughout the river with bright, fresh chinook still available in the lower river.

But the Eel reputation has been built and sustained on its winter steelhead fishery. Steelheading is excellent in all three major portions of the Eel system—the Eel, the South

Fork and the Van Duzen. Metalheads move in starting in November. Action picks up in December with the run peaking in January.

The average Eel River steelie weighs 8 to 10 pounds. Fish in the 12-16 pound class are common, and hook-ups with fish over 20 pounds are made each year from shore and boat. In a typical year, most of the steelhead are caught by early January because heavy rains later in the season make the river unfishable. During the late January through March period, data suggests that the Eel is only fishable 60% of the time.

When the Eel and South Fork are high and muddy, some anglers head over to the Van Duzen. It doesn't blow out as easily as the other branches and clears much more quickly. The Van Duzen is located 14 miles upstream from the mouth of the Eel. It's total length is about 50 miles. But the best fishing is usually below Bridgeville. Bank access is excellent via Hwy. 36. And shore anglers do very well because the river is relatively narrow, so most holes can be easily identified and reached with modest casts. Anglers seeking more solitude should consider the Van Duzen, especially when the Eel is fishable. You may find you're all alone and catching up to 16 pound metalheads.

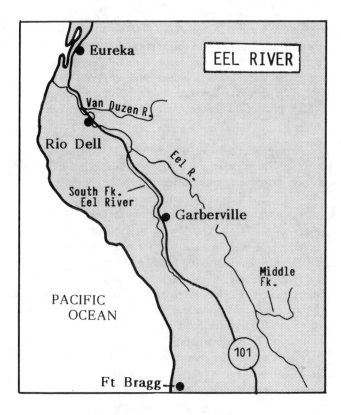

Eel and Van Duzen anglers use about 12 pound line when the river is up, and drop down to 8 or 10 pounds when it is low and clear. On days when the Eel is murky, big spinners, bright plugs and spoons can produce. When the water is clear, fresh roe can't be beat. Good steelhead holding holes have about 3 to 7 feet of moving water over a rocky bottom. Look for steelies behind the many boulders in tailouts in the Eel. They'll be there just treading water and looking. Steelhead don't like deep holes.

Eel River Facts

Location: The mouth is located 15 miles south of Eureka. The Eel River watershed flows for over 100 miles, mostly in a northern direction, in Humboldt and Mendocino Counties.

Species: King salmon and steelhead

Fishing Areas: Almost all of the Eel is accessible including its tributary, the Van Duzen River. But the South Fork, along Hwy. 101, may be the most popular. Anglers scan the river from their vehicles, park, walk down to a hole, and fish. Drift boats are also common on the South Fork. Improved and unimproved launching sites are available about every 4 to 5 miles.

Best Times: Steelhead fishing is good from November through March, with the peak in January. Salmon runs go from September through December.

Communities: Eureka, Fortuna, Rio Dell, Weott, Garberville, Leggett

Information: Bucksport Sporting Goods, Eureka, (707) 442-1832, Department of Fish and Game, Eureka, (707) 445-6493, Northern California River Guides Association, Santa Rosa, CA, (707) 539-9534

Klamath River (maps - p. 188, 189)

The mighty Klamath River, more than 200 miles long from the ocean to the Oregon border, provides a wide variety of steelhead and salmon fishing experiences. The Lower Klamath, which runs from Weitchpec at the mouth of the Trinity (a tributary of the Klamath) to the ocean, is the largest and probably the most heavily fished section. The waters here average about 100-200 feet wide. The mouth of the Klamath has been the scene of legendary salmon fishing since early this century. Zane Gray caught a 57 pound salmon here. Today, shore anglers are shoulder to shoulder, and small boats crowd the tidal waters. Bank anglers cast Bear Valley spinners, Kastmasters or Panther Martins. Aluminum boats with small motors troll anchovies or large spinners like Bear Valleys. A spreader bar with up to 16 ounces of lead keeps the rig down in the strong currents. Anglers need a salmon punch card to fish the Klamath River. The best bank fishing locations and launching ramps along the Lower Klamath are shown on the accompanying map.

The Klamath is known for the number of steelhead rather than size. But the river does produce many 8 to 10 pounders each year. The average catch is 3 to 6 pounds. In October, the river hosts a run of "half-pounders." These juvenile steelhead actually weigh from 1 1/2 to 2 1/2 pounds, and are most numerous below Happy Camp. In the middle river, bank anglers can easily locate places to fish by driving along Hwy. 96 beside the river. Mostly public lands border the Klamath as it flows through sections of the Klamath and Six Rivers National Forest. One, two and three day guided drift trips are also popular along the middle river.

Steelhead are caught in the upper section of the Klamath as early as September and can still be caught, in good years, as late as April. Best fishing is from early November through March. This 40 mile stretch runs from the base of Iron Gate Dam downriver to Hamburg, and consists of a multitude of deep pools and long riffles. There are good opportunities for bank and boat anglers using bait, lures or flies. The upper river clears quickly following storms, sometimes in a matter of hours.

Fishing is a primary industry in the Klamath River basin. There are numerous campsites, R.V. parks, motels, lodges, drift boat services, tackle stores, launching sites, gas stations and restaurants. Most are concentrated in or near the small river communities. Beauty and wilderness are part of the Klamath also. The drive along the river on Hwy. 96 is dramatic. River canyons are steep, rugged and heavily timbered. There is an abundance of wildlife including bear, cougar, deer, otter, eagle, osprey, fox, badger, and more. The smells and sounds of forests and the river are unforgettable.

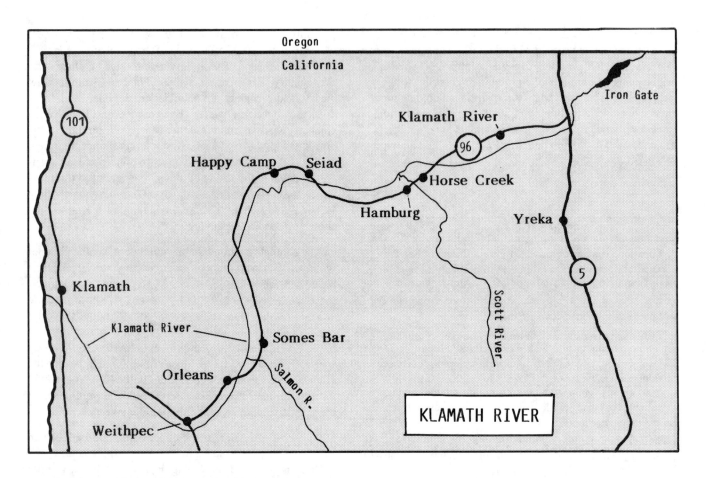

Klamath River

KLAMATH RIVER

Klamath River Facts

Location: The mouth is located 60 miles north of Eureka and 20 miles south of Crescent City off Hwy. 101. Much of the Klamath is paralleled by Hwy. 96 from Weitchpec to I-5.

Species: King salmon and steelhead, along with resident trout

Fishing Areas: The lower 10 miles on either side of Hwy. 101; the middle river along Hwy. 96 (Somes Bar, Happy Camp, Hamburg); the upper river (20 miles on either side of I-5)

Best Times: Salmon start running in July. Lower river runs are usually strongest in August and early September. The initial run of smaller steelhead begins in late summer and continues through October. The winter run of 4 to 10 pound fish enters the river in November through February.

Communities: Klamath, Weitchpec, Somes Bar, Happy Camp, Hamburg, Klamath River

Information: Del Norte Chamber of Commerce, (707) 464-3174; Jury's Ace Hardware, Hoppa, (530) 625-4387; Siskiyou County Visitor's Bureau, (800) 446-7475; Ron's Bait and Tackle, Happy Camp, (530) 493-2409

Mad River (map - p. 190)

The Mad River has just recently become known as a prolific steelhead stream—both in quantity and quality. The winter steelhead run produces plenty of fish, with many in the 8 to 20 pound class. Somehow this doesn't seem possible in an era of declining fisheries. But it is possible, due to the productivity of the local Mad River Hatchery. This hatchery has rejuvenated a dying steelhead fishery and is working to improve the troubled fall chinook run. The Mad River Hatchery came on line in the early 1970's. It's about one mile south of Blue Lake.

Up until a few years ago, only the locals knew about the steelhead run on the Mad. But now anglers come from all over the state to get in on the fun. There are crowds on weekends, especially near the hatchery, but the metalhead population has been holding up very well despite all the fishing pressure.

Steelhead fishing is concentrated in the 15 miles of the river between the hatchery and the ocean. Above the

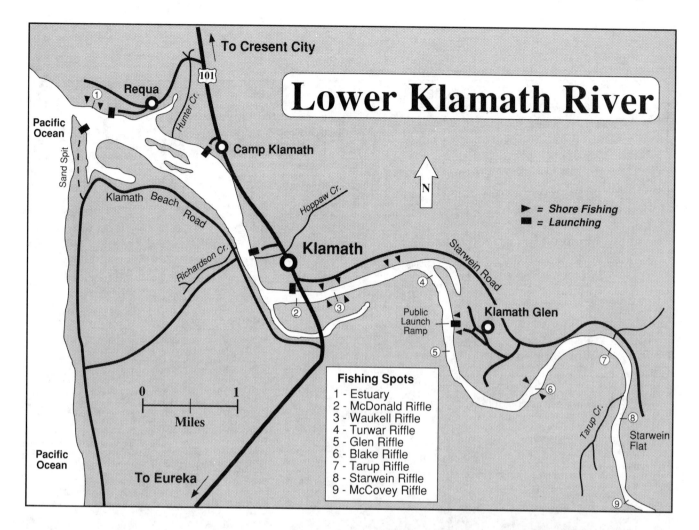

Lower Klamath River

To Cresent City

Requa

Pacific Ocean

Sand Spit

Hunter Cr.

Camp Klamath

Klamath Beach Road

Hoppaw Cr.

Richardson Cr.

Klamath

N

► = Shore Fishing
■ = Launching

Starwein Road

Klamath Glen

Public Launch Ramp

Tarup Cr.

Starwein Flat

Fishing Spots
1 - Estuary
2 - McDonald Riffle
3 - Waukell Riffle
4 - Turwar Riffle
5 - Glen Riffle
6 - Blake Riffle
7 - Tarup Riffle
8 - Starwein Riffle
9 - McCovey Riffle

0   1
Miles

Pacific Ocean

To Eureka

hatchery access is limited. There are very few roads, and the river runs through private property. But it is possible to wade up from the hatchery when the water is low and safe. The Mad River is excellent for bank angling. Access is good and so is wading. By far, the best fishing is located below the hatchery off Hwy. 299. Simply drive along 299 and scout out good holes. It's good all the way down to Hwy. 101. Steelhead lay in water 3 to 8 feet deep. Look for tailouts, the edges of riffles and moving currents at river bends.

The technique of choice on the Mad is drift fishing. Cast upstream and let your offering drift naturally downstream. A pause in the drift usually signals a steelhead. Flies, roe, nightcrawlers, corkies, okies, Spin-N-Glos, Birdy Drifters and other standards all work. When the river is high and off-color, use larger and brighter lures. 12-14 pound test monofilament is recommended by local pros.

If there is one negative to the Mad, it's winter storms. The stream bed up river is unstable, so high flows muddy the water quickly and make it slow to clear.

Mad River Facts

Location: The mouth is located 15 miles north of Eureka in Humboldt County. The headwaters are about 100 miles southeast at Ruth Lake

Species: Steelhead, king and silver salmon, resident trout

Best Times: Excellent run of winter steelhead from December through March

Fishing Areas: The best steelhead waters are from the Mad River Hatchery downstream 15 miles to the north.

Bank Fishing: Very good access from Hwy. 101 all the way up to the hatchery. Also, wading upstream above the hatchery.

Boat Fishing: Boaters can launch at the Blue Lakes Bridge and drift downstream to the Hwy. 101 bridge.

Communities: Eureka, Blue Lake, Arcata, McKinleyville

Information: Mad River Hatchery, (707) 822-0592; Bucksports, Eureka, (707) 442-1832, New Outdoor Store, Arcata, (707) 822-0321

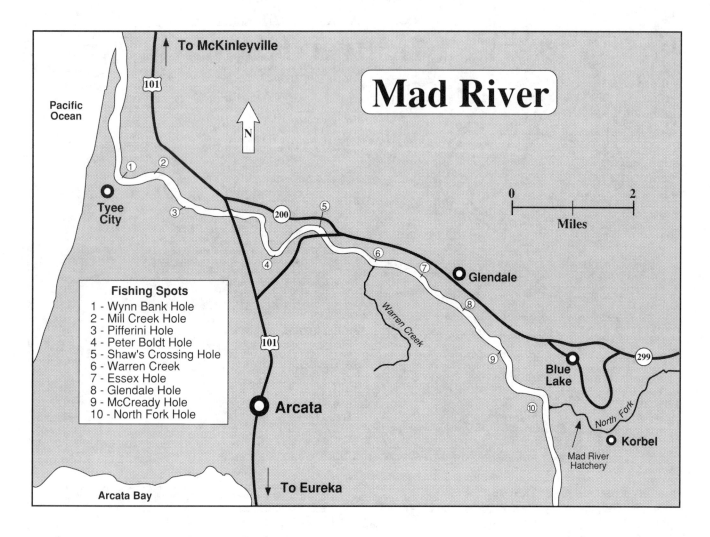

Mattole River

The Mattole is a small, remote coastal river that produces large, hard fighting, *native* steelhead. This is a free-flowing river with no dams and very little civilization. The countryside along the Mattole and its steelhead population are probably very much like what all of the major coastal rivers were like 50 years ago. Wildlife abounds in this area. Bear, deer, mountain lion, Roosevelt elk, game birds and sea birds flourish. And the metalheads are big, plentiful and tough.

Actually, I had second thoughts about including the Mattole in this book. No, I'm not trying to keep it a secret for selfish reasons, but there is a school of thought that suggests that this river will be better off if fewer people know about its existence. On the other hand, maybe awareness by enough people will help create a protective attitude toward one of the

last completely natural steelhead resources in the state. Use and abuse are two different things. So if you choose to fish the Mattole, respect it. And respect its fish. Wild steelhead are special. Many steelhead caught today are hatchery fish that just don't have the fighting spirit of their naturally spawned and reared relatives. I urge you to release all steelhead caught in the Mattole. Use barbless hooks to facilitate the process. You can flatten barbed hooks with a pliers. To release deeply hooked fish, cut the leader at the fishes' mouth.

Bank access is good along the Mattole via Mattole Road between Petrolia and Honeydew. Drift boats also work here. There are about 9 major creeks flowing in the Mattole in these 23 miles. Each presents a great fishing opportunity. Boats are also effective below Petrolia, drifting toward the Mattole river mouth.

```
┌─────────────────────────────────────────┐
│            Mattole River Facts            │
├─────────────────────────────────────────┤
```

Location: On the "Lost Coast" in southwestern Humboldt County, with headwaters in the King Range National Conservation Area. The main river is due west of Humboldt Redwood State Park.

Species: Native winter run steelhead in the 8 to 24 pound range

Fishing Areas: The entire river is about 40 miles long. Best fishing is in the 23 mile section from Honeydew to Petrolia.

Best Times: January through March

Camping: A.W. Way Campground is located on Mattole Road about halfway between Petrolia and Honeydew.

Communities: Petrolia, Honeydew, Dyerville

Information: Department of Fish and Game, Eureka, (707) 445-6493; Brown's Sporting Goods, Garberville, (707) 923-2533

Russian River

The Russian River is the southernmost of the major coastal rivers. Probably because of this it runs through more populated areas, and has been abused more than most of the others. Also, it flows through more gentle terrain than the streams farther north. It can be fished from shore and by boat. Access is good along parts of the river, but private property prevents bank anglers access to some good stretches and pools.

Unlike other coastal streams, the Russian is more than a salmon/steelhead/trout stream. It supports a healthy population of smallmouth bass and has shad and striper runs. There are also catfish and even some sturgeon.

Many experts say that a major negative impact on the Russian River fisheries occurred when the Coyote Dam was completed in 1957. It created Lake Mendocino and wiped out much of the upper river spawning grounds for salmon and steelhead. Add in silt and human pollution, and things were grim for a time. Surprisingly, another dam project has helped breathe new life into the river. Warm Springs dam created Lake Sonoma on Dry Creek several years back. And it did a few other things. The new Warm Springs Hatchery below the dam is greatly improving the steelhead fishing, and Lake Sonoma is providing a controlled flow down Dry Creek and into the main Russian watershed.

The winter steelhead fishing is good and improving on the Russian. It usually gets into gear around Thanksgiving,

and runs through February. Don't be fooled by the look of the river. Almost all of the water is slow and flat, not likely looking steelhead holes. But there are outstanding runs and glides on the Russian.

All conventional methods work including drifting roe, drift bobbers, and salmon eggs. Casting spoons and spinners are also good. And when the water is clear, even wet flies will provoke strikes. Speaking of water clarity, the Russian is one of the fastest rivers to muddy and the slowest to clear. Count on 10 days to almost 2 weeks after a major rainfall for the Russian to be fishable.

The first really productive area for steelhead is from Duncan Mill to Monte Rio. Pools and riffles such as Freezeout, Browns, Austin Creek, and Moscow are accessible and good. Monte Rio has a paved ramp. But from here up to Guerneville, access is very limited for shore anglers. But boat anglers find it a good drift. Public ramps, in addition to Monte Rio, are at Hacienda and Guerneville. Access is fair from Guerneville up to Wohler Road bridge, but is almost nonexistent from there on up to Healdsburg.

Near Healdsburg is the most productive steelhead spot on the entire river. There are five excellent holes downstream from the mouth of Dry Creek. They are all walkable. Drift boats are put in about a half mile up from Dry Creek. On up, the river access is spotty. Fitch Mountain Road in Healdsburg provides limited access. Then upstream to Alexander Valley Road access is nonexistent except for drift boaters. Other spots to reach the river are in Geyersville, Asti, the Cloverdale Airport, and in Cloverdale. A final good spot is the mouth of Sulfur Creek. A popular drift is from Asti down to Geyersville.

The Dry Creek hatchery program for salmon has not been very successful, to date. But some silver and king salmon start their migrations in late September and run through October into early November.

Smallmouth fishing is a pleasant bonus. Bronzebacks inhabit almost the entire river from the tidal pools all the way up to Cloverdale. Slower flowing sections of the river are the best bets. Crankbaits, Git Zits, small jigs, crawdads and nightcrawlers all work. When water is clear in the upper river, the smallies will spook, so stalk them like stream trout. Smallmouth can be taken all year long.

The shad fishing is hot on the Russian from mid-April to mid-June. They are in the entire lower river, from Healdsburg on down to the mouth. Most steelhead waters are also good for shad. Fish waters about 3 to 5 feet deep with shad darts, small jigs and spinners. In the early spring and early fall striper inhabit the lower river from near Monte Rio on down to the tidal basin. From shore, use cut baits or cast out broken-back Rebels. Boaters troll jigs and plugs. Catfish, bluegill and crappie provide angling opportunities in the summertime. The lower river is best.

Dams and other degradations have eliminated trout fishing on most of the Russian. But there is a good put-and-take fishery on the East Fork above Lake Mendocino where it parallels Hwy. 20 to Potter Valley Road. In the rest of the Russian, anglers who think they are catching small trout are probably catching steelhead smolts in the 8-10 inch range. These should be released.

Russian River Facts

Location: It flows southward from its headwaters at Lake Mendocino paralleling Hwy. 101 to Healdsburg, and then flows westward along Hwy. 116. The Russian mouth is at Jenner on Hwy. 1 in Sonoma County.

Species: Steelhead, king and silver salmon, smallmouth bass, shad, catfish, striped bass, sturgeon

Fishing Areas: There are good sections up and down the river. See the adjoining description for details. By the way, the "North Bay Counties" California State Automobile Association (CSAA) map features a detailed Lower Russian River map, including fishing holes. Several other commercial fishing maps are also available at local tackle shops.

Best Times: The Russian is a four season river, but heaviest use is during the winter steelhead run from late November through February. See adjoining material for additional details.

Communities: Cloverdale, Healdsburg, Guerneville, Jenner

Information: Department of Fish and Game, (707) 944-2011; Warm Springs Hatchery, (707) 433-6325; Western Angler in Santa Rosa, (707) 542-4432; King's Sports Shop in Guerneville, (707) 869-2156; Healdsburg Chamber of Commerce, (707) 433-6935; Eagle's Sport World in Cloverdale, (707) 894-2041

Smith River (map - p. 193)

The Smith is the farthest north of California's major salmon and steelhead streams. But often it's worth the trip because the Smith produces some of the Pacific coast's largest sea-run fish. The state record steelhead came from the Smith in 1976. It weighed in at a whopping 27 pounds 4 ounces. Trophy class steelhead, in excess of 20 pounds, are caught here each year. The Smith also produced the state's second largest chinook salmon—86 pounds. Average kings run about 20 to 36 pounds with several in excess of 60 pounds being caught each year.

One desirable feature of the Smith, besides the number and large size of its fish, is the quickness with which it clears after a winter storm. Often it is clear and fishable within a few days following a major storm. Some other streams take up to two weeks to clear. The Smith clears so quickly because most of its stream bed is solid rock.

During the early salmon season the Smith is low and clear, not at all like the high, fast flowing river of winter. Salmon come in on high ocean tides, then hold at Baily Hole (the first major stopover in the river) or at the mouth of Rowdy Creek. Fishing tidal water is the same as described for the Klamath, but usually less weight is needed to keep trolled offerings down.

Early fall rains bring the river up allowing the salmon to move up throughout the river. Then they stock up in the deeper holes waiting for the heavier rains that will provide water for them so they can continue up feeder streams. Salmon holding when water is low and clear are tough to catch. Higher waters of late November usually allow the salmon to move at will. Sometimes in late November and early December, 40 to 60 pound salmon move in and through the lower river making for some awesome angling. Anglers use 15 to 25 pound line during normal water flows. Go lighter during low flow times.

Steelhead begin showing up about when the salmon are dropping off. The peak is in January. From February on, a larger portion of fish are post-spawners moving on downstream. As with salmon, the best fishing can be found in the lower river, from the South Fork down to the mouth. Fish the same stretches as for salmon, only different waters. Steelhead anglers work the tailouts and broken waters, while salmon chasers concentrate on the deep holes. Steelhead seek cover. Fish the heads of holes

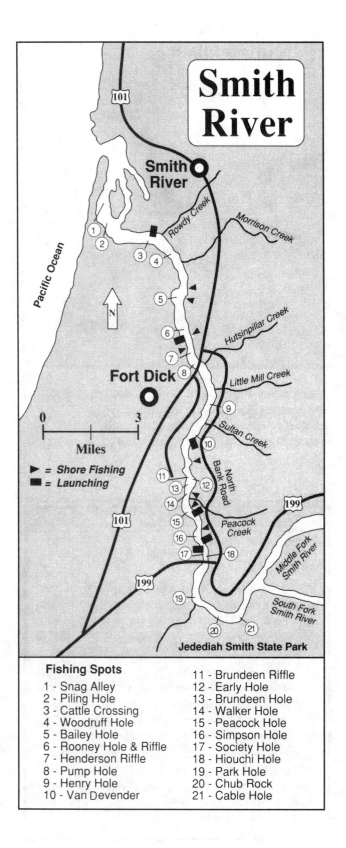

Fishing Spots

1 - Snag Alley
2 - Piling Hole
3 - Cattle Crossing
4 - Woodruff Hole
5 - Bailey Hole
6 - Rooney Hole & Riffle
7 - Henderson Riffle
8 - Pump Hole
9 - Henry Hole
10 - Van Devender

11 - Brundeen Riffle
12 - Early Hole
13 - Brundeen Hole
14 - Walker Hole
15 - Peacock Hole
16 - Simpson Hole
17 - Society Hole
18 - Hiouchi Hole
19 - Park Hole
20 - Chub Rock
21 - Cable Hole

and where the water goes over. Steelhead usually lay on the current line next to fast water. 10 to 15 pound test line is about right for most conditions. Access to some good holes on the Middle Mork is via Hwy. 199.

Smith River Facts
Location: The Smith is located in Del Norte County; its mouth is five miles south of the Oregon border and 10 miles north of Crescent City.
Species: Known for its large king salmon and steelhead
Best Times: The salmon run starts in late August, peaks in November, and ends in late December. Steelhead begin showing in early December and run through March.
Bank Fishing: Reasonable access along much of the river below the South Fork. Top bank fishing spots are Bailey Hole, Early Hole, just below Jedediah Smith State Park and Van Deventer County Park, and Hiouchi Hole.
Boat Fishing: The Smith is navigable in the lower 15 miles below the confluence with the South Fork. Popular launching and take-outs are at the South Fork, Jedediah Smith State Park, Van Deventer County Park, Smith River Outfitters and Rowdy Creek.
Camping: Jedediah Smith State Park is most popular.
Communities: Crescent City, Smith River, Gasquet
Information: Department of Fish and Game, Eureka, (707) 445-6493; Smith River Outfitters (707) 487-0935; Del Norte Chamber of Commerce, (707) 464-3174

Trinity River (map - p. 194)

The Trinity River is a good salmon, steelhead and trout fishery. This is true despite the fact that its headwaters are a huge manmade reservoir (Trinity Lake) and its mouth is not the Pacific Ocean, but rather the Klamath River. Prior to the damming of the Trinity in the early 1960's, the Trinity had a reputation as one of the finest salmon, steelhead and trout rivers in the West. Fishing obviously is not like that today. But this long, winding tributary of the Klamath is a major fishing resource and it's getting better.

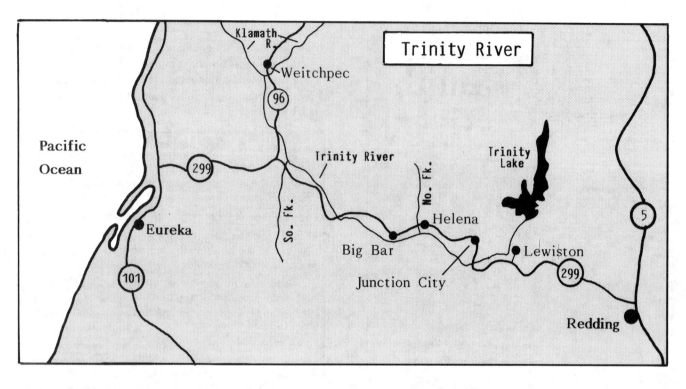

In early September the Trinity begins receiving its annual fall king salmon run. Average fish are in the 9 to 12 pound range and provide light tackle anglers with many exciting hook-ups. The technique of choice here is drifting bait (fresh roe, sardines, crawfish tails, nightcrawlers, tuna balls) through major, deep holding pools that separate swift flowing riffles and glides. Hardware anglers also catch their share on glow bugs, spinners, plugs and weighted spoons. Action takes place all the way from Willow Creek to Junction City, so there is more room for anglers to spread out, than at the Lower Klamath or Lower Smith, for example. Major salmon holding waters are at Willow Creek, the South Fork, Hawkins Bar, Grays Falls, Cedar Flat, Big Bar, Helena and Junction City. A major key to success is to keep on moving along Hwy. 299 until you find fish. Concentrate on deep holding water and pools.

In October, silver salmon join in on the run. They're great fighters and jumpers, and average 5 to 8 pounds. Most salmon taking methods will work, but more cohos are taken on medium-sized spinners than on anything else. Silvers move up the river system quite quickly so timing and luck are critical factors. A note about regulations: Regulations for salmon on the Trinity can and do change. Some sections may be closed to fishing, and a salmon punch card is required. So be informed.

By the middle of October, many steelhead have usually arrived in the Trinity. Anglers work the many swift flowing riffles and tailouts. Trying different waters and moving along 299 are again important. Generally, on the Trinity it is best to fish the upper river after a major rain or water fluctuation from the dam, while the lower river is

---

Trinity River Facts

Location: The Trinity River flows generally from east to west from Trinity Lake at Lewiston to its confluence with the Klamath River at Weitchpec.

Species: Steelhead, king and silver salmon, trout

Best Times: Fall king salmon from late September through early November. Winter steelhead and silver salmon start showing in mid-October and last through December. Spring king salmon are available in May through early August.

Fishing Areas: Most of the river parallels Hwy. 299 providing excellent access for over 100 miles between Lewiston Lake and Willow Creek.

Communities: Lewiston, Weaverville, Junction City, Big Bar, Del Loma, Burnt Ranch, Willow Creek

Camping: Forest Service, BLM and private campgrounds are located all along the Trinity River.

Information: Shasta Casacade Wonderland Association, Redding, (530) 365-7500 or (800) 474-2782; Brady's Sports Shop, Weaverville, (530) 623-3121

often best during low water or dry fall conditions. Major steelhead locales include the month of the South Fork, Group Falls, Big Bar, Cedar Flat, Helena, Junction City and Douglas City. Most all steelhead techniques work, as do flies, if the river is in the proper condition. In fact, the Trinity can be one of the best fly fishing waters for steelhead in the West.

Two other Trinity fisheries are also worth noting. First there is the spring run of king salmon. These are smaller than the fall run, averaging 6 to 7 pounds. But the fish are in the river in great numbers. Then there are the resident brown and rainbow trout. Both of these species are present in good numbers along the river, and the "fly

fishing only" stretch below Lewiston Dam is one of the top trout spots in the state. The best section of river for browns is from Lewiston Dam downstream to Douglas City. But trout are taken as far downstream as the confluence with the North Fork. Check the current *Fish and Game Regulations* for spring salmon and resident trout seasons.

Other Steelhead Streams

Besides the major steelhead and salmon rivers detailed in this section, there are streams that provide good steelhead fishing in the fall/winter months. These are summarized in the table below.

SALMON AND STEELHEAD PORTS AND STREAMS

Coastal Streams and Their Tributaries; Main Streams Listed From North to South, Tributaries Listed From Upstream Down

Stream	Steel-head	Silver Salmon	King Salmon	Time of Salmon and Steelhead Runs and Other Comments
SMITH RIVER	Yes	Yes	Yes	At the mouth and in the lagoon there is a large skiff fishery. King salmon are the biggest attraction. Best fishing for kings is late Sept. through Oct.; silvers run about a month later. Some steelhead are taken in the lagoon. Sea-run cutthroat fishing fall, winter, and spring; best March through May. Above the lagoon fishing for salmon, steelhead, and cutthroat fall and winter. Most of the Smith system is in canyons.
KLAMATH RIVER	Yes	Yes	Yes	At the mouth and in the lagoon there is a large skiff fishery for king salmon, best in Aug. and Sept.; silvers late Sept. through Oct.; sea-run cutthroat fishing Sept. through April; best in March and April. Fall steelhead run is best in the lower river in Aug. and Sept.; about a month later near Copco Dam. Some summer steelhead available. Winter steelhead best in Jan. and Feb.; but high water usually bothers fishermen. Upriver salmon fishing fair in fall.
SCOTT RIVER	Yes	Yes	Yes	Runs through farming country. Much of the bottom has been gold dredged. Salmon and steelhead in fall. Some winter steelhead. Canyon below farming area is best.
SALMON RIVER	Yes	Yes	Yes	Some summer steelhead. Good steelhead and salmon stream in the fall. The mouth of the Salmon River is an especially good spot.
Wooley Creek	Yes		Yes	Spring-run salmon, summer steelhead, no winter fishing, no roads.
TRINITY RIVER	Yes	Yes	Yes	Spring-run king salmon available near Lewiston May through summer. Kings also available through most of the river in the fall. Some silver salmon in the lower parts of the Trinity. Some summer steelhead. Best steelhead fishing from the first fall rains through the winter.
SOUTH FORK TRINITY RIVER	Yes	Yes	Yes	Some spring-run king salmon, good fall run of kings. Some silvers in lower part of South Fork. Steelhead in fall and winter.
REDWOOD CREEK	Yes	Yes	Yes	Best in fall and winter. A dry fall may delay the runs. Good sea-run cutthroat fishing in tidewater fall, winter, and early spring.
Little River	Yes	Yes		Fall and winter—runs start after first heavy rains.
MAD RIVER	Yes	Yes	Yes	Fall and winter. A dry fall may delay the runs.
Elk River	Yes	Yes	Few	Fall and winter—runs start after first heavy rains.
EEL RIVER	Yes	Yes	Yes	Trolling for king salmon in tidewater late Aug. through Oct. Kings are caught further upstream fall and winter. Half-pounder fishing below the Van Duzen late summer and early fall. Larger steelhead below the Van Duzen in the fall. Winter fishing for steelhead throughout the river system.
MIDDLE FORK EEL RIVER	Yes		Yes	Salmon and steelhead fishing fall and winter. Some summer steelhead near Covelo and above.
SOUTH FORK EEL RIVER	Yes	Yes	Yes	Fall and winter fishing for steelhead and salmon.
VAN DUZEN RIVER	Yes	Yes	Yes	Fall and winter fishing for steelhead and salmon. Some summer steelhead above Bridgeville.
Bear River	Yes	Yes	Yes	November or later, depending on rains.
MATTOLE RIVER	Yes	Yes	Yes	November or later, depending on rains.
TEN MILE RIVER	Yes	Yes		November or later, depending on rains.
NOYO RIVER	Yes	Yes		November or later, depending on rains.
BIG RIVER	Yes	Yes		November or later, depending on rains.
ALBION RIVER	Yes	Yes		November or later, depending on rains.
NAVARRO RIVER	Yes	Yes		November or later, depending on rains.
Greenwood Creek	Yes			November or later, depending on rains.
Alder Creek	Yes			November or later, depending on rains.
Brush Creek	Yes			November or later, depending on rains.
GARCIA RIVER	Yes	Yes	Few	November or later, depending on rains.
GUALALA RIVER	Yes	Yes		November or later, depending on rains.
RUSSIAN RIVER	Yes	Yes		Fall and winter—runs apt to be delayed by late rains. Silver salmon confined roughly to lower 40 miles of river.
Salmon Creek	Yes	Yes		Fall and winter—depending on rains and water flow.
Walker Creek	Yes	Yes		Fall and winter—depending on rains and water flow.
PAPERMILL CREEK	Yes	Yes		Fall and winter—depending on rains and water flow.
NAPA RIVER	Yes			Fall and winter—runs start after first heavy rains.
Alameda Creek	Yes			Late fall and winter—Recommended only for local people.
San Gregorio Creek	Yes			Late fall and winter—Recommended only for local people.
Pescadero Creek	Yes	Few		Late fall and winter—Recommended only for local people.
Scott Creek	Yes	Few		Late fall and winter—Recommended only for local people.
SAN LORENZO RIVER	Yes	Few		Fall and winter—Recommended only for local people.
Soquel Creek	Yes	Few		Late fall and winter—Recommended only for local people.
Pajaro River	Yes			Late fall and winter—Recommended only for local people.
CARMEL RIVER	Yes			Fall and winter—depending on rains and water flow.
BIG SUR RIVER	Yes			Fall and winter—depending on rains and water flow.

Central Valley River Fishing

The Central Valley rivers of Northern California offer some of the finest fishing in the entire state. The most productive waters are the Sacramento River and its tributaries, the American and the Feather Rivers. In these waters fishing is almost a year-round activity. There's steelhead and salmon beginning in late summer and running through winter. Striped bass, sturgeon and shad make spring spawning runs into the Sacramento system. And if the migratory fish aren't enough, there's catfishing, smallmouth bass, rainbow and brown trout fishing in these rivers. See the accompanying map.

The key to successful fishing is to be there when the action is hot. Salmon, steelhead, striper, sturgeon and shad are migrating through the Central Valley Rivers to get to their spawning grounds. So they're on the move. In addition, most of the best fishing takes place during the rainy season, so stream conditions can change rapidly. Keep in touch with fishing tackle stores, fishing guide services and bait shops in the stretches of river you want to fish, for up-to-date information. Shore fishing is possible in selected areas, but boats are used by many to increase coverage, and to reach spots that flow through the many farms and ranches. But boating these rivers during high water flow months requires experience and skill.

Lower Sacramento River (map - p. 197)

The Lower Sacramento River is the largest and most important waterway in California. It runs from near Redding all the way down to Rio Vista in the Delta. As the crow flies, this measures 180 miles, so the river channel is probably in excess of 200 miles. A lot of water flows in the Sacramento since on its way south it takes in the flows of the Pit, McCloud, Feather, Yuba, Bear and the American rivers. Of course, because of dams, and the domestic and agricultural diversion of water in all these systems, there is less flow and it is now controlled.

As with all of California's rivers, fishing in the Sacramento was better in days gone by than it is today. But on balance, the Lower Sacramento is still an excellent fishing resource. I'm sure anglers in many other states would love to fish for Sacramento River salmon, steelhead, striped bass, shad, sturgeon, rainbow trout, catfish, black bass and panfish. In this section, the portion of the Lower Sacramento River between Lake Shasta and Sacramento is covered. The southern portion, from Sacramento to Rio Vista, is covered in the "Delta" chapter. And the Upper Sacramento River,

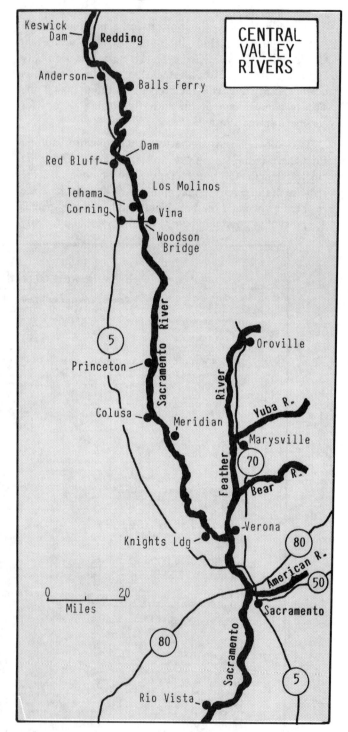

above Lake Shasta, is covered in the "Northeast Freshwater Fishing" chapter.

Almost 60% of all the king salmon caught off the coast of Northern California were spawned in the Lower Sacramento River. Of course, many Sacramento River salmon are not caught in the ocean, and it is these 3 or 4 year-old chinook that come back under the Golden Gate Bridge, pass through San Francisco Bay and Delta, and eventually provide such great sport all the way up to Redding. The major run usually begins in August and continues through October. Fish range from 12 to 50 pounds or more, with the average in the 12 to 20 pound range. The state record king, a whopping 88 pounds, was taken below Red Bluff in 1978.

King salmon are taken all along the river, from Sacramento on up. But in most of this long, wide waterway, the action is inconsistent. Maybe because the salmon are spread out and continually on the move up river. The most productive and consistent salmon waters on the Sacramento River are from Los Molinos north to the fishing cut-off line at the Deschutes Road bridge near Anderson. In this section of the river, bank access is limited by private property, so most anglers use boats. Anyway, boats are almost a necessity to properly work the deep holes. Backtrolling Flatfish, Kwikfish or salmon roe are the usual techniques.

There is a launch ramp at Los Molinos off Tehama—Vina Road. Good salmon holes in the vicinity include Salmon Hole, Car Body Hole and Salt Creek Hole. There is also launching at Bend where Seven Mile Hole and Paynes Creek Hole produce fish. The last stretch of river from Bend on up is probably the best of all. Great holes include the Barge Hole and the Old Mouth of Battle Creek. Other good spots are the House Hole under the Jelly Ferry Bridge and Jelly's Hole. Launching is at either Ball's Ferry Fishing Resort or at Rooster's Landing. In total, there are 10 launch ramps available to the public in Shasta and Tehama Counties.

Steelhead are also prevalent in the Sacramento. The best time of year is mid-December through February. Generally, the up river areas hold more promise. Battle Creek, which used to be a favorite spot for steelhead, is currently closed year around. Riffles, cutbanks, pools, runs below feeder stream mouths, as well as heads of drifts and above tailouts, are the most sought after spots. Most productive approaches are backtrolling plugs and drift fishing roe from an anchored boat.

Rainbow trout fishing on the Sacramento has blossomed into a marvelous sport. Most weigh from 1 to 1 1/2 pounds, but fish up to 5 pounds are taken. The best waters are from the Keswick Dam on down to Balls Ferry. These trout are resident and are caught year around, whenever the river isn't

Fishing Spots
1 - Bridge Riffle
2 - Conveyor Belt Riffle
3 - Tobiason Hole
4 - Clear Creek Riffle
5 - Hawes Hole
6 - Anderson River Pk.
7 - Deschutes Bridge Riffle
8- Kimberly-Clark Riffle
9 - Power Line Riffle
10 - Balls Ferry Hole
11 - Reading Island
12 - Old Mouth of Battle Creek
13 - Ink's Cr. Riffle
14 - Jelly's Ferry Rifle
15 - Perry Riffle
16 - Bend Riffle
17 - Anderson Riffle
18 - Public access via Le Claire
19 - Tennison Riffle
20 - Mill Cr. Park
21 - Tehama #1 Riffle
22 - Tehama #2 Riffle
23 - Corning Riffle

Sacramento River
Redding to Corning

► = *Shore Fishing*
■ = *Launching*

0   5
Miles

too high or too muddy. But spring, especially April and May when high winter flows are reduced to a fishable level (in the 5,000 to 12,000 cubic feet per second range), produces prime rainbow action.

Shad dominate the action during the middle of May through June and most of July in the upper river from the Red Bluff Diversion Dam down to Los Molinos. Most fish are in the 2 1/2 to 4 pound range. Boats are used to get to good spots where anglers wade or fish from anchored boats. Shad fishing is also good on down the river. As the shad move northward, hot spots include Freeport, the Sacramento area, Verona at the mouth of the Feather, Colusa, Princeton, and from Butte City on up to Hamilton City. There are many shore fishing access spots at all of the lower river locales, but boat fishing is also popular.

Spring is the prime time for striped bass in the Sacramento River above the city of Sacramento. Some of California's fastest and most consistent striper action takes place between mid-March and early June. The Sacramento is the major spawning river for California's striper bass population, with the predominant stretch being from Knights Landing to Princeton. May is the main spawning month, but early arrivals usually reach the Knights Landing waters by the last week of March. In low water years, most fish stay below Colusa. Wet springs or higher releases of water from Shasta Dam will move most spawning stripers up between Grimes and Princeton. Some small fish may even move all the way up to the Red Bluff Diversion Dam. The offering of choice is large Rebel minnow plugs with long plastic bills. The 5 1/2 inch size is about perfect. Black or blue-backed plugs with silver sides are favorites. Troll deep, bouncing on the bottom once in awhile. Other trolling options are Cordell Fin-Deeps and Bomber minnow-style plugs. Filleted anchovies are used by anchored boat anglers and by bank anglers. Use enough weight to hold bait on the inside or outside of bends. Bank access for shore anglers is abundant in the good striper sections of the Lower Sacramento.

Sturgeon spawn in many of the same spawning areas as the striped bass. Fishing hot spots for these winter spawners are in the Princeton/Colusa/Meridian section of the Sacramento River. Ghost shrimp is fished right on the bottom using a sliding sinker rig. Sturgeon hold in deep holes in the daytime and then move onto shallower gravel bars at night-time to feed.

Lower Sacramento River Facts

Location: The Lower Sacramento River flows from the foot of Shasta Dam near Redding all the way down through Sacramento, and finally to the Delta at Rio Vista.

Species: King salmon, steelhead, rainbow trout, shad, striped bass, sturgeon, catfish, panfish

Fishing Areas: The entire length of the river offers good fishing. Best locations depend on season and species.

Best Times: Fall king salmon run from August to November. Steelhead are best from mid-December to February. Rainbow trout are taken all year but peak in April and May. Shad season runs from May through July. Striped bass run from mid-March to early June, following the winter sturgeon run.

Communities: Redding, Red Bluff, Colusa, Sacramento, Rio Vista

Information: Shasta-Cascade Wonderland Association, Redding, (530) 365-7500 or (800) 474-2782; tackle dealers in towns along the Sacramento River.

Lower Feather River (map - p. 199)

The Lower Feather River has a great deal in common with its big sister, the Lower Sacramento River. The species (salmon, steelhead, shad, striper, etc.) and fishing seasons are quite similar. Both rivers run from north to south in the Sacramento Valley. And both have their origins in a major reservoir. Differences are in degree. The Feather is shorter, but still flows over 50 miles, as the crow flies. Its water flow is lower making boating more difficult, especially for the less experienced. A final and pleasant difference is that the Feather doesn't seem to attract the crowds that the Sacramento does, probably because it gets less publicity.

King salmon typically start entering the Feather at Verona in August. However, the best fishing often takes place in October, before the mid-month spawning closure north of Honcut Creek. After this closure many anglers switch to steelhead, but there are still salmon action in areas like Shanghai Bend from both boat and bank. In the latter part of the season salmon get darker, and most anglers release them to spawn.

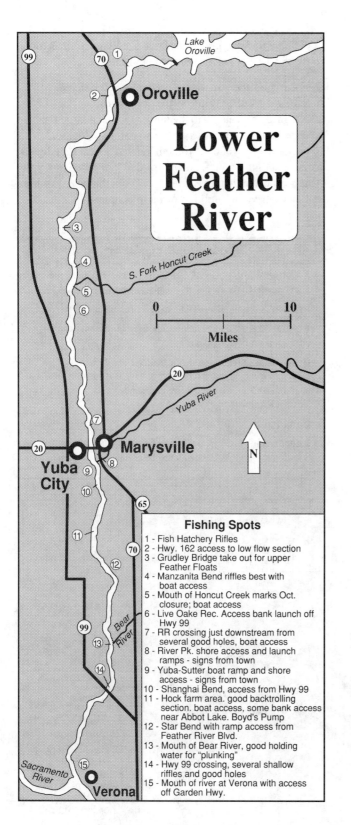

The mouth of the Feather at Verona is a great spot for migratory species. Boat anglers work salmon, steelhead, stripers and shad. Another popular spot is the Star Bend/ Shanghai Bend area. Due to private property restrictions, most anglers fish with boats from Verona up to Shanghai Bends' rapids, south of the Yuba River confluence. Good boat fishing spots south of Yuba City include deep holes below the rapids of Boyd's Pump, above the rapids, above the mouth of the Yuba River, and above and below Star Bend. Above Yuba City two good areas are the Car Body Hole and the Long Hole.

Bank anglers do well just below and above Shanghai Bend. Another good shore fishing area is in the riffles from the Gridley Bridge up to Thermolito Afterbay. Just downstream of the Thermolito outlet is a good spot to cast large, weighted spinners.

The lower Feather is one of the finest smallmouth waters in all of the West. These 1 to 2 pound fighters are anywhere there is cover (stumps, under brushy banks, etc.). They are in the river all year and can be taken all year long. April and May are prime months for smallmouth bass fishing in the lower Feather. Air temperatures are comfortable and river flow is low enough to form channels, so that smallmouth are concentrated in the numerous pools and runs. The best fishing takes place when water releases are less than 4,000 cubic feet per second, with about 3,000 being ideal. Anglers fish from shore, use waders, or small drift boats.

Fishing Spots

1 - Fish Hatchery Rifles
2 - Hwy. 162 access to low flow section
3 - Grudley Bridge take out for upper Feather Floats
4 - Manzanita Bend riffles best with boat access
5 - Mouth of Honcut Creek marks Oct. closure; boat access
6 - Live Oake Rec. Access bank launch off Hwy 99
7 - RR crossing just downstream from several good holes, boat access
8 - River Pk. shore access and launch ramps - signs from town
9 - Yuba-Sutter boat ramp and shore access - signs from town
10 - Shanghai Bend, access from Hwy 99
11 - Hock farm area. good backtrolling section. boat access, some bank access near Abbot Lake. Boyd's Pump
12 - Star Bend with ramp access from Feather River Blvd.
13 - Mouth of Bear River, good holding water for "plunking"
14 - Hwy 99 crossing, several shallow riffles and good holes
15 - Mouth of river at Verona with access off Garden Hwy.

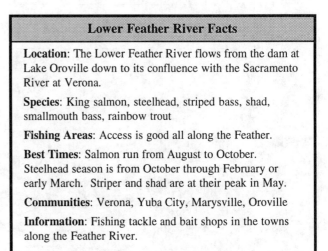

Lower Feather River Facts

Location: The Lower Feather River flows from the dam at Lake Oroville down to its confluence with the Sacramento River at Verona.

Species: King salmon, steelhead, striped bass, shad, smallmouth bass, rainbow trout

Fishing Areas: Access is good all along the Feather.

Best Times: Salmon run from August to October. Steelhead season is from October through February or early March. Striper and shad are at their peak in May.

Communities: Verona, Yuba City, Marysville, Oroville

Information: Fishing tackle and bait shops in the towns along the Feather River.

American River (map - p. 200)

The Lower American River offers one of the best metropolitan angling experiences in the entire United States. It flows about 22 miles from the Nimbus Dam in Fair Oaks to its confluence with the Sacramento River, just north of downtown Sacramento. Salmon, steelhead, striper and shad visit the river, and trout, smallmouth bass and catfish make it their permanent home.

Many anglers use drift boats, putting in near the Nimbus Basin. These boaters fish holes such as Upper Sunrise, Bridge Street, Lower Sunrise, Sacramento Bar, Rossmoor Bar and the mouth at Sacramento. But the American also offers great shore fishing possibilities. Some of the best spots are the Nimbus Basin, Sailor Bar Park, Upper and Lower Sunrise, Rossmoor Bar, Goethe Park, the end of Arden Way, Watt Avenue bridge, Howe Avenue bridge, Paradise Beach, the area behind Cal Expo and the Discovery Park area.

There is a closure on the American River from Nimbus Basin downstream about 8 miles to just below Hoffman Park from November 1st to January 1st. This closure allows salmon and steelhead to spawn in the upper river during these months. Salmon fishing is usually best before the closure, and the large steelhead are usually taken after the closure. A shad and striper hot spot is the Discovery Park area. Two strains of steelhead use the American. The Coleman strain usually makes its way up the American from

September to November. The large Eel River strain is found in the river from December through March.

Fishing on the American, particularly for steelhead, has fallen off considerably during the dry years of the late 1980's. This is in sharp contrast to the fantastic runs of large fish that were present in the early 1980s, and before. Hopefully, this is primarily a cyclical problem related to rainfall levels. Another point—don't expect to find solitude along the American when fishing is good. After all, this river is within an hour's drive of a million or more people.

Lower American River

Location: From Folsom Lake to its confluence with the Sacramento River in the city of Sacramento.

Species: Salmon, steelhead, striped bass, shad

Fishing Areas: Good bank and boat fishing along the entire length of 22 miles.

Best Times: King salmon run from September to December, steelhead are best from January through March, shad are taken in May and June, and stripers in July and August.

Communities: City of Sacramento

Information: Fishing tackle and bait shops in the city of Sacramento and its eastern suburbs

---

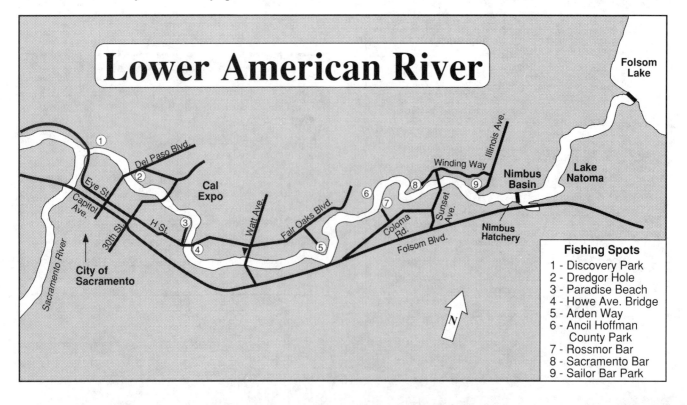

Lower American River

Fishing Spots
1 - Discovery Park
2 - Dredgor Hole
3 - Paradise Beach
4 - Howe Ave. Bridge
5 - Arden Way
6 - Ancil Hoffman County Park
7 - Rossmor Bar
8 - Sacramento Bar
9 - Sailor Bar Park

Special: Sacramento River Sloughs

Catfishing is very good in the Sacramento River. And according to some polls, catfish are the most sought after gamefish in the entire state. Why not—"cats" are fun to catch and great eating.

But there are times during each year when catfishing is better in the sloughs, creeks, and drainage ditches that flow into the Sacramento River, than in the river itself. That's because huge numbers of big catfish move up into tributary flows of the Sacramento River to feed on threadfin shad, minnows, and everything else coming off rice fields (e.g. drowned mice) and other cyclical wetlands.

Surprisingly, many California anglers are overlooking this catfish bonanza. But this Fishing in Northern California special report tells you the "where's," "when's," and "hows" you need so you can get in on the fun.

First let's look at the "where." We're talking about the system of canals, creeks, sloughs, and ditches that are between the Sacramento River and Hwy. 99 on the west and east, and between Chico and Knights Landing on the north and south. In this vast area, two of the most noteworthy catfish hot spots are:

- Sutter National Wildlife Refuge—It begins just south of Hwy. 20 and runs south to Hwy. 113. Here the east and west canals, or east and west Sutter Sloughs, flank the Sutter Bypass (see AAA Sacramento Valley Region map).

- Butte Creek between Durham and the Butte Sink (see AAA Feather River and Yuba River Regions map).

The above two areas combine for over 50 miles of excellent catfish waters. But there are also literally hundreds of miles of other sloughs, canals, creeks, and drainage ditches, some even unmarked and unnamed on the maps, that produce good numbers of large catfish. Scout around and you'll find them.

Much of these waters are on private land, but many owners permit fishing when asked. Additionally, countless miles of canals, drains, and bypasses are open to the public. Water companies often leave graveled levee access roads open and public roads crisscross most waters. Ditches and canals range in size from "jump-overs" to boatable waters.

Now for the "when." Catfishing in the Sacramento River valley drainage is a rainy season affair. The water is flowing and chocolate brown. Often fall rains result in quickly rising flows in late October and November. Another good time is spring (late March through early May). This is when rice farmers are draining off fields which fill ditches, canals, bypasses, and creeks.

Finally, the "how." High water catfish hit just about as well throughout the day as they do at night. It is important, however, to keep your offering on or near the bottom. Some anglers walk the creeks or canals dipping baited rigs below a bobber. Adjust the drop so the bait is drifting along with the current just off the bottom. Among the best baits for big channel cats are crayfish, chicken livers, mackerel, and clams. Beef or lamb brains are also a local favorite. Here are some of the best types of spots to try:

- Where water is pumped out of or into a larger body of water

- Below control dams, or any other type of obstruction

- Beneath piles of driftwood or around snaggy sections of back waters

- The junction of flowing culverts and pools

- The confluence of two drains, or the base of any kind of spillway

- The seams that separate fast currents from slower ones.

High-water catfish fillets, dipped in beer and flour batter and fast-fried in a buttered skillet, marks a great way to top off a day of winter catfishing in the Sacramento Valley.

Delta Fishing

The Sacramento-San Joaquin Delta is a very large area of diked islands, elevated levee roads and meandering interlocking waterways, where the Sacramento and San Joaquin Rivers come together. There are almost 1000 miles of navigable waterways. Fishing in these waterways and rivers is excellent. Striped bass (to 30-40 pounds) and sturgeon (to several hundred pounds) are the most prized catches. But the Delta also provides excellent black bass, catfish and panfish, as well as an occasional migrating salmon.

The Sacramento-San Joaquin River Delta extends from Walnut Grove on the north to Tracy on the south, and from Stockton on the east to Pittsburg on the west. The Sacramento and San Joaquin are the two major inflowing rivers, but there are also inputs from the Calaveras, Mokelumne and Cosumnes rivers. More than 125 resorts, marinas and boat harbors are scattered throughout the Delta. Food services in the towns and resorts range from fine restaurants to quaint coffee shops. R.V. sites and campgrounds abound, anchored by Brannan Island State Park near Rio Vista. Houseboating is very popular as is cruising, sailboating, wind surfing, jet skiing and waterskiing. But on the other side of the levees on the islands, agriculture is still king.

Striped Bass

Striped bass run in the Delta from April through June. A second run takes place sometime in September and can continue on past the end of the year. Routine catches are in the 5 to 25 pound size range. A catchable number of striped bass are in the Delta throughout the year. Some experts relate this to the rising Delta population of the threadfin shad, an excellent forage fish introduced into California waters over 20 years ago. Around the Delta, bait fishing and trolling are the two most popular fishing methods for stripers. Bait fishing is most often practiced from an anchored boat using shad, mudsuckers, sculpines (bullheads) or shrimp. Trollers use minnow-shaped plugs such as Bombers, Rebels and Rapalas. Anglers pursuing largemouth bass, at times, hook stripers on crankbaits, spinnerbaits and plastic worms.

Stripers feed most actively on moving water, so it's best to fish when there is a big tide swing. When still fishing for stripers from a boat, fish right where a sandbar drops off. Position your boat (anchored) on the upstream side of the bar on an incoming tide, and on the downstream drop-off on an outgoing tide. If tide movements are modest, trolling might be a better option. You can cover more water to locate fish by trolling. Remember striper are bottom feeders, so whether you're fishing with bait or trolling, make sure your offering is near the bottom.

Striper fishing is most consistent from November through May. The Rio Vista/Decker Island area is a best bet early in the season. In late winter and early spring more "up river" locations are favored. These include the Sacramento River near Sacramento, the San Joaquin River near Stockton, the Grant Line Canal and the Old River north of Tracy. Move "down river" again in late spring. in cooler months when the Delta water is cooler, striper are found along the shallower edges of channels. But in the hot Delta summer, the big bass are in deeper, cooler water.

A final note—the striper fishing has declined dramatically in recent years. Both the number and size of fish is down for a lot of reason that are beyond the scope of this book. But the implications to anglers should be obvious. First, use lighter tackle. Most fish will be less than 10 pounds. Second, release most fish. Bait caught fish using a sliding sinker rig will be hooked deep. Cut the line at the fishes' mouth to release these, if they are not bleeding. Badly bleeding fish should be kept.

Sturgeon

January through March is prime time for sturgeon fishing in the Delta. White sturgeon that spend most of their time in San Francisco, San Pablo and Suison Bays move up into the Delta, and even on up in the Sacramento River as far as Colusa to spawn in the winter. These sturgeon prefer deep channels. Anglers work waters in the 25 to 50 foot range. And water muddied by heavy rain runoff doesn't seem to hurt the bite. In fact, at times it seems to help it. There are many good spots including Decker Island, Sherman Island, the Antioch Bridge, False River, Frank's Tract, the main channel of the San Joaquin (San Andreas Shoal, Santa Clara Shoal, West Island, mouth of Mayberry Slough) on through Mile Slough, on the Sacramento River (Hwy. 12 bridge at Rio Vista, Isleton, Clarksburg, Freeport), Cache Slough, Prospect Slough and Miner Slough.

It was mainly after the striper fishing declined that anglers in large numbers turned their attention to sturgeon. And the rewards have been worth the effort required to learn how, when, and where to catch these prehistoric giants. Mind you, a legal keeper sturgeon must be over 40 inches long. And many fish are taken weighing 50, 100 or even over 150 pounds. We're talking big fish!

Catfish

Catfishing in the Delta is an all season possibility, although it's probably most popular in summer months. The water is warmer so the catfish seem to feed more actively. And the other more glamorous species are either absent, or at least difficult to locate. Catfish, however, are all over the Delta in good numbers.

There are two prominent varieties of catfish in Delta waters—channel cats and blue catfish. Channel cats are larger, ranging from three to five pounds or more. Blue cats usually run around a pound or less. Fish for channel cats in deeper, faster moving water. Chicken livers, mackerel, shrimp, crawfish or shad on a 1/0 or 3/0 hook is about right. Blues are more likely to be found in slower water and closer to bushes, tules or rocks, as close as 4 to 6 feet from shore. Best baits on #2 or #4 hooks include clams, anchovies or mackerel. But don't be surprised to catch channel cats on "blue cat bait," and visa versa. After dark, catfish will move into shallows to feed, so anglers concentrate in areas out of the main flow of the tides. Remember, catfish are bottom feeders, so always use enough lead to keep your bait down.

Largemouth Bass, Panfish, Carp

Largemouth bass in the 1 to 3 pound range, with some going much larger, lurk all over the Delta. Hot spots vary seasonally depending on water clarity, temperature and tidal activity (especially in the west Delta). Sloughs with some current are usually better than dead water. Many veteran bassers concentrate on river channels and the lower section of tributary streams. Structure, as is true with all largemouth angling, is critical. Levees, jetties, pilings, docks, retaining walls, drop-offs, fallen trees, stumps, and tule beds are some of the top hangouts. There is lots of water in the Delta, probably more than 3000 miles of shoreline, so don't stay in one spot if there is no action. Crawdads are a dietary staple of Delta largemouth. So jigs and crankbaits that imitate crawfish are consistent producers. Plastic worms, spinnerbaits and grubs are also winners. Large tidal swings typically improve black bass action, and most experts suggest fishing the incoming tide. Anglers who want even more variety pursue panfish and carp in the quiet, backwater sloughs.

Maps

The locations marked for specific species on the accompanying map are meant to highlight those specific sloughs that are consistently good producers. But, the sloughs and rivers in the Delta are miles and miles long. So keep moving in a particular slough until you find fish. Also, the indicated locations are not the only places you can find fish. For example, catfish and stripers (especially in late winter/early spring) can be found in many places in the Delta. And any of the back sloughs will produce panfish. The maps in this section are intended only to show choice fishing spots. See Hal Shell's Delta Map for facilities and some navigational information. Navigational maps, published by the National Oceanic and Atmospheric Administration, are also available for the Delta. Marine supply dealers are a good source. A list of some of the most popular Delta launch ramps is included below.

Delta Launch Ramps	
Location	Comments
Antioch Public Ramp	2 lanes concrete
B & W Resort Marina	3 lanes concrete
Bethel Harbor	Elevator
Big Break Marina	
Boathouse in Locke	Elevator
Brannan Island Public Ramp	6 lanes concrete
Buckley Cove Public Ramp	1 lane concrete
Carol's Harbor	Sling hoist
Collinsville Resort	
Del's Boat Harbor	3 lanes concrete
Delta Marina Yacht Harbor	1 lane concrete
Delta Resort	2 lanes concrete
Discovery Bay Yacht Harbor	2 lanes concrete
Discovery Park, Sacramento	6 lanes concrete
Eddo's Boat Harbor	1 lane concrete
Garcia Park Public Ramp	4 lanes concrete
Haven Acres	
Hennis Marina	Elevator
Herman & Helen's Marina	
Hogback Public Ramp	2 lanes concrete
Holland Riverside Marina	
Ko-Ket Resort	
Korth's Pirates Lair	1 lane concrete
Lauritzen Yacht Harbor	
Lazy M Marina	
Louis Park Public Ramp	2 lanes concrete
Miller Park Public Ramp	2 lanes concrete
New Hope Landing	1 lane
Orwood Resort	2 lanes concrete
Paradise Point Marina	2 lanes concrete
Pittsburg Public Ramp	2 lanes concrete
Rancho Marina	Elevator
Rio Vista Public Ramp	2 lanes concrete
Sandy Beach Public Ramp	
Snug Harbor	
Tiki Lagun Resort	
Tower Park Marina	Elevator
Tracy Oasis Marina	
Uncle Bobbie's	1 lane concrete
Vieira's Resort	
Walnut Grove Marina	1 lane concrete
West Sacramento Public Ramp	2 lanes concrete
Whiskey Slough Harbor	
Wimpy's Marina	2 lanes concrete
Windmill Cove	
Yolo County Public Ramp	1 lane concrete

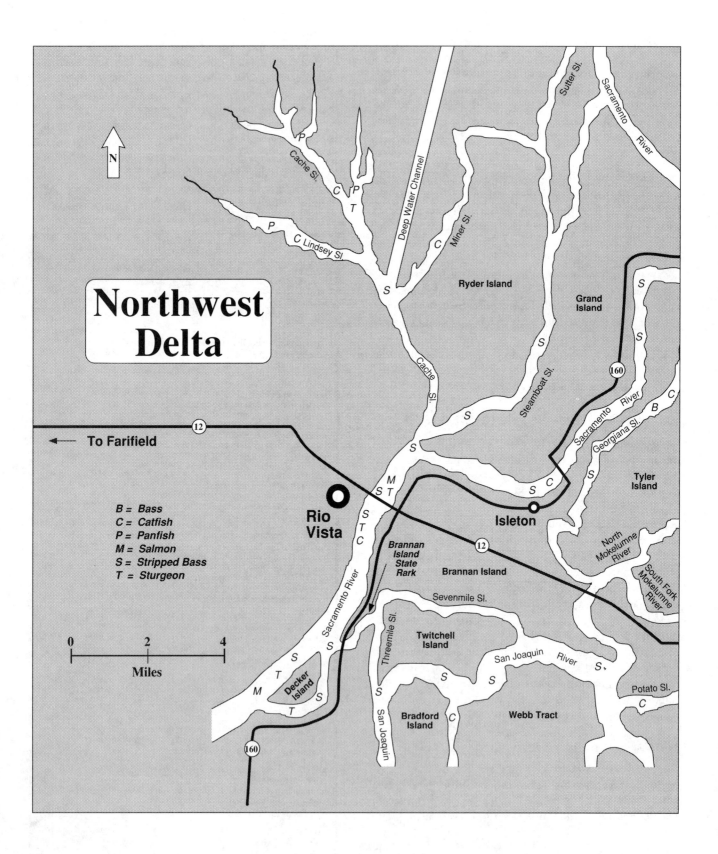

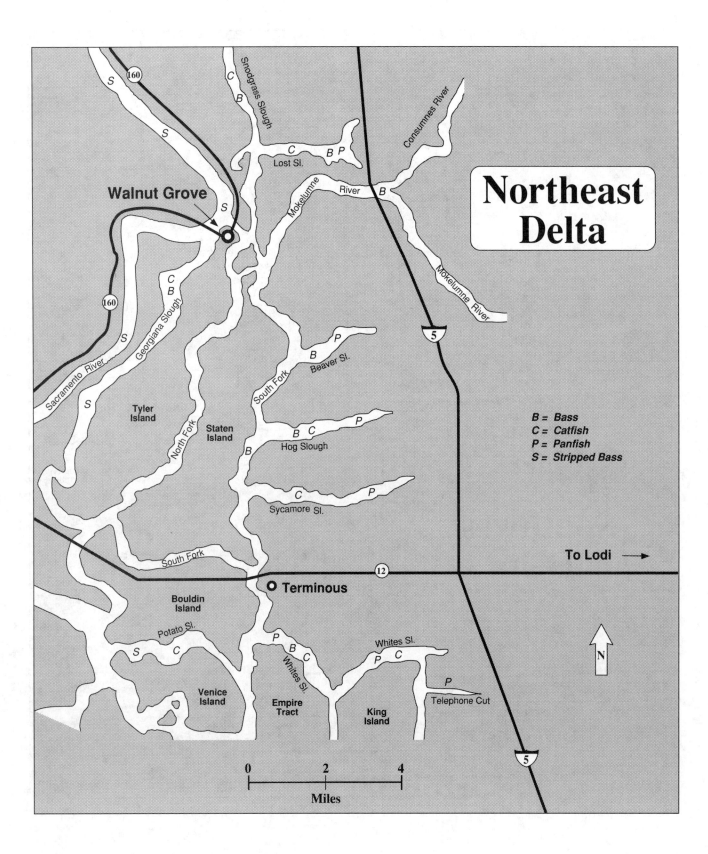

Northeast Delta

Walnut Grove

Terminous

To Lodi →

B = Bass
C = Catfish
P = Panfish
S = Stripped Bass

Snodgrass Slough
Consumnes River
Lost Sl.
Mokelumne River
Mokelumne River
Sacramento River
Georgiana Slough
North Fork
South Fork
Beaver Sl.
Tyler Island
Staten Island
Hog Slough
Sycamore Sl.
South Fork
Bouldin Island
Potato Sl.
Venice Island
Empire Tract
Whites Sl.
Whites Sl.
King Island
Telephone Cut

N

0   2   4
Miles

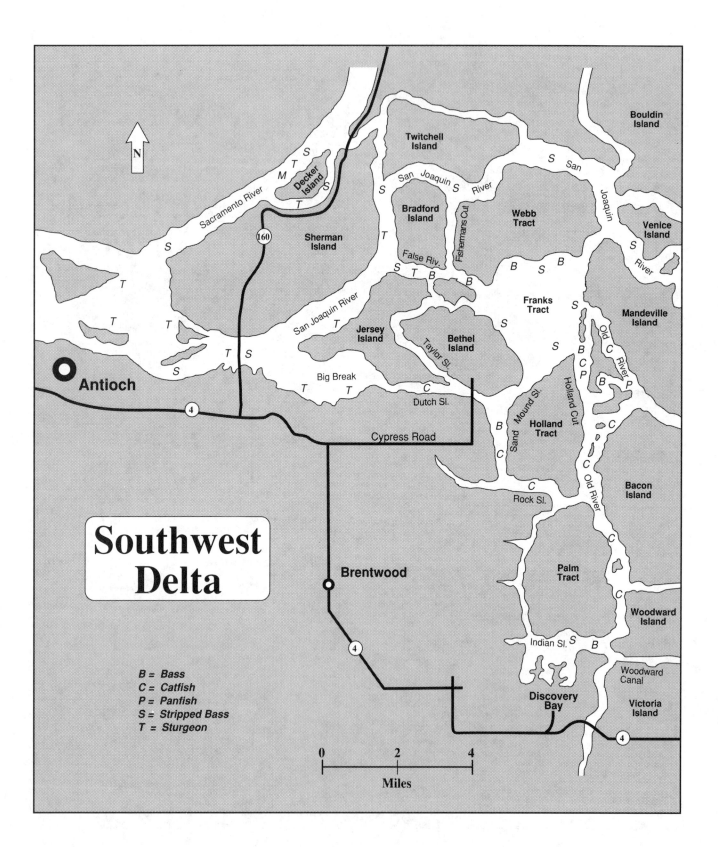

Southwest Delta

B = Bass
C = Catfish
P = Panfish
S = Stripped Bass
T = Sturgeon

0   2   4
Miles

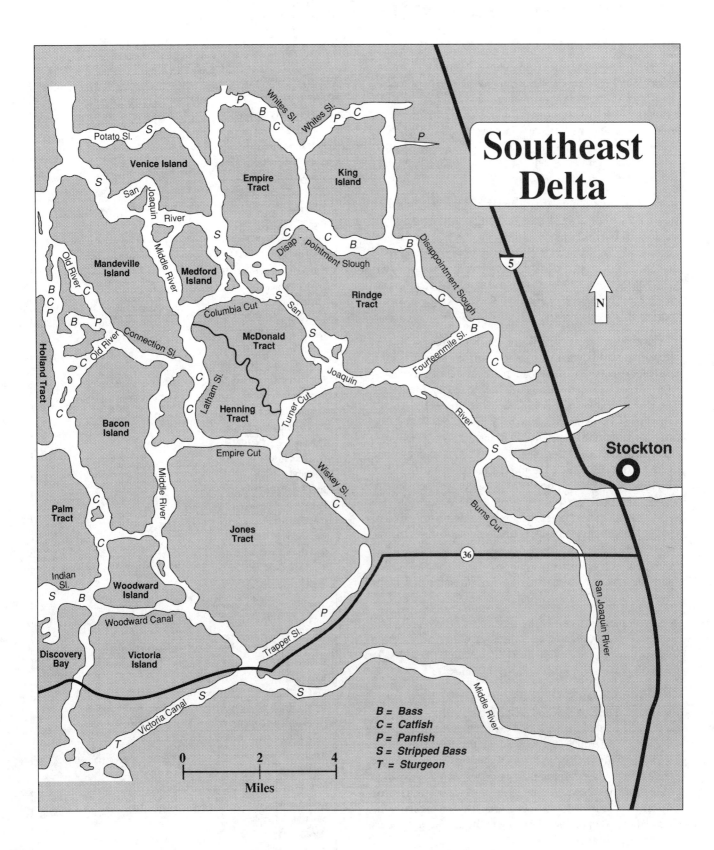

Southeast Delta

B = Bass
C = Catfish
P = Panfish
S = Stripped Bass
T = Sturgeon

0   2   4
Miles

San Francisco Bay Fishing

San Francisco Bay, California's largest estuary, technically is divided into three connecting bays—San Francisco Bay proper, San Pablo Bay and Suisun Bay. These bays receive runoff from the extensive Sacramento and San Joaquin River systems that drain California's Central Valley and have their source in the Sierra Nevada. In general, most of the San Francisco Bay system is very shallow— the average depth is 20 feet—and there are extensive mudflats in San Pablo Bay and South San Francisco Bay.

The two most sought after game fish in the San Francisco Bay area are the striped bass and chinook salmon. Most salmon fishing takes place in the ocean outside the Golden Gate, while San Francisco Bay is practically the unrivaled domain of the striped bass angler. Other fish such as sturgeon, starry flounder, surfperch, jacksmelt, topsmelt, white croaker, rockfish, sharks and rays also offer a great deal of sport to Bay Area anglers.

The angler certainly will not find this area lacking in recreational fishing facilities. Piers, skiff rental, concessions and launching facilities are scattered around the bay's perimeter, and scores of party boats operate out of Bay Area ports. There are sizeable sport fishing fleets near the Fisherman's Wharf in San Francisco, along the Sausalito waterfront, and at the Berkeley and Emeryville marinas. Many of these boats fish out in the ocean for chinook and coho salmon; some make rockfish trips to the Farallon Islands; and most also fish for striped bass when good runs develop. In the northern reaches of the bay, party boats operating out of San Pablo Bay and Carquinez Strait ports fish exclusively for striped bass, sturgeon and starry flounder. Charters can usually be arranged at harbors from which boats operate, although in San Francisco, trips are usually arranged through bait and tackle shops because of parking and other logistics problems in the city.

San Francisco, San Pablo and Suisun Bays provide a wonderful year-round fishery. The keys to successful fishing in these bays, beyond using the right techniques, is to fish in the right place and to fish at the right times.

Fishing during the prime tidal movements is extremely important. The best time to fish these bays is during the two-week cycle of extreme water movement that is a result of the maximum difference between high and low tide. More rapidly moving waters move bait and this produces more active feeding for all game fish in the bays. Concentrate fishing from the 2-3 hours before the high water slack period until an hour or two after the ebb starts. This will produce the best results. This period is even more productive if it occurs at first light or dusk.

Location	Sport Fishing Boats	Pier Fishing	Boat Rental	Launch Ramp	Jetty Fishing
Richardson Bay (1)*	X		X	X	
Turney Street Ramp (2)				X	
Sausalito Y.H. (3)	X			X	
Fort Baker (4)		X			X
Fort Point, Presidio (5)		X			X
Golden Gate Y.H. (6)	X			X	
S.F. Small Craft Har, (7)				X	
Fisherman's Wharf (8)	X	X		X	
Pier #7, S.F. (9)		X			
Ferry Building, S.F. (10)		X			
Mission Rock Area (11)			X	X	
Hunter's Point, S.F. (12)			X	X	
Oyster Point (13)				X	
Coyote Point (14)				X	
San Mateo Pier (15)		X			
Redwood Creek (16)		X		X	
Palo Alto Harbor (17)				X	
Alviso (18)				X	
San Leandro Marina (19)		X		X	X
Doolitle Drive (20)			X	X	
Grand St., Alameda (21)			X		
Pacific Mar. Alam. (22)			X		
Ballena Y.C., Alam. (23)			X		
Oakland In. Harbor (24)			X		
Oakland Marina (24)	X			X	
Jack London Marina (25)				X	
Emeryville Marina (26)	X				
Berkeley Marina (27)	X	X		X	X
Richmond Marina (28)				X	
Red Rock Marina (29)	X	X		X	
San Pablo Y.H. (30)	X				
Rodeo (31)	X	X	X	X	
Crockett, Dowrelio's (32)	X	X			
White's Resort (33)		X	X		
Martinez (34)		X	X	X	
Benecia Boat Ramp (35)				X	
Vallejo (36)				X	
Vallejo (37)	X			X	
Vallejo Heights (38)			X		
Vallejo Mun. Pier (39)	X				
Dutchman Slough (40)			X	X	
Mud Slough (41)			X		
Petaluma River (42)				X	
Gallinas Creek (43)				X	
China Camp (44)		X	X		
Loch Lomond Mar. (45)	X			X	
San Rafael Creek (46)				X	
Paradise Pier (47)		X			
Angel Island State Pk. (48)		X			

* Map fishing facilities

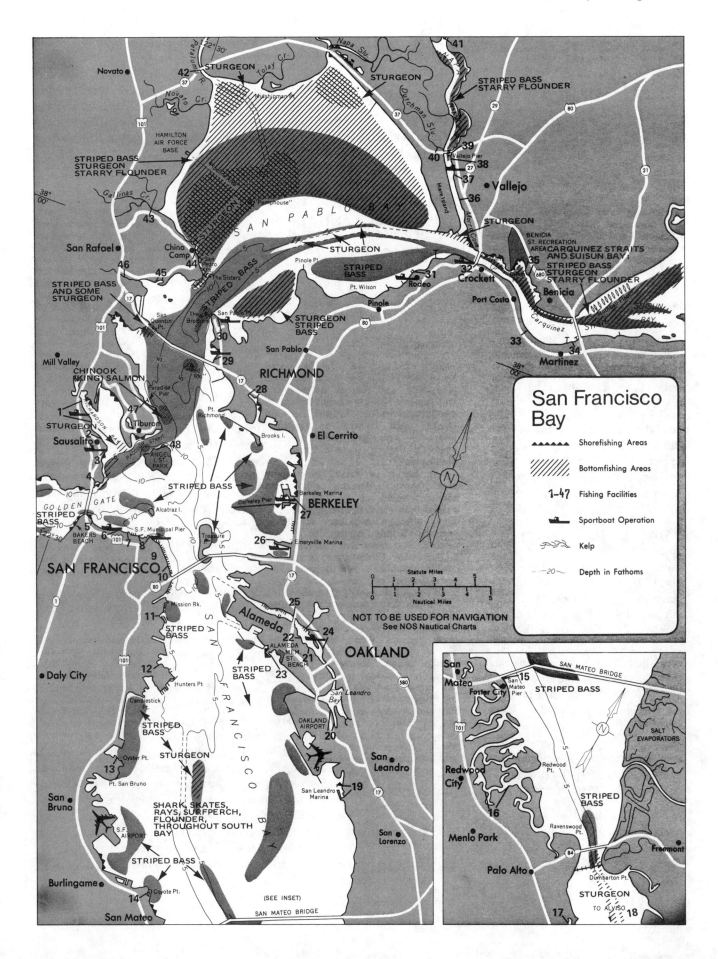

San Francisco Bay

Shorefishing Areas

Bottomfishing Areas

1-47 Fishing Facilities

Sportboat Operation

Kelp

—20— Depth in Fathoms

NOT TO BE USED FOR NAVIGATION
See NOS Nautical Charts

Striped Bass

Striped bass spawn from about April to mid-June in fresh waters of the Sacramento and San Joaquin Rivers. After spawning, the fish move back down into the saltwater bays; some venture out into the ocean. They spend most of the summer and fall in salt water before returning once again to brackish water and freshwater sloughs and rivers. Although best fishing times vary with area, in general, the fishing season extends from March to December, with best fishing from mid-August to November. October has been the best striped bass fishing month consistently since 1969.

In San Pablo Bay, Carquinez Strait, and Suisun Bay, striped bass are caught year-round with best fishing usually in October and November, with a lesser run of fish in June, July and August. Most spring and summer fish are caught trolling in the late afternoon. Fall-run fish are caught still fishing or drifting, primarily with live bait such as staghorn sculpin (known locally as "bullheads").

In the Napa River and nearby brackish-water sloughs along the northern shore of San Pablo Bay, striped bass are caught throughout the year although weather sometimes restricts fishing during the winter months. Best times are considered to be September, October and November, usually peaking in late October. Fish are taken by bait fishing and trolling from boats, or bait casting from shore.

Within San Francisco Bay proper, in such areas as the Golden Gate Bridge (south tower), Raccoon Strait (over Raccoon Shoal), Berkeley flats and off Alcatraz and Treasure Islands, fishing usually starts in June and extends through October into November. Most fish are caught after mid-August, with peak catches in October. A popular fishing method is drifting with live bait (anchovies or shiner surfperch) in areas where an abrupt change in depth occurs and when the current is running swiftest. Anglers also troll for stripers and some will even get out their plug casting gear when a surface-feeding school is located. From Angel Island north to The Brothers, good striped bass fishing can usually be had in September, October and November by drifting live bait and trolling as fish migrate through on their way back to the Sacramento-San Joaquin Delta. Shore and pier fishermen cast lures and bait for striper from selected spots on both sides of the bay. (See chart for shore fishing areas and piers.)

The striped bass season in South San Francisco Bay extends from June through September, and in some years fishing may last until November or December. Fishing usually reaches a peak around the San Mateo Bridge area in June and July and around the Dumbarton Bridge in September and October. Most striper fishing in South San Francisco Bay is a trolling affair with some plug casting when a school is found. Also, a growing number of anglers are fishing from shore for striped bass in spring, and again in late summer around San Francisco Airport and Coyote Point.

Sturgeon

Sturgeon fishing has become very popular in the Bay Area over the years, especially in San Pablo Bay, Carquinez Strait and Suisun Bay. A small but growing sturgeon fishery is also developing in South San Francisco Bay from off Oyster Point (San Bruno Shoals) south to the entrance of Alviso Slough. Both green and white sturgeon are taken; the white sturgeon is the most prized.

Although sturgeon are caught throughout the year in the upper bays, best fishing is usually in the fall and winter when the biggest fish are taken. In San Pablo Bay, they appear to move in over the flats in early fall, and fishing usually lasts from November to May, with best catches from about January to March. The flats along the north side of the bay from Mare Island ("Rockwall") to China Camp are especially productive at high tide during the winter. Other good spots in San Pablo Bay are the "pump house" and around the odd-numbered buoys that mark the north side of the main channel with cuts through the middle of the bay. There is also year-round fishing in Carquinez Strait over the flats along the northern shore. Smaller fish are taken in summer, larger ones in winter.

In Suisun Bay, fishing usually starts in spring around April and lasts until October or November, about the time of the first rains. In summer, most Suisun sturgeon are sublegal size (less than 40 inches long) with about one "keeper" out of every ten caught. Larger fish are taken in the fall. The "mothball fleet" and the channel buoys along the edges of sand bars near the entrance to the bay are good areas to fish. In South San Francisco Bay from San Bruno Shoals south to Alviso Slough, the season extends from about November to March. Early season fishing is usually best in the northerly areas; late season fishing is usually best in the more southerly areas along the edge of the channel. Sometimes during the Pacific herring runs, which occur anytime between December and March, sturgeon are taken from boats and shore in the central part of the bay in such areas as Richardson Bay and along the Sausalito waterfront. There is a closure of the sturgeon fishing season in some bay waters during January, February and March. Be aware of regulations.

Other Bay Sport Fish

Although most salmon are taken outside the Golden Gate, migrating chinook salmon are sometimes caught deep trolling with whole anchovies in the area from the Golden Gate to Raccoon Strait and off the Tiburon Peninsula north to the Richmond Bridge during late summer. The area off the eastern side of the Tiburon Peninsula (called "California City" by anglers) is heavily fished when the salmon are running.

Sharks, skates and rays are plentiful throughout the bay; some of the more common types are leopard, brown, smoothhound and seven gill sharks, spiny dogfish, bat ray and big skate. These are especially numerous in South San Francisco Bay all year. Most fishing, however, takes place in summer and fall. Starry flounder are abundant, especially over the flats in San Pablo and Suisun bays and in the Napa River and adjacent sloughs. An assortment of surfperch are taken, as well as white croaker ("kingfish"), jacksmelt, topsmelt, English sole, sand sole, small lingcod and brown and black rockfish.

Pacific Ocean Fishing

The coastal waters of the Pacific Ocean offer an immense variety of fishing opportunities. There are salmon, bottom fishing for rock cod and lingcod, albacore fishing 20-30 miles offshore, pier and rock fishing for all kinds of fish depending on location and season, and finally surf fishing for striped bass and perch.

But ocean fishing can be dangerous. Fishermen are lost every year. Breakers wash anglers off rocks. People fall overboard. Increased winds are foolishly ignored. Equipment fails. But don't let this scare you away from fishing. Do enjoy the marvelous experience of ocean fishing, but be prepared, be careful and error on the side of caution.

Salmon fishing can get hot anytime during the season, but more predictable is the size of the catch. Bigger salmon move closer to shore starting in July. August and September are the months when most of the twenty pound plus king salmon are taken. Ocean fishing for striper is probably best near shore and in the surf in the Pacifica area, and when anchovies move into the shallow waters (as shallow as 10 feet) of ocean bays like Monterey and Tomales. The albacore season is short and unpredictable, so stay alert or you'll miss the season. Rock cod and lingcod can be caught all year. But the best lingcod season is in fall and winter when these fish move into shallow water (50-150 feet) to spawn.

Central Coast Ocean Fishing
(map - p. 213)

Ocean fishing along the Central Coast, from about San Simeon down to about Pt. Conception, is covered in this section. Although this stretch of ocean is actually in the southern half of the state, fish species and techniques are more akin to those of Northern California. Pt. Conception is often described as an ecological dividing point for marine life. South of the Point is the subtropical zone; north of it is the temperate zone. Many coastal pelagic fish such as Pacific barracuda and yellowtail that are common to the waters off Southern California and Baja California, Mexico are taken only rarely north of Pt. Conception. Conversely, some pelagic northern marine and anadromous species such as coho salmon are taken only in small numbers southeast of Pt. Conception in late winter and early spring.

The coastline alternates between broad sandy beaches and rocky headlands and is backed by low rolling hills. Shore anglers cast from sandy beaches for surfperch, and bait cast and poke pole along rocky shores. Offshore bottom fishing is good year-round, and albacore, salmon and bonito are available seasonally. In some years, white sea bass also add to the sport catch. In addition to angling, abalone picking and clamming are very popular in this region, which has one of the heaviest concentrations of pismo clams along the California coast.

Point Sal to Point Buchon: The San Luis Obispo Bay area has offshore bottom fishing for rockfish, and to a lesser degree, lingcod and cabezon. California halibut are taken over sandy bottoms in San Luis Obispo Bay and areas to the south; bonito and white sea bass are sometimes taken from summer to late fall. Boats go out for king salmon from early spring to midsummer. Fishing is available at Pismo Beach pier, the county pier in Avila and Port San Luis pier. Surf anglers cast for surfperch at Pismo Beach and lingcod and cabezon at Shell Beach and Avila.

Location	Sport Fishing Boats	Pier Fishing	Boat Rental	Launch Ramp	Jetty Fishing
Pismo Beach Pier (1)*		X			
Avila County Pier (2)		X			
Port San Luis Pier (3)	X	X		X	X
Morro Bay (4)	X	X	X	X	X
Cayucos (5)		X			
San Simeon (6)	X	X		X	

* Map fishing facilities

Morro Bay Area: Morro Bay party boats operate year-round, many fishing exclusively for albacore when it runs off the coast, with the best times in September and early October. Inside Morro Bay, skiff anglers catch starry flounder, California halibut, jacksmelt, sharks, rays and surfperch. Outside the bay, the catch consists of rockfish, cabezon and lingcod. There is pier, dock and bank fishing along the shores of Morro Bay for starry flounder, jacksmelt and surfperch. The power plant outfall on the north side of Morro Rock is another productive place for surfperch and occasionally striped bass. Ocean shore fishing for surfperch takes place along the sandy spit that separates the bay from the sea. This is also a popular clamming area. Access is by way of a road approaching from the south or by boat.

Areas to the North: North of Morro Bay the shoreline is characterized by sandy beaches interrupted by rock and boulder-strewn shores affording excellent fishing. Surf-

This section is based on Angler's Guide to the United States Pacific Coast (U.S. Dept. of Commerce).

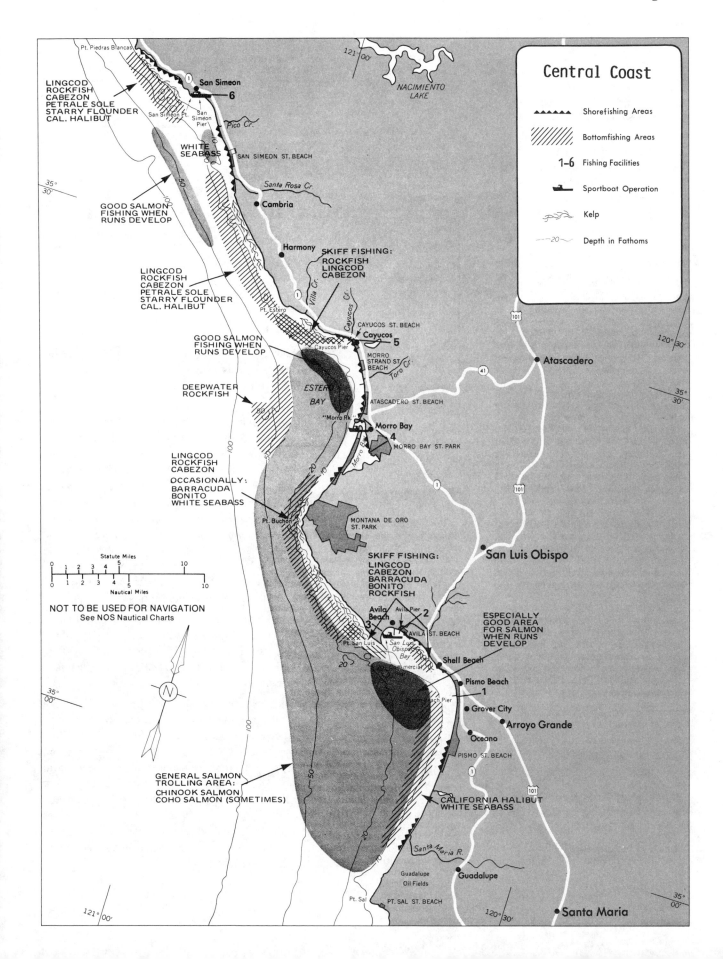

Central Coast

▲▲▲▲▲ Shorefishing Areas

////// Bottomfishing Areas

1-6 Fishing Facilities

Sportboat Operation

Kelp

—20— Depth in Fathoms

LINGCOD
ROCKFISH
CABEZON
PETRALE SOLE
STARRY FLOUNDER
CAL. HALIBUT

WHITE
SEABASS

GOOD SALMON
FISHING WHEN
RUNS DEVELOP

LINGCOD
ROCKFISH
CABEZON
PETRALE SOLE
STARRY FLOUNDER
CAL. HALIBUT

SKIFF FISHING:
ROCKFISH
LINGCOD
CABEZON

GOOD SALMON
FISHING WHEN
RUNS DEVELOP

DEEPWATER
ROCKFISH

LINGCOD
ROCKFISH
CABEZON
OCCASIONALLY:
BARRACUDA
BONITO
WHITE SEABASS

SKIFF FISHING:
LINGCOD
CABEZON
BARRACUDA
BONITO
ROCKFISH

ESPECIALLY
GOOD AREA
FOR SALMON
WHEN RUNS
DEVELOP

GENERAL SALMON
TROLLING AREA:
CHINOOK SALMON
COHO SALMON (SOMETIMES)

CALIFORNIA HALIBUT
WHITE SEABASS

Statute Miles
0 1 2 3 4 5 10
0 1 2 3 4 5 10
Nautical Miles

NOT TO BE USED FOR NAVIGATION
See NOS Nautical Charts

N

Pt. Piedras Blancas
San Simeon
6
San Simeon Pt.
San Simeon Pier
Pico Cr.
SAN SIMEON ST. BEACH
Santa Rosa Cr.
Cambria
Harmony
Villa Cr.
Pt. Estero
Cayucos Cr.
CAYUCOS ST. BEACH
Cayucos
5
Cayucos Pier
MORRO STRAND ST. BEACH
Toro Cr.
ESTERO BAY
ATASCADERO ST. BEACH
"Morro Rk."
Morro Bay
4
Morro Bay
MORRO BAY ST. PARK
Pt. Buchon
MONTANA DE ORO ST. PARK
San Luis Obispo
Avila Beach
Avila Pier
2
3
AVILA ST. BEACH
Pt. San Luis
San Luis Obispo Bay
Commercial
Shell Beach
Pismo Beach
1
Beach Pier
Grover City
Arroyo Grande
Oceano
PISMO ST. BEACH
Santa Maria R.
Guadalupe Oil Fields
Guadalupe
Pt. Sal
PT. SAL ST. BEACH
Santa Maria

NACIMIENTO LAKE
121°00'
101
120°30'
Atascadero
35°30'
41
1
101
1
101

35°30'
35°00'
121°00'
120°30'
35°00'

perch are taken along sandy shores, and bait casting produces cabezon, surfperch, rockfish and kelp greenling. At the Cayucos Pier, jacksmelt, white croaker, queenfish, staghorn sculpin and bocaccio are the usual fare. Cayucos Beach is the northernmost beach in California with grunion runs occurring during spring and summer. From Point Estero to San Simeon there is little beach access. At San Simeon, pier fishermen produce starry flounder, halibut, skates and surfperch. Stream mouths in this area produce steelhead during years of heavy rainfall. Party boats operate from San Simeon during the summer. Along the rocky stretch of coastline from San Simeon north to Pt. Piedras Blancas, shore fishing is excellent for surfperch, kelp greenling, rockfish and cabezon. Most shore areas are open to the public. North of Pt. Piedras Blancas the topography becomes precipitous as Rte. 1 winds its way toward the towering cliffs of the Big Sur coast. There is little access to shore along this majestic route for over 60 miles until one reaches Point Lobos and the Carmel-Monterey Bay area.

Monterey Bay Area Coast (map - p. 215)

Along this scenic stretch of California coast rainy days alternate with days of crisp sunshine during winter, while spring brings blustery weather as prevailing northwesterly winds intensify. During summer fog cools most of the coast, while autumn days are often warm and sunny as the on-shore winds decrease, bringing little fog to the area. The weather along the northern shore of Monterey differs somewhat, particularly around Santa Cruz, which is protected from the prevailing winds by the curve of the land. This area is almost fog-free during summer.

Monterey Bay is an important recreational fishing area, and an impressive number and variety of marine game fish are taken here. Most sport fishing from party boats is for bottom fish (particulary rockfish) although albacore, bonito and chinook salmon are also landed in season. In some years salmon are abundant in the bay in spring, and good fishing may last until late summer. In general, the major marine sport fish caught from boats and from shore are rockfish, chinook salmon, California halibut, Pacific sanddab, surfperch, lingcod, kelp greenling, white croaker and albacore.

Shore and Pier Fishing: As one approaches the Monterey Bay area from the south, there is little access to shore along this rugged section of the coast as Hwy. 1 makes a gradual descent out of the mountainous Big Sur country, and then passes through rolling coastal hills before dropping down to

Location	Sport Fishing Boats	Pier Fishing	Boat Rental	Launch Ramp	Jetty Fishing
Pacific Grove (1) *			X		
Monterey Harbor (2)	X	X	X	X	
Moss Landing Harbor (3)	X		X	X	X
Kirby Pk., Elkhorn Sl. (4)				X	
Seacliff Pier (5)		X			
Capitola Pier (6)	X	X	X	X	
Santa Cruz Harbor (7)	X			X	
Santa Cruz Pier (8)	X	X	X		

* Map fishing facilities

sea level about a mile south of Carmel. Where the shoreline can be reached there is excellent rocky-shore fishing for lingcod, kelp greenling, cabezon, striped surfperch and rockfish.

Shore fishermen can reach the beaches of the Monterey Peninsula from the south by way of 17-Mile Drive (toll road), which is a south entrance at Carmel, or by approaching from the northeast through the town of Monterey. Along scenic 17-Mile Drive, shore fishing is allowed at Fanshell Beach just north of Cypress Point, in Pacific Grove at Asilomar State Beach, and between Point Pinos and Lover's Point. Some of the more common species taken by shore anglers at these locations are striped surfperch, kelp greenling, cabezon and blue rockfish. Sometimes steelhead are caught around the mouth of the Carmel River in fall after heavy rains, but fishing even at its best is considered spotty.

The town of Monterey has 2 public piers, but most fishing takes place from Municipal Pier #2 at the eastern end of the harbor. Here the catch is young bocaccio, blue rockfish, surfperch, jacksmelt, white croaker, and in some years, jack mackerel in summer.

Broad sandy beaches rim the coast from the Monterey Peninsula north along the inner curve of the bay all the way to Seacliff State Beach. Most beaches offer excellent fishing for a variety of sandy-shore fish. Striped bass sometimes are taken by surf casters during the summer along beaches from Monterey north to the Salinas River. (Check locally about fishing the Fort Ord area—beach front restrictions change from day to day.) All beaches north of the Salinas River offer excellent surf fishing for sand sole, jacksmelt and surfperch. There is also surf netting for night smelt in summer along beaches adjacent to Moss Landing.

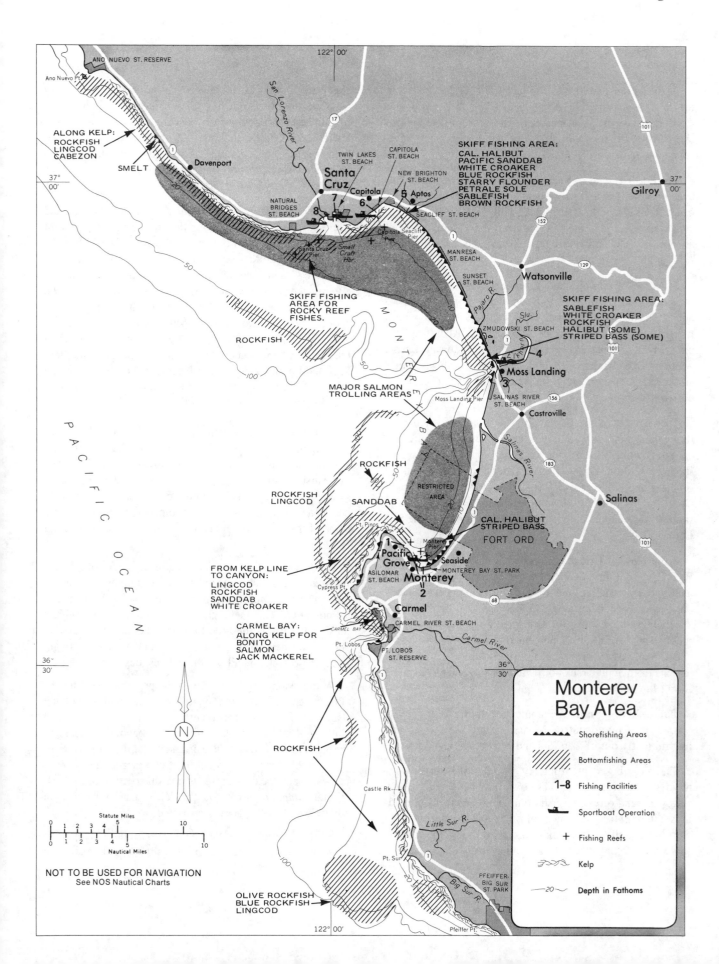

ANO NUEVO ST. RESERVE

Ano Nuevo Pt.

ALONG KELP:
ROCKFISH
LINGCOD
CABEZON

SMELT

Davenport

San Lorenzo River

17

SKIFF FISHING AREA:
CAL. HALIBUT
PACIFIC SANDDAB
WHITE CROAKER
BLUE ROCKFISH
STARRY FLOUNDER
PETRALE SOLE
SABLEFISH
BROWN ROCKFISH

101

Gilroy

TWIN LAKES ST. BEACH

CAPITOLA ST. BEACH

Santa Cruz

NEW BRIGHTON ST. BEACH

Capitola

NATURAL BRIDGES ST. BEACH

7

6

5 Aptos

8

Small Craft Hbr.

SEACLIFF ST. BEACH

Santa Cruz Pier

Capitola Seacliff Pier

MANRESA ST. BEACH

152

129

Watsonville

Pajaro R.

SKIFF FISHING AREA FOR ROCKY REEF FISHES.

SUNSET ST. BEACH

SKIFF FISHING AREA:
SABLEFISH
WHITE CROAKER
ROCKFISH
HALIBUT (SOME)
STRIPED BASS (SOME)

ROCKFISH

ZMUDOWSKI ST. BEACH

50

4

101

MONTEREY

3

Moss Landing

MAJOR SALMON TROLLING AREAS

Moss Landing Pier

SALINAS RIVER ST. BEACH

156

Castroville

PACIFIC

OCEAN

ROCKFISH

ROCKFISH
LINGCOD

SANDDAB

RESTRICTED AREA

Salinas River

183

Salinas

101

CAL. HALIBUT
STRIPED BASS

FORT ORD

Pt. Pinos

1

FROM KELP LINE TO CANYON:
LINGCOD
ROCKFISH
SANDDAB
WHITE CROAKER

Pacific Grove

Monterey Pier

Seaside

MONTEREY BAY ST. PARK

ASILOMAR ST. BEACH

Monterey

2

68

Cypress Pt.

CARMEL BAY:
ALONG KELP FOR
BONITO
SALMON
JACK MACKEREL

Carmel

CARMEL RIVER ST. BEACH

CARMEL BAY

Carmel River

Pt. Lobos

PT. LOBOS ST. RESERVE

1

N

ROCKFISH

Castle Rk

Little Sur R.

Statute Miles
0 1 2 3 4 5   10

0 1 2 3 4 5   10
Nautical Miles

NOT TO BE USED FOR NAVIGATION
See NOS Nautical Charts

Pt. Sur

1

100

20

OLIVE ROCKFISH
BLUE ROCKFISH
LINGCOD

PFEIFFER-
BIG SUR
ST. PARK

Big Sur R.

Pfeiffer Pt.

Monterey Bay Area

▲▲▲▲ Shorefishing Areas

▨ Bottomfishing Areas

1-8 Fishing Facilities

🚢 Sportboat Operation

✛ Fishing Reefs

〰 Kelp

～20～ Depth in Fathoms

At the entrance to Moss Landing harbor, anglers fish from the jetty for surfperch, starry flounder, and occasionally California halibut and striped bass. There is also fishing from shore inside Elkhorn Slough for surfperch, plus shark, rays, sand sole and starry flounder.

The northern end of Seacliff State Beach near Aptos has a fishing pier (actually a cement ship) from which anglers catch Pacific sanddab, surfperch, white croaker, jacksmelt, small bocaccio, jack mackerel (during some summers), and an occasional California halibut, starry flounder, lingcod, salmon and steelhead.

Rocky outcroppings and low bluffs begin to interrupt sandy beaches north of Aptos, and rocky-shore fish start to appear in the angler's catch, finally replacing sandy-shore fish in importance as one proceeds westward. At the Capitola pier, which is mostly over sandy bottom, the usual fare is white croaker, jacksmelt, small bocaccio, walleye, shiner surfperch, cabezon, staghorn sculpin and an occasional barred surfperch.

To the west of the Santa Cruz pier, anglers catch both rocky and sandy-shore fish such as surfperch, lingcod, cabezon, young bocaccio, kelp rockfish, topsmelt, jacksmelt, staghorn sculpin, skates, Pacific sanddab, sand sole, starry flounder and white croaker. Rockfish are taken from Santa Cruz Small Craft Harbor jetties, and in some years, coho salmon and steelhead are taken around the mouth of the San Lorenzo River.

From Natural Bridges State Beach north to Ano Nuevo Point, the shoreline changes rather abruptly to a predominantly rocky coastline, and fog and blustery northwest winds once again sweep the coast. This rocky shoreline offers excellent shore fishing for kelp greenling, cabezon, grass rockfish and surfperch. Where the rocky shoreline is broken occasionally by short stretches of sandy beach, netters work the surf from Scott Creek northward for surf and night smelts from March to October.

Party Boat Fishing: Commercial sport fishing boats operate year-round out of Monterey and Santa Cruz and intermittently out of Capitola and Moss Landing.

The fleet based at Monterey, which fishes mainly for rockfish, has expanded its range over the past 10 years. Blue, yellowtail and olive rockfish dominate the party boat landings, although an assortment of other rockfish species also contribute to the catch. Those taken in the shallower near-shore areas along the kelp are blue, olive, black, copper,

starry and rosy rockfish. In deeper water spots in Monterey Bay and off Point Sur, the yellowtail, blue, and bocaccio predominate. Monterey party boat anglers also take lingcod, Pacific sanddab, Pacific bonito (in summer with September being the best month), sablefish and albacore (late summer). In most years, albacore schools appear about 10-15 miles offshore, usually in water about 61 to 64^{0}F.

Along the north shore of Monterey Bay, Santa Cruz and Capitola party boats fish over the rocky reefs from Point Santa Cruz north to Ano Nuevo Point for rockfish, lingcod and cabezon. The Ano Nuevo grounds are exceptionally good for lingcod and blue and black rockfish. Other rockfish entering the party boat catch along the northern section of the coast include copper, olive, brown, yellowtail, widow, green-spotted, bocaccio and chilipepper—the last five in deep-water areas. Party boats also go after chinook salmon during the season when good runs develop (best catches usually in May and June). Along the north shore, the party boats catch other fish such as bonito, sablefish, petrale sole, rock sole, Pacific sanddab and kelp greenling.

Skiff Fishing: Most of the Monterey Bay area skiff catch is made up of several species of rockfish, Pacific sanddab, chinook salmon and lingcod. Most small boat fishing takes place inside Monterey Bay, although on calm days Monterey skiff anglers occasionally venture out around the peninsula between Point Pinos and Cypress Point to fish for lingcod and some of the near-shore rockfish, or try their luck in Carmel Bay.

Inside Carmel Bay, skiffs work along the edge of the kelp for lingcod and rockfish; sometimes in summer, jack mackerel and bonito make a showing in the bay. Occasionally salmon are taken when a good run develops. Skiff anglers making the trip around the Monterey Peninsula to Carmel Bay are warned that the return trip can be extremely rough, if not impossible, on all but the calmest days.

Within Monterey Bay from early spring to late summer, skiff anglers troll for chinook salmon in areas shown on the map. Pacific sanddabs are plentiful over a sandy bottom, and California halibut are taken trolling just beyond the surf line during summer and fall. The area south of the Salinas River is closed by the military when Fort Ord target ranges are in use, so check locally before fishing this section of the bay. Warning flags are flown from the Coast Guard breakwater in Monterey when this area is restricted.

Skiff anglers out of Moss Landing on Elkhorn Slough fish both the tidewater section of the slough and outside in

Monterey Bay. The area around the entrance is particularly good for Pacific sanddab, sablefish, white croaker and occasionally California halibut. Salmon trolling is very popular with Moss Landing skiff anglers, who actively fish in the bay for chinook salmon during the season (June and July considered best). Surfperch are particularly abundant inside the slough. Jacksmelt, sand sole, staghorn sculpin, starry flounder, sharks and rays are also common in the estuary. A shark derby is held in Moss Landing each year.

To the north and west, skiff anglers who fish off Capitola bring in a mixed catch of blue rockfish, white croaker, petrale sole and sablefish. To the west, Santa Cruz small-boat anglers fish mainly the reef and kelp areas for rockfish (blue, grass and brown), lingcod and cabezon, or troll along the sandy beaches to the east for halibut in summer. During the salmon season, boats work the area between Sunset Beach and Davenport.

San Francisco Area Coast (map - p.218)

The climate along this coast is cool and temperate with little seasonal variation in air temperature. During summer, San Francisco's famous fog funnels in through the Golden Gate morning and evenings, drawn inland by the warmings of the Central Valley.

Most offshore recreational fishing is for chinook salmon from spring through fall, although bottom fish tend to dominate the sport catch in areas south of San Pedro Point where salmon runs occur less predictably. In most years, migrating albacore are taken around the Farallon Islands in fall.

Pigeon Point to Half Moon Bay: The main angling activities from Pigeon Point to Bean Hollow State Park are rock fishing and poke poling from shore. From Bean Hollow State Park north to Pillar Point the shore is alternately sandy beach and rocky outcroppings. Along this coast, striped bass begin to enter the shore angler's catch during summer and early fall; some of the better locations are Pescadero State Beach, San Gregorio State Beach, Martins Beach and Half Moon Bay State Beaches. These are also good areas for

Location	Sport Fishing Boats	Pier Fishing	Boat Rental	Launch Ramp	Jetty Fishing
Princeton, HMB(1)*	X	X	X	X	X
San Pedro Point (2)			X	X	
Pacifica Pier (3)		X			

* Map fishing facilities

surfperch and for netting surf and night smelts (March to October).

Pillar Point Harbor on Half Moon Bay is the major recreational fishing port along this section of coast, and party boats based at the harbor fish over near shore and offshore reefs for lingcod, cabezon and rockfish (blue, copper, olive and yellowtail). Occasional bottom-fish trips are made to the Farallon Islands, and albacore are sometimes taken west of the Farallons from August to October. Small-boat anglers actively fish for salmon when the fish make a showing near shore, or fish on the bottom around the entrance to the harbor and north along Pillar Point for rockfish, lingcod, cabezon and white croaker.

Inside Pillar Point Harbor, anglers fish from the Princeton Pier for Pacific sanddab, white croaker, surfperch, jacksmelt, topsmelt, brown smoothhound shark, skates, staghorn sculpin and rockfish. Anglers also fish from the east and west jetties that partially enclose the harbor. At the west jetty the catch consists mainly of striped surfperch, kelp greenling, cabezon, grass rockfish, and occasionally lingcod. From the east jetty they catch sandy bottom species such as white croaker, starry flounder, sand sole and rubberlip surfperch.

Pillar Point North to the Golden Gate: North of Pillar Point the coast becomes rocky once again until you reach Montara State Beach—a narrow, coarse sand beach backed by sandstone bluffs. Here surf casters take surfperch and catch striped bass during the summer.

North of the State Park, Hwy. 1 is above steep sandstone cliffs, and access to shore is difficult, if not dangerous, especially around the Devil's Slide area.

At Point San Pedro on Shelter Cove, skiffs can be rented and launched when weather permits. The area off the point is especially good for rockfish, lingcod and white croaker. During good salmon years, chinook are landed off the point in spring and summer; striped bass are taken from boats and from shore during late summer and fall.

The coast north of Point San Pedro has no party boat operations, skiff rentals or launching facilities; all these facilities are in San Francisco Bay. However, a public fishing pier offers good angling at Pacifica. From Pacifica north to the Golden Gate, the coast is mostly sandy beach, and it is along these beaches that the heaviest runs of striped bass occur in the surf. The map shows some of the more popular fishing spots, although this entire coast is good for striped bass when they are running. One of the most heavily fished

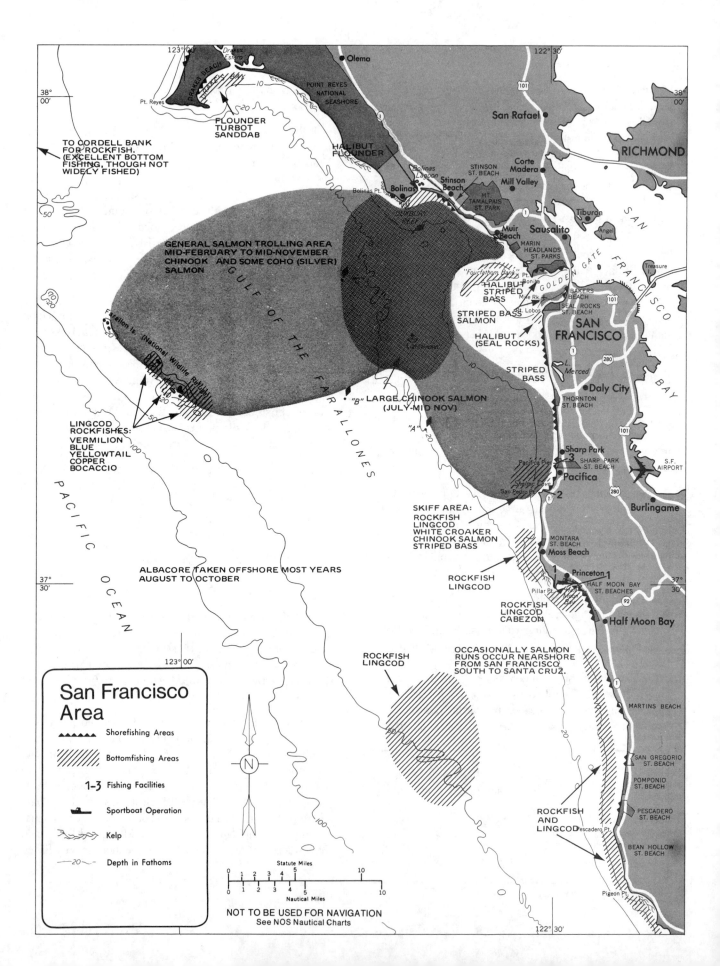

TO CORDELL BANK
FOR ROCKFISH.
(EXCELLENT BOTTOM
FISHING, THOUGH NOT
WIDELY FISHED)

FLOUNDER
TURBOT
SANDDAB

HALIBUT
FLOUNDER

GENERAL SALMON TROLLING AREA
MID-FEBRUARY TO MID-NOVEMBER
CHINOOK AND SOME COHO (SILVER)
SALMON

LINGCOD
ROCKFISHES:
VERMILION
BLUE
YELLOWTAIL
COPPER
BOCACCIO

"B" LARGE CHINOOK SALMON
(JULY-MID NOV)

"A"

HALIBUT
STRIPED
BASS

STRIPED BASS
SALMON

HALIBUT
(SEAL ROCKS)

STRIPED
BASS

SKIFF AREA:
ROCKFISH
LINGCOD
WHITE CROAKER
CHINOOK SALMON
STRIPED BASS

ROCKFISH
LINGCOD

ROCKFISH
LINGCOD
CABEZON

ALBACORE TAKEN OFFSHORE MOST YEARS
AUGUST TO OCTOBER

ROCKFISH
LINGCOD

OCCASIONALLY SALMON
RUNS OCCUR NEARSHORE
FROM SAN FRANCISCO
SOUTH TO SANTA CRUZ.

ROCKFISH
AND
LINGCOD

PACIFIC OCEAN

RICHMOND

Olema
San Rafael
Corte Madera
Mill Valley
Tiburon
Sausalito
SAN FRANCISCO
Daly City
Burlingame
S.F. AIRPORT
Sharp Park
Pacifica
Moss Beach
Princeton
Half Moon Bay
Martins Beach
San Gregorio St. Beach
Pomponio St. Beach
Pescadero St. Beach
Bean Hollow St. Beach
Pigeon Pt.

San Francisco Area

▲▲▲▲ Shorefishing Areas

///// Bottomfishing Areas

1-3 Fishing Facilities

Sportboat Operation

Kelp

—20— Depth in Fathoms

Statute Miles
0 1 2 3 4 5   10

Nautical Miles
0 1 2 3 4 5   10

NOT TO BE USED FOR NAVIGATION
See NOS Nautical Charts

places is Bakers Beach near the Golden Gate Bridge. These ocean beaches are also good bait-casting areas for redtail surfperch during winter and spring, and at times, for jacksmelt and other surfperch.

The Gulf of the Farallons is fished primarily by San Francisco Bay party boats and occasionally boats from Half Moon Bay. This area produces the most consistent ocean sport fishing for salmon in the state. Most fishing is for chinook salmon, although some coho are also landed. The season extends from mid-February through mid-November (check state regulations), and there are two major chinook runs—one in the spring and one in the fall. During the height of the spring run from about March to June, most fishing occurs offshore between Duxbury Reef and the Farallon Islands, while from July to mid-October the fish are taken closer to shore. The most productive area for large fall-run chinook extends from the San Francisco light buoy, or "light bucket," former site of the San Francisco lightship, to the Marin County beaches and north to Duxbury Reef, where fishing is best from July through September. The Golden Gate area, especially around Mile Rock and the south tower of the bridge, is also a good fishing spot in midsummer and fall for striped bass and occasionally salmon.

When salmon are not running, boats may fish for rockfish and lingcod around the Farallon Islands, and occasionally travel as far west as Cordell Bank about 20 miles west of Point Reyes.

There is some skiff fishing for chinook salmon off Muir and Stinson Beaches in late summer, but weather and sea often restrict small boat fishing in the ocean. Fourfathom Bank (also called Potato Patch Shoal) can get particularly rough on windy days, but in calm weather this sandy shoal area is a good fishing spot for California halibut and striped bass. California halibut are also taken around Seal Rocks and to the south (July and August being the best months).

Shore Fishing North of the Golden Gate: Only a limited amount of shore fishing takes place along the rugged rocky coast from the Golden Gate Bridge north to Stinson Beach. Access is difficult in most places. Striped bass occasionally are caught from shore in summer and fall along isolated sandy coves near the Golden Gate (Fort Baker, Fort Barry, Fort Cronkite and at Muir Beach). From Muir Beach to Stinson Beach, where rocky shores can be reached, anglers fish for blue rockfish, lingcod, cabezon, kelp greenling and surfperch, or poke pole for monkeyface eels at low tide. This stretch of coastline can be dangerous during rough weather;

it is advisable to fish here only on calm days and always keep an eye out for changing sea conditions.

At Stinson Beach State Park, rocky shores abruptly give way to a long and wide expanse of sandy beach where surf anglers cast for surfperch. To the north along the sandy shores of the Point Reyes Peninsula, there is bait casting for surfperch.

Point Reyes to Fort Ross (map - p. 220)

Along this rural and often wind-swept part of the coast, party boats operate year-round, weather permitting, out of Bodega Harbor and Dillon Beach. Most offshore fishing is for bottom fish—particularly rockfish or "rock cod." Some boats also fish for chinook salmon when the fish are running, but in general, salmon appear less predictably here than off San Francisco and areas to the north.

The range of the party boat fleet extends south to off Point Reyes and north to Fort Ross. Areas most frequented by the fleet are Tomales Point, the 27-fathom reefs off the western shore of Point Reyes Peninsula, and areas north along the coast from Bodega Head to Fort Ross. Occasionally, special trips are made to Cordell Bank, about 23 miles southwest of the Bodega Harbor entrance. Most of the party boat catch is made up of rockfish. Other rocky bottom fish such as cabezon and lingcod are also caught along with an occasional chinook. Lingcod appear to be more plentiful in the northern areas off Fort Ross than in areas to the south, and flatfish are sometimes taken incidentally as boats drift over from a rocky to sandy bottom.

Skiff Fishing: Skiff fishing is generally limited to the confines of Tomales Bay and around the entrance to Bodega Harbor. Experienced boat anglers familiar with the area sometimes venture farther out to fish for salmon or bottom fish, but this practice is not without its risks. Many people (up to 13 in 1 year) have lost their lives at the entrance to Tomales Bay, where huge waves are known to appear and capsize boats with little warning. Strangers to the area would do well to stay within the protection of the bay.

Inside Tomales Bay, small-boat anglers fish for sharks and rays, California halibut (June to October), sand sole, turbot, jacksmelt (September to November best) and an assortment of surfperch. Sharks are particularly plentiful in the bay, and every year a shark and stingray derby is sponsored by local civic groups. Striped bass are sometimes

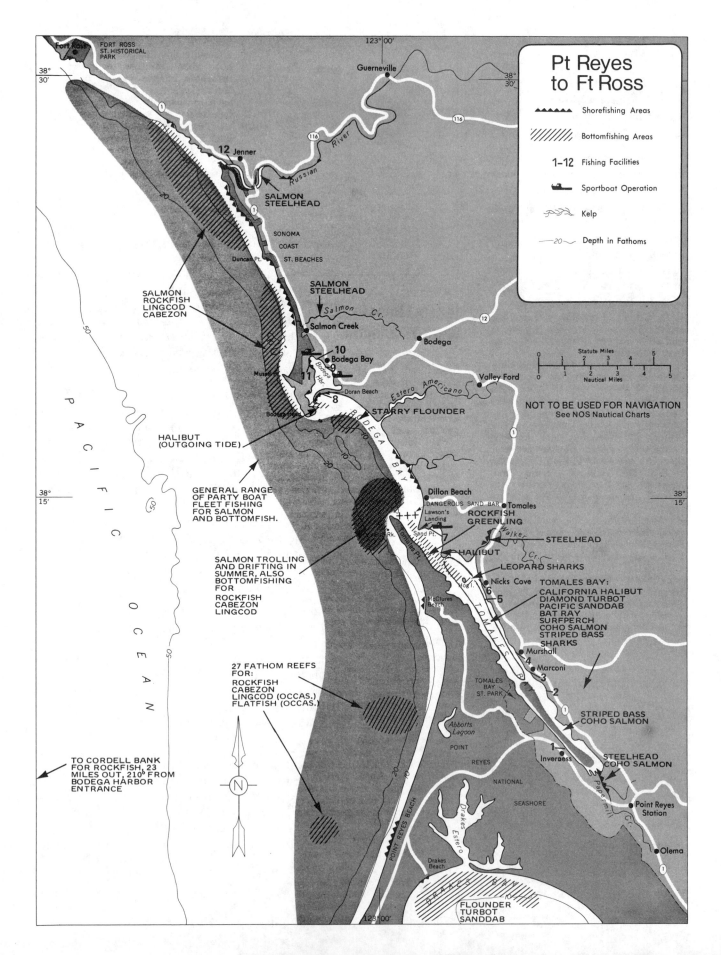

Pt Reyes to Ft Ross

Shorefishing Areas
Bottomfishing Areas
1-12   Fishing Facilities
Sportboat Operation
Kelp
20   Depth in Fathoms

FORT ROSS ST. HISTORICAL PARK
Fort Ross
38° 30'
123° 00'
Guerneville
38° 30'
116
1
12 Jenner
Russian River
SALMON STEELHEAD
SONOMA COAST ST. BEACHES
Duncan Pt.
SALMON STEELHEAD
Salmon Cr.
SALMON ROCKFISH LINGCOD CABEZON
Salmon Creek
Bodega
10
Bodega Bay
9
12
Mussel Pt.
11
Bodega Hbr.
Doran Beach
8
Valley Ford
Estero Americano
STARRY FLOUNDER
Bodega Head
HALIBUT (OUTGOING TIDE)
BODEGA BAY
GENERAL RANGE OF PARTY BOAT FLEET FISHING FOR SALMON AND BOTTOMFISH.
NOT TO BE USED FOR NAVIGATION
See NOS Nautical Charts

Statute Miles
Nautical Miles

38° 15'
Dillon Beach
DANGEROUS SAND BAR
Tomales
Lawson's Landing
ROCKFISH GREENLING
Rk.
Sand Pt.
7
Walke
STEELHEAD
SALMON TROLLING AND DRIFTING IN SUMMER, ALSO BOTTOMFISHING FOR ROCKFISH CABEZON LINGCOD
Tomales Pt.
HALIBUT
LEOPARD SHARKS
Dog I.
6
Nicks Cove
5
TOMALES BAY:
CALIFORNIA HALIBUT
DIAMOND TURBOT
PACIFIC SANDDAB
BAT RAY
SURFPERCH
COHO SALMON
STRIPED BASS
SHARKS
McClures Beach
Murshall
4
Marconi
3
27 FATHOM REEFS FOR:
ROCKFISH CABEZON LINGCOD (OCCAS.) FLATFISH (OCCAS.)
TOMALES BAY ST. PARK
2
STRIPED BASS COHO SALMON
Abbotts Lagoon
POINT
REYES
1
Inverness
STEELHEAD COHO SALMON
TO CORDELL BANK FOR ROCKFISH, 23 MILES OUT, 210° FROM BODEGA HARBOR ENTRANCE
N
NATIONAL
SEASHORE
Point Reyes Station
Papermill Cr.
Olema
Point Reyes Beach
Drakes Estero
Drakes Beach
FLOUNDER TURBOT SANDDAB
DRAKES BAY
38° 15'
123° 00'

PACIFIC OCEAN
50
50
50

caught in the southern reaches of the bay in summer. The lower bay also has a small run of coho salmon which are caught trolling during October and November, and some steelhead are taken as they make their way to Papermill Creek to spawn (November to February).

In Bodega Harbor, a narrow channel cuts through this shallow lagoon to the boat basin at the town of Bodega Bay and into deeper water at the harbor's northwest corner. There is a limited amount of skiff fishing for surfperch and starry flounder in deep-water parts of the lagoon, and steelhead occasionally are taken around areas of freshwater seepage.

To the north, skiffs and launching are available at Jenner on the Russian River. In addition to winter steelhead and salmon fishing (September to November), there is skiff fishing inside the tidal lagoon for surfperch and starry flounder. Small boats do not venture into the ocean because the outlet, or "bar," at the Russian River mouth is often too narrow for skiffs.

Shore Fishing: Selected areas of this coast offer many different types of shore fishing, including casting along sandy beaches for surfperch, pier and dock fishing in bays and harbors, stream and river fishing for salmon and steelhead, poke poling and bait casting along rocky shores, and netting smelts around river and creek mouths. Spring and early summer are best for surfperch, steelhead fishing is best in fall and winter following heavy rains, coho salmon appear in the fall from September to November, surf and night smelts are netted March through October, and most rocky-shore fish are taken year-round.

The sandy beaches along the Point Reyes Peninsula provide good surf fishing. Most of the peninsula is within the boundaries of the Point Reyes National Seashore, and though much of the land is still under the private ownership of ranchers, some beaches are open to the public and it is expected that even more shore areas will be open in the future.

Along the Tomales Bay shore, pier and dock fishing is available at some of the small-boat harbors and wharfs. Jacksmelt and surfperch are the most common pier-caught species. At the very southern end of the bay, coho salmon are taken near the entrance of Papermill Creek (October to November) and winter steelhead fishing is often productive in deep pools just inside the creek mouth.

Location	Sport Fishing Boats	Pier Fishing	Boat Rental	Launch Ramp	Jetty Fishing
Inverness (1) *			X	X	
Tomales Boat Basin (2)			X	X	
Marconi Cove (3)				X	
Marshall (4)		X			
North Shore Boats (5)		X	X		
Nick's Cove (6)		X			X
Lawson's Landing (7)	X	X	X	X	
Doran Park (8)				X	X
Tides Wharf (9)	X	X			
Shaws Marina (10)	X			X	
Westside Park (11)				X	X
Jenner (12)				X	

* Map fishing facilities

On the eastern shore near the entrance to Tomales Bay, surfperch are taken by shore casting along beaches north of Sand Point, and fishing is excellent for rockfish and greenling where the sandy beach gives way to a predominantly rocky coastline north of Dillon Beach. This is also a good place for poke poling monkeyface eels and other crevice-seeking fish. Anglers usually reach this shore area by hiking north from Dillon Beach since most of the land adjacent to this rocky stretch of coast is privately owned.

The next opportunity for shore fishing as you approach Bodega Bay from the south is found at Doran Beach Park. Most fishing takes place around the east jetty at the mouth of the harbor where the usual fare is shiner and silver surfperch, jacksmelt, starry flounder, rockfish and greenling. Anglers also fish from the west jetty on the other side of the harbor entrance for the same species.

In the town of Bodega Bay, the public is allowed to fish from the local wharf where the main species taken are jacksmelt, young bocaccio and surfperch. There is some fishing along the breakwater on the western shore of Bodega Harbor for shiner, surfperch and black rockfish.

On beaches along the Sonoma coast, anglers catch surf-perch, lingcod, rockfish, and flounder. This stretch of coast is also good for netting surf and night smelts around the mouth of coastal streams. Steelhead and a few salmon are sometimes taken from these streams.

In the Russian River, migrating steelhead are caught just inside the mouth of the river from the south bank, and in selected areas, up river. Striped bass and sturgeons are occasionally landed from boats in the estuary and from the beach adjacent to the river mouth. Surfperch and flounder are taken in the tidal lagoon section, and runs of chinook have occurred in the river during late summer and early fall in the last few years.

North of Jenner the coast becomes steep and rugged, and most of the land is privately owned. At Fort Ross State Park and areas to the north where the shore can be reached, anglers cast for rockfish, greenling, cabezon, surfperch and occasionally lingcod. This rocky coastline is also very popular with skin divers and shore pickers who hunt for red abalone.

Fort Ross to Cape Mendocino
(map - p. 223)

Here the shoreline is predominantly rocky backed by high grassy bluffs. These rugged headlands are sharply indented with numerous gulches, and public access to shore occurs infrequently because of the steep terrain and the many privately owned areas adjacent to the coast. Most shore fishing occurs at coves and beaches where coastal streams and rivers empty into the sea. Winters are wet and chilly, and in summer the coast is usually fogbound. Fall is the sunniest and most pleasant time of the year.

Most ocean sport fishing takes place out of the town of Fort Bragg, and to a lesser extent, at Albion, Point Arena and Shelter Cove. Bottom fishing along this rocky coast is excellent and salmon trolling is very popular.

Where the shore can be reached, rock anglers seek ling-cod, cabezon and small rockfish, and where rocky shores are interrupted by stretches of sandy beach, surf casters fish for redtail surfperch during spring and summer (April and May are considered best). Surf netters work the breakers for surf and night smelts around the mouths of streams; best catches of night smelt are made from February to April, and for surf (day) smelt, from April through August. Steelhead run in rivers between early December and the end of February, with fishing usually at its peak around New Year's Day.

Location	Sport Fishing Boats	Pier Fishing	Boat Rental	Launch Ramp	Jetty Fishing
Point Arena (1)*		X	X	X	
Albion (2)	X		X		
Noyo Harbor (3)	X	X	X	X	X
Shelter Cove (4)			X	X	

* Map fishing facilities

Fort Ross to Point Arena: The first access to shore north of Fort Ross is at Salt Point State Park which has a small bluff-protected cove where skiffs can be launched over the beach in calm weather. Fishing is not allowed inside this cove (Gerstle Cove), but when weather and sea are favorable, anglers venture out around the rocky points on either side of the cove in search of lingcod, blue rockfish, kelp greenling and cabezon. From Salt Point to Gualala, all land is part of a private development of houses and rental units, although there is public access to a tiny stretch of rock and driftwood-strewn beach at the northern end of the development.

The Gualala River has excellent runs of winter steelhead and the tidewater section is a popular fishing area. Access is by way of dirt road at the north end of the Hwy. 1 bridge that leads out to the gravel bar near the mouth. Small boats can be launched here (no ramp), and the pools near the south bank are considered the most productive.

At Anchor Bay, owners of the property allow anglers access for a fee, and skiffs can be launched over the beach on the north side of the cove in calm weather. Here, skiff anglers catch such rocky-shore species as kelp greenling, blue and black rockfish, lingcod and cabezon. Because of the steep terrain, access to the shore is limited north of Anchor Bay to the Point Arena area.

Point Arena: The main fishing activities at Point Arena are pier and skiff fishing at Arena Cove. The cove would be a more important fishing port if it were not for its vulnerability to southerly and westerly winds. Skiffs are available for rent at the pier, which also has a boat hoist. Skiff anglers fish over the reef areas for bottom fish, and during July and August, there is a limited amount of trolling for salmon out to about 15 fathoms. The small pier at Arena Cove is over rocky bottom and attracts such rocky-shore species as striped and walleye surfperch, kelp greenling, black rockfish, ling-

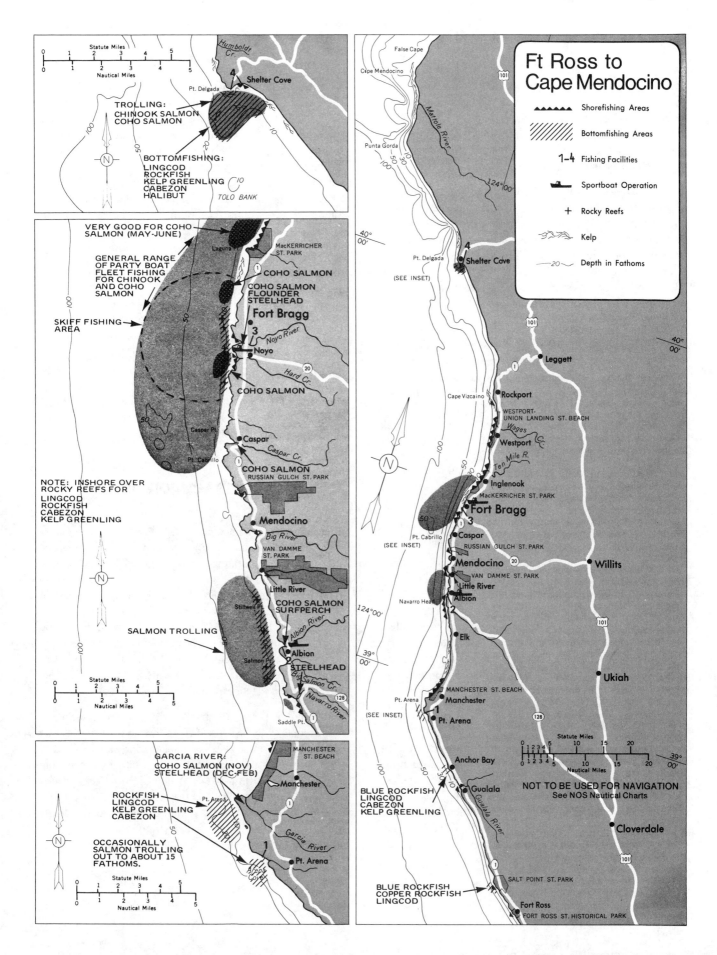

TROLLING:
CHINOOK SALMON
COHO SALMON

BOTTOMFISHING:
LINGCOD
ROCKFISH
KELP GREENLING
CABEZON
HALIBUT

TOLO BANK

Statute Miles
Nautical Miles

VERY GOOD FOR COHO
SALMON (MAY-JUNE)

GENERAL RANGE
OF PARTY BOAT
FLEET FISHING
FOR CHINOOK
AND COHO
SALMON

SKIFF FISHING
AREA

NOTE: INSHORE OVER
ROCKY REEFS FOR
LINGCOD
ROCKFISH
CABEZON
KELP GREENLING

SALMON TROLLING

MacKERRICHER
ST. PARK

COHO SALMON

COHO SALMON
FLOUNDER
STEELHEAD

Fort Bragg

Noyo River

Hard Cr.

COHO SALMON

Caspar Cr.

Caspar

COHO SALMON
RUSSIAN GULCH ST. PARK

Mendocino

Big River

VAN DAMME
ST. PARK

Little River

COHO SALMON
SURFPERCH

Albion River

Albion

STEELHEAD

Big Salmon Cr.

Navarro River

Saddle Pt.

Statute Miles
Nautical Miles

GARCIA RIVER:
COHO SALMON (NOV)
STEELHEAD (DEC-FEB)

MANCHESTER
ST. BEACH

Manchester

ROCKFISH
LINGCOD
KELP GREENLING
CABEZON

Pt. Arena

OCCASIONALLY
SALMON TROLLING
OUT TO ABOUT 15
FATHOMS.

Garcia River

Pt. Arena

Statute Miles
Nautical Miles

Ft Ross to Cape Mendocino

▲▲▲▲ Shorefishing Areas

/////// Bottomfishing Areas

1-4 Fishing Facilities

⛴ Sportboat Operation

+ Rocky Reefs

〰 Kelp

—20— Depth in Fathoms

False Cape

Cape Mendocino

Mattole River

Punta Gorda

Pt. Delgada

Shelter Cove
(SEE INSET)

Leggett

Cape Vizcaino

Rockport

WESTPORT-
UNION LANDING ST. BEACH

Wages

Westport

Ten Mile R.

Inglenook

MacKERRICHER ST. PARK

Fort Bragg

(SEE INSET)

Pt. Cabrillo

Caspar

RUSSIAN GULCH ST. PARK

Mendocino

Willits

VAN DAMME ST. PARK

Little River

Navarro Head

Albion

Elk

Ukiah

124°00'

39°
00'

MANCHESTER ST. BEACH

Pt. Arena

Manchester

Pt. Arena

(SEE INSET)

Anchor Bay

BLUE ROCKFISH
LINGCOD
CABEZON
KELP GREENLING

Gualala

Gualala River

Statute Miles
Nautical Miles

NOT TO BE USED FOR NAVIGATION
See NOS Nautical Charts

Cloverdale

BLUE ROCKFISH
COPPER ROCKFISH
LINGCOD

SALT POINT ST. PARK

Fort Ross
FORT ROSS ST. HISTORICAL PARK

cod and occasionally cabezon. To the north at Manchester State Beach, smelts are netted in the surf along sandy stretches, and good rock fishing spots can be found at the north end. About a mile north of the state beach boundary at Alder Creek, fishing is good for surf smelt, redtail surfperch and migrating salmon and steelhead around the creek mouth.

Fort Bragg and Albion: Sport fishing boats operate out of Noyo Harbor in Fort Bragg, and in some years, out of Albion when weather permits. Most fishing is during the summer. The rocky reefs along this coast are extremely productive for lingcod, cabezon, kelp greenling and rockfish. Reef areas around rocky points adjacent to the Noyo and Albion rivers' mouths are excellent spots for lingcod and red rockfish.

Offshore, anglers troll for chinook and coho salmon from May to October in water 10 to 60 fathoms deep. At the height of the season in July and August, coho move inshore to feed over reef areas, and during October and November they congregate around river and creek mouths such as the Ten Mile River, Noyo River, Albion River, Caspar Creek and the Navarro River. During this time skiff fishing reaches its peak around the Noyo River mouth. Most ocean skiff fishing (for both salmon and bottom fish) occurs within 3 miles of the whistle buoy about a mile west of the mouth of the Noyo River. To the south at Albion River, small-boat anglers are warned that the dangerous bar at the entrance can be crossed only during certain tide stages, and then only during calm weather.

Tidewater fishing takes place in both the Noyo and Albion rivers. Inside the Noyo River, coho are taken from October to mid-December, and starry flounder are caught year-round with March bringing the best catches. Surfperch are caught in winter and spring (April and May being the best months). Surfperch, jacksmelt and flounder are taken from the north jetty at the river entrance for surfperch, kelp greenling and small black rockfish. Striped surfperch show around the jetty during spring. The Albion River has tidewater fishing for coho in October and November; surfperch and flounder are also taken here, as in the Noyo River.

Shore anglers looking for spots to fish on the coast around the Fort Bragg-Albion area can try their luck between the towns of Elk and Albion and at the state parks. Most of these areas have good rock fishing and poke poling places, and beaches can be good for redtail surfperch and calico surfperch, as well as surf and night smelt. North of Mackerricher Park, smelt are surf netted around the mouths of practically all creeks—especially those between Westport and Rockport (Wages, DeHaven, Hardy and Juan Creeks). Juan Creek and the Ten Mile River also have good surf fishing for redtail surfperch, and the Ten Mile River mouth has good fall fishing for coho. North of Rockport, Hwy. 1 turns inland through mountainous terrain and redwood forest, meeting up with U.S. 101 at Leggett. Twenty-seven miles north of Leggett an access road (not shown on the map) leads to Shelter Cove—this is the last fishing outpost along this section of coast.

Shelter Cove: Shelter Cove affords reasonably good shelter from northwesterly winds, but like Arena Cove, it is exposed to the full force of southerly and westerly winds. Skiffs can be rented during the summer. Bait and tackle are also available. Though Shelter Cove is isolated and has no docking or wharf facilities, skiff fishing here is excellent—particularly for bottom fish. Such rocky-bottom types as lingcod, cabezon, greenling and rockfish abound over the rocky reefs, and in July and August, skiffs work the cove for coho and chinook salmon. Pacific halibut are sometimes caught by skiffs, and redtail and other surfperch are taken by surf casters on the beach.

Eel River to the Oregon Border
(map - p. 225)

North of Cape Mendocino, dark sand beaches begin to interrupt rocky headlands more frequently, and large rivers, famous for their migrating salmon and steelhead, empty into the sea. The terrain is less steep near the ocean than areas to the south, but the coastline still maintains a rugged beauty of its own. Along this coast, the magnificent coastal redwood trees thrive in the cool and very damp climate of the Pacific Northwest. Salmon is by far the most important game fish in this region, and both chinook and coho salmon are taken during summer and fall. Rockfish and other bottom fish also enter the sport catch, especially in the north.

Redtail surfperch are abundant and are available year-round along sandy beaches and in tidewater, with spring and early summer bringing the best catches. Surf smelt are netted from March through September, and night smelt run from February through mid-May. Along the occasional rocky stretches, black and grass rockfish and kelp and rock greenling are taken by rock anglers. In most places there is year-round fishing in tidewater for starry flounder and surfperch, with spring bringing the best catches. Eulachon, or candle-

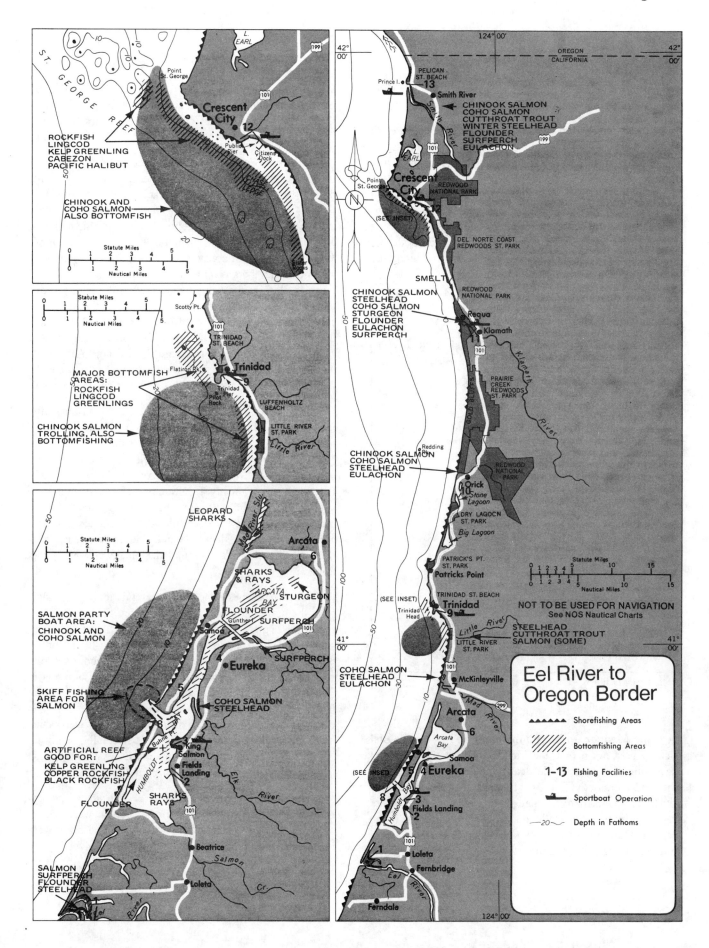

ROCKFISH
LINGCOD
KELP GREENLING
CABEZON
PACIFIC HALIBUT

CHINOOK AND
COHO SALMON
ALSO BOTTOMFISH

MAJOR BOTTOMFISH
AREAS:
ROCKFISH
LINGCOD
GREENLINGS

CHINOOK SALMON
TROLLING, ALSO
BOTTOMFISHING

LEOPARD
SHARKS

SHARKS
& RAYS

STURGEON

FLOUNDER
SURFPERCH

SURFPERCH

SALMON PARTY
BOAT AREA:
CHINOOK AND
COHO SALMON

SKIFF FISHING
AREA FOR
SALMON

COHO SALMON
STEELHEAD

ARTIFICIAL REEF
GOOD FOR:
KELP GREENLING
COPPER ROCKFISH
BLACK ROCKFISH

FLOUNDER

SHARKS
RAYS

SALMON
SURFPERCH
FLOUNDER
STEELHEAD

OREGON
CALIFORNIA

PELICAN
ST. BEACH

CHINOOK SALMON
COHO SALMON
CUTTHROAT TROUT
WINTER STEELHEAD
FLOUNDER
SURFPERCH
EULACHON

REDWOOD
NATIONAL PARK

DEL NORTE COAST
REDWOODS ST. PARK

SMELT

REDWOOD
NATIONAL PARK

CHINOOK SALMON
STEELHEAD
COHO SALMON
STURGEON
FLOUNDER
EULACHON
SURFPERCH

PRAIRIE
CREEK
REDWOODS
ST. PARK

CHINOOK SALMON
COHO SALMON
STEELHEAD
EULACHON

REDWOOD
NATIONAL PARK

DRY LAGOON
ST. PARK

PATRICK'S PT.
ST. PARK

Patricks Point

TRINIDAD ST. BEACH

STEELHEAD
CUTTHROAT TROUT
SALMON (SOME)

LITTLE RIVER
ST. PARK

COHO SALMON
STEELHEAD
EULACHON

NOT TO BE USED FOR NAVIGATION
See NOS Nautical Charts

Eel River to Ocean Border

▲▲▲▲ Shorefishing Areas

////// Bottomfishing Areas

1-13 Fishing Facilities

⛴ Sportboat Operation

—20~ Depth in Fathoms

fish, are dip netted in Redwood Creek and the Klamath, Smith and Mad rivers in April and May.

Winter steelhead run in most rivers October through March, with peak fishing in December and January. Summer steelhead run in the Klamath and Eel rivers from July through September, and sea-run cutthroat trout occur in the more northerly rivers, fall through spring. Mud flats and beaches along this stretch of coast are famous for their gaper, Washington, littleneck, soft-shell and razor clams. Crabbing for Dungeness crab is also popular along this coast during winter and spring, especially at Crescent City, Humboldt Bay and in the Eel River Lagoon.

Location	Sport Fishing Boats	Pier Fishing	Boat Rental	Launch Ramp	Jetty Fishing
Crab Pk. Eel R. (1)*				X	
Fields Lndg. Eureka (2)				X	
King Salmon, Eureka (3)	X	X	X	X	X
Ft. of Com. St (4)				X	
Samoa Access (5)				X	
Arcata (6)				X	
Mad River (7)				X	
Humboldt Bay (8)					X
Trinidad Harbor (9)	X	X	X	X	
Stone Lagoon (10)			X		
Klamath River (11)	X		X	X	X
Crescent City Harbor (12)	X	X	X	X	X
Smith River (13)	X	X	X	X	

*Map fishing facilities

Cape Mendocino to Humboldt Bay: The first coastal fishing area north of Cape Mendocino that is reasonably accessible is at Centerville Beach and around the mouth of the Eel River. In the Eel River Lagoon, most fishing is from skiffs, although there is shore fishing also. Steelhead are caught in summer and fall with larger fish landed late in the season. During most years chinook salmon enter the lagoon in August and run through October; coho salmon begin to appear later, around November. Starry flounder and surfperch are also taken in the lagoon. South of the Eel River there is surf netting for surf (day) smelt and casting for redtail surfperch along the sandy beach at Centerville County Park.

North of the Eel River, U.S. 101 turns toward the coast as it approaches the town of Eureka, a center of fishing activity during the salmon season. A sizeable party boat and skiff fishery operates out of Humboldt Bay, and boats fish almost exclusively for chinook and coho. Standard fishing methods are trolling and drifting with chinook being the first to show. July and August are considered the best fishing months as significant numbers of coho begin to be caught. Salmon move in close to the beaches and around the jetties at the harbor entrance as the season progresses. During this time skiffs venture out into the ocean to join the party boat fleet and the entrance channel soon becomes a favorite spot for chinook fishing. Small-boat fishermen are warned not to negotiate the harbor entrance on an outgoing tide—larger breakers form along the bar and make this a highly dangerous area.

Inside Humboldt Bay there is tidewater fishing from skiffs for jacksmelt, sharks, rays and surfperch. Sharks are plentiful in Arcata Bay, and leopard shark fishing is excellent in Mad River Slough during summer. Sturgeons sometimes are taken around the ruins of the old Arcata Channel. South Humboldt Bay is mostly a clamming area, but there is also angling for some of the species mentioned above as well as rockfish, which are taken consistently by anglers over the artificial reef during slack tide and when the water is clear. Rockfish are also taken around the breakwater at Buhne Point.

The ocean beaches adjacent to the Humboldt Bay entrance from the north and south spits have shore fishing. On the south spit, anglers cast for surfperch, and net surf and night smelt in the surf. The south jetty is a popular fishing spot for blue and black rockfish, kelp greenling, lingcod, cabezon, surfperch, jacksmelt and coho and chinook salmon (in summer). Species caught from the north spit are similar to those taken along the south spit, but permission from the Coast Guard is needed to fish the tip of the spit as well as the north jetty where grass rockfish are especially plentiful. Another jetty on the bay side of the north spit is a good spot for lingcod, kelp greenling, cabezon and rockfish.

A popular shore fishing site on the eastern side of the bay is at Buhne Point around the electric power plant warm-water outfall, where good numbers of surfperch are taken, as well as other bay fish. Shore anglers also catch a variety of surfperch around the railroad bridge that spans Eureka Slough. Pier fishing is allowed at a number of docks at Fields Landing, Buhne Point and Eureka, where the catch consists usually of jacksmelt, topsmelt, staghorn sculpin, kelp greenling and surfperch.

Mad River: At Mad River, most fishing is in the lagoon section for coho and winter run steelhead (January to March) although a few chinook are landed. Along beaches adjacent to the river mouth and north to Little River State Beach, there is good shore casting for surfperch and netting for surf and night smelt. Steelhead run in Little River in winter, sea-run cutthroat trout appear in spring, and salmon occasionally run up the river in fall.

About a mile north of Little River at the southern end of Luffenholtz Beach (a sandy beach bordered by rock outcroppings), access to shore is difficult in places, but there is good cabezon and kelp greenling fishing, excellent smelt netting, and surf casting for redtail surfperch along the sandy-shore section.

Trinidad Harbor offers ocean salmon fishing and bottom fishing in summer, and pier and rocky-shore fishing year-round. The salmon catch is mostly coho, and best fishing is in July and August. Blue and black rockfish, lingcod, kelp greenling and cabezon are caught in the salmon fishing areas and inshore over rocky reefs. There is pier fishing in this harbor for jacksmelt, surfperch, kelp greenling and cabezon.

To the north, rockfish, greenling and surfperch are taken from rocky beaches at Trinidad State Beach and Patricks Point State Park.

North of Patricks Point: North of Patricks Point the shore becomes lined with sand dunes, and beaches have excellent runs of surf and night smelt and redtail surfperch. The large brackish-water lagoons along this section of the coast have sporadic year-round fishing for cutthroat trout and small steelhead. Big Lagoon and Stone Lagoon sometime break open to the sea during high water, at which time salmon and steelhead move in. North of Dry Lagoon State Park, beaches backed by evergreen-crowned bluffs have good runs of surf and night smelt and redtail surfperch—particularly the Gold Bluffs area (reached by way of Fern Canyon Road).

The Klamath River is famous for its excellent runs of chinook salmon and steelhead. The tidewater section of the river is heavily fished by skiff and shore anglers—there is no skiff fishing in the ocean. Chinook start running in mid-July or August and continue through October. Although most fish are landed from skiffs which jam the lower river during the height of the season (August to September), many are also taken by anglers casting from shore around the river mouth. Coho enter the catch in mid to late September, and the run may last until July and continue to run through November or later, depending on river conditions. Other fish caught in tidewater include surfperch, starry flounder, white and green sturgeon and eulachon. Along beaches adjacent to the Klamath River mouth, surf netters strain the breakers for surf and night smelt, and bait casters fish for redtail surfperch and starry flounder. North of the Klamath, near the south border of Del Norte Coast Redwoods State Park, netters, rock anglers and surf casters fish from shore around the mouth of Wilson Creek. Within the creek, chinook and coho salmon, summer steelhead and sea-run cutthroat trout are taken.

Crescent City: The harbor at Crescent City is well protected from sea and weather by extensive seawalls which flank its perimeter and by the Point St. George headland. The fishing fleet is based at Crescent City Boat Basin between the east seawall and the public fishing pier, an area known as Citizen's Dock. Party boat and skiff anglers fish for salmon and bottom fish, weather permitting. Salmon trolling (mainly for chinook) usually begins in June and continues through September, with best catches made in July and August. Lingcod, cabezon, kelp greenling, rockfish and Pacific halibut are also taken in the salmon areas, but best bottom fishing is found usually farther inshore close to rocky Sister Rocks to the harbor entrance and along the 10-fathom curve from Chase Ledge north to St. George's Reef. Species of rockfish that enter the catch include black, blue, china, vermillion and bocaccio.

Shore anglers take blue and black rockfish, lingcod, and kelp and rock greenling from the west breakwater and along rocky shores north to Point St. George. There is pier fishing at Citizen's Dock for starry flounder, kelp greenling, surfperch and jacksmelt. Occasionally, large schools of surf smelt appear around the dock and are taken by snagging; herring are taken during late winter and early spring. Pier anglers also trap Dungeness crab in ring nets during winter and spring. Both surf and night smelt are netted along beaches south of the harbor and north of Point St. George, with surf smelt predominating along northern beaches.

The Smith River: The Smith River mouth and the tidewater lagoon section have considerable skiff fishing during the salmon season. Chinook is the most sought after, and fish weighing 25 to 30 pounds are not uncommon. The season usually extends from September through December; late September and October are peak fishing times in tidewater. Some coho are also taken; most are landed in October and November. Sea-run cutthroat trout are caught from shore and skiffs from September through May, with peak fishing in March and April. A few winter steelhead are caught in the lagoon from December through March, and eulachon are dip netted during their run in spring. Starry flounder, surfperch and cabezon are caught year-round in tidewater, and redtail surfperch as well as surf and night smelt are taken along the beach south of the river mouth. North along the coast, anglers fish the rocky shores of Pelican State Beach for black rockfish and other rocky-shore fish, and for night smelt along sandy stretches.

Fish Cleaning

There's a syndrome among some anglers that I like to call, "The Fear of Filleting." It's not unlike "The Fear of Flying." But fortunately, it's a lot easier to overcome. It just takes a little knowledge, a little willingness and an extra sharp filleting knife.

But don't be mislead, filleting is not the end-all or be-all of fish cleaning. It's only one of several basic approaches (all are presented here, in detail), and filleting is not even desirable or appropriate for some fish.

Field Dressing

Actually, the word dressing is not accurate, but we're stuck with it. Field dressing means removing the entrails and gills of a fish just after catching. This process is generally reserved for large fish (several pounds or more). It's purpose is to preserve the fish at its height of freshness. Field dressing, for example, is quite common among ocean salmon anglers. It's the kind of thing that's desirable but not absolutely necessary—especially if your catch is kept cold.

Here's how it's done. With the fish pointing away from you, put the tip of your knife in the anal vent and cut through the belly (leaving the intestines as undisturbed as possible) up to where the gills come together under the chin of the fish.

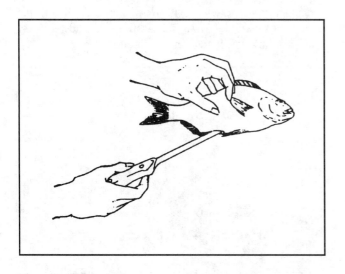

Next, with short cuts, free the bottom of the gills from the chin flesh and from the belly flesh, as illustrated in the following diagram.

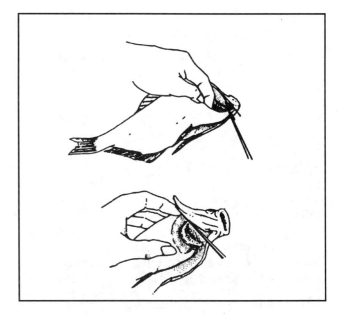

Now, pull open the gill cover on each side of the fish and cut the top of the gills free from the head. The gills and entrails can now be lifted or slid out of the fish in one unit. Now, remove the strip of reddish tissue near the backbone in the intestinal cavity (these are the fishes' kidneys). You may have to cut through a thin layer of tissue covering this area. As a last step, rinse off the fish. It is now ready for icing down.

Traditional Fish Cleaning

This approach is basically an extension of field dressing. As a young boy, my earliest memory of fish cleaning was the assembly line my dad set up with my brother and myself to clean a stringer of well over 100 Lake Michigan perch (about 1/2 to 1 pound each). Here are the steps:

1. **Scaling**—Using a knife (not necessarily real sharp) or a fish scaler, scrape from the tail towards the head. This is best done out-of-doors since the scales fly around. Actually some fish (like salmon and sanddabs) can be scaled with the spray from a garden hose nozzle. It's quick and easy.

2. **Gutting**—This is actually the same as the beginnings of field dressing. Open the belly from anal vent to gills.

3. **Be-Heading**—The entrails are slid forward and out of the body cavity, and then with a sharp knife, cut

perpendicular to the backbone at the top of the gill cover, cut off the entrails, gills and head.

4. **Rinsing**—Rinse inside and outside of fish after removing red flesh in body cavity (see Field Dressing section).

5. Fish is now ready for cooking and preserving.

Filleting

Filleting is simple and has many advantages. For example, scaling is not necessary since the skin (and scales) will be removed. It can and often is done without even gutting or field dressing the fish first. It produces boneless or almost bone-free slabs of meat. And filleting works great on fish of all sizes and both round-bodied and flat-bodied fish.

Here are the steps in filleting:

1. Make the first cut just behind the gills. Cut down to the backbone, then turn the knife toward the tail of the fish and slice above the spine (feeling for it as you proceed) all the way to the tail. One flank of the fish will now be removed. Flip the fish over and repeat the process. This step is illustrated below.

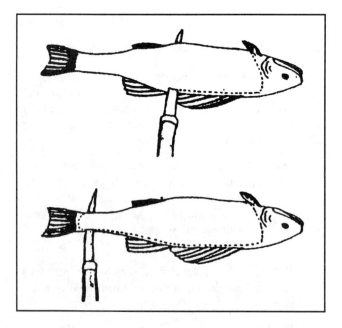

2. Now cut away the rib cage from each fillet. Insert the knife at the top of the rib cage and slice down following close to ribs.

3. Lastly, remove the skin. Lay fillet skin side down on cutting board. Insert the knife just about one-half inch from the tail and cut down to the skin. Now, firmly holding the tail end, turn the blade forward and work the knife along the skin, "lifting" the meat from the skin all the way to the large end of the fillet.

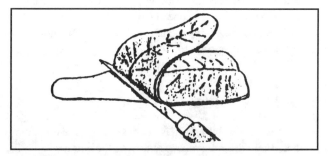

With a little practice, filleting becomes second nature. For a great visual display, watch the pros do it when a party boat docks after a day of fishing. You'll be amazed. Successful filleting depends on two things once you understand the principles: 1) Use a good fish fillet knife; and 2) keep the knife very sharp.

Steaking

Steaking simply means cutting a fish into similar-sized parts by making parallel cuts that are all perpendicular to the spine! Just joking! I know only math freaks and geometry teachers could understand that definition.

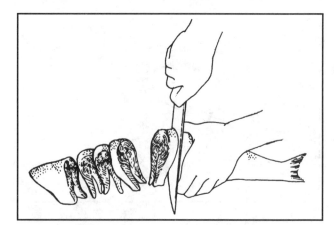

The first step in steaking (which, by the way, is usually reserved only for large fish) is to remove the head (this is done after field dressing) right at the gill cover. Now just lay the fish flat and divide it into about one-inch thick pieces. The tail section (where the steaks are small) can be filleted. Some varieties need to be scaled before steaking.

Keeping Fish Fresh

Fish is delicious. But it is also one of the most perishable of foods. So, from the time a fish is caught until it is served, care must be taken to preserve its freshness.

Freshness on the Water

If possible, the best way to keep a fish fresh, while continuing to fish, is to keep your catch alive. This can be done in several ways:

- For pan fish, use a collapsible basket. A fully submerged burlap bag will also serve the purpose.

- The best stringers are those that have large safety pin type clasps, and some type of swivel mechanism so fish are less likely to get twisted up.

- The proper stringing technique is to run the stringer through both the upper and lower lip. This allows the fish to open and close its mouth, thereby forcing water through its gills to breathe. Never run a stringer through the fishes' gills. This prevents it from closing its mouth and therefore starving it of oxygen.

- Let out the full stringer. Even add a rope if extra length is needed to keep the fish down deep in the water. The water is cooler and more oxygenated down deeper.

- If you move your boat quickly, lift the stringer out of the water during a short trip.

- Surf and river anglers who use a stringer move the fish along with them, always placing the fish back into the deepest water available.

- When using a creel, bed and surround fish in dry grass. Canvas creels or fishing vests should be moist to maintain coolness.

- There are some hazards to be aware of when keeping fish in water:

- Fish on stringers have been known to be eaten by turtles. Never string fish in warm lake water. Summertime surface water temperatures in some Northern California lakes are in the 80s!

- Stringers are taboo in salt waters. It's just feeding the sharks. Rather, use a cooler or fish box, preferably with ice in it.

Freshness During Travel

If you're traveling for any length of time, follow these simple steps to ensure freshness:

- Field dress the fish.

- Dry the fish thoroughly.

- Cover each fish with foil or plastic.

- Surround each package of fish in a cooler with crushed or cubed ice.

Refrigeration

Fish do not do particularly well under prolonged refrigeration. So it's best to either eat fresh caught fish, or freeze them. Refrigerated fish should be covered with heavy foil, freezer paper or plastic to prevent moisture from escaping.

Freezing

There are basically two ways to freeze fresh fish. With either approach you can freeze whole-field cleaned fish, fish fillets, steaks or chunks.

The first method is more conventional. Wrap fish in packaging materials with high barriers to moisture and vapor transmission. A good quality freezer wrapping paper or heavy foil is recommended. Wrap tightly and tape securely. This method is adequate. Defrost slowly in a refrigerator. Better flavor and preservation can be achieved by repeatedly dipping and freezing unwrapped fish in water until a layer of ice is formed. Then wrap securely.

Actually, the best and simplest way to freeze fish is to utilize old milk cartons or similar liquid holding containers.

Fresh and well-cleaned fish can be placed in the container up to an inch from the top. Now, simply fill the container with water (or a brine solution of 1/3 cup of table salt to one gallon of water) and shake to make sure there are no air bubbles.

Seal up container and freeze. Thawing is best done on a drain rack so the fish does not sit in cold water. Date fish packages you put in the freezer. Store them at 0^0F or lower, and plan to use within 2 months for best flavor.

Cooking Fish

There are numerous fish cookbooks jam-packed with recipes. But matching your favorite catch to an unfamiliar or inappropriate recipe often leads to less than enjoyable eating. Rather than special recipes, successful fish cooking depends on adhering to two simple principles:

1. Know when the fish is done—too often fish is overcooked.

2. Match cooking method to the fish flavor, fish size and fat level.

First, let's address the "when fish is done" issue. Fish by its very nature is more tender than red meat or poultry. It doesn't contain fibers that need to be broken down by extensive cooking. Some cooking experts say fish should be considered more like egg than like meat. So, as in cooking egg, just enough heat needs to be applied to firm up the protein. Overcooking makes eggs tough and dry; it does the same for fish.

So how dow you tell when fish is cooked for just the right length of time? It's easy. Fish is cooked properly when it flakes when probed with a fork. By flaking, I mean separated into its natural layers or divisions. This test should be done often at the center, or thickest part of the fish fillet, steak or whole fish.

Matching Fish to Cooking Method

Now the second key principle of successful fish cooking: matching the specific fish to the specific cooking method. Fish caught in Northern California have a wide variety of flavor levels, fish size and fat level. Typically, all fish is considered a low-fat source of protein. But there are pronounced differences in fat content that do affect taste and texture. Flavor level also varies generally from very mild to quite pronounced. This influences cooking method and seasoning selection. Fortunately, all these fish can be grouped into four cooking categories.

Category One: In this category are the delicate, mild flavored, lean and generally small cuts of fish. Specific examples include sole, sanddabs, flounder and halibut. Cuts of fish in this category are generally thin and oval shaped. The exception is halibut which is thicker and has a heavier texture.

Category One fish are very good sauteed. Sole fillets are so delicate that some only need to be cooked on one side. A flour coating promotes browning. Thicker cuts can have a flour, crumb, cornmeal or egg-wash coating before frying. Oven frying or foil baking also works well, as does poaching.

Category Two: Fish in this second group are generally of medium density, yet still light in flavor. We're talking about lingcod, the whole family of rockfish, surfperch, salmon, trout, catfish, striped bass and steelhead. Both steaks and fillets from larger fish in this category are good poached, cooked in foil or oven-fried. Pan frying is good with a coating like crumbs or egg-wash to add flavor, texture and enhance browning. Small, whole fish are good baked or foil cooked. The most oily fish in this category, salmon, is very good barbecued.

Category Three: Here we have the Northern California fish that are more dense with a darker meat and more pronounced flavor. Three ocean-going fish—the tunas (albacore, yellowfin, etc.), bonito and mackerel—make up this third category. To be honest with you, many fishermen don't even like the robust (some say strong) flavor of these fish. But those who do usually barbecue them. Fresh caught barbecued tuna is quite tasty, but some would say that it's not as good as "good old Charlie The Tuna."

Category Four: Now we're into the large fish that result in thick cuts (1 to 1 1/2 inch) of dense meat. Northern California fish in this category are the sturgeon and shark (leopard and blue). Cuts of these fish brown nicely in a frying pan without any coating, and you can barbecue them directly on a greased grill. In fact, cubes can be skewered for kabobs. Meal-sized pieces are good baked, poached or cooked in foil.

The preceding categories and guidelines have wide latitude. That's why for each fish covered in the "How To Catch . . ." chapter, specific cooking information is given.

Sauteing

This method is often called frying, but frying is quite distinct. More on this in the pan frying section below. Sauteing is cooking fish in a frying pan, usually in a small amount of melted butter, over moderate or high heat.

This is one of the fastest and simplest ways to prepare fish. And, it is well suited for either lean or fat fish. The fish is sprinkled with salt and pepper and dipped in flour on both sides. Cooking time per side varies from 1 minute to 3 minutes. A sauce can be prepared in the pan after the fish are removed to a warm platter.

Frying (both Pan and Deep)

Frying fish means immersing either partially or completely in cooking oil. This process results in a thicker, more crusty covering of the fish than with sauteing or oven frying. Frying usually involves a batter made with a beaten egg and a small amount of milk. The dipped fish pieces are rolled in bread crumbs, crack crumbs or a purchased coating mix.

One eighth inch of shortening or salad oil should be heated to between 350 and 375 degrees in a substantial frying pan. Or, if deep-frying, use enough shortening or salad oil in a deep fryer to cover the fish. Heat to the same temperature. Finished fish should be golden brown and flake when tested.

Some pitfalls to avoid: Don't let the oil temperature fall; it results in a greasy or soggy coating. Too much fish put in the oil at one time can lower the cooking temperature where the fish can't cook properly. Too high an oil temperature will result in a dark coating or burnt flavor. If batter falls off, the fish pieces may have been too wet. So, pat dry before battering.

Oven Frying

Everybody knows how to oven-fry chicken, so everybody knows how to oven-fry fish. This method is simple and doesn't cause fat spattering, if that's a problem with you.

Fish should be serving-sized pieces. Dip each piece in milk, drain, sprinkle with salt and pepper, then roll in bread crumbs or cracker crumbs. Melt enough butter or margarine in a shallow baking pan to generously coat the bottom. Now, turn the crumb-coated fish over in the melted butter or margarine and arrange the pieces in the pan. Bake in a hot oven (about 500°F) until the fish flakes (from 5 to 15 minutes). Turn each piece one time so it browns evenly.

Baking

Foil wrapped or covered-dish oven cooking is the typical fish baking approach. The covering or enclosure is needed to prevent the fish from drying out. This is an ideal method for baking fish with vegetables, herbs or tomato sauce. The steam that is developed helps produce a tasty sauce. Oven temperature is usually about 450°F.

Barbecuing or Grilling

Rich, full-flavored fish such as salmon, trout or tuna are most desirable for barbecuing since they're fatter and the smoke enhances the taste. Milder-tasting fish might be overcome by the smoke flavor. Serving-sized fillets, steaks and whole fish can be barbecued.

Some people like to grill directly over the coals, while others put the fish on a sheet of heavy aluminum foil. The foil method works well in a covered grill because it prevents any sticking or turning problems.

Some helpful hints: Make sure the coals are hot and the grill is hot—fish stick like magnets to a cold grill. Start fillets skin side up (if no foil is used) and turn only once. If foil is used, fillet skin should be down (that is, touching foil). While cooking, the fish is basted with melted butter or your favorite sauce.

Broiling

Broiling, of course, is much akin to barbecuing, except that the heat is above the fish. Any fish can be broiled, but leaner fish must be basted often to prevent it from drying out. Fillets are often broiled on only one side, while steaks are turned once. Broil 2 to 3 inches from the heat.

Poaching

Poaching is simmering fish gently in a flavorful liquid. The liquid is never boiled, however. Fish prepared this way is very good served hot with a fish sauce made from the poaching liquid. Any fish with a low fat content, and salmon of course, is delicious prepared this way. And as an extra bonus, cold, poached fish like tuna is great.

Pieces of fish are often poached in cheese cloth while large, whole fish are done in a poaching pan that has a special rack for lowering and removing the fish. Again, the flake test will reveal when the fish is cooked properly. Fillets should be tested after about 5 minutes.

An easy way to poach a steak or fillet is to put it in lightly salted water in a wide saucepan or skillet on top of the stove (it's much less fuss than the classic oven poach). Frozen fish pieces can even be defrosted and poached at the same time. Poaching is complete (for frozen or fresh fish) when the meat has turned from translucent to opaque, and it feels somewhat springy rather than squishy. Cooked pieces are patted dry and served with melted butter or in other more elaborate ways.

Smoking

Many avid, and some not so avid, anglers own and use fish smokers. They are simple to use and quite modestly priced. And they produce delicious smoked fish. All commercially available smokers come with detailed instruction manuals. It is also possible to convert such items as 55 gallon drums, or a discarded refrigerator and a hot plate into a smoker. Instructions for these do-it-yourself projects can be found in smoking-oriented cookbooks in your local library.

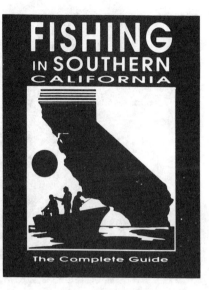

Fishing in Southern California
- How to catch all game fish
- The best techniques, lures and bait, rigging
- Complete coverage of streams, rivers, lakes, ocean
- 63 maps, many illustrations
- 256 pages, 8 1/2"x11"

Bass Fishing in California
- Secrets of the Western Pros
- Best techniques. What? Where? Why?
- "How to fish" the top 40 lakes in the state
- 40 maps, many illustrations
- 256 pages, 8 1/2" x 11"

OUR BESTSELLERS -in detail

Expanded and Updated Edition
Fishing in Southern California
By Ken Albert

Here is a new enlarged and updated version of the premier SoCal fishing book.

- **More lakes**
- **More maps**
- **More "where to go" info**
- **More tips**

"At last, a basic information book for Southern California ...every angler should have a copy."
—UNITED ANGLERS OF CALIF.

"Southern California should delight in...FISHING IN SOUTHERN CALIFORNIA."
—The Editors
CALIFORNIA ANGLER MAGAZINE

Both the veteran anglers and beginners are finding this book an information bonanza. It explains in detail how, when and where to catch SoCal abalone, barracuda, largemouth bass, bluegill, bonito, calico bass, catfish, crappie, grunion, halibut, marlin, rockfish, striped bass, trout (in streams, in lakes and golden) and yellowtail.

This book covers SoCal lakes (44 of the best with full page fishing maps), mountain trout streams and lakes (with maps), the Salton Sea, Colorado river lakes (with full page fishing maps), the Pacific coast (with detailed info and 8 full page maps) as well as surf fishing, pier fishing, rockfishing, party boat fishing, Baja fishing trips, fish cleaning and fish cooking.

This book has become a bestseller because it details the nitty-gritty of SoCal fishing; how to rig up, when to fish, equipment and tackle, best techniques, lures and bait and more.

8 1/2 x 11 inches, 256 pages

Expanded and Updated Edition
Bass Fishing in California
By Ron Kovach

Here is the expanded and updated edition of the bible of bass fishing in California.

At last, a bass fishing book just for California anglers—both beginners and veterans. Bass fishing inCalifornia is unique and special, and now there's a book that tells it all. How? What? Where? and Why?

This book explains in detail how to catch bass using crankbaits, plastic worms, top-water lures, spinner baits, spoons, jigs and live bait. Plus there are chapters on equipment, electronics, tips and tricks, and more. There is also a chapter detailing sure-fire ways to catch smallmouth bass.

"This book really does detail the secrets of the Western pros. These are the tricks we use out there every day."
—Bobby Garland
Top Touring Pro and Lure Manufacturer

"This book is a must for any bass angler who would like to learn what it takes to catch fish in our manmade waters. It has more about finesse fishing with worms and other baits than any other book."
—Don Iovino
Top Touring Pro and Professional Guide

But most valuable to Caiifornians, this is a guide to over 3 dozen of the best bass lakes, up and down the state. Two full pages are devoted to each lake, including a large fishing map and numerous fishing tips.

Ron Kovach is highly successful professional bass fisherman and outdoor writer. In this book he tells, in simple terms, exactly how the Western bass pros catch so many big fish. And how the weekend angler can do it too.

8 1/2 x 11 inches, 256 pages

more ..

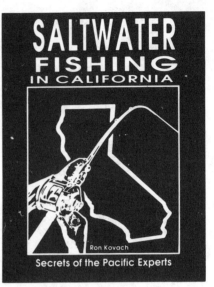

Trout Fishing in California
- Secrets of the Top Western anglers
- Best techniques. What? Where? Why?
- Major "Where to fish" sections
- 50 maps, many illustrations
- 240 pages, 8 1/2" x 11"

Saltwater Fishing in California
- Secrets of the Pacific Experts
- Best techniques. What? Where? Why?
- Complete Mexico-Oregon "Where-to" sections
- 15 full - page maps; many illustrations
- 256 pages, 8 1/2" x 11"

OUR BESTSELLERS -in detail

Expanded and Updated Edition
Trout Fishing in California
Secrets of the Western Anglers
by Ron Kovach

Trout fishing is special in California. And now there is a special book for the California trout angler - both veteran and beginner. Trout fishing is number one all up and down California. This book answers all the"Hows", "Whats", "Wheres", and "Whys" for angling, from the Oregon border down to San Diego.

It covers, in detail, how to catch trout in lakes or streams, with lures or bait, or flies, by trolling, casting or still fishing, from boat or shore. Plus there are chapters on reading the water, tips and tricks, cleaning and cooking, and more. There are also chapters on pack-in trout fishing and ice fishing. And even better for California anglers, this is a guide to the best trout waters all over California. Detailed information and precise maps are featured. The entire state is devided into manageable regions, and then specific trout fishing particulars are presented for highly productive waters in each region.

"There are more secrets and tricks in this book than a person will ever be able to use in a lifetime."
—Jon Minami
California Record Holder, 1983-1987

"It will give you that edge in catching the trophy of a lifetime."
—Bob Bringhurst
World Record Holder, 1977-1984

Ron Kovach is a highly successful professional angler and outdoor writer. *Trout Fishing in California* follows on the heels of his best selling *Bass Fishing in California*, also proudly published by Marketscope Books.

And now, this essential book has been expanded and updated!

1/2 x 11 inches, 240 pages

Saltwater Fishing in California
Secrets of the Pacific Experts
By Ron Kovach

California is blessed with over 800 miles of Pacific Ocean coastline. This is a marvelous resource for all Golden State anglers. And now there is a book that covers it all. Surf fishing. Kelp fishing. Harbor and Bay fishing. Poke poling. And more. Don't go saltwater fishing without it.

Both veteran anglers and beginners are finding this book a necessity. It explains, in detail, how to catch albacore, barracuda, bass, bonito, halibut, rockfish,sharks, salmon, stripers, yellowtail and striped marlin. And there is a large "How-To and Where-To" Guide for hot spots all along the coast. And don't be without the Saltwater Sportfish I.D. Section.

"Saltwater Fishing in California belongs in every angler's tackle box"
—Bob Robb, Editor
Peterson's Fishing Magazine

"Finally - a comprehensive, informative book that addresses all aspects...of saltwater angling."
—Larry Green
KCBS

This book has become a standard because it explains in simple, straightforward language how to catch fish in the Pacific, off California.

8 1/2 x 11 inches, 256 pages

Great Books (for more details see p.236)

Fishing in Northern California

RKOE / MARKETSCOPE publishes the bestselling **Fishing in Northern California** (8 1/2 x 11 inches, 240 pages). It includes "How To Catch" sections on all freshwater fish as well as salmon, steelhead, sturgeon, shad, kokanee, lingcod, clams, sharks, rock crab, crawdads, stripers, etc. Plus, there are sections on all major NorCal fishing waters (over 50 lakes, the Delta, Coastal Rivers, Valley Rivers, Mountain Trout and the Pacific Ocean). All these waters are mapped in detail!

Fishing in Southern California

RKOE / MARKETSCOPE also publishes the bestselling **Fishing in Southern California** (8 1/2 x 11 inches, 256 pages). It includes "How To Catch" sections on all freshwater fish as well as barracuda, bonito, calico bass, grunion, halibut, marlin sea bass and yellowtail. Plus, there are sections on major SoCal fishing waters (45 lakes, the Salton Sea, Colorado River, Mountain Trout and the Pacific Ocean). All these waters are mapped in detail!

Bass Fishing in California

At last, a bass fishing book just for Californians—both beginners and veterans. This book explains in detail how to catch more and larger bass in California's unique waters. But, most valuable, it includes a comprehensive guide, with maps, to 40 of California's best bass lakes, up and down the state. 8 1/2 x 11, 240 pages.

Trout Fishing in California

Trout fishing is special in California and now there is a special book for the California trout anglers. It covers, in detail, how to catch trout in lakes or streams, with line, bait or flies, by trolling, casting or still fishing, from boat or shore. And even better for California anglers, this is a guide to the best trout waters all over the state. Detailed info and precise maps are featured. 8 1/2 x 11, 224 pages.

Saltwater Fishing in California

California is blessed with over 800 miles of Pacific Ocean coastline. This is a marvelous resource for all Golden State anglers. And now there is a book that covers it all. Surf fishing. Kelp fishing. Harbor and Bay fishing. Poke poling. And more. Don't go saltwater fishing without it. Both veteran anglers and beginners are finding this book a necessity. It explains, in detail, how to catch albacore, barracuda, bass, bonito, halibut, rockfish, sharks, salmon, stripers, yellowtail and striped marlin. And there is a large "How-To and Where-To" Guide for hot spots all along the coast. And don't be without the Saltwater Sportfish I.D. Section. This book has become a standard because it explains in simple, straightforward language how to catch fish in the Pacific, off California. 8 1/2 x 11, 256 pages.

Order your Copies Today!

	Price	Sales Tax	Total Price	Qty	Total Amount
___ **Fishing in Northern California**	$14.95	$1.20	$16.15	___	_____
___ **Fishing in Southern California**	$14.95	$1.20	$16.15	___	_____
___ **Bass Fishing in California**	$14.95	$1.20	$16.15	___	_____
___ **Trout Fishing in California**	$14.95	$1.20	$16.15	___	_____
___ **Saltwater Fishing in California**	$14.95	$1.20	$16.15	___	_____
					_____

Postage & Handling (1st book $3.00; no charge on 2 or more books) . . . .   _____ *

Check Enclosed . . . .   _____

*Special Offer (order 2 books, any combination, and we'll pay **all** postage & handling)

Name _____ Address _____

Send Your Order To: **RKOE / MARKETSCOPE, P.O. Box 3118, HUNTINGTON BEACH, CA 92605-3118**

fnc   (Permission is granted to xerox this page.)

```
HELP MAKE IT A FAIR FIGHT . .



      It's the FISH against - Water diversion,
                              Habitat degradation,
                              Sewage,
                              Dredge spoils,
                              Chemicals,
                              Poaching,
                              Gill netting,
                              Bureaucracy,
                              Special interests,
                              And More!
```

UNITED ANGLERS OF CALIFORNIA

Is the largest fishery conservation organization in the state working to restore, protect and enhance all of our state's sport fisheries. We represent 80,000 sport anglers in California who demand that our fisheries be restored. They support UAC because we are providing the organizational and political strength to see that fishery resources were properly protected and wisely managed. United Anglers has demonstrated that by joining together we can raise the voice of anglers across the state to have proper attention paid to these resources. As our membership grows, our voice becomes louder and our ability to reach all of our goals grows stronger. The future of our fisheries depends on your support.

Call 408-371-0331